Salesforce Apex Design Patterns

*Architecting Salesforce solutions
with Apex design patterns*

Chamil Madusanka

bpb

www.bpbonline.com

First Edition 2025

Copyright © BPB Publications, India

ISBN: 978-93-65896-138

To View Complete
BPB Publications Catalogue
Scan the QR Code:

www.bpbonline.com

Dedicated to

My baby girl
Abhima Sanaya Wickramaarachchi

My wife
Dr Prarthana Liyanaarachchi

My mom
K.L.A Swarnalatha

About the Author

Chamil Madusanka holds the distinction of being the very first Sri Lankan Salesforce MVP, a title he has proudly held since 2019. A certified Salesforce.com Professional, Chamil embarked on his Salesforce journey in 2011. In 2012, he took the pioneering step of founding the Sri Lankan Salesforce Ohana, a community-driven initiative. He is leading the Colombo Developer Community Group under Sri Lankan Salesforce Ohana. Chamil's vision is to elevate Salesforce competency within Sri Lanka, fostering a nurturing environment for Salesforce professionals and students to flourish within the Salesforce ecosystem.

At present, Chamil assumes the roles of Head of Salesforce Practice and Salesforce Architect at iTelasoft Pvt. Ltd. His professional trajectory includes notable tenures at Dazeworks Technologies Pvt. Ltd., Rizing (formerly known as attune Lanka Pvt. Ltd., and Sabre Technologies Pvt. Ltd. (where he started Salesforce Journey). He serves as a visiting lecturer at the University of Moratuwa, Sri Lanka, offering his expertise in subjects such as Innovation Management and Multidisciplinary Design.

Chamil's remarkable contributions extend beyond his roles, as evidenced by his authorship of two impactful works: Visualforce Developer's Guide and Learning Force.com Application Development. His invaluable expertise has been instrumental as a technical reviewer for four distinct books focusing on Salesforce technologies. These publications stand as a testament to his commitment to knowledge sharing and his dedication to enhancing the Salesforce landscape.

Educationally, Chamil secured a BSc in computer science from the University of Colombo, School of Computing, Sri Lanka (UCSC) and MBA in Management of Technology from the University of Moratuwa, Sri Lanka. His academic journey kindled his fascination with cloud computing, semantic web technologies, Ontology-based systems, Innovation Management, Knowledge Management, Innovation Performance and Market Orientation

Geographically, hailing from the ancient city of Polonnaruwa in Sri Lanka, Chamil currently resides in Colombo, within the Western province of the country. Beyond his tech pursuits, he finds solace in consuming technology literature and playing and watching cricket.

About the Reviewers

❖ **Subramani Kumarasamy** is a Certified Salesforce Application Architect with a strong focus on automating critical business processes and delivering end-to-end solutions. Known for managing complex projects with precision, he is committed to building scalable, technical debt-free systems. His deep knowledge of the Salesforce core platform, integrations, and license management positions him as a trusted expert in the ecosystem. Beyond his technical work, Subramani is passionate about teaching and has trained professionals worldwide, from beginners to experienced users. His talent for simplifying complex topics and delivering practical, hands-on learning has earned him respect and recognition within the Salesforce community.

Beyond his professional pursuits, Subramani enjoys indulging in his favorite television shows, such as Game of Thrones and Suits, during his leisure time. However, his true joy lies in spending quality moments with his family and friends, as he understands the importance of work-life balance and cherishes the relationships that matter most to him.

❖ **Ila Anmol Verma** is a result-driven Salesforce Technical Professional with over 8 years of experience in designing, implementing, and maintaining Salesforce solutions across telecommunications, insurance, and healthcare industries. Skilled in Apex (classes, triggers), Aura components, Lightning Web Components (LWC), Visualforce, Flows, Workflows, and Process Builder.

With expertise in Sales Cloud, Service Cloud, Experience Cloud, and Health Cloud, Ila has successfully integrated FileNet, CloudSense, Apttus CPQ, and Conga into Salesforce, enhancing system capabilities. As a Technical Architect and Solution Designer, Ila has led teams of developers and testers, ensuring smooth execution and optimization of Salesforce implementations. She also has worked as a Release Manager responsible for strategically planning and maintaining salesforce orgs performing release updates and deployments.

Passionate about scalability, automation, and seamless integrations, Ila collaborates closely with cross-functional teams, and multiple Scrum teams, managing iterative CRM enhancements. With strong problem-solving, documentation, and communication skills, Ila is dedicated to delivering efficient, scalable Salesforce solutions that drive business success and improve customer experiences.

- ❖ **Nipunu Wijesingha** is an accomplished Salesforce professional with over 12 years in the IT industry, including 8 years specializing in Salesforce solutions. He holds multiple certifications, including Salesforce Platform Developer and Administrator, as well as AWS Cloud Practitioner. As a 2x Trailhead Ranger, Nipunu is committed to continuous learning and staying at the forefront of Salesforce technologies. His expertise spans Sales, Service, and Experience/Community Cloud, as well as Field Service Lightning (FSL) and Salesforce integration, making him a versatile asset to complex, large-scale projects.

Nipunu is a Salesforce Technical Lead at iTelaSoft Australia, passionate about driving business transformation through innovative Salesforce solutions. He brings deep expertise in Apex, Lightning Web Components (LWC), and integration tools, along with a strong focus on DevOps. With hands-on experience using Gearset, Copado, Git, and Salesforce DX, he has built efficient deployment frameworks and automation strategies. Previously at Micado in New Zealand, Nipunu developed scalable, enterprise-grade Salesforce applications and led integrations with external systems. His background also includes academic roles where he introduced Salesforce training to university programs, reflecting his commitment to knowledge sharing. As a technical lead and mentor, Nipunu blends technical excellence with collaboration and best practices, ensuring teams are empowered to deliver impactful solutions.

Acknowledgement

I would like to express my deepest gratitude to everyone who has contributed to realizing this book, Salesforce Apex Design Patterns.

First and foremost, I immensely thank my family and friends for their unwavering support, patience, and encouragement throughout this journey. Your understanding and inspiration have been the cornerstone of our efforts.

I extend my heartfelt thanks to the individuals whose insights, expertise, and constructive feedback played a crucial role in shaping the content of this book. Your contributions have been invaluable in enhancing the depth and quality of this work.

I am profoundly grateful to BPB Publications for their guidance and professionalism in navigating the intricacies of the publishing process. Your support has been instrumental in bringing this book to life.

Special acknowledgment goes to the reviewers, technical experts, and editors who meticulously examined the manuscript, offering valuable suggestions and refinements. Your dedication has significantly elevated the standards of this book.

Finally, to our readers and the Salesforce community, your enthusiasm and commitment to learning and innovation inspire us daily. This book is a tribute to your passion for building scalable, efficient, and maintainable solutions.

Thank you to everyone who has been a part of this journey. Your encouragement and belief in this project have been the driving force behind its completion.

Preface

In the ever-evolving landscape of technology, Salesforce has emerged as a leading platform for delivering innovative, cloud-based solutions. As Salesforce continues to empower organizations to streamline their operations, develop scalable solutions, and adapt to the ever-changing demands of the business world, the need for robust design principles and patterns in Salesforce development becomes increasingly apparent.

Salesforce Apex Design Patterns is a comprehensive guide that bridges the gap between theoretical design principles and practical implementation in the context of Salesforce. This book is born out of our desire to share knowledge, experience, and best practices with developers, architects, and anyone aspiring to build scalable and maintainable applications on the Salesforce platform.

The primary goal of this book is to equip readers with a deep understanding of design patterns and their practical application in Apex programming. By exploring patterns such as Singleton, Factory, Builder, Proxy, and many others, this book aims to help developers craft clean, efficient, and reusable code that adheres to Salesforce's best practices and limitations. Each chapter delves into real-world scenarios, offering clear explanations, code examples, and insights into how design patterns can address common challenges in Salesforce development.

Whether you are a seasoned Salesforce professional looking to refine your approach or a newcomer eager to learn best practices, this book is designed to be a valuable resource for all. It covers a range of topics, from foundational concepts to advanced design strategies, ensuring that readers at every skill level can benefit.

We have written this book with a strong emphasis on practicality, aiming to provide actionable insights and solutions. Our intention is to empower developers to create solutions that are not only functional but also elegant, scalable, and future-proof.

We hope that Salesforce Apex Design Patterns serves as both a guide and a source of inspiration as you navigate the complexities of Salesforce development. As you turn these pages, we invite you to explore, experiment, and embrace the power of design patterns to unlock the full potential of Salesforce.

Chapter 1: Foundation of Apex Design Patterns- This chapter introduces design patterns and their role in Salesforce development, emphasizing improved code reusability, scalability, and maintainability. It outlines how Apex patterns support best practices and performance. Readers are also guided through the book's structure, preparing them to apply design patterns effectively in real-world Salesforce scenarios.

Chapter 2: Understanding Design Patterns- This chapter lays the foundation for understanding design patterns, defining their structure, principles, and classification into creational, structural, and behavioral types. It emphasizes their benefits in Apex development, such as improved modularity and faster development. Readers gain a clear conceptual framework for applying design patterns effectively in Salesforce projects.

Chapter 3: Apex Fundamentals- This chapter introduces the fundamentals of Apex, covering syntax, data types, variables, operators, and control structures like loops and conditionals. It equips readers with essential programming knowledge, offering a solid foundation for understanding design patterns and their practical use in Salesforce development through clear explanations of Apex's core components.

Chapter 4: Apex Design Principles- This chapter explores core design principles essential to effective Apex development, including modularity, encapsulation, and maintainability. It emphasizes clean, efficient code and highlights the importance of separation of concerns. The SOLID principles are introduced, demonstrating how they enhance code structure, clarity, and quality, preparing readers for applying design patterns.

Chapter 5: Creational Design Patterns- This chapter delves into creational design patterns in Apex, including singleton, factory method, builder, abstract factory, and prototype. Each pattern is explored with practical application, illustrating how they streamline object creation, enhance flexibility, and promote scalability. Readers gain a solid grasp of optimizing object instantiation in Apex development.

Chapter 6: Structural Design Patterns- This chapter explores structural design patterns in Apex, including adapter, decorator, facade, composite, bridge, and flyweight. Each pattern is examined for its role in enhancing code structure, flexibility, and maintainability. Readers learn how these patterns simplify complex systems and promote scalable, efficient Apex development through practical application.

Chapter 7: Behavioral Design Patterns- This chapter examines behavioral design patterns in Apex, including Observer, Strategy, Command, Chain of Responsibility, State, and Iterator. Each pattern is tailored to manage object interactions and enhance adaptability. Readers learn how these patterns promote flexible, decoupled architectures, empowering dynamic behavior and streamlined communication within Apex applications.

Chapter 8: Apex Specific Patterns- This chapter focuses on design patterns uniquely suited to Apex and Salesforce development. It covers custom settings for dynamic configurations, the trigger and handler pattern for separating logic, bulkification strategies for performance optimization, and exception management for robust error handling. Readers gain practical insights into applying these patterns effectively in Apex.

Chapter 9: Architectural Patterns in Salesforce- This chapter explores key architectural patterns for structuring large-scale Apex applications, including MVC for separating concerns, the Service Layer for encapsulating business logic, and DAO for abstracting data access. Readers gain strategic insight into building scalable, maintainable Salesforce solutions through organized, modular, and efficient application architecture.

Chapter 10: Integrating Patterns in Apex Projects- This chapter guides readers on integrating design patterns into real-world Apex projects, emphasizing scalability, maintainability, and best practices. It explores combining patterns for optimal solutions and presents case studies illustrating practical applications. Readers learn to select appropriate patterns based on specific scenarios, ensuring effective, goal-aligned Salesforce development.

Chapter 11: Anti-Patterns and Pitfalls in Apex Development- This chapter highlights common mistakes and anti-patterns in Apex development, offering guidance on avoiding pitfalls to ensure code quality and efficiency. It covers the process of refactoring, improving maintainability, and systematically eliminating bad practices. Readers also learn best practices for sustaining code quality through continuous improvement and code reviews.

Chapter 12: Future Trends in Apex Design Patterns- This chapter explores the future of design patterns in Apex development, focusing on emerging patterns, technologies, and methodologies shaping the landscape. It highlights how new Salesforce features can be integrated with design patterns for innovative solutions. Readers gain insights into adapting to technological changes, ensuring their Apex applications remain resilient and future-ready.

Code Bundle and Coloured Images

Please follow the link to download the
Code Bundle and the *Coloured Images* of the book:

https://rebrand.ly/634b39

The code bundle for the book is also hosted on GitHub at
https://github.com/bpbpublications/Salesforce-Apex-Design-Patterns.
In case there's an update to the code, it will be updated on the existing GitHub repository.

We have code bundles from our rich catalogue of books and videos available at
https://github.com/bpbpublications. Check them out!

Errata

We take immense pride in our work at BPB Publications and follow best practices to ensure the accuracy of our content to provide with an indulging reading experience to our subscribers. Our readers are our mirrors, and we use their inputs to reflect and improve upon human errors, if any, that may have occurred during the publishing processes involved. To let us maintain the quality and help us reach out to any readers who might be having difficulties due to any unforeseen errors, please write to us at :

errata@bpbonline.com

Your support, suggestions and feedbacks are highly appreciated by the BPB Publications' Family.

Piracy

If you come across any illegal copies of our works in any form on the internet, we would be grateful if you would provide us with the location address or website name. Please contact us at **business@bpbonline.com** with a link to the material.

If you are interested in becoming an author

If there is a topic that you have expertise in, and you are interested in either writing or contributing to a book, please visit **www.bpbonline.com**. We have worked with thousands of developers and tech professionals, just like you, to help them share their insights with the global tech community. You can make a general application, apply for a specific hot topic that we are recruiting an author for, or submit your own idea.

Reviews

Please leave a review. Once you have read and used this book, why not leave a review on the site that you purchased it from? Potential readers can then see and use your unbiased opinion to make purchase decisions. We at BPB can understand what you think about our products, and our authors can see your feedback on their book. Thank you!

For more information about BPB, please visit **www.bpbonline.com**.

Join our book's Discord space

Join the book's Discord Workspace for Latest updates, Offers, Tech happenings around the world, New Release and Sessions with the Authors:

https://discord.bpbonline.com

Table of Contents

CHAPTER 1
Foundation of Apex Design Patterns

Introduction

The first chapter of **Apex design patterns** introduces the fundamental concepts behind this book. We will discuss the importance of design patterns in software development, highlighting their role in improving code reusability and maintainability. We then focus on how these patterns are crucial in Salesforce development, helping developers address complex challenges and improve efficiency and scalability. Additionally, we provide an overview of the book's structure and content to guide readers through various chapters covering design patterns, Apex principles, and real-world applications.

Structure

The chapter covers the following topics:

- Significance of design patterns in software development
- Importance of Apex design patterns in Salesforce development

Objectives

By the end of this chapter, readers will understand the significance of design patterns in Apex development and get a glimpse of what is to come in the book.

Significance of design patterns in software development

In the ever-evolving world of software development, where innovation and complexity are the norm, it becomes important to establish structured approaches to tackle common challenges. Design patterns are standardized, reusable solutions to recurring software design challenges. For example, patterns help developers manage platform constraints. Using design patterns is one such approach that has stood the test of time and remains as relevant as ever. This section explores the profound significance of design patterns and their crucial role in shaping how we craft software solutions.

Following is the significance of design patterns in software development:

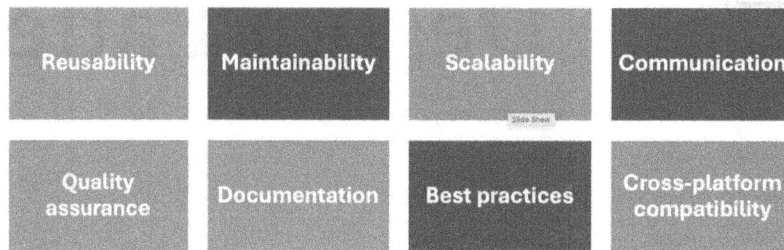

Figure 1.1: The significance of design patterns in software development

Design patterns hold great significance in software development for the following reasons:

- **Reusability:** Design patterns provide proven solutions to common problems in software development. By using these patterns, developers can reuse well-established designs and code structures, saving time and effort. This leads to more efficient development processes and reduces the risk of errors. One of the key advantages of design patterns is their ability to enhance code reusability. When developers apply these patterns, they create modular and reusable components that can be employed across different parts of a project or in entirely new projects. This not only accelerates development but also reduces the likelihood of duplicating code and introduces consistency into the codebase.

- **Maintainability:** Maintaining software over time can be a daunting task, especially as projects grow in complexity. Design patterns promote maintainability by encouraging clean, organized, and well-structured code. When developers follow established patterns, it becomes easier for them and their colleagues to understand, modify, and extend the codebase. This results in fewer bugs, smoother updates, and a reduced risk of introducing unintended issues during maintenance.

- **Scalability:** In today's fast-paced technological landscape, software must be adaptable and scalable to meet changing requirements. Design patterns provide a foundation for creating flexible and extensible architectures. They also help in creating software architectures that can scale to accommodate future requirements. They provide a framework for building flexible and extensible systems, making it easier to add new features or adapt to changing business needs without major code overhauls.

By employing these patterns, developers can design systems that accommodate future features, scale with increased user loads, and adapt to evolving business needs without undergoing major overhauls.

- **Communication:** Design patterns act as a common language among developers. They provide a shared vocabulary for discussing and documenting software design decisions. This enhances communication and collaboration within development teams and helps ensure that everyone understands the design choices being made.

- **Quality assurance:** By following established design patterns, developers can create code that is more robust and less prone to errors. This contributes to higher-quality software that is less likely to have defects or security vulnerabilities.

- **Documentation:** Design patterns serve as a form of documentation. When a developer encounters a particular pattern in the codebase, they can quickly understand its purpose and how it fits into the overall design. This reduces the need for extensive documentation and makes the codebase more self-explanatory.

- **Best practices:** Design patterns encapsulate best practices and proven solutions from experienced software engineers. They embody collective wisdom and expertise, allowing developers to benefit from the lessons learned by others in the field.

- **Cross-platform compatibility:** Some design patterns are platform-agnostic, making it easier to develop software that can run on different platforms or adapt to various environments.

Importance of Apex design patterns in Salesforce development

Salesforce development encompasses a diverse range of projects, from simple data management applications to complex, enterprise-level solutions. Regardless of the project's scale or complexity, the use of Apex design patterns holds the utmost importance. These patterns are not just coding guidelines but serve as a foundation for robust, scalable, and maintainable applications.

Following are some key reasons why Apex design patterns are essential in Salesforce development:

- **Scalability and maintainability:** Design patterns provide a structured framework for building Apex code, ensuring that your application remains agile and adaptable as it grows. They help prevent the development of monolithic, difficult-to-maintain code by promoting modularization.

- **Best practices:** Design patterns encapsulate best practices that have evolved over time. These practices result in more efficient, readable, and reliable code. By following established patterns, developers can avoid common pitfalls and ensure code consistency.

- **Code reusability:** One of the primary benefits of design patterns is the creation of reusable code components. These components can be employed throughout your application or even in other projects. Code reuse saves time and fosters consistency in functionality across various parts of your application.

- **Separation of concerns:** Design patterns encourage the separation of concerns, a fundamental principle in software design. This separation involves isolating different aspects of your code, such as business logic, data access, and user interface. The result is code that is easier to understand, test, and modify.

- **Performance optimization:** Certain design patterns focus on optimizing performance. They aim to reduce resource consumption and enhance execution speed. This can be particularly important in Salesforce development, where efficient processing is key to delivering a responsive user experience.

- **Error handling and testing:** Many design patterns include guidelines for error handling and testing. Proper error handling ensures that issues are identified and addressed systematically, leading to more robust and reliable applications. Testing becomes more straightforward and effective when following established patterns.

- **Team collaboration:** In collaborative development environments, design patterns act as a common language and set of guidelines. They facilitate communication and understanding among team members, making it easier for developers to collaborate effectively and maintain code consistency.

- **Flexibility:** Different projects have different requirements. Design patterns provide developers with the flexibility to choose the pattern that best aligns with the specific needs of their project. Whether it is a simple CRUD application, a complex integration, or custom business logic, the right design pattern can be selected.

- **Security:** Some design patterns incorporate security considerations, helping to safeguard sensitive data and operations. This is particularly vital in Salesforce development, where data protection and security compliance are important.

- **Industry standards:** Salesforce applications often need to adhere to industry standards and regulatory requirements. Many design patterns can help ensure compliance with these standards, simplifying the development process and reducing the risk of non-compliance.

In conclusion, Apex design patterns are indispensable in Salesforce development, as they promote good development practices, elevate code quality, and ensure the creation of scalable and maintainable solutions. By adhering to these patterns, developers can craft efficient, reliable, and adaptable applications on the Salesforce platform, regardless of the project's size or complexity.

Conclusion

In this chapter, we covered the fundamental concepts behind this book. We discussed the importance of design patterns in software development, highlighting their role in improving code reusability and maintainability. We then focused on how these patterns are crucial in Salesforce development, helping developers address complex challenges and improve efficiency and scalability.

In the next chapter, we will learn the fundamentals of design patterns which will cover the definition and characteristics of design patterns, the types of design patterns, and the benefits of using design patterns in Apex development.

Points to remember

- Design patterns are reusable solutions to common software development problems, providing structure and clarity in your code.

- Design patterns help achieve reusability, maintainability, scalability, and readability, leading to efficient and cleaner codebases.

- Apex design patterns adapt these principles to Salesforce development by promoting best practices specific to the platform's architecture and limitations.

- Apex design patterns help manage platform constraints like governor limits, execution context, and multi-tenancy.

- Using patterns like separation of concerns, error handling, and modularization ensures scalable and testable Apex applications.

- Design patterns act as a common vocabulary for teams, improving communication, collaboration, and adherence to best practices.

Questions

1. What is a design pattern, and why is it important in software development?

2. How do design patterns contribute to code reusability and maintainability?

3. Why are Apex design patterns especially important in Salesforce development?

4. Explain how design patterns improve team collaboration and code consistency.

5. What are some examples of software engineering principles supported by Apex design patterns?

6. How do design patterns assist in handling complexity and platform limitations in Salesforce?

7. What are the benefits of separating concerns in your Apex application?

8. In what ways do design patterns contribute to testing and debugging efforts?

9. How do design patterns ensure compliance with industry standards or regulations?

10. Can design patterns influence the performance of your Apex application? If so, how?

Join our book's Discord space

Join the book's Discord Workspace for Latest updates, Offers, Tech happenings around the world, New Release and Sessions with the Authors:

https://discord.bpbonline.com

CHAPTER 2
Understanding Design Patterns

Introduction

In this section of *Apex design patterns*, the emphasis turns towards understanding design patterns. The definition and unique characteristics of these patterns will be introduced, illuminating their structural elements and guiding principles. The taxonomy of design patterns is examined, covering creational, structural, and behavioral categories. The advantages of utilizing design patterns in the context of Apex development are underscored, demonstrating their ability to improve code modularity, streamline solutions, and accelerate development processes. As readers advance through this chapter, they cultivate a deeper understanding of the conceptual framework and the benefits associated with design patterns in Apex development.

Structure

The chapter covers the following topics:

- Definition and characteristics of design patterns
- Types of design patterns
- Benefits of using design patterns in Apex development

Objectives

By the end of this chapter, readers will understand the definitions and characteristics of design patterns, the different types of design patterns, and their benefits in Apex development.

Definition and characteristics of design patterns

Design patterns in software development are recurring solutions to common design problems that arise while developing software systems. They encapsulate best practices and provide proven approaches for designing software that is maintainable, scalable, and adaptable to change. We will provide a detailed exploration of the definition and characteristics of design patterns.

Defining design patterns

Design patterns refer to recurring solutions to common problems encountered in software design. They represent best practices, capturing expert knowledge and proven solutions to specific design challenges. These solutions are formalized to facilitate their reuse in various contexts.

Design patterns are essentially templates for solving problems in a particular context. They encapsulate the collective experience of skilled software developers, offering a standardized approach to recurring design challenges. These patterns are not blueprints or finished designs but rather guidelines for structuring code to solve a particular problem efficiently. At their core, design patterns provide a common vocabulary and abstractions that help developers communicate more effectively about software architecture and design. They contribute to creating flexible, maintainable, and scalable software systems.

Relationship with architecture and software engineering

Design patterns are crucial in the broader fields of software architecture and engineering. Let us look at an explanation of how design patterns are related to architecture and software engineering:

- **Architecture:** Design patterns are building blocks of software architecture. They guide architects in structuring systems, defining relationships between components, and ensuring the architecture is robust and adaptable. By incorporating design patterns, architects can create scalable and maintainable systems.

- **Software engineering:** In software engineering, design patterns act as tools that facilitate the software development process. They help manage complexity, promote code reusability, and ensure that software is functional, well-organized, and easy to understand. Design patterns contribute to the overall efficiency and effectiveness of the software engineering process.

In essence, design patterns bridge the gap between high-level architectural decisions and the nitty-gritty details of software implementation. They provide a shared language for developers, architects, and other stakeholders, fostering a more cohesive and efficient software development process.

Purpose of design patterns

The purpose of design patterns in software development is multifaceted, encompassing fundamental objectives that enhance the quality, maintainability, and scalability of software systems. Design patterns serve as guiding principles and proven solutions to common design challenges, fulfilling the following key purposes:

- **Improving software design**: Design patterns serve as guidelines to create well-structured and efficient software designs. They encapsulate best practices and proven solutions, allowing developers to leverage established approaches to common design problems. By incorporating design patterns, software designs become more modular, flexible, and adaptable, leading to higher-quality architectures.

- **Promoting code reuse**: One of the primary goals of design patterns is to promote code reuse. By encapsulating solutions to recurring problems, design patterns allow developers to reuse proven and tested code in different parts of an application or even across multiple projects. This not only saves time and effort but also enhances the consistency and reliability of the software.

- **Facilitating communication among developers**: Design patterns provide a common vocabulary and set of abstractions that facilitate communication among developers. When a team of developers is familiar with design patterns, they can express design ideas more clearly and concisely. This shared understanding promotes effective collaboration, as team members can discuss and implement solutions using a standardized and widely recognized set of concepts.

Enhancing maintainability and scalability

Design patterns contribute significantly to the maintainability and scalability of software systems. Refer to the following points for a better understanding:

- **Maintainability:** By promoting modular and well-organized code, design patterns make it easier to understand, update, and maintain software. Changes in one part of the system are less likely to have unintended consequences in other areas, leading to a more maintainable codebase.

- **Scalability:** Design patterns provide scalable solutions to common design challenges. As software requirements evolve or the scale of a system increases, design patterns offer guidance on how to extend and adapt the architecture without compromising its integrity. This scalability is crucial for systems that need to grow and handle increased complexity over time.

In summary, the purpose of design patterns goes beyond solving specific design problems; they are essential tools for improving the overall quality, maintainability, and scalability of software systems. They promote a systematic and efficient approach to software development, contributing to the success of projects in both the short and long term.

Types of design patterns

Design patterns are general reusable solutions to common problems that occur in software design. They represent best practices and provide a way to create flexible, efficient, and maintainable software. Design patterns are typically categorized into three main types: creational, structural, and behavioral.

The following figure illustrates the overall main types and sub types of design pattens:

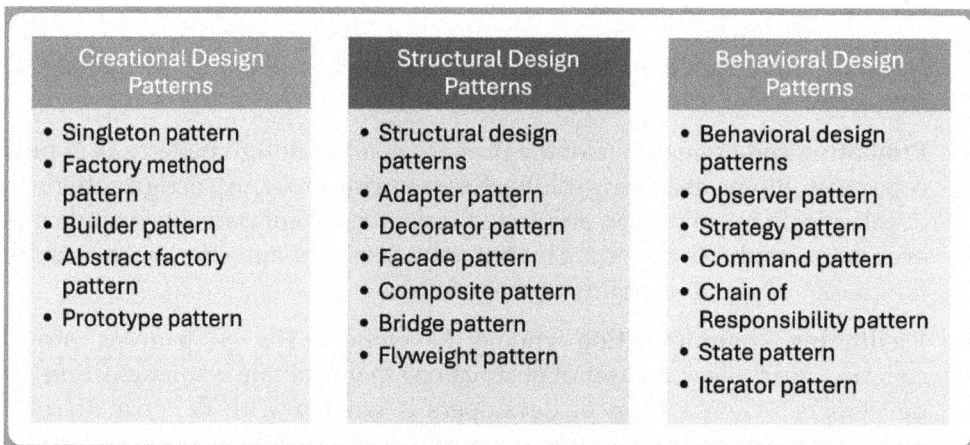

Creational Design Patterns	Structural Design Patterns	Behavioral Design Patterns
• Singleton pattern • Factory method pattern • Builder pattern • Abstract factory pattern • Prototype pattern	• Structural design patterns • Adapter pattern • Decorator pattern • Facade pattern • Composite pattern • Bridge pattern • Flyweight pattern	• Behavioral design patterns • Observer pattern • Strategy pattern • Command pattern • Chain of Responsibility pattern • State pattern • Iterator pattern

Figure 2.1: Main types & sub types of design patterns

Creational design patterns

Creational design patterns are concerned with the process of object creation in software development. They deal with the best way to instantiate objects, providing mechanisms for class instantiation while making the system independent of how its objects are created, composed, and represented.

Following are some common creational design patterns:

- **Singleton pattern:** The singleton pattern ensures that a class has only one instance throughout the application and provides a centralized, global access point to it. This is useful for managing shared resources or configurations.

- **Factory method pattern:** The factory pattern provides a way to create objects without specifying the exact class of object that will be created. This approach is useful for abstracting the instantiation logic, making the code more flexible and maintainable.

- **Abstract factory pattern:** This pattern provides a way to create families of related or dependent objects without specifying their exact class. It helps in maintaining consistency across related objects.

- **Builder pattern:** The builder pattern simplifies the creation of complex objects by separating the construction process from their final representation. It allows different representations to be built using the same construction process.

- **Prototype pattern:** This pattern creates new objects by duplicating existing ones, known as prototypes. It is useful when creating objects is resource-intensive or involves complex initialization.

Structural design patterns

Structural design patterns are concerned with simplifying the organization of classes and objects to form larger structures. They help in defining the composition of classes or objects to create more flexible and efficient systems.

Following are some common structural design patterns:

- **Adapter pattern:** It allows the interface of an existing class to be used as another interface.

- **Bridge pattern:** It separates an object's abstraction from its implementation so that the two can vary independently.

- **Composite pattern:** It composes objects into tree structures to represent part-whole hierarchies.

- **Decorator pattern:** It attaches additional responsibilities to an object dynamically. Decorators provide a flexible alternative to subclassing for extending functionality.

- **Facade pattern:** It provides a simplified interface to a set of interfaces in a subsystem, making it easier to use.

- **Flyweight pattern:** It minimizes memory usage or computational expenses by sharing as much as possible with related objects to support large numbers of fine-grained objects efficiently.

Behavioral design patterns

Behavioral design patterns are concerned with the interaction and communication between objects, defining patterns of communication between them. These patterns help in distributing responsibilities among objects and making the system more flexible and extensible.

Following are some common behavioral design patterns:

- **Observer pattern:** It defines a one-to-many dependency between objects so that when one object changes state, all its dependents are notified and updated automatically.

- **Strategy pattern:** It defines a family of algorithms, encapsulates each one, and makes them interchangeable. Strategy lets the algorithm vary independently from clients that use it.

- **Command pattern:** It encapsulates a request as an object, thereby allowing for parameterization of clients with different requests, queuing of requests, and logging of the parameters.

- **State pattern:** It allows an object to alter its behavior when its internal state changes. The object will appear to change its class.

- **Chain of responsibility pattern:** It passes a request along a chain of handlers. Upon receiving a request, each handler decides either to process the request or to pass it to the next handler in the chain.

- **Iterator pattern:** It provides a way to access elements of an aggregate object (such as a list or collection) sequentially without exposing the underlying representation of that object.

These design patterns help in solving specific problems and promote design principles such as encapsulation, abstraction, and flexibility in software development. It is common to use a combination of these patterns in a real-world application to address various design challenges. These topics will be discussed in detail in the next set of chapters.

Benefits of using design patterns in Apex development

Design patterns play a crucial role in software development, including Apex development in the Salesforce platform.

Following are some benefits of using design patterns in Apex development:

- **Reusability:** Design patterns promote code reuse by providing proven solutions to common problems. This reduces the need to reinvent the wheel for similar functionalities, leading to more efficient and maintainable code.

- **Scalability:** Design patterns help in building scalable solutions. They provide a structured approach to development, making it easier to scale the application as business requirements grow or change.

- **Maintainability:** Code developed using design patterns is often more modular and easier to maintain. Changes to one part of the system are less likely to have a ripple effect on other parts, making it simpler to update or enhance the codebase.

- **Consistency:** Design patterns encourage a consistent coding style and structure across an application or a development team. This consistency makes it easier for developers to understand each other's code, facilitating collaboration and reducing the learning curve for new team members.

- **Solving common problems:** Design patterns provide solutions to recurring problems in software design. In Apex development, patterns like the singleton pattern, factory pattern, and observer pattern can be applied to address specific challenges, such as managing the global state, creating objects, or handling event notifications.

- **Testability:** Code built using design patterns is often more testable. Patterns such as **Dependency Injection** (**DI**) facilitate the use of mock objects and make it easier to write unit tests for individual components, ensuring the reliability of the code.

- **Adaptability to change:** Design patterns make the codebase more adaptable to changes in requirements. Since they provide a modular structure, it becomes easier to replace or extend individual components without affecting the entire system.

- **Best practices:** Design patterns encapsulate best practices in software development. By adhering to these patterns, developers can benefit from the collective experience and wisdom of the software development community, resulting in more robust and efficient code.

- **Performance optimization:** Some design patterns can contribute to performance optimization. For example, the Flyweight pattern can be used to reduce memory consumption by sharing common data among multiple objects.

- **Community support:** Using design patterns in Apex development aligns your code with industry best practices. This makes it easier to find support and resources in the Salesforce community, as developers are more likely to be familiar with and understand code structured using well-known design patterns.

In summary, incorporating design patterns in Apex development can lead to more maintainable, scalable, and efficient code, while also promoting collaboration and adherence to best practices within the development community.

Conclusion

In this chapter, we covered the definition of design patterns and the characteristics of the design patterns. We discussed the formal definition, the relationship of the design patterns with architecture and software, and the purpose of design patterns. Additionally, we provided high-level information about the types of design patterns followed by the benefits of using design patterns in Apex development.

In the next chapter, we are going to learn the essentials of the Apex programming language. A brief introduction to Apex will be provided, including its core characteristics and functionalities.

Points to remember

- Design patterns are recurring solutions to common software design problems. They encapsulate best practices and proven approaches and also facilitate code reuse and improve maintainability and scalability.

- Creational design patterns include singleton, factory method, abstract factory, builder, and prototype.

- Structural design patterns include adapter, bridge, composite, decorator, facade, and flyweight.

- Behavioral design patterns include observer, strategy, command, state, chain of responsibility, and iterator.

- The benefits of using design patterns in Apex development are that they are reusability, scalability, maintainability, and consistency. Solving common problems efficiently. They also enhance testability and adaptability to change, along with encapsulating best practices and optimizing performance.

- The relationship between design patterns, architecture, and software engineering is that design patterns play a fundamental role in structuring software architecture. They aid in managing complexity and promoting code reusability. Design patterns bridge high-level architectural decisions with detailed software implementation.

Questions

1. What are design patterns in software development, and why are they important?

2. How are design patterns categorized, and what are examples of each category?

3. What benefits do design patterns offer in Apex development specifically?

4. How do design patterns contribute to software maintainability and scalability?

5. Why is it beneficial for developers to use a common set of design patterns in a project?

Join our book's Discord space

Join the book's Discord Workspace for Latest updates, Offers, Tech happenings around the world, New Release and Sessions with the Authors:

https://discord.bpbonline.com

CHAPTER 3
Apex Fundamentals

Introduction

The essentials of the Apex programming language are unveiled in this chapter. A brief introduction to Apex is provided, acquainting readers with its core characteristics and functionalities. The spectrum widens to encompass data types, variables, and operators, offering insights into the foundational elements that underpin Apex code. Furthermore, exploring control structures, including loops and conditional statements, ensues, presenting readers with the means to orchestrate program flow. As readers traverse this chapter, a comprehensive understanding of Apex's fundamental components is fostered, laying a solid groundwork for subsequent discussions on design patterns and their practical implementation.

Structure

The chapter covers the following topics:

- Introduction to Apex
- Data types and variables
- Control structures
- Exception handling
- Apex triggers

- Salesforce Object Query Language
- Governor limits
- Integration with external system
- Best practices and design patterns

Objectives

By the end of this chapter, readers will understand the fundamentals of Apex. The reader will understand the data types, variables, operators, and control structures (loops and conditional statements) in Apex.

Introduction to Apex

Salesforce Apex is a powerful, strongly typed, **object-oriented programming (OOP)** language designed for the Salesforce platform. It serves as the backend code for customizing and extending the functionality of Salesforce applications. Apex allows developers to add business logic to Salesforce objects, create custom web services, and perform database operations. The primary purpose of Apex is to enable the development of robust, scalable, and data-centric applications within the Salesforce ecosystem.

Integration with Salesforce platform

Apex is tightly integrated with the Salesforce platform, forming the backbone of various customization and automation features. It seamlessly interacts with the underlying Salesforce database, supporting the manipulation of records, execution of complex algorithms, and the implementation of custom workflows.

Key aspects of Apex integration with the Salesforce platform include the following:

- **Event-driven execution:** Apex is often event-driven, responding to actions such as record updates, button clicks, and system events. For instance, developers can write triggers in Apex to execute logic before or after records are inserted, updated, or deleted.

- **Access to salesforce objects:** Apex provides access to Salesforce objects (standard and custom) using **Salesforce Object Query Language (SOQL)** for querying and **Data Manipulation Language (DML)** for modifying records.

- **Customization of user interface:** Developers can use Apex to create custom controllers and extensions to enhance the functionality of Visualforce pages and Lightning components, allowing for a tailored user experience.

- **Integration with external systems:** Apex supports integration with external systems through various mechanisms, including web service callouts, REST, and **Simple Object Access Protocol (SOAP)**, enabling seamless communication with third-party services.

- **Governor limits:** Salesforce enforces governor limits to ensure fair usage of resources. These limits are an integral part of Apex development, preventing resource-intensive or poorly optimized code from affecting the overall performance of the Salesforce platform.

Key features of Apex are as follows:

- **OOP**: Salesforce Apex is fundamentally rooted in OOP principles, which brings several advantages to developers. Key features related to its object-oriented nature include the following:

  o **Classes and objects:** Apex follows the class-based model, where classes act as blueprints for creating objects. Objects, in turn, are instances of classes, encapsulating data and behavior.

  o **Inheritance:** Apex supports inheritance, allowing developers to create new classes based on existing ones. This promotes code reuse and the creation of a hierarchical structure.

  o **Encapsulation:** Apex promotes encapsulation by allowing developers to hide the implementation details of a class and expose only what is necessary. This enhances code modularity and reduces dependencies.

  o **Polymorphism:** This allows the use of a single interface to represent different types of objects. In Apex, polymorphism enables developers to design flexible and extensible code.

  o **Abstraction:** This involves simplifying complex systems by modeling classes based on real-world entities. Developers can use abstract classes and interfaces in Apex to achieve abstraction and build scalable systems.

- **Event-driven development:** This is a paradigm where events, such as user interactions or system events determine the flow of the program. In the context of Salesforce Apex, event-driven development is a key aspect that enables dynamic and responsive applications. Important features related to event-driven development include the following:

  o **Triggers:** Apex triggers are a fundamental part of event-driven development in Salesforce. Triggers respond to events, such as the creation, updating, or deletion of records, and execute custom logic.

  o **Asynchronous processing:** Apex provides mechanisms for handling events asynchronously, allowing developers to design applications that respond to events without blocking the main execution thread. This is crucial for scalable and efficient processing.

  o **Visualforce controllers and lightning components:** In the context of user interfaces, Apex controllers for Visualforce pages and Lightning components allow developers to respond to user interactions and events on the client side.

o   **Platform events:** Salesforce supports the creation and consumption of platform events, which are messages that represent events in a Salesforce organization. Developers can use platform events for building loosely coupled event-driven architectures.

Apex class structure

Apex classes are the building blocks of custom functionality in the Salesforce platform. They encapsulate methods and variables, enabling developers to organize code and define behavior. Let us explore the anatomy of an Apex class, focusing on member variables and methods.

Refer to the following:

- **Class declaration:**

```
public class MyClass {
    // Class body
}
```

  o   The **public** keyword specifies the access modifier, determining the visibility of the class.

  o   The class name (**MyClass** in this example) follows standard naming conventions.

  o   The class body is enclosed in curly braces **{}**.

- **Class modifiers:**

```
public with sharing class MyClass {
    // Class body
}
```

  o   The **with sharing** or **without sharing** keywords define the sharing setting for the class, controlling how data access is enforced.

- **Class variables (member variables):**

  o   Member variables store data within a class. They are defined with a data type and can have access modifiers such as public, private, or protected.

```
public class MyClass {
        public String name; // Public variable
        private Integer age; // Private variable
}
```

  o   Member variables store data within a class.

- o   They have data types (String and Integer in this example) and can have access modifiers like public or private.

- **Methods:**

```
public class MyClass {
    public String greetUser(String userName) {
        return 'Hello, ' + userName + '!';
    }
}
```

- o   Methods contain executable code within a class.

- o   They have a return type (**String** in this example), a name (**greetUser**), and can have parameters (**String userName**).

- **Constructors:**

```
public class MyClass {
    public MyClass() {
        // Constructor logic
    }
}
```

- o   A constructor initializes an object when it is created.

- o   It has the same name as the class and does not have a return type.

- **Access modifiers:**

```
public class MyClass {
    public String publicVariable;
    private Integer privateVariable;

    public void publicMethod() {
        // Public method logic
    }

    private String privateMethod() {
        // Private method logic
        return 'Private Result';
    }
}
```

- o   Access modifiers control the visibility of variables and methods.

- o   **public** and **private** are examples of access modifiers.

- **Static methods:**

```
public class MyClass {
    public static void staticMethod() {
        // Static method logic
    }
}
```

  o A static method is associated with the class rather than an instance.

  o It is called the class itself and can be used without creating an instance of the class.

- **Annotations:**

```
@AuraEnabled
public class MyClass {
    // Class body
}
```

  o Annotations provide metadata about the class.

  o **@AuraEnabled** is an example used for Lightning components.

- **Interfaces and inheritance:**

```
public class MyClass implements MyInterface {
    // Class body
}
```

  o Apex supports interfaces and inheritance.

  o The implements keyword is used for interfaces, and the extends keyword is used for inheritance.

- **Comments:**

```
/*
 * This is a multiline comment
 */
public class MyClass {
    // This is a single-line comment
}
```

  o Comments are used for documentation.

  o They can be single-line (//) or multiline (/* */).

Data types and variables

In Salesforce Apex, data types and variables play a crucial role in defining and manipulating data. Let us explore these concepts in more detail.

Data types in Apex are as follows:

- **Primitive data types**: They represent single values and are the building blocks for more complex data structures. Salesforce Apex supports the following primitive data types:

  o **Boolean**: It represents a true or false value.

  o **Date**: It represents a date (day, month, and year).

  o **DateTime**: It represents both date and time.

  o **Decimal**: It represents a fixed-point number with a decimal point.

  o **Double**: It represents a 64-bit floating-point number.

  o **Integer:** It represents a whole number (32-bit signed integer).

  o **Long**: It represents a 64-bit integer (larger than Integer).

  o **String**: It represents a sequence of characters (text).

  o **Time**: It represents a specific time of day.

  Example:
  ```
  Boolean isActive = true;
  Date currentDate = Date.today();
  Integer quantity = 10;
  String message = 'Hello, Salesforce!';
  ```

- **Collections (Lists, Sets, Maps)**: Collections allow you to work with multiple values or data sets. Salesforce Apex provides several collection data types, as follows:

  o **List**: An ordered collection that can contain duplicate values.

  o **Set**: An unordered collection that stores unique values (no duplicates).

  o **Map**: A collection of key-value pairs, where each key is associated with a value.

  Example:
  ```
  List<String> fruits = new List<String>{'Apple', 'Banana', 'Orange'};
  Set<Integer> uniqueNumbers = new Set<Integer>{1, 2, 3};
  Map<String, Integer> employeeSalaries = new Map<String,
  Integer>{'Alice' => 50000, 'Bob' => 60000};
  ```

- **Custom objects**: They are user-defined data structures created to store specific data tailored to your organization's needs. They are created using the Salesforce Object Manager and can have custom fields, relationships, and behaviors.

Example:

```
// Custom object Account__c with custom fields
List<Account__c> accounts = [SELECT Id, Name, Custom_Field__c FROM
Account__c WHERE Custom_Field__c = 'Value'];
```

Declaring variables

In Apex, variables are used to store data temporarily.

Following is how you declare and work with variables:

- **Variable naming conventions**:
  - Variable names must start with a letter and can contain letters, numbers, and underscores.
  - Names are case-insensitive but conventionally written in CamelCase for classes and PascalCase for variables.
  - Avoid using reserved keywords.

  Example:

  ```
  String firstName;
  Integer accountNumber;
  ```

- **Initialization and assignment**:
  - Variables can be initialized and assigned values when declared or at a later stage.
  - Initialization involves providing an initial value to a variable.
  - Assignment involves changing the value of a variable.

  Example:

  ```
  String greeting = 'Hello';
  Integer count;
  count = 42;
  ```

Operators in Apex

In Apex, operators are essential components that allow you to perform various operations on variables and values. These operations can include arithmetic calculations, comparisons, logical operations, and more. Understanding how to effectively use operators in Apex is critical for writing efficient and maintainable code. This section will cover the different types of operators available in Apex, providing examples and explanations to help you master their usage.

- **Arithmetic operators:**

  - + (Addition), - (Subtraction), * (Multiplication), / (Division): Perform basic arithmetic operations.

  - % (Modulus): Returns the remainder of a division operation.

  - ++ (Increment), -- (Decrement): Increase or decrease the value of a variable by 1.
    ```
    Integer a = 5;
    Integer b = 3;
    Integer sum = a + b; // sum = 8
    Integer remainder = a % b; // remainder = 2
    a++; // a = 6
    ```

- **Comparison operators:**

  - == (Equal to), != (Not equal to), > (Greater than), < (Less than), >= (Greater than or equal to), <= (Less than or equal to): Compare values and return true or false.
    ```
    Integer x = 5;
    Integer y = 3;
    Boolean isEqual = x == y; // isEqual = false
    Boolean isGreaterThan = x > y; // isGreaterThan = true
    ```

- **Logical operators:**

  - && (AND), || (OR), ! (NOT): Combine Boolean expressions to produce a Boolean result.
    ```
    Boolean condition1 = true;
    Boolean condition2 = false;
    Boolean result = condition1 && condition2; // result = false
    ```

Understanding data types, variables, and operators in Salesforce Apex is fundamental for writing effective code and building robust applications on the Salesforce platform.

Control structures

In Salesforce Apex, control structures are used to control the flow of code execution. They allow you to make decisions, execute code conditionally, and repeat code blocks. Here are the primary control structures in Apex.

Conditional statements

Conditional statements are a fundamental concept in Apex that allows developers to control the execution flow based on specific conditions. By using conditional statements, you can create flexible and dynamic code that responds differently depending on the values of variables or the outcome of expressions. This section will explore the various types of conditional statements available in Apex, such as if, else, and switch statements. It will also provide examples to demonstrate how to implement them effectively in your programs.

Refer to the following:

- **if-else statement:**

  o The **if-else** statement allows you to execute different blocks of code based on a condition.

  o In the following example, the code inside the **if** block is executed if the condition **(age >= 18)** is true. Otherwise, the code inside the **else** block is executed.

```
Integer age = 25;

if (age >= 18) {
    System.debug('You are an adult.');
} else {
    System.debug('You are a minor.');
}
```

- **Switch statements:**

  o A **switch** statement provides a way to evaluate multiple conditions based on the value of an expression.

  o In the following example, the switch statement evaluates the **dayOfWeek** variable and executes the code block associated with the matching case. The **break** statement is used to exit the **switch** statement once a match is found.

```
String dayOfWeek = 'Monday';

switch (dayOfWeek) {
    case 'Monday':
        System.debug('It\'s the start of the week.');
        break;
    case 'Friday':
        System.debug('It\'s almost the weekend.');
```

```
            break;
        default:
            System.debug('It\'s a regular day.');
    }
```

Loops

Loops in Apex are powerful constructs that allow you to repeatedly execute a block of code while a specific condition is met or for a predefined number of iterations. They help simplify tasks such as iterating over collections, performing repetitive operations, or handling large datasets efficiently.

In this section, we will explore the different types of loops available in Apex, including for, while, and do-while loops, and provide practical examples to illustrate how to use them in your applications.

Refer to the following:

- **For loops:**

  o A for loop is used to iterate over a range of values, such as a collection or a numerical range.

  o In this example, the **for** loop initializes a counter **i** to 0 and iterates as long as **i** is less than 5, incrementing **i** by 1 in each iteration.

  ```
  for (Integer i = 0; i < 5; i++) {
      System.debug('Iteration ' + i);
  }
  ```

- **While loops:**

  o A **while** loop repeatedly executes a block of code as long as a specified condition is true.

  o The **while** loop continues to execute as long as the **counter** is less than 3. The **counter** is incremented in each iteration to prevent an infinite loop.

  ```
  Integer counter = 0;

  while (counter < 3) {
      System.debug('Count: ' + counter);
      counter++;
  }
  ```

- **Do-while loops:**

  o A **do-while** loop is similar to a **while** loop but guarantees that the loop body is executed at least once before checking the condition.

- o In this example, the loop body is executed once even though **num** is initially 5.

```
Integer num = 5;

do {
    System.debug('Number is: ' + num);
    num--;
} while (num > 0);
```

Control structures are fundamental for controlling the flow of your Apex code, allowing you to create dynamic and responsive applications by making decisions and handling repetitive tasks based on specific conditions.

Exception handling

Exception handling in Salesforce Apex is a crucial aspect of writing robust code. It allows you to gracefully handle unexpected situations or errors that may occur during the execution of your code. Here is an overview of exception handling in Apex, including try-catch blocks and common exception types.

try-catch blocks

In Apex, handling errors and exceptions gracefully is crucial to maintaining a robust and reliable application. Try-catch blocks are designed to help you catch and handle exceptions that may occur during the execution of your code. By using try-catch blocks, you can prevent unexpected runtime errors from crashing your application and provide meaningful responses or fallback behavior. This section will cover how to implement try-catch blocks in Apex, including best practices for handling specific exceptions and ensuring that your code remains resilient in various scenarios.

- The **try** block encloses the code that may generate an exception.
- If an exception is thrown within the **try** block, control is transferred to the **catch** block.
- **ExceptionType** is the specific type of exception you expect to handle (e.g., **DmlException**, **NullPointerException**), refer to the following code for the same:

```
try {
    // Code that might throw an exception
} catch (ExceptionType e) {
    // Exception handling code
}
```

Common exception types

Following are some common exception types that you may encounter in Salesforce Apex:

- **Exception (Generic exception):**
  - This is a generic exception class that can catch various types of exceptions.
  - It is often used when you want to handle multiple exceptions in a single catch block. Refer to the following code for a better understanding:

```
try {
    // Code that might throw an exception
} catch (Exception e) {
    // Handle the exception
    System.debug('An exception occurred: ' +
e.getMessage());
}
```

- **DmlException (Database exception):**
  - Thrown when a **Database Manipulation Language** (**DML**) operation (e.g., insert, update, delete) fails.
  - It provides detailed information about which records caused the exception. Refer to the following code for a better understanding:

```
try {
    // DML operation
    insert new Account(Name = 'Test Account');
} catch (DmlException e) {
    // Handle DML exception
    System.debug('DML Exception: ' + e.getMessage());
}
```

- **NullPointerException:**
  - It occurs when you attempt to access or manipulate a null object.
  - It is essential to check for null values before using objects to avoid this exception. Refer to the following code for a better understanding:

```
try {
    // Attempting to access a null object
    String s = null;
    Integer length = s.length(); // Throws a
NullPointerException
} catch (NullPointerException e) {
    // Handle null pointer exception
```

```
        System.debug('Null Pointer Exception: ' +
    e.getMessage());
    }
```

- **ListException:** This is thrown when there is an issue with list operations, such as accessing elements beyond the list's bounds. Refer to the following code for a better understanding:

```
try {
    List<Integer> numbers = new List<Integer>{1, 2, 3};
    Integer value = numbers[5]; // Throws a ListException
} catch (ListException e) {
    // Handle list exception
    System.debug('List Exception: ' + e.getMessage());
}
```

- **IndexOutOfBoundsException:** It occurs when you attempt to access a list element using an index that is outside the valid range. Refer to the following code for a better understanding:

```
try {
    List<Integer> numbers = new List<Integer>{1, 2, 3};
    Integer value = numbers[5]; // Throws an
IndexOutOfBoundsException
} catch (IndexOutOfBoundsException e) {
    // Handle index out of bounds exception
    System.debug('Index Out of Bounds Exception: ' +
e.getMessage());
}
```

- **LimitException:** Thrown when you exceed governor limits set by Salesforce, such as limits on the number of queries, DML operations, or CPU time. The code for the same is mentioned below:

```
try {
    // Code that may exceed governor limits
} catch (LimitException e) {
    // Handle limit exception
    System.debug('Limit Exception: ' + e.getMessage());
}
```

These are some of the common exception types in Salesforce Apex. The complete set of Apex in-built exceptions is listed in the Salesforce developer section: **https://developer. salesforce.com/docs/atlas.en-us.apexref.meta/apexref/apex_classes_exception_ methods.htm**

Handling exceptions appropriately is essential for building reliable and robust applications on the Salesforce platform, as it allows you to gracefully handle errors and prevent unexpected failures.

Apex triggers

Let us explore the basics of Apex triggers, including trigger events, trigger context variables, and best practices for writing triggers, as well as considerations for bulk processing.

Trigger basics

Apex triggers are pieces of code that are executed in response to specific events occurring in Salesforce, such as record insertions, updates, or deletions. The following are some fundamental aspects of Apex triggers:

- **Trigger events**: They define when a trigger should run. Common trigger events include the following:
  - o **before insert**: This trigger runs before records are inserted.
  - o **before update**: This trigger runs before records are updated.
  - o **before delete**: This trigger runs before records are deleted.
  - o **after insert**: This trigger runs after records are inserted.
  - o **after update**: This trigger runs after records are updated.
  - o **after delete**: This trigger runs after records are deleted.
  - o **after undelete**: This trigger runs after records are undeleted.

    You can specify one or more trigger events when creating a trigger.

- **Trigger context variables:** They provide information about the trigger's execution context. Common trigger context variables include the following:
  - o **Trigger.new**: Contains the new versions of records being inserted or updated.
  - o **Trigger.old**: Contains the old versions of records being updated or deleted.
  - o **Trigger.newMap**: A map of new records, where the record ID is the key.
  - o **Trigger.oldMap**: A map of old records, where the record ID is the key.
  - o **Trigger.isInsert, Trigger.isUpdate, Trigger.isDelete, Trigger.isBefore, Trigger.isAfter**: Boolean flags indicating the trigger's context.

Writing triggers

Triggers in Apex are powerful tools that allow you to automate processes and enforce business logic by responding to specific events on Salesforce objects, such as record insertions, updates, or deletions. Triggers enable you to interact with data at a deeper level, making it possible to perform actions like validation, updates, or sending notifications when certain conditions are met. In this section, we will discuss how to write efficient and well-structured triggers, explore trigger context variables, and discuss best practices to avoid common pitfalls such as recursion and governor limits:

- **Best practices:** When writing Apex triggers, it is essential to follow best practices to ensure maintainability and performance, some are mentioned as follows:

    o **Use a trigger handler pattern**: Organize your code by implementing a trigger handler pattern to separate trigger logic from the trigger itself. This improves code readability and testability.

    o **Bulk-friendly code**: Write your triggers to handle bulk operations efficiently. Avoid using SOQL queries or DML statements inside loops to prevent hitting governor limits.

    o **Governor limits**: Be mindful of Salesforce governor limits and design your triggers to work within these limits. Implement strategies like query optimization and data aggregation.

    o **Error handling**: Implement robust error handling to handle exceptions gracefully. Use try-catch blocks to capture and log errors.

    o **Testing and code coverage**: Always write unit tests to ensure adequate code coverage for your triggers. Test various scenarios, including bulk operations and edge cases.

- **Bulk processing considerations:** When dealing with bulk operations in triggers, consider the following:

    o **Bulk trigger events**: Ensure your triggers can handle bulk events with multiple records. Use collections and bulk processing techniques to optimize performance.

    o **Avoid SOQL queries inside loops**: Refrain from querying records inside a loop. Instead, query the necessary data before entering the loop and use collections to process records.

    o **DML operations**: Minimize the number of DML operations. You can often update multiple records with a single DML statement.

    o **Recursive triggers**: Prevent infinite loops by using static variables to track trigger recursion.

    o **Trigger order**: Be aware of the order in which triggers are executed if multiple triggers are on the same object. Use trigger handler patterns to control execution order.

Apex triggers are a powerful way to automate and customize behavior in Salesforce, but they should be designed and written carefully to ensure reliable and efficient execution. Following best practices and considering bulk processing scenarios is crucial for successful trigger development.

Salesforce Object Query Language

SOQL is a query language used in Salesforce to retrieve data from Salesforce objects (records) such as standard objects e.g., accounts, contacts, opportunities, and custom objects. It is similar in syntax to **Structured Query Language** (**SQL**) but is tailored for querying Salesforce data.

Querying Salesforce objects

To query Salesforce objects using SOQL, you use the **SELECT** statement.

Following is a basic example of querying **Account** records:

```
SELECT Id, Name, Industry FROM Account
```

- **SELECT**: Specifies the fields to retrieve.
- **FROM**: Specifies the object to query (in this case, the **Account** object).

Filtering and sorting results

SOQL allows you to filter and sort query results using various clauses, refer to the following points for a better understanding:

- **WHERE Clause (Filtering):** You can use the **WHERE** clause to filter records based on specific conditions, as shown below:

```
SELECT Id, Name FROM Account WHERE Industry = 'Technology'
```

- **ORDER BY Clause (Sorting):** The **ORDER BY** clause allows you to sort the results in ascending or descending order based on one or more fields, as shown below:

```
SELECT Id, Name FROM Account ORDER BY CreatedDate DESC
```

Relationship queries

Salesforce objects often have relationships with other objects. SOQL allows you to query related data using relationship fields, as follows:

- **Parent-to-child relationship (lookup relationship):** You can query child records related to a parent record using a relationship field. For example, querying **Contacts** related to an **Account**, as shown below:

```
SELECT Id, Name, (SELECT Id, FirstName, LastName FROM
    Contacts) FROM Account
```

- **Child-to-parent relationship (lookup relationship):** You can also query the parent record from a child record using a relationship field. For example, querying the **Account** associated with a **Contact**, as shown below:

```
SELECT Id, FirstName, LastName, Account.Name FROM Contact
```

- **Cross-object relationships (master-detail and lookup relationships):** You can traverse multiple relationships in a single query to retrieve related data from multiple objects. For example, querying **Opportunities** related to an **Account** and the associated **Contact**, as follows:

```
SELECT Id, Name, (SELECT Id, Name FROM Contacts), (SELECT Id,
Name FROM Opportunities) FROM Account
```

SOQL provides a flexible and powerful way to query Salesforce data, allowing you to retrieve, filter, and sort records based on your specific needs. Understanding relationships between objects is key to constructing complex queries to fetch related data efficiently.

Data Manipulation Language

Data Manipulation Language (DML) in Salesforce refers to the set of operations used to manipulate data within Salesforce objects (records). DML operations include inserting, updating, and deleting records, as well as handling transactions. Let us explore these concepts:

Inserting and updating records

In Salesforce, managing data through Apex often involves inserting new records and updating existing ones. Using DML operations, such as insert and update, developers can efficiently handle record transactions. Whether you are adding new data to the database or modifying existing information, understanding how to perform these actions properly is crucial for maintaining data integrity and optimizing performance. This section will guide you through the process of inserting and updating records using DML statements in Apex, while also highlighting best practices to avoid common pitfalls, such as hitting governor limits or causing unnecessary record locking.

Refer to the following:

- **Inserting records:**

  o In order to insert new records into Salesforce objects, you use the **insert** DML statement.

  o You create a new record using the appropriate object type (e.g., **Account**), set the field values, and then use the **insert** statement to add it to the database. The following is an example of inserting a new **Account** record:

    ```
    Account newAccount = new Account(Name = 'Sample Account');
    insert newAccount;
    ```

- **Updating records:**

  o In order to update existing records in Salesforce objects, you use the **update** DML statement.

  o You query the record you want to update, modify its field values, and then use the update statement to save the changes to the database. Here is an example of updating an existing **Contact** record:

```
Contact existingContact = [SELECT Id, FirstName, LastName
FROM Contact WHERE LastName = 'Smith' LIMIT 1];
existingContact.FirstName = 'John';
update existingContact;
```

Deleting records

In order to delete records from Salesforce objects, you use the **delete** DML statement. You query the record you want to delete and then use the **delete** statement to remove it from the database.

Following is an example of deleting a **Contact** record:

```
Contact contactToDelete = [SELECT Id FROM Contact WHERE LastName =
'Johnson' LIMIT 1];
delete contactToDelete;
```

Handling transactions

In Salesforce, DML operations are typically performed within transactions. Transactions are sequences of one or more DML operations executed as a single unit.

Following are some key aspects of handling transactions:

- **Implicit transactions:**
  - Salesforce implicitly wraps individual DML operations (insert, update, delete) in a transaction.
  - If any part of the transaction fails (e.g., due to an exception or validation rule), the entire transaction is rolled back, and no changes are saved.
- **Explicit transactions:**
  - You can also define explicit transactions using the **Database** class methods:
  - **Database.insert():** This allows you to insert records in bulk and specify how to handle errors.
  - **Database.update():** This allows you to update records in bulk and specify error handling.
  - **Database.delete():** This enables bulk deletion of records with error handling.
  - **Database.rollback(savepoint):** This rolls back to a specific savepoint within a transaction.
- **Savepoints:**
  - Savepoints can be used within a transaction to create checkpoints that you can roll back to if an error occurs.
  - This helps in handling complex transactions more effectively.

```
Savepoint sp = Database.setSavepoint();
try {
    // DML operations
} catch (Exception e) {
    // Handle the exception
    Database.rollback(sp);
}
```

Handling DML operations and transactions effectively ensures data integrity and reliability in Salesforce applications. Proper error handling and bulk processing considerations are important for managing data manipulations efficiently.

Governor limits

Governor limits are a set of runtime constraints enforced by the Salesforce platform to ensure that resource usage is fair, efficient, and does not negatively impact the overall performance and stability of the platform. Understanding and working within these limits is crucial when developing applications on the Salesforce platform.

This section is an overview of Salesforce governor limits, common limits, and best practices to avoid hitting these limits.

Overview of limits

Salesforce enforces a wide range of limits across various aspects of the platform.

The following figure illustrates the types of governor limits in Salesforce:

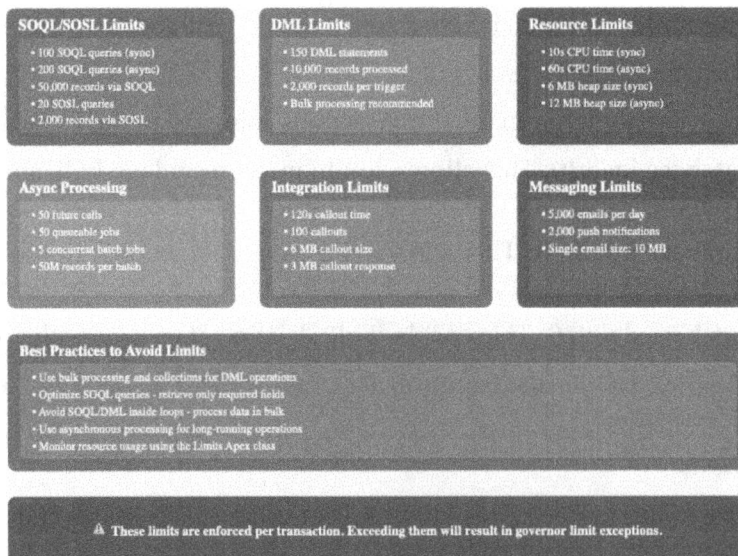

SOQL/SOSL Limits
- 100 SOQL queries (sync)
- 200 SOQL queries (async)
- 50,000 records via SOQL
- 20 SOSL queries
- 2,000 records via SOSL

DML Limits
- 150 DML statements
- 10,000 records processed
- 2,000 records per trigger
- Bulk processing recommended

Resource Limits
- 10s CPU time (sync)
- 60s CPU time (async)
- 6 MB heap size (sync)
- 12 MB heap size (async)

Async Processing
- 50 future calls
- 50 queueable jobs
- 5 concurrent batch jobs
- 50M records per batch

Integration Limits
- 120s callout time
- 100 callouts
- 6 MB callout size
- 3 MB callout response

Messaging Limits
- 5,000 emails per day
- 2,000 push notifications
- Single email size: 10 MB

Best Practices to Avoid Limits
- Use bulk processing and collections for DML operations
- Optimize SOQL queries - retrieve only required fields
- Avoid SOQL/DML inside loops - process data in bulk
- Use asynchronous processing for long-running operations
- Monitor resource usage using the Limits Apex class

⚠ These limits are enforced per transaction. Exceeding them will result in governor limit exceptions.

Figure 3.1: Types of Governor Limits in Salesforce

Some of the most common governor limits include the following:

- **Apex limits:**
    - Maximum CPU time per transaction.
    - Maximum heap size (memory) per transaction.
    - Maximum number of SOQL queries and DML statements per transaction.
    - Maximum number of asynchronous and batch Apex jobs.
    - Maximum trigger depth (recursive triggers).

- **Data limits:**
    - Maximum number of records retrieved in a SOQL query.
    - Maximum number of records processed in a DML operation (e.g., insert, update, delete).
    - Maximum number of custom fields per object.
    - Maximum number of custom objects per organization.

- **Email limits:**
    - Maximum number of outbound emails sent per day.
    - Maximum number of recipients in an email.

- **API limits:**
    - Maximum number of API requests made per day.
    - Maximum number of API requests made per minute.

- **Storage limits:**
    - Maximum data storage capacity for an organization.
    - Maximum file storage capacity for an organization.
    - Maximum number of custom settings and metadata components.

Best practices to avoid limits

In order to work within Salesforce governor limits and avoid hitting them, consider the following best practices:

- **Bulk processing**: Use bulk processing techniques when working with data. Minimize the number of DML operations and SOQL queries within loops.

- **Query optimization**: Write efficient SOQL queries to retrieve only the necessary data. Use selective **WHERE** clauses and indexes where applicable.

- **Data volume considerations**: Design data models that can handle future growth. Consider archiving or deleting old data if necessary.

- **Asynchronous processing**: Use asynchronous processing, such as batch Apex, to perform long-running operations and avoid hitting CPU and heap size limits.

- **Limit monitoring**: Implement monitoring and logging mechanisms to track your application's resource usage and detect issues early.

- **Error handling**: Implement robust error handling to handle exceptions gracefully. Roll back transactions when needed.

- **Testing and code coverage**: Write unit tests to ensure code coverage and validate that your code works correctly within limits.

- **Design patterns**: Implement design patterns like trigger handlers and service layers to organize and optimize code execution.

- **Governor limit exceptions**: Use appropriate try-catch blocks to catch governor limit exceptions and handle them gracefully.

- **Consult salesforce documentation**: Refer to Salesforce documentation for specific limits and best practices for each limit type.

By following these best practices, you can ensure that your Salesforce applications are efficient, scalable, and reliable while staying within the platform's governor limits. Proper planning and monitoring are key to successfully working within these constraints.

Integration with external systems

Integration with external systems is a common requirement in Salesforce applications, allowing you to exchange data and functionality with other services or platforms. Salesforce provides several mechanisms for integrating with external systems, including web service callouts, REST and SOAP integration, and asynchronous Apex. Let us explore each of these integration options.

Web service callouts

Web service callouts enable your Salesforce application to interact with external web services or APIs to exchange data. Salesforce supports both outbound and inbound web service callouts:

- **Outbound web service callouts:**
  - **REST API callouts**: HTTP requests to external RESTful APIs can be made using Apex. Here is an example of making a REST API callout:

    ```
    Http http = new Http();
    HttpRequest request = new HttpRequest();
    request.setEndpoint('https://api.example.com/resource');
    request.setMethod('GET');
    HttpResponse response = http.send(request);
    ```

o   **SOAP API callouts**: SOAP-based web service callouts to external SOAP APIs can also be made using Apex. Salesforce provides tools to generate Apex classes from WSDL files for SOAP integration.

- **Inbound web service callouts:**

o   Inbound web service callouts allow external systems to invoke Apex classes in your Salesforce org.

o   You can expose custom Apex RESTful web services or SOAP web services for this purpose.

REST and SOAP integration

Salesforce provides robust support for both REST and SOAP-based integrations, as follows:

- **REST integration**:

o   RESTful integration allows you to work with external systems using HTTP methods (GET, POST, PUT, DELETE) and standard data formats like JSON and XML.

o   Custom RESTful services can be built in Salesforce using Apex and exposed to external systems.

o   Salesforce also supports external REST APIs. You can make HTTP requests to external REST services using Apex.

- **SOAP integration**:

o   SOAP integration is a standardized protocol for exchanging structured information in web services.

o   Apex classes can be generated from WSDL files provided by external SOAP services to enable SOAP-based callouts from Salesforce.

Asynchronous Apex

Asynchronous Apex is used for performing long-running operations, such as integrations or data processing, in the background without blocking the user interface. There are several ways to implement asynchronous processing in Salesforce, as follows:

- **Future methods:** The following code can be run asynchronously in the background using future methods. **@future** annotations can be applied to methods to make them asynchronous:

```
@future
public static void myAsyncMethod() {
    // Perform asynchronous tasks here
}
```

- **Queueable Apex:** Jobs can be added to the Apex job queue using Queueable Apex, offering greater control and flexibility over asynchronous processing, as follows:

```
public class MyQueueable implements Queueable {
    public void execute(QueueableContext context) {
        // Perform asynchronous tasks here
    }
}
```

- **Batch Apex:** Thus is used for processing large sets of records in chunks, often in the context of data integration, by using the following code:

```
public class MyBatch implements Database.Batchable<SObject> {
    public Database.QueryLocator start(Database.BatchableContext
context) {
        // Define query to fetch records for processing
    }

    public void execute(Database.BatchableContext context,
List<SObject> scope) {
        // Process records in chunks
    }

    public void finish(Database.BatchableContext context) {
        // Post-processing logic
    }
}
```

By utilizing asynchronous Apex, time-consuming tasks, including integrations with external systems, can be offloaded to background jobs, while maintaining the responsiveness of your Salesforce application.

Integrating with external systems and conducting asynchronous processing are fundamental capabilities in Salesforce development, allowing for the creation of powerful and efficient solutions that connect and interact with various external services and platforms.

Best practices and design patterns

Best practices, design patterns, and **test-driven development** (**TDD**) are crucial aspects of Apex development in Salesforce. They help ensure code quality, maintainability, and reliability. Here is a more detailed look at each of these topics.

Code organization

Let us look at the organization of the code, as follows:

- **Modularization:** Break down your code into modular components, such as classes and methods, each with a clear and specific responsibility. This enhances code reusability and maintainability.

- **Use of comments:** Add meaningful comments and documentation to your code to explain complex logic, assumptions, and any potential gotchas.

- **Naming conventions:** Follow consistent naming conventions for variables, methods, classes, and other elements. This promotes code readability and makes it easier for others to understand your code.

- **Trigger handler pattern:** Adopt the trigger handler pattern to separate trigger logic from trigger code. Create trigger handler classes to encapsulate logic, making it easier to test and maintain.

- **Service layer:** Implement a service layer to centralize and abstract business logic. This promotes code reusability and maintainability and ensures consistent interactions with external systems or custom logic.

- **Custom settings and metadata:** Store configuration settings in custom settings or custom metadata types to make your code more dynamic and configurable.

Design patterns for maintainability

Design patterns are reusable solutions to common software design problems. There are design patterns that can help improve maintainability and code organization, some of them are mentioned, as follows:

- **Singleton pattern:** This ensures that a class has only one instance and provides a global point of access to that instance.

- **Factory method pattern:** This defines an interface for creating an object but lets us subclasses alter the type of objects that will be created.

- **Builder pattern:** This allows the construction of a complex object step by step. It separates the construction of a complex object from its representation.

- **Abstract factory pattern:** This provides an interface for creating families of related or dependent objects without specifying their concrete classes.

- **Prototype pattern:** This creates new objects by copying an existing object, known as the prototype, and modifying it as needed.

- **Adapter pattern:** This allows objects with incompatible interfaces to work together. It acts as a bridge between two interfaces.

- **Decorator pattern:** This adds functionality to objects dynamically without altering their structure. It is used to extend the behavior of classes in a flexible way.

- **Facade pattern:** This provides a simplified interface to a complex system, making it easier to interact with the system without needing to understand its internal complexities.

- **Composite pattern:** This allows you to treat individual objects and compositions of objects uniformly. It creates a tree structure of objects.

- **Bridge pattern:** This separates an object's abstraction from its implementation, allowing both to vary independently. It is used when you want to avoid a permanent binding between an abstraction and its implementation.

- **Flyweight pattern:** This is used to reduce memory usage or computational expenses by sharing as much as possible with similar objects. It treats objects with shared states uniformly.

- **Observer pattern:** This defines a one-to-many dependency between objects, where one object (the subject) maintains a list of its dependents (observers) and notifies them of state changes.

- **Strategy pattern:** This defines a family of algorithms, encapsulates each one, and makes them interchangeable. It allows you to choose the appropriate algorithm at runtime.

- **Command pattern:** This encapsulates a request as an object, thereby allowing for the parameterization of clients with queues, requests, and operations.

- **Chain of responsibility pattern:** This passes a request along a chain of handlers. Each handler decides either to process the request or to pass it to the next handler in the chain.

- **State pattern:** This allows an object to change its behavior when its internal state changes. It encapsulates states into separate classes and delegates the state-specific behavior to these classes.

- **Iterator pattern:** This provides a way to access elements of an aggregate object (such as a list or collection) sequentially without exposing the underlying representation of that object.

Note: These design patterns will be explained in the next set of chapters.

Test-driven development in Apex

TDD is a software development methodology that emphasizes writing tests before implementing the actual code. In Apex, TDD helps ensure that your code is reliable, maintainable, and meets the desired functionality by first outlining tests that define expected behavior. By developing tests upfront, you can catch bugs early, enforce business logic, and improve code quality. In this section, we will explore how to apply the principles of TDD in Apex, including writing unit tests, using test data, and achieving high code coverage. You will also learn the best practices for structuring your test classes and leveraging the test class to create effective and scalable test methods in the following section:

1. **Write a test first**: Begin by writing a test class that defines test methods for the expected behavior of the code you plan to implement. Ensure that the test initially fails because the functionality is not yet implemented.

2. **Implement the code**: Write the actual code to make the test pass. Follow the Red-Green-Refactor cycle:

    a. **Red**: The test fails because the functionality is not implemented.

    b. **Green**: The test passes after writing the code.

    c. **Refactor**: Improve the code without changing its behavior while keeping the tests passing.

3. **Repeat**: Repeat the TDD cycle for each new feature or change in your codebase.

Ensuring that your code behaves as expected and is testable from the start is facilitated by TDD. Documentation for your code's intended behavior is also provided, and regressions can be caught when making future changes. Robust, maintainable, and high-quality Salesforce applications can be created by following best practices, utilizing design patterns, and incorporating TDD in your Apex development process.

Conclusion

In this chapter, we covered a brief introduction to the Apex programming. We discussed the data types, variables, operators, Loops, and conditional statements in apex. Additionally, we provided high-level information about Exception handling, apex triggers, SOQL, DML, Governor limits, possibilities of integration with Apex, and best practices in Apex.

In the next chapter, we are going to learn the writing clean, maintainable, and efficient Apex code the importance of separation of concerns, and SOLID principles and their application in Apex.

Points to remember

- Apex is a strongly typed, OOP language designed for the Salesforce platform.

- It allows developers to add business logic, create custom web services, and perform complex database operations within Salesforce.

- Apex is tightly integrated with Salesforce objects (both standard and custom), enabling developers to perform DML operations and SOQL queries.

- It supports event-driven execution via triggers and allows integration with external systems through web service callouts (REST/SOAP).

- Apex supports key OOP principles like encapsulation, inheritance, polymorphism, and abstraction.

- Classes, objects, and interfaces form the building blocks of Apex applications.

- Apex supports various control structures such as **if-else**, **switch**, **for**, **while**, and **do-while** loops for controlling the flow of code.

- Proper use of control structures ensures efficient and dynamic application behavior.

- Exception handling in Apex is done using **try-catch** blocks to gracefully handle runtime errors.

- Common exceptions include **DmlException**, **NullPointerException**, **ListException**, and **LimitException**.

- Triggers allow automation by responding to data manipulation events (e.g., insert, update, delete) on Salesforce objects.

- Best practices include handling bulk operations and avoiding recursion by using static variables.

- SOQL is used to query Salesforce records while DML is used to modify records (insert, update, delete).

- Efficient queries and bulk DML operations are essential to avoid hitting governor limits.

- Salesforce imposes governor limits on resources like CPU time, heap size, SOQL queries, and DML operations.

- Writing bulk-friendly code and optimizing queries are crucial for staying within these limits.

- Use design patterns like singleton, factory method, and trigger handler patterns to ensure code maintainability.

- Modularize code, avoid SOQL/DML in loops and ensure that code is bulk-safe and testable.

- TDD emphasizes writing tests before coding. It ensures that code meets desired functionality, improves maintainability, and helps identify bugs early.

Questions

1. What is Apex, and how does it integrate with the Salesforce platform?

2. How does Apex differ from other programming languages in terms of its use within Salesforce?

3. What are the primary data types available in Apex, and how are they used in coding?

4. How do you declare a variable in Apex, and what are the rules for naming variables?

5. Explain the different types of operators in Apex and provide examples of arithmetic, comparison, and logical operators.

6. How do conditional statements like if-else and switch work in Apex?

7. What are the differences between a for loop, while loop, and do-while loop in Apex? Provide examples of when each type should be used.

8. What is the purpose of exception handling in Apex, and how does a try-catch block work?

9. Describe common types of exceptions in Apex, such as DmlException and NullPointerException. How would you handle these exceptions in a program?

10. What are triggers in Apex, and what types of events can they respond to?

11. Explain the importance of writing bulk-safe triggers. What are some best practices for handling bulk data processing in triggers?

12. How is SOQL used to query data in Salesforce? Provide an example of a simple SOQL query.

13. What is the difference between the insert and update DML operations? Provide code examples of each.

14. What are the risks of using SOQL queries or DML operations inside loops, and how can you mitigate them?

15. What are governor limits, and why are they important in Salesforce Apex development?

16. How can you optimize your code to avoid hitting governor limits related to SOQL queries and DML operations?

17. What are classes and objects in Apex, and how do they help in organizing code?

18. Explain the concept of inheritance in Apex. How does it promote code reuse?

19. How does polymorphism work in Apex, and why is it useful?

20. Why is it important to follow the trigger handler pattern when writing triggers in Apex?

21. How does the use of design patterns (like singleton and Factory) improve the maintainability of Apex code?

22. What is TDD, and how can it be applied in Apex development?

23. What are the benefits of writing tests before writing the actual code in TDD?

Join our book's Discord space

Join the book's Discord Workspace for Latest updates, Offers, Tech happenings around the world, New Release and Sessions with the Authors:

https://discord.bpbonline.com

CHAPTER 4
Apex Design Principles

Introduction

In this chapter, we will explore the fundamental principles that guide Apex code design, focusing on writing clean, maintainable, and efficient code. By following best practices, developers can produce Apex code that is both elegant and effective, ensuring long-term scalability and ease of maintenance.

A key emphasis is placed on the **separation of concerns**, a principle essential for structuring code in a clear and manageable manner. This chapter also introduces the **SOLID principles**, a set of five core guidelines that enhance software design by promoting modularity and reducing dependencies. These principles, **Single Responsibility, Open/ Closed, Liskov Substitution, Interface Segregation, and Dependency Inversion** are examined in the context of Apex development, demonstrating how they contribute to better code organization and maintainability.

By the end of this chapter, readers will have a strong foundation in the core design principles that underpin effective Apex development. This understanding sets the stage for the subsequent chapters, where we will discuss design patterns that further refine and optimize Apex applications.

Structure

The chapter covers the following topics:

- Writing clean, maintainable, and efficient Apex code
- Importance of separation of concerns
- SOLID principles and their application in Apex

Objectives

By the end of this chapter, readers will understand how to write clean, maintainable, and efficient Apex code. The reader will understand the importance of the separation of concerns and SOLID principles along with their application in Apex.

Writing clean, maintainable and efficient Apex code

Writing clean, maintainable, and efficient Apex code is crucial for creating high-quality Salesforce applications. Clean code is not only easier to read and understand but also reduces the likelihood of bugs and makes it simpler to maintain and extend your codebase.

Following are the best practices for achieving these goals:

- **Descriptive naming:** Descriptive naming is a fundamental aspect of writing clean, maintainable, and efficient Apex code. Well-chosen names for variables, methods, classes, and other identifiers can significantly improve code readability and make it easier for other developers (including your future self) to understand your code.

  Following are some guidelines for using descriptive naming in your Apex code:

  o **Use meaningful and clear names**: Use meaningful and descriptive names for variables, methods, classes, and other identifiers. Names should convey the purpose and intent of the element. Avoid single-letter or cryptic names that require additional context to understand, as follows:

    ```
    // Good naming example
    String customerName = 'Chamil Madusanka';

    // Poor naming example
    String cn = 'CM';
    ```

  o **Follow a consistent naming convention:** Adhere to a consistent naming convention throughout your codebase. Common conventions include CamelCase for class names and variables and CamelCase for method names and instance variables, as follows:

```
// Consistent naming convention
public class OrderProcessor {
    public void processOrder(Order order) {
        // Method and variable names are consistent with
the convention.
    }
}

// Inconsistent naming convention
public class Order_processor {
    public void Process_Order(Order Order_) {
        // Inconsistent naming makes the code harder to
read.
    }
}
```

o **Use descriptive variable names:** Variables should have names that convey their purpose and the data they hold. Avoid generic or ambiguous names, as follows:

```
// Descriptive variable names
Integer numberOfItems = 10;
Decimal totalPrice = 250.50;

// Ambiguous variable names
int n = 10;
double t = 250.50;
```

o **Name methods verbosely:** Method names should describe the action they perform. Use verbs and be explicit about what the method does, as follows:

```
// Descriptive method name
public Decimal calculateTotalPrice(Integer quantity,
Decimal unitPrice) {
    // Method calculates the total price.
}

// Ambiguous method name
public Decimal calc(Integer q, Decimal p) {
    // The purpose of the method is unclear.
}
```

○ **Avoid abbreviations unless commonly accepted:** Avoid using abbreviations unless they are widely recognized and accepted in your domain. Abbreviations can be confusing and may lead to misunderstandings, as follows:

```
// Full and clear variable name
String customerName = 'John Doe';


// Abbreviated and unclear variable name
String custNm = 'John Doe';
```

○ **Be mindful of acronyms:** If your code includes acronyms or initialisms, ensure that they are well-known and consistently capitalized, as follows:

```
// Properly capitalized acronym
String JSONData = '{"name": "John"}';


// Inconsistent or lowercase acronym
String jsonData = '{"name": "John"}';
```

○ **Use comments when necessary:** While good naming is important, there may be situations where additional context is needed. In such cases, consider adding comments to explain the purpose of variables, methods, or classes, as follows:

```
// This variable stores the customer's name.
String customerName = 'John Doe';
```

The following table shows the summary for descriptive naming, that is, dos and don'ts:

Best practice	Do's	Don'ts
Use meaningful names	String customerName;	String cn;
Follow naming conventions	public void processOrder();	public void Process_Order();
Be descriptive	Decimal totalPrice;	double t;
Use Clear Method Names	calculateTotalPrice();	calc();
Avoid Uncommon Abbreviations	customerName;	custNm;
Maintain Acronym Consistency	JSONData;	jsonData;

Table 4.1: Descriptive naming, dos and don'ts

- **Consistent formatting:** Consistent formatting is a critical aspect of writing clean, maintainable, and efficient Apex code. A consistent coding style throughout your codebase improves readability, reduces confusion, and makes it easier for developers to collaborate on the same project.

Following are some key formatting guidelines for maintaining consistency in your Apex code:

- o **Indentation and spacing:** Use consistent indentation throughout your code, typically with two or four spaces per level of indentation. Choose one style and stick with it. Maintain a consistent space after keywords, before and after operators, and around parentheses and brackets, as follows:

```
// Consistent indentation and spacing
if (condition) {
    // Code block
} else {
    // Code block
}


// Inconsistent indentation and spacing
if(condition) {
// Code block
}else{
// Code block
}
```

- o **Braces and brackets:** Place opening braces at the same line as the statement they belong to (Allman style) or on the next line (K&R style), but be consistent within your project. Maintain consistent spacing before and after braces and brackets, as follows:

```
// Allman style
if (condition)
{
    // Code block
}

// K&R style
if (condition) {
    // Code block
}
```

- o **Line length:** Limit line length to a reasonable number of characters, such as 80 or 120 characters per line, to enhance readability and avoid horizontal scrolling. If a line exceeds the recommended limit, consider breaking it into multiple lines with proper indentation, as follows:

```
// Keeping lines within recommended length
String message = 'This is a long string that should not
exceed the recommended line length ' +
    'to maintain code readability and prevent horizontal
scrolling.';


// Breaking long lines into multiple lines
String message =
    'This is a long string that is broken into multiple
lines for readability and ' +
    'to prevent excessive line length.';
```

o **Blank lines:** Use blank lines to separate logically related code sections, such as methods, classes, or sections of code with distinct purposes. Be consistent in the number of blank lines you use to separate sections, as follows:

```
// Separating methods with blank lines
public void method1() {
    // Code for method1
}

public void method2() {
    // Code for method2
}
```

o **Comments:** Follow a consistent style for comments, such as placing comments above the code they refer to or using inline comments. Ensure that comments are aligned consistently and do not create visual clutter, as follows:

```
// Consistent style for comments
// This is a comment

// Inconsistent style for comments
//This is a comment

// Proper alignment of comments
// Comment 1
// Comment 2
```

o **File and class structure:** Maintain a consistent structure for your Apex classes, including the order of class members, for example, variables, methods and the placement of inner classes. Following a standard Apex class structure improves maintainability and ensures that code remains organized and scalable:

```
//Recommended Class Structure
public class ExampleClass {
    // Static variables
    public static Integer MAX_RECORDS = 100;

    // Instance variables
    private String instanceVariable;

    // Constructor
    public ExampleClass(String instanceVariable) {
        this.instanceVariable = instanceVariable;
    }

    // Public methods
    public void performAction() {
        // Method implementation
    }

    // Private helper methods
    private void helperMethod() {
        // Helper logic
    }
}
```

o **Automating formatting consistency:** To enforce formatting standards automatically, developers can use linter tools such as:

* **PMD for Apex**: A static code analysis tool that detects formatting and style issues.

* **Checkmarx**: Ensures security and consistency in Apex development.

* **Visual Studio Code Apex Plugin**: Provides auto-formatting and linting features.

Tip: Using tools like PMD can help enforce formatting standards and ensure code consistency across a team.

The following table shows the summary for the formatting guidelines, that is, do's and don'ts:

Best practice	Do's	Don'ts
Indentation	Use 2-4 spaces per level	Mix indentation styles
Braces & Brackets	Stick to Allman or K&R style	Switch styles inconsistently
Line Length	Keep lines under 120 characters	Write excessively long lines
Blank Lines	Separate logical sections	Add unnecessary blank lines
Comments	Use clear and aligned comments	Place comments inconsistently
Trigger Formatting	Maintain structured trigger logic	Use inconsistent spacing

Table 4.2: Formatting guidelines, dos and don'ts

- **Comments and documentation:** Comments and documentation are essential components of writing clean, maintainable, and efficient Apex code. They provide context, explanations, and guidance to both developers and maintainers of the code. Following are some guidelines for effectively using comments and documentation in your Apex code:

  o Comments for clean and maintainable code, consider the following:

    ▪ **Use comments sparingly:** Avoid excessive comments that merely restate what the code does. Instead, focus on explaining why the code does something or providing context for complex logic.

    Good comment explaining intent:

    ```
    // Using a Map to store customer data for efficient
    lookups.
    Map<String, Customer__c> customerMap = new Map<String,
    Customer__c>();
    ```

    Poor comment restating the obvious:

    ```
    // This is a for loop that iterates over a list of
    accounts.
    for (Account acc : accountList) {
        processAccount(acc);
    }
    ```

    ▪ **Document intent and high-level design:** Use comments to describe the purpose and intent of classes, methods, and complex algorithms and explain why certain decisions were made in the code, as follows:

    ```
    // Good comment explaining the intent
    // We're using a Map to store customer data for
    efficient lookups.
    ```

```
// Poor comment restating the obvious
// This is a for loop that iterates over a list of
accounts.
```

- **Inline comments for clarity:** Use inline comments to clarify tricky or non-obvious parts of the code. These comments should explain what is happening in a specific line or block of code, as follows:

```
// Check if the email address is valid
if (isValidEmail(email)) {
    // Process the email
    sendEmail(email);
}
```

- **TODO and FIXME comments:** Use TODO comments to indicate tasks or features that need to be addressed in the future. Use FIXME comments to highlight known issues or bugs that should be fixed, as follows:

```
// TODO: Implement error handling here.
// FIXME: This section crashes on certain inputs;
investigate and fix.
```

The following table shows the summary for the commenting and documentation, that is, do's and don'ts:

Best practices	Do's	Don'ts
Explain why, not what	Use comments to clarify intent	State what the code already shows
Be concise	Keep comments short and meaningful	Write long, unnecessary explanations
Use standard tags	Use TODO and FIXME for future fixes	Leave unclear or incomplete comments
Follow a style guide	Place comments where they improve readability	Scatter comments randomly

Table 4.3: commenting and documentation, do's and don'ts

- **Documentation for maintainability:** Documentation for maintainability involves creating clear, concise, and comprehensive documentation that enables developers to understand, update, and manage a system or application efficiently. It includes detailed explanations of the architecture, design patterns, code structure, and functionality, along with well-documented APIs, workflows, and configurations.

Such documentation ensures seamless knowledge transfer, simplifies debugging, and facilitates future enhancements, contributing to the long-term sustainability of the project.

- o **Class and method documentation:** Document classes and public methods with comments that include a brief description, parameters, return values, and any exceptions thrown, as follows:

```
/**
 * Calculates the total price of an order.
 * @param quantity The quantity of items ordered.
 * @param unitPrice The price of one unit.
 * @return The total price.
 * @throws InvalidInputException If quantity or unitPrice
is negative.
 */
public Decimal calculateTotalPrice(Integer quantity,
Decimal unitPrice) {
    // Implementation here
}
```

- o **Method signatures:** Ensure that method signatures are self-explanatory. Use meaningful method and parameter names to reduce the need for extensive documentation, as follows:

```
// Well-named method signature
public void processOrder(Order order)

// Less descriptive method signature
public void process(into)
```

- o **Javadoc comments:** If you are using a tool like Salesforce's ApexDocs, follow Javadoc-style comments to generate external documentation for your Apex code. This is especially useful for documenting APIs, as follows:

```
/**
 * This is a Javadoc-style comment.
 * You can include additional details here.
 */
```

- o **README and documentation files:** Consider creating README files or documentation files within your project to provide high-level overviews, installation instructions, and usage guidelines for your codebase.

Following is the content for Salesforce project README:

- o **Project overview:** Purpose, scope, and key features.

o **Prerequisites:** Required tools, for example, Salesforce CLI, API versions, connected apps.

o **Setup instructions:** Steps for configuring the development environment.

o **Deployment steps:** How to deploy the code to different Salesforce environments.

o **Usage examples:** Instructions for running batch jobs, invoking classes, or interacting with APIs.

o **Known issues and troubleshooting:** Common errors and their resolutions.

The following table shows the summary of the documentation for the maintainability, that is, do's and don'ts:

Best practice	Do's	Don'ts
Document purpose	Focus on **why** the code exists or decisions were made.	Restate **what** the code is doing.
Readable signatures	Use meaningful and clear method/parameter names.	Create ambiguous or cryptic names.
Use ApexDocs	Generate external documentation for APIs and workflows.	Skip API documentation for key components.
Include a README	Provide setup, usage, and deployment instructions.	Leave high-level instructions incomplete.
Comment configurations	Describe flows, validation rules, and metadata usage.	Leave configuration-heavy components undocumented.

Table 4.4: documentation for the maintainability, dos and don'ts

- **Avoid long methods:** Avoiding long methods is an important principle in writing clean, maintainable, and efficient Apex code. Long methods can be challenging to understand, debug, and maintain.

Following are some strategies and best practices for avoiding long methods in your Apex code:

o **Single Responsibility Principle (SRP):** Follow the SRP, which states that a method should have one clear and specific responsibility. Break down complex methods into smaller, focused methods, each handling a specific task, as follows:

```
// Long method with multiple responsibilities
public void processOrder(Order order) {
```

```
    // Complex logic for order processing
    // ...
}


// Breaking down the method into smaller, focused methods
public void processOrder(Order order) {
    validateOrder(order);
    calculateTotalPrice(order);
    applyDiscounts(order);
    // ...
}
```

- **Meaningful method names:** Choose meaningful method names that describe what the method does. A well-named method can serve as documentation for its purpose, as follows:

```
// Unclear method name
public void method1() {
    // ...
}


// Clear and descriptive method name
public void validateOrder(Order order) {
    // ...
}
```

- **Limit method length:** Aim to keep methods relatively short, ideally no longer than 20-30 lines of code. However, the optimal length may vary depending on the context. If a method becomes too long, consider refactoring it into smaller methods or splitting it into multiple methods.

- **Use helper methods**: Encapsulate repeated or complex logic in helper methods. This not only reduces method length but also promotes code reuse, as follows:

```
// Repeated logic within a method
public void processOrder(Order order) {
    if (order.getStatus() == 'Pending') {
        // Handle pending order
        // ...
    } else {
        // Handle other cases
        // ...
    }
```

```
        }

        // Using a helper method
        public void processOrder(Order order) {
            if (isPendingOrder(order)) {
                handlePendingOrder(order);
            } else {
                handleOtherCases(order);
            }
        }

        private Boolean isPendingOrder(Order order) {
            return order.getStatus() == 'Pending';
        }
```

o **Refactor when necessary:** Regularly review your codebase, and if you encounter long methods, consider refactoring them to improve readability and maintainability.

The following table shows the summary of avoiding long methods, that is, do's and don'ts:

Best practice	Do's	Don'ts
Refactor regularly	Break down methods using the SRP.	Write methods that handle multiple responsibilities.
Descriptive naming	Use **meaningful and descriptive method names** for clarity.	Use cryptic names like method1 or doSomething.
Concise code	Keep methods concise, ideally **20-30 lines of code**.	Create long methods with hundreds of lines, making them hard to read.
Encapsulate logic	Use **helper methods** for repetitive or complex logic.	Copy-paste similar code blocks across methods.
Frequent reviews	Refactor methods regularly during code reviews.	Ignore refactoring opportunities when methods grow too long.
Standard naming	Use **consistent naming conventions** for helper methods and logic.	Name helper methods inconsistently, leading to confusion.
Unit testing	Test smaller methods independently for improved test coverage.	Rely solely on testing long methods that cover multiple responsibilities.

Table 4.5: Avoiding long methods, dos and don'ts

- **Error handling:** Error handling is a critical aspect of writing clean, maintainable, and efficient Apex code. Effective error handling ensures that your code behaves predictably in exceptional situations, provides meaningful feedback to users or administrators, and helps identify and resolve issues promptly.

  Following are some best practices for error handling in Apex:

  ```
  try {
      // Code that may throw an exception
  } catch (CustomException1 e1) {
      // Handle CustomException1
  } catch (CustomException2 e2) {
      // Handle CustomException2
  } catch (Exception genericException) {
      // Handle other exceptions
  }
  ```

  o **Handle exceptions appropriately:** Determine the appropriate action to take when an exception occurs. This may involve logging the exception, notifying users, rolling back transactions, or gracefully degrading functionality, as follows:

  ```
  try {
      // Code that may throw an exception
  } catch (CustomException e) {
      // Log the exception for debugging
      System.debug('An error occurred: ' + e.getMessage());

      // Notify the user
      ApexPages.addMessage(new ApexPages.Message(ApexPages.
      Severity.ERROR, 'An error occurred. Please try again
      later.'));

      // Rollback any changes made in the current transaction
      Database.rollback(sp);

      // Rethrow the exception if necessary
      throw e;
  }
  ```

  o **Provide user-friendly error messages:** When displaying error messages to users, use clear and concise language. Avoid technical jargon that may confuse non-technical users, as follows:

```
ApexPages.addMessage(new ApexPages.Message(ApexPages.
Severity.ERROR, 'The order could not be processed. Please
check your input.'));
```

o **Log errors for debugging:** Use system logs or custom log objects to record details of exceptions, including the error message, stack trace, and context information. Logging helps in diagnosing and debugging issues in production environments, as follows:

```
try {
    // Code that may throw an exception
} catch (Exception e) {
    // Log the exception details for debugging
    System.debug('Exception Message: ' + e.getMessage());
    System.debug('Stack Trace: ' +
e.getStackTraceString());

    // Additional logging or actions as needed
}
```

o **Avoid empty catch blocks:** Avoid empty catch blocks without any error handling or logging. They make it difficult to identify and diagnose issues, as follows:

```
try {
    // Code that may throw an exception
} catch (Exception e) {
    // Empty catch block - no error handling or logging
}
```

o **Use custom exceptions:** Define custom exception classes to represent specific error conditions in your application. This makes it easier to handle and differentiate between different types of exceptions, as follows:

```
public class CustomException extends Exception {
    public CustomException(String message) {
        super(message);
    }
}
```

o **Bulk processing considerations:** When dealing with bulk operations, handle exceptions in a way that ensures the processing of valid records continues while errors are logged or reported separately, as follows:

```
for (Order order : ordersToProcess) {
    try {
        processOrder(order);
```

```
        } catch (Exception e) {
            // Log the error and continue processing other
    orders
            logError(order, e.getMessage());
        }
    }
```

- o **Governor limits:** Be aware of Salesforce governor limits and handle exceptions that might arise due to reaching these limits gracefully. Consider using batch processing or asynchronous Apex for large data volumes.

Effective error handling improves the reliability of your Apex code and enhances the user experience by providing informative messages and minimizing downtime. It is an essential aspect of writing maintainable and efficient Apex code.

The following table shows the summary of error handling, that is, do's and don'ts:

Best practices	Do's	Don'ts
Logging	Log detailed error information.	Leave catch blocks empty.
Clear messaging	Provide user-friendly error messages.	Use overly technical language in messages.
Custom exceptions	Use custom exceptions for clarity.	Overload generic exception handlers.
Bulk-friendly handling	Test error handling in bulk scenarios.	Ignore exceptions in bulk processing.
Dynamic exception handling	Handle governor limit exceptions.	Hardcode error messages.

Table 4.6: Error handling, do's and don'ts

- **Avoid hardcoding:** Avoiding hardcoded values and using named constants or custom settings is crucial in writing clean, maintainable, and efficient Apex code. Hardcoded values can lead to code that is difficult to maintain, less flexible, and error-prone.

Following are some best practices for avoiding hardcoded values in your Apex code:

- o **Use named constants:** Replace magic numbers and strings with named constants that have meaningful names. Define constants at the top of your class or in a separate **Constants** class for better organization, as follows:

```
// Hardcoded value
Integer discount = 10;
```

```
// Named constant
public static final Integer DEFAULT_DISCOUNT = 10;
```

- o **Custom settings:** Use custom settings to store configuration data, such as application settings, preferences, or values that may change over time. Custom settings provide a way to make configuration changes without modifying code, as follows:

```
// Hardcoded email addresses
String supportEmail = 'support@example.com';

// Custom setting for email addresses
CustomSetting__c settings = CustomSetting__c.
getInstance('EmailSettings');
String supportEmail = settings.SupportEmail__c;
```

- o **Hierarchical custom settings:** If you need different settings for different profiles or users, consider using hierarchical custom settings. These settings allow you to define values for specific profiles or users, making your application more configurable.

- o **Custom metadata types:** Custom metadata types are another option for storing configuration data that may change over time. They are especially useful for dynamic configurations, such as feature flags or dynamic picklist values.

- o **Environment variables:** In Salesforce DX or Heroku-based applications, you can use environment variables to store configuration values, such as API keys or secrets. These variables are accessible through code but can be changed without code changes.

- o **Resource bundles:** For multilingual applications, consider using resource bundles or custom labels to store and manage strings for different languages, as follows:

```
// Hardcoded error message
String errorMessage = 'An error occurred.';

// Custom label for error message
String errorMessage = Label.Error_Message;
```

- o **Dynamic queries:** When building dynamic SOQL queries, avoid concatenating user inputs directly into queries, as it can lead to security vulnerabilities and SQL injection. Use bind variables or parameterized queries to safely include user inputs, as follows:

```
// Hardcoded query with concatenation (avoid this)
String name = 'John';
String query = 'SELECT Id FROM Contact WHERE Name = \'' +
name + '\'';

// Parameterized query (safer)
String name = 'John';
List<Contact> contacts = [SELECT Id FROM Contact WHERE
Name = :name];
```

o **Test coverage:** Ensure that your tests cover different configurations and scenarios, including changes to named constants or custom settings. This helps validate that your code behaves correctly with various configurations.

The following table shows the summary of avoiding hardcoding, that is, do's and don'ts:

Best practices	Do's	Don'ts
Named constants	Use named constants for reusable values.	Hardcode sensitive data like API keys.
Custom settings/ metadata	Store configuration in custom settings or metadata.	Hardcode application settings or URLs.
Resource bundles	Use resource bundles for multilingual applications.	Hardcode strings for different locales.
Parameterized queries	Use parameterized queries to prevent SOQL injection.	Directly concatenate user inputs in SOQL.
Testing configurations	Ensure test coverage for various configurations.	Ignore edge cases in dynamic configurations.

Table 4.7: Avoiding hardcoding, do's and don'ts

By avoiding hardcoded values and adopting these practices, you can make your Apex code more maintainable, configurable, and adaptable to changing requirements. This leads to cleaner and more efficient code that is easier to maintain and less error-prone.

- **Testing:** Testing is a crucial aspect of writing clean, maintainable, and efficient Apex code in Salesforce. Testing ensures that your code behaves as expected, catches regressions when making changes, and helps maintain code quality.

Following are some best practices for testing in Salesforce Apex:

o **Write unit tests:** Salesforce requires that you have at least 75% code coverage for your Apex classes and 1% code coverage for triggers. To achieve this, write unit tests for your Apex code. Unit tests should focus on testing individual methods and classes in isolation.

o **Use descriptive test method names:** Name your test methods clearly and descriptively to indicate what you are testing. Follow a naming convention like `MethodName_WhenCondition_ExpectedOutcome`.

o **Use the @isTest annotation:** Annotate your test class and test methods with `@isTest` to let Salesforce know that these are test classes and methods. This annotation ensures that your tests are executed in a separate test context and do not consume your organization's limits, as follows:

```
@isTest
public class MyTestClass {
    @isTest
    public static void myTestMethod() {
        // Test code here
    }
}
```

o **Test positive and negative scenarios:** Ensure that your tests cover both positive and negative scenarios, including edge cases and error conditions. Test for expected behavior when inputs are invalid or unexpected.

o **Use test data factory patterns:** Implement a test data factory to create test records in a structured and reusable way. Avoid relying on existing data in your tests, as it may not be consistent across environments, as follows:

```
@isTest
public class TestFactory {
    public static Account createTestAccount() {
        Account acc = new Account(Name = 'Test Account');
        insert acc;
        return acc;
    }
}
```

o **Bulk testing:** When applicable, test the behavior of your code with bulk data by creating multiple test records. Ensure that your code performs efficiently and adheres to Salesforce governor limits in bulk scenarios. Example code is as follows.

```
@isTest
public class BulkTestExample {
    @isTest
    public static void testBulkTrigger() {
        List<Account> accounts = new List<Account>();
```

```
        for (Integer i = 0; i < 200; i++) {
                accounts.add(new Account(Name = 'Test Account
' + i));
        }
        insert accounts;

        // Validate results
        System.assertEquals(200, [SELECT Count() FROM
Account]);
    }
}
```

- o **Use assertions:** Include assertions in your test methods to verify that your code produces the expected results. Assertions help ensure that your code remains correct as it evolves, as follows:

```
@isTest
public class MyTestClass {
    @isTest
    public static void calculateTotalPrice_WithValidInput_
ReturnsTotalPrice() {
        Decimal totalPrice = MyService.
calculateTotalPrice(5, 10.0);
        System.assertEquals(50.0, totalPrice);
    }
}
```

- o **Test error handling:** Test how your code handles exceptions and error conditions by deliberately causing exceptions in your test methods. Verify that exceptions are caught and handled correctly.

  The example code is as follows:

```
@isTest
public class ErrorHandlingTest {
    @isTest
    public static void testErrorHandling() {
        try {
            MyService.processWithError();
            System.assert(false, 'Expected an exception to
be thrown.');
        } catch (CustomException e) {
            System.assertEquals('Expected error message',
```

```
e.getMessage());
        }
    }
}
```

o **Test asynchronous code**: When you have asynchronous code, for example, triggers or async methods, write tests that ensure the correct behavior of that code. Use the **@future** or Queueable interface to test asynchronous code execution.

The example code is as follows:

```
@isTest
public class AsyncTestExample {
    @isTest
    public static void testAsyncExecution() {
        Test.startTest();
        MyAsyncClass.asyncMethod();
        Test.stopTest();

        // Validate the results of asynchronous execution
        System.assert(...);
    }
}
```

o **Test permissions and sharing rules**: Verify that your code respects Salesforce's security model by testing permissions and sharing rules in your test methods. Ensure that users can only access data they are authorized to access.

The example code is as follows:

```
@isTest
public class PermissionsTest {
    @isTest
    public static void testUserPermissions() {
        System.runAs(new User(Id = 'UserId')) {
            // Perform actions as the user and verify
access
            System.assert(...);
        }
    }
}
```

- o **Test setup and teardown:** Use test setup methods for creating common test data used across multiple test methods. Leverage test teardown methods to clean up test data after test execution to ensure test isolation.

- o **Continuous integration and automation:** Integrate automated testing into your development pipeline to run tests automatically with each deployment. Tools like Salesforce DX, Jenkins, and Travis CI can help automate testing.

- o **Code coverage analysis:** Monitor code coverage regularly and strive for high code coverage to ensure that most of your code is tested. Use tools like Salesforce's Developer Console or VS Code extensions to analyze code coverage.

The following table shows the summary of testing, that is, do's and don'ts:

Best practice	Do's	Don'ts
Write Unit Tests	Write unit tests with at least 75% coverage but always try to achieve 100%.	Rely on existing org data in your tests.
Descriptive method names	Use descriptive and meaningful test method names.	Skip testing error handling or edge cases.
Use @isTest Annotation	Use the @isTest annotation for isolation.	Hardcode test data or avoid reusable patterns.
Test scenarios	Cover positive and negative scenarios.	Ignore security tests for permissions/sharing.
Test data factory	Implement test data factories.	Overload production org with debug logs.
Bulk testing	Test bulk scenarios for governor limits.	Skip testing for governor limits or scalability.
Use ssertions	Write assertions to validate expected behavior.	Use vague or incomplete assertions that do not fully validate outcomes.

Table 4.8: Testing, do's and don'ts

By following these testing best practices, you can ensure that your Apex code is reliable, maintainable, and efficient. Testing helps catch issues early in the development process, making it easier to deliver high-quality code to your Salesforce organization:

- **Bulk and governor limits:** Handling bulk data and adhering to Salesforce governor limits is crucial when writing clean, maintainable, and efficient Apex code. Salesforce imposes various limits to ensure the platform's stability and performance. Failing to account for these limits can result in runtime exceptions and application instability.

Following is how to handle bulk data and governor limits in your Apex code:

- o **Bulk-friendly code design**: Design your code to be bulk-friendly, and capable of processing large volumes of data efficiently. Minimize the use of SOQL and DML operations within loops, as these can quickly lead to hitting governor limits, as follows:

```
// Non-bulk-friendly code (SOQL query inside a loop)
for (Account acc : accountsList) {
    List<Contact> contacts = [SELECT Id FROM Contact WHERE
AccountId = :acc.Id];
    // Process contacts
}

// Bulk-friendly code (query outside the loop)
List<Id> accountIds = new List<Id>();
for (Account acc : accountsList) {
    accountIds.add(acc.Id);
}
List<Contact> contacts = [SELECT Id FROM Contact WHERE
AccountId IN :accountIds];
for (Contact con : contacts) {
    // Process contacts
}
```

- o **Batch Apex**: For processing large datasets, consider using Batch Apex, which divides the data into manageable chunks (batches) to prevent governor limit violations. Batch jobs can be scheduled and provide robust error handling. An example code is as follows:

```
global class AccountBatchJob implements Database.
Batchable<SObject> {
    global Database.QueryLocator start(Database.
BatchableContext context) {
        return Database.getQueryLocator('SELECT Id, Name
FROM Account WHERE Industry = \'Technology\'');
    }
    global void execute(Database.BatchableContext context,
List<Account> scope) {
        for (Account acc : scope) {
            acc.Name += ' - Processed';
        }
        update scope;
    }
```

```
global void finish(Database.BatchableContext context) {
    System.debug('Batch processing completed.');
}
}
```

o   **Query optimization**: Optimize your SOQL queries to fetch only the necessary fields and records. Use indexing when filtering data and consider using **LIMIT** clauses to limit the number of records retrieved.

o   **Bulk API**: If you need to work with large data volumes programmatically, consider using the Salesforce Bulk API, which is specifically designed for bulk data operations. Bulk API can be more efficient than standard Apex DML operations. Here are some real-world relevance for Bulk API in Apex.

  •   Migrating data during system implementation.

  •   Processing millions of records efficiently via external systems using the Bulk API.

o   **Limit DML operations**: Minimize DML operations within loops, and instead, perform bulk DML operations whenever possible. Use **Database.insert**, **Database.update**, and **Database.delete** methods to handle large collections of records efficiently, as follows:

```
// Non-bulk DML operations (inside a loop)
for (Account acc : accountsList) {
    insert acc; // Inefficient for bulk data
}

// Bulk DML operation
insert accountsList; // More efficient for bulk data
```

o   **Aggregate queries**: Utilize aggregate queries, for example, **GROUP   BY**, **COUNT()**, **SUM()** when you need to perform calculations or aggregations on large datasets. The following code represents the aggregate queries:

```
// Aggregate query example
AggregateResult[] results = [
    SELECT Industry, COUNT(Id)
    FROM Account
    GROUP BY Industry
];
for (AggregateResult result : results) {
    System.debug('Industry: ' + result.get('Industry') +
', Count: ' + result.get('expr0'));
}
```

o **Governor limit monitoring**: Continuously monitor governor limits in your production and sandbox environments, especially when dealing with large data volumes. Use tools like Salesforce Health Check or custom monitoring solutions to proactively identify potential limit issues.

The following are some of the tools for monitoring Salesforce governor limits:

- **Debug logs**: Use Debug Logs to monitor SOQL and DML operations in triggers and batch classes.

- **Developer Console**: Use the **Execution Overview** tab in the Developer Console to view governor limit usage for each transaction.

- **Custom monitoring**: Create a monitoring system using Apex classes and custom objects to track operations nearing governor limits.

o **Test for bulk scenarios**: In your unit tests, ensure that your code performs correctly and efficiently with bulk data. Create test data in bulk and simulate bulk operations to validate the behavior of your code under different conditions.

The following example explains creating test data in bulk:

```
@isTest
public class TestBulkProcessing {
    @isTest
    public static void testBulkProcessing() {
        List<Account> accounts = new List<Account>();
        for (Integer i = 0; i < 200; i++) {
            accounts.add(new Account(Name = 'Test Account
 ' + i));
        }
        insert accounts;

        Test.startTest();
        AccountBatchJob batchJob = new AccountBatchJob();
        Database.executeBatch(batchJob, 100);
        Test.stopTest();
    }
}
```

o **Bulk data testing**: Test your code with real bulk data to ensure it can handle the expected volumes and that it does not reach governor limits in a production environment.

    ○ **Exception handling**: Implement robust error handling and recovery mechanisms for bulk data processing. Log errors, handle exceptions gracefully, and consider implementing retry logic when appropriate.

The following table shows the summary of Bulk and governor limits, that is, do's and don'ts:

Best practices	Do's	Don'ts
Bulk-friendly design	Perform SOQL/DML operations outside loops.	Perform DML or SOQL queries inside loops.
Batch processing	Use Batch Apex for large datasets.	Overload synchronous processing for large datasets.
Query optimization	Optimize SOQL queries with indexed filters.	Retrieve unnecessary fields or records in queries.
Bulk data testing	Test with bulk data scenarios and governor limits	Ignore governor limits during testing.
Aggregate queries	Use aggregate queries for calculations.	Hardcode queries for large datasets without filters.

Table 4.9: Bulk and governor limits, do's and don'ts

By following these guidelines and best practices, you can write clean, maintainable, and efficient Apex code that is capable of handling bulk data and complying with Salesforce's governor limits, ensuring the stability and reliability of your applications.

- **Code reviews:** Code review is a critical step in ensuring that your Apex code is clean, maintainable, and efficient. A well-structured code review process helps catch issues, promotes best practices, and fosters collaboration within your development team.

Following are some guidelines for conducting effective code reviews in the context of writing clean, maintainable, and efficient Apex code:

    ○ **Set clear standards and guidelines**: Establish a set of coding standards, best practices, and guidelines specific to your organization's Apex development. Document these standards and make them accessible to all team members.

    ○ **Use code linting and analysis tools**: Employ code analysis tools, such as Salesforce's Apex **Programming Mistake Detector (PMD),** to automatically identify common coding issues and enforce coding standards. Integrate these tools into your development process and include the results in your code reviews.

    ○ **Assign a reviewer**: Assign a knowledgeable and experienced developer to review each pull request or code change. Reviewers should be well-versed in both Apex development and your organization's coding standards.

o **Review for code quality**: Check for adherence to coding standards, naming conventions, and best practices. Look for issues related to error handling, bulk data processing, governor limits, and performance optimization.

o **Review for maintainability**: Assess code readability and organization. Ensure that the code is easy to understand and well-documented. Evaluate the use of meaningful variable and method names, comments, and clear code structures.

o **Review for efficiency**: Verify that the code is efficient and performs well, especially when dealing with bulk data operations. Look for potential performance bottlenecks and suggest improvements.

o **Ensure test coverage:** Confirm that the code is adequately covered by unit tests. Each code change should have corresponding test coverage. Review test methods for completeness, accuracy, and coverage of edge cases.

o **Check for security**: Scrutinize the code for potential security vulnerabilities, such as SOQL injection or data exposure. Ensure that the code respects Salesforce's security model and adheres to data-sharing rules.

o **Review exception handling**: Examine how exceptions and errors are handled in the code. Verify that exceptions are caught, logged, and handled appropriately. Ensure that error messages are meaningful and user-friendly.

o **Encourage feedback and discussion**: Promote an open and collaborative environment where developers can provide constructive feedback and ask questions. Encourage the author and reviewer to discuss code changes, potential improvements, and alternative solutions.

o **Use code review tools**: Leverage code review tools or platforms for example, GitHub, GitLab, Bitbucket, to facilitate the code review process. These tools provide features for commenting on code, tracking changes, and managing discussions.

o **Document review findings**: Record review findings and recommendations in a systematic manner, either within the code review tool or in a shared document. Ensure that the author understands the feedback and has a chance to address any issues.

o **Consider automation**: Explore automation options for routine code checks and validations, such as automated testing and continuous integration pipelines.

o **Educate and train team members**: Provide training and education to team members on coding standards, best practices, and any new technologies or tools being used.

o **Review iteratively**: Consider iterative reviews where code changes are reviewed multiple times during the development process to catch issues early.

- Be respectful and constructive: Maintain a respectful and constructive tone during code reviews. The goal is to improve code quality, not criticize developers.

- Follow-up: Ensure that code changes are reviewed and approved before they are merged into the codebase. Follow up on review comments to verify that issues have been addressed.

  By implementing a robust code review process, you can enhance the quality, maintainability, and efficiency of your Apex code, promote best practices, and foster a culture of collaboration and continuous improvement within your development team.

- **Continuous improvement:** Continuous improvement is a fundamental principle in writing clean, maintainable, and efficient Apex code. It involves ongoing efforts to enhance your development practices, code quality, and team collaboration.

  Following are the key strategies for achieving continuous improvement in Apex development:

  - Regular code reviews: Conduct regular code reviews to assess code quality, adherence to coding standards, and best practices. Use feedback from reviews to identify areas for improvement and educate team members.

  - Automated testing: Invest in test automation to ensure that your code remains robust and reliable over time. Set up automated test suites that run with each code change and provide immediate feedback on regressions.

  - Performance monitoring: Implement monitoring and profiling tools to keep an eye on the performance of your Apex code in production. Identify and address performance bottlenecks and optimization opportunities.

  - Documentation: Maintain up-to-date documentation for your Apex code, including code comments, API documentation, and architecture diagrams. Ensure that documentation is accessible and comprehensive for both current and future team members.

  - Coding standards and guidelines: Continuously refine and update your coding standards and guidelines based on evolving best practices and Salesforce platform updates. Educate team members about changes and encourage adherence.

  - Education and training: Provide ongoing training and educational opportunities for your development team. Stay informed about Salesforce releases, new features, and best practices through courses, webinars, and certifications.

  - Code analysis tools: Use code analysis and linting tools to automatically identify and fix coding issues. Integrate these tools into your development process to catch problems early.

o **Refactoring and technical debt**: Regularly review your codebase for technical debt and opportunities for refactoring. Allocate time to address technical debt to prevent it from accumulating.

o **Performance optimization**: Keep an eye on Salesforce governor limits and performance bottlenecks. Implement optimizations as needed to ensure your code operates efficiently, especially when dealing with large data volumes.

o **Peer learning and collaboration**: Encourage peer learning and collaboration within your development team. Share knowledge, experiences, and solutions to common challenges.

o **Retrospectives**: Hold regular retrospectives or post-implementation reviews to evaluate completed projects and identify areas for improvement. Use these sessions to celebrate successes and learn from challenges.

o **Version control and branching strategies**: Maintain a well-organized version control system and adhere to clear branching and merging strategies. Ensure that code changes are tracked and versioned effectively.

o **Feedback loops**: Establish feedback loops with stakeholders, product owners, and end-users to gather input and continuously refine requirements and features.

o **Innovation and experimentation**: Encourage innovation by allowing team members to experiment with new technologies, tools, and approaches in a safe environment. Share learnings from experiments with the team.

o **Quality metrics and Key Performance Indicators (KPIs)**: Define and track quality metrics and KPIs related to code quality, testing coverage, and performance. Use these metrics to set goals for improvement and measure progress.

o **Code reviews for learning**: Use code reviews as opportunities for learning and mentorship. Pair junior developers with experienced team members during reviews to facilitate knowledge transfer.

o **Continuous Integration and Deployment (CI/CD)**: Implement CI/CD pipelines to automate the building, testing, and deployment of code changes. Ensure that code is continuously delivered to production in a controlled and reliable manner.

o **Feedback culture**: Foster a culture where feedback is welcomed, constructive, and regular. Encourage team members to provide feedback on processes, tools, and coding practices.

By consistently applying these principles and strategies, your development team can achieve continuous improvement in writing clean, maintainable, and efficient Apex code. Embracing change, learning from experiences, and adapting to new challenges is key to ensuring the long-term success of your Apex development efforts.

By following these best practices, you can create clean, maintainable, and efficient Apex code that not only meets immediate requirements but also stands the test of time as your application evolves.

Importance of separation of concerns

The separation of concerns is a fundamental design principle in software engineering, including Apex development in Salesforce. It refers to the practice of dividing a software system into distinct and independent modules or components, each responsible for a specific aspect or concern of the application.

In the context of Apex, understanding and implementing separation of concerns is of paramount importance for several reasons, as follows:

o **Modularity and maintainability**: Separation of concerns leads to modular code where each component focuses on a specific task or functionality. This modularity makes the codebase easier to understand, maintain, and extend over time.

o **Code readability and clarity**: When code is organized around specific concerns, it becomes more readable and clearer. Developers can quickly understand the purpose and functionality of each module, making it easier to troubleshoot and enhance.

o **Reusability**: Well-separated concerns often result in reusable code components. Reusable modules can be leveraged across different parts of an application, reducing duplication and promoting consistency.

o **Collaboration and parallel development**: Separated concerns facilitate parallel development, allowing multiple developers to work on different parts of the application concurrently. This speeds up development cycles and promotes collaboration within development teams.

o **Testability**: Isolating concerns simplifies the testing process. Developers can write focused unit tests for individual modules. It becomes easier to cover edge cases, identify issues, and ensure code correctness.

o **Error isolation and debugging**: When an issue arises, it is easier to isolate the problem to a specific module or concern. Debugging becomes more efficient, as you can narrow down the scope of the investigation.

o **Scalability and extensibility**: Separated concerns enable the system to scale and evolve more gracefully. New features or changes can be added to specific modules without affecting the entire application.

o **Flexibility and adaptability**: When concerns are separated, it is easier to adapt to changing requirements or business rules. Modifications can be made to individual components without causing a ripple effect throughout the application.

- o **Security and data integrity**: By separating concerns, you can enforce security measures at different levels. Access control, validation, and data integrity checks can be implemented in a granular manner.

- o **User experience**: Separation of concerns can lead to better user experiences. Front-end and back-end concerns can be separated, allowing for more responsive user interfaces.

In the context of Salesforce Apex, following are some examples of concerns that should be separated:

- **Data access**: Isolating database access code from business logic is a fundamental practice to ensure code modularity, reusability, and maintainability. This approach helps to create a clear separation of concerns and simplifies debugging, testing, and future enhancements.

  Consider the following principles:

  - o Separate data access code, including SOQL queries and DML operations, from other parts of your Apex code.

  - o Isolate database interactions in dedicated classes or methods that encapsulate database operations.

  - o This separation ensures that database-related logic is modular and can be reused without mixing it with other business logic.

- **Business logic**: Ensuring that business rules and logic are distinct from presentation and user interface code is a best practice for creating maintainable and scalable applications. This separation promotes clarity, reusability, and testability.

  Key principles are as follows:

  - o Keep your business rules, calculations, and workflow logic in distinct classes or methods.

  - o Business logic should be independent of specific data access or presentation concerns.

  - o Separating business logic promotes code reusability and makes it easier to test and maintain.

- **Trigger logic:** Triggers in Salesforce are powerful tools used to automate processes in response to data changes. To maintain clarity and ease of management, it is essential to separate trigger logic from the underlying business logic.

  Following is the code snippets for trigger logic example:

```
// Trigger
trigger AccountTrigger on Account (before insert, before update)
{
    AccountTriggerHandler.handleTrigger(Trigger.new, Trigger.
```

```
oldMap);
}

// Trigger Handler Class
public class AccountTriggerHandler {
    public static void handleTrigger(List<Account> newAccounts,
Map<Id, Account> oldAccounts) {
        if (Trigger.isInsert) {
            validateAccounts(newAccounts);
        }
        if (Trigger.isUpdate) {
            updateRelatedContacts(newAccounts, oldAccounts);
        }
    }

    private static void validateAccounts(List<Account> accounts)
{
        for (Account acc : accounts) {
            if (String.isBlank(acc.Name)) {
                acc.addError('Account Name cannot be blank.');
            }
        }
    }

    private static void updateRelatedContacts(List<Account>
newAccounts, Map<Id, Account> oldAccounts) {
        // Logic for updating related contacts
    }
}
```

Key practices are as follows:

o   In Salesforce, triggers are often used to automate processes based on data changes.

o   It is crucial to separate trigger logic from the underlying business logic to ensure clarity and maintainability.

o   Place trigger-related code in trigger handler classes, which can be designed to handle specific objects and events.

• **Integration logic:** When integrating your Salesforce application with external systems, it is essential to maintain a clear separation between integration-specific code and core business logic. This approach ensures better organization and easier maintenance.

Following is the code snippets for integration logic example:

```
public class ExternalServiceIntegration {
    public static String getExchangeRate(String currencyCode) {
        HttpRequest req = new HttpRequest();
        req.setEndpoint('https://api.exchangeratesapi.io/
latest?base=' + currencyCode);
        req.setMethod('GET');
        HttpResponse res = new Http().send(req);

        if (res.getStatusCode() == 200) {
            Map<String, Object> response = (Map<String, Object>)
JSON.deserializeUntyped(res.getBody());
            return String.valueOf(response.get('rates'));
        } else {
            throw new CustomException('Failed to fetch exchange
rate.');
        }
    }
}
```

Key points to consider are as follows:

o   If your Salesforce application integrates with external systems, for example other APIs, third-party services, keep integration-related code separate.

o   Use dedicated classes or components to encapsulate integration details, such as making HTTP requests or parsing responses.

o   Separating integration logic allows for easier maintenance and updating of integration endpoints or protocols.

By adhering to the principle of separation of concerns in Apex development, you can create cleaner, more maintainable, and more efficient code that is better equipped to handle evolving requirements and challenges.

SOLID principles and its application

SOLID principles are a set of five design principles in software development that aim to improve the maintainability and scalability of software systems. These principles are widely recognized and applied in various programming languages, including Apex in the context of Salesforce development.

Following figure illustrates the SOLID principles:

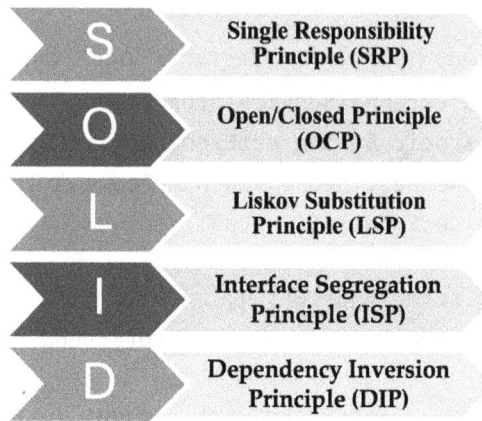

Figure 4.1: SOLID principles

Let us explore each SOLID principle and its application in Apex, as follows:

- **Single Responsibility Principle (SRP):**
  - **Principle**: A class should have only one reason to change, meaning it should have only one responsibility.

  - **Application in Apex**: In Apex, adhere to the SRP by ensuring that each class or method has a single, well-defined responsibility. For example, separate data access code from business logic, and keep trigger handlers focused on handling trigger events without incorporating extensive business logic.

    Adhering to SRP in Apex helps create cleaner, more maintainable, and more understandable code.

    Following is how to apply SRP in Apex:
    - **Separate data access and business logic:** Create separate classes or methods for data access and business logic. For example, use one class to handle database queries, for example, using SOQL and another to perform data processing.

      Refer to the following code:
      ```
      // Example of a class for data access
      public class EmployeeDataAccess {
          public List<Employee__c> getEmployees() {
              return [SELECT Id, Name, Email FROM
      Employee__c];
          }
      }
      ```

```
// Example of a class for business logic
public class EmployeeProcessor {
    public Decimal calculateBonus(List<Employee__c>
employees) {
        // Business logic for calculating bonuses
        // ...
    }
}
```

- **Avoid mixing concerns:** Ensure that a class or method focuses on a single aspect of functionality and does not mix unrelated concerns. For example, avoid mixing user interface code with data access or complex calculations.

- **Keep methods cohesive:** Within a class, individual methods should also follow SRP. Each method should have a Single Responsibility and perform a specific task.

    Refer to the following code:

```
public class OrderProcessor {
    public void processOrder(Order__c order) {
        validateOrder(order);
        updateInventory(order);
        calculateTax(order);
        sendConfirmationEmail(order);
    }

    private void validateOrder(Order__c order) {
        // Validation logic
    }

    private void updateInventory(Order__c order) {
        // Inventory update logic
    }

    private void calculateTax(Order__c order) {
        // Tax calculation logic
    }

    private void sendConfirmationEmail(Order__c order) {
```

```
            // Email sending logic
        }
    }
```

- **Use helper classes:** If a class becomes too large or starts to handle multiple responsibilities, consider refactoring it into smaller helper classes. These helper classes can focus on specific tasks or concerns.

  The following code is a Salesforce-specific example where helper classes are used for trigger logic.

```
public class OpportunityTriggerHandler {
    public static void
handleBeforeInsert(List<Opportunity> newOpportunities)
{
        OpportunityValidator.
validateOpportunities(newOpportunities);
    }
}


public class OpportunityValidator {
    public static void
validateOpportunities(List<Opportunity> opportunities)
{
        for (Opportunity opp : opportunities) {
            if (opp.Amount <= 0) {
                opp.addError('Opportunity Amount must
be greater than zero.');
            }
        }
    }
}
```

- **Focus on single unit tests:** When writing unit tests, ensure that each test case focuses on testing a single unit of functionality, corresponding to a Single Responsibility. This promotes clarity and makes tests easier to maintain.

- **Review and refactor:** Regularly review your codebase for violations of SRP and refactor as needed to ensure that each class and method has a clear and Single Responsibility. The following is an example of a class that violates SRP, followed by its refactored version.

```
// SRP Violation: Mixing data access and business logic
public class EmployeeManager {
    public List<Employee__c> getEmployees() {
        return [SELECT Id, Name, Email FROM
Employee__c];
    }

    public Decimal calculateBonus(List<Employee__c>
employees) {
        // Business logic for calculating bonuses
        // ...
    }
}


// Refactored Code with SRP
public class EmployeeDataAccess {
    public List<Employee__c> getEmployees() {
        return [SELECT Id, Name, Email FROM
Employee__c];
    }
}

public class EmployeeProcessor {
    public Decimal calculateBonus(List<Employee__c>
employees) {
        // Business logic for calculating bonuses
        // ...
    }
}
```

o **Common Pitfalls for SRP:** While adhering to SRP, be mindful of over-engineering by avoiding the creation of excessively granular classes. Each class should balance a focused responsibility with practical usability in the codebase.

By applying SRP in Apex development, you create code that is easier to understand, maintain, and extend. Each class and method has a well-defined purpose, which makes it more predictable and less prone to unintended side effects when changes are made. Additionally, it enhances the testability of your code, as each unit of functionality can be tested in isolation.

- **Open/Closed Principle (OCP):**

  o **Principle**: Software entities (classes, modules, functions) should be open for extension but closed for modification.

  o **Application in Apex**: Design classes and modules in a way that allows for extensions or customizations without modifying the existing code. Utilize interfaces, abstract classes, and polymorphism to enable the introduction of new functionality through extension rather than modification. This principle promotes code maintainability, scalability, and flexibility.

  Following is how you can apply the open/closed principle in Apex:

  - **Use inheritance and interfaces:** Inheritance and interfaces are essential tools for applying the OCP in Apex. Design your classes and interfaces with the expectation that they can be extended or implemented by subclasses without changing the base class's behavior. Base classes and interfaces should define abstract or virtual methods that can be overridden or implemented by subclasses to provide specific functionality, as follows:

    ```
    // Example of an interface that follows OCP
    public interface BonusCalculator {
        Decimal calculateBonus(Employee__c employee);
    }
    ```

  - **Create abstract or virtual methods:** Define abstract or virtual methods in base classes or interfaces to represent the behavior that can be extended. Subclasses can then override these methods to provide customized implementations, as follows:

    ```
    // Example of a base class with a virtual method
    public virtual class BonusCalculator {
        public virtual Decimal calculateBonus(Employee__c
    employee) {
            // Default bonus calculation logic
            return 0;
        }
    }
    ```

  - **Extend base classes or implement interfaces**: When you need to introduce new functionality, create subclasses or implement interfaces that extend or implement the base classes or interfaces. In these subclasses or implementations, override the abstract or virtual methods to provide the desired behavior, as follows:

```
// Example of a subclass extending the BonusCalculator
public class PerformanceBonusCalculator extends
BonusCalculator {
    public override Decimal calculateBonus(Employee__c
employee) {
        // Custom bonus calculation logic based on
performance
        return employee.Performance_Rating__c * 100;
    }
}
```

- **Utilize dependency injection:** In cases where you need to change the behavior of a class at runtime or inject different implementations, use **dependency injection** (**DI**). Pass instances of the extended or specialized classes or interfaces to the client code that depends on them, as follows:

```
// Example of dependency injection
public class BonusCalculatorClient {
    private BonusCalculator calculator;

    public BonusCalculatorClient(BonusCalculator
calculator) {
        this.calculator = calculator;
    }

    public Decimal calculateBonus(Employee__c employee)
    {
        return calculator.calculateBonus(employee);
    }
}
```

- **Avoid conditional statements:** Instead of using conditional statements (if-else or switch) to determine behavior, favor using polymorphism and method overriding to achieve different behaviors based on the actual type of the object.

o **Common Pitfalls for SRP:** While adhering to OCP, it is important to understand that the principle applies to stable, tested code. Experimental or frequently changing code may require modifications until it stabilizes. Avoid creating too many small interfaces that overcomplicate the design. Strive for a balance between granularity and usability.

The open/closed principle in Apex helps ensure that your codebase remains stable and maintainable as new features or requirements emerge. It promotes the creation of modular and extensible code that allows you to introduce new functionality by extending existing classes or implementing interfaces without altering the existing code. This results in more robust and flexible Apex applications.

- **Liskov Substitution Principle (LSP):**

   o **Principle**: Subtypes must be substitutable for their base types without altering the correctness of the program.

   o **Application in Apex**: When creating custom objects or classes that inherit from standard Salesforce objects for example, SObject, ensure that the custom objects can be used interchangeably with their base types. Follow Salesforce's inheritance hierarchy and respect platform conventions to maintain compatibility. In other words, if a class follows the LSP, you should be able to use its derived classes interchangeably with the base class, and the behavior of the program should remain consistent.

   Following is how you can apply the Liskov Substitution Principle in Apex:

   - **Inheritance hierarchy:** Define a clear inheritance hierarchy where the derived class (subclass) inherits from the base class (superclass). The base class typically represents a more general or abstract concept, while the derived class represents a more specialized or concrete concept, as follows:

```apex
// Example of a base class
public virtual class Shape {
    public virtual Decimal calculateArea() {
        return 0;
    }
}


// Example of a derived class
public class Circle extends Shape {
    public Decimal calculateArea() {
        // Custom implementation for calculating the
area of a circle
        return Math.PI * radius * radius;
    }
}
```

- **Method overriding:** In the derived class, override methods from the base class when necessary. The overriding methods should provide specialized behavior while maintaining the same method signature as the base class, as follows:

```
// Example of method overriding in a derived class
public override Decimal calculateArea() {
    // Custom implementation for calculating the area
of a circle
    return Math.PI * radius * radius;
}
```

- **Maintain method contracts:** Ensure that the overridden methods in the derived class adhere to the method contracts defined in the base class. This means that the method parameters and return types in the derived class should match or be more specific than those in the base class, as follows:

```
// Base class method
public virtual Decimal calculateArea() {
    return 0;
}


// Derived class method adheres to the method contract
public override Decimal calculateArea() {
    // Custom implementation for calculating the area
of a circle
    return Math.PI * radius * radius;
}
```

- **Substitute objects:** You should be able to substitute an object of the derived class for an object of the base class wherever the base class is expected. This substitution should not introduce unexpected behavior or errors in the program, as follows:

```
Shape myShape = new Circle(); // LSP-compliant
substitution
Decimal area = myShape.calculateArea(); // Calls the
overridden method in Circle
```

- **Respect salesforce inheritance rules:** When working with Salesforce objects like custom objects, follow the Salesforce inheritance hierarchy and conventions. Ensure that custom objects and classes adhere to Salesforce's platform-specific rules and interfaces.

- o **Common pitfalls for LSP**: Common pitfalls when applying LSP include overriding base class methods without preserving their expected behavior and introducing additional constraints or side effects that prevent seamless substitution of the base class with its subclass.

- **Interface Segregation Principle (ISP):**

  - o **Principle**: Clients should not be forced to depend on interfaces they do not use. In other words, keep interfaces specific to their clients' needs.

  - o **Application in Apex**: When defining interfaces in Apex, keep them focused and small in scope. Avoid creating overly general interfaces that require implementing unnecessary methods. Use multiple interfaces if needed to provide specific functionality to different clients. In other words, an interface should have a specific and focused set of methods that are relevant to the clients that implement it. Apex supports interfaces, and you can apply ISP principles to create cohesive and specialized interfaces.

    Following is how you can apply the Interface Segregation Principle in Apex:

    - **Create focused interfaces**: Design interfaces to have a clear and specific purpose, focusing on a single aspect of functionality. Avoid creating overly general interfaces with a large number of methods that may not be relevant to all implementing classes, as follows:

      ```
      // Example of a focused interface (good)
      public interface Printable {
          void print();
      }


      // Avoid overly general interfaces (not ideal)
      public interface GeneralOperations {
          void performOperation1();
          void performOperation2();
          void performOperation3();
      }
      ```

    - **Implement only relevant methods:** When implementing an interface, implement only the methods that are relevant to the class's functionality. If a method is not needed or applicable to the class, leave it unimplemented. This prevents unnecessary dependencies, as follows:

      ```
      // Example of implementing a focused interface
      public class Report implements Printable {
          public void print() {
              // Implementation specific to printing a report
      ```

```
        }
    }
```

- **Use multiple interfaces, if needed:** If a class requires functionality from multiple interfaces, it is better to implement those interfaces separately rather than combining them into a single, monolithic interface, as follows:

```
// Example of implementing multiple interfaces
public class Invoice implements Printable, Exportable {
    public void print() {
        // Implementation specific to printing an
invoice
    }

    public void export() {
        // Implementation specific to exporting an
invoice
    }
}
```

- **Avoid forcing irrelevant implementations:** Do not force classes to implement methods that are irrelevant to their purpose. If a class needs to provide default or empty implementations for certain methods, consider using abstract base classes or providing default behavior in the interface itself, as follows:

```
// Avoid forcing irrelevant methods (not ideal)
public interface Payable {
    void makePayment();
    void trackPayment();
}

// Better approach with default method implementations
public interface Payable {
    void makePayment();

    default void trackPayment() {
        // Default implementation for tracking payments
    }
}
```

- **Common pitfalls for ISP:** Common pitfalls when applying ISP include creating overly broad interfaces that force classes to implement unnecessary methods and splitting interfaces excessively, leading to fragmented and hard-to-manage code.

By following the Interface Segregation Principle in Apex, you create interfaces that are focused, relevant, and cohesive. This results in cleaner and more maintainable code, as clients (classes implementing the interfaces) only need to depend on the methods that are meaningful to their specific functionality. It also reduces the risk of unintentional dependencies and promotes code readability and clarity.

- **Dependency Inversion Principle (DIP):**

  o **Principle**: High-level modules should not depend on low-level modules. Both should depend on abstractions. Abstractions should not depend on details. Details should depend on abstractions.

  o **Application in Apex**: In Apex, use DI to invert dependencies, allowing higher-level classes to depend on abstractions or interfaces rather than concrete implementations. Favor interfaces and abstract classes for dependencies to promote flexibility and decouple components. Additionally, abstractions should not depend on details, and details should depend on abstractions. In the context of Apex, DIP can be applied to create flexible and maintainable code by decoupling dependencies.

  Following is how you can apply DIP in Apex:

  - **Use interfaces or abstract classes:** Define interfaces or abstract classes to represent abstractions or contracts for dependencies. High-level modules (classes or components) should depend on these abstractions rather than concrete implementations, as follows:

    ```
    // Example of an interface representing an abstraction
    public interface Logger {
        void log(String message);
    }
    ```

  - **Implement concrete classes:** Create concrete classes that implement the interfaces or extend the abstract classes defined in first step. These concrete classes provide the actual implementations of the dependencies, as follows:

    ```
    // Example of a concrete class implementing the Logger
    interface
    public class FileLogger implements Logger {
        public void log(String message) {
            // Implementation for logging to a file
        }
    }
    ```

- **Use DI:** Inject instances of the dependencies (concrete classes) into the high-level modules that require them. This can be done through constructor injection, method injection, or property injection, as follows:

```
// Example of constructor injection
public class OrderProcessor {
    private Logger logger;

    public OrderProcessor(Logger logger) {
        this.logger = logger;
    }

    public void processOrder(Order__c order) {
        // ...
        logger.log("Order processed: " + order.Name);
    }
}
```

- **Decouple high-level modules:** High-level modules should not be tightly coupled to specific concrete implementations. Instead, they rely on the abstractions provided by the interfaces or abstract classes. This decoupling allows you to switch or extend implementations without modifying the high-level module.

- **Favor composition over inheritance:** When dealing with dependencies, favor composition (using object composition) over inheritance (subclassing) to assemble complex objects. This promotes flexibility, as you can change the behavior of a class by swapping out its dependencies without changing its inheritance hierarchy.

- **Use DI containers (Optional):** For more complex dependency management, consider using DI containers or frameworks like Salesforce's built-in DI framework or third-party libraries. By applying the DIP in Apex, you achieve loose coupling between components, making your code more adaptable to changes and easier to test. High-level modules depend on abstractions, allowing you to substitute different implementations without affecting the core logic. This principle is particularly useful in Apex when dealing with external services, data access, or custom business logic, as it promotes modularity and maintainability.

o **Common pitfalls for DIP:** Common pitfalls when applying DIP include creating unnecessary layers of abstraction for straightforward cases and using DI even when concrete implementations rarely change.

Suppose you have a Salesforce application that involves data access and processing. Following is how you can follow SOLID principles:

- Separating data access code into dedicated classes or methods.

- Designing interfaces for data access and ensuring that business logic classes depend on these abstractions, not concrete data access implementations.

- Using DI to provide the necessary data access implementations to business logic classes, making them more flexible and testable.

- Ensuring that custom objects or classes you create extend or implement base Salesforce types in a way that adheres to LSP.

By applying SOLID principles in your Apex development, you can create more maintainable, extensible, and testable code that is adaptable to changing requirements and scalable for future enhancements.

Conclusion

In this chapter, we explored the foundational principles and best practices for writing clean, maintainable, and efficient Apex code, which serves as the cornerstone for robust Salesforce applications. We delved into the importance of creating modular and well-organized code by following practices like descriptive naming, consistent formatting, meaningful comments, and efficient error handling. By avoiding hardcoding, adhering to bulk processing principles, and staying within governor limits, we emphasized the necessity of writing scalable and performance-driven code.

We also underscored the significance of the separation of concerns, a core principle in software development. By isolating data access, business logic, trigger logic, and integration-specific logic, developers can achieve better code readability, reusability, and testability. This ensures a clear distinction between various components, enabling teams to work collaboratively and efficiently on different parts of the application.

A key highlight of this chapter was the application of SOLID principles in Apex development. We analyzed how these principles Single Responsibility, Open/Closed, Liskov Substitution, Interface Segregation, and Dependency Inversion serve as guiding frameworks for building systems that are easier to extend, maintain, and adapt to evolving business requirements. Practical examples accompanied each principle to illustrate its relevance and impact on Apex-based solutions.

By integrating these concepts into the development process, readers can establish a strong foundation for writing Apex code that is functional, clean, modular, and scalable. These principles and practices ensure that your applications can grow with your organization while remaining easy to maintain and enhance over time.

In the next chapter, the spotlight turns toward creational design patterns and passive constructs for object creation. It will cover the singleton pattern, factory method pattern, builder pattern, abstract factory pattern, and prototype pattern.

Points to remember

- Descriptive naming enhances code readability and understanding.
- Consistent formatting improves collaboration and reduces confusion.
- Avoid long methods by breaking them into smaller, focused methods.
- Use comments sparingly and for clarity, not redundancy.
- Avoid hardcoding; use named constants, custom settings, or metadata.
- Always handle exceptions appropriately and provide user-friendly error messages.
- Log errors for debugging and avoid empty catch blocks.
- Use custom exceptions for specific error scenarios.
- Write bulk-friendly code to handle large data volumes efficiently.
- Avoid SOQL/DML operations inside loops; leverage Batch Apex for large datasets.
- Write unit tests to achieve high code coverage.
- Cover positive, negative, and edge-case scenarios.
- Use test data factory patterns and assertions for effective testing.
- Conduct regular code reviews to maintain quality.
- Use tools like Apex PMD to enforce standards.
- Incorporate continuous integration and automated testing.
- Isolate data access, business logic, trigger logic, and integration logic into distinct modules.
- Modular code promotes readability, maintainability, and scalability.
- **SRP**: Ensure each class or method has a Single Responsibility.
- **OCP**: Allow classes to be extended without modifying their existing code.
- **LSP**: Derived classes should be substitutable for their base classes.
- **ISP**: Design interfaces with specific purposes; avoid forcing irrelevant dependencies.
- **DIP**: High-level modules should depend on abstractions, not concrete implementations.

Questions

1. What is the importance of writing clean, maintainable, and efficient Apex code?
2. Explain the principle of separation of concerns and its significance in Apex development.

3. Describe the purpose of SOLID principles in software design.

4. Why is error handling critical in Apex development, and what are the best practices?

5. How can descriptive naming improve code readability in Apex?

6. Provide an example of refactoring a long method to follow the SRP.

7. How would you implement DI in Apex to adhere to the Dependency Inversion Principle?

8. Write an example of a bulk-friendly SOQL query to avoid governor limits.

9. A trigger is mixing business logic with data access. How would you refactor it to follow the separation of concerns principle?

10. If a new requirement involves adding a custom bonus calculation for specific employees, how can you implement this change using the open/closed principle?

11. How would you ensure that your custom objects in Salesforce adhere to the Liskov Substitution Principle?

12. How can adopting clean coding practices and SOLID principles improve team collaboration in a Salesforce project?

13. Discuss a scenario where not adhering to the Interface Segregation Principle could lead to issues in an Apex application.

14. How does continuous improvement contribute to the long-term success of an Apex development team?

Join our book's Discord space

Join the book's Discord Workspace for Latest updates, Offers, Tech happenings around the world, New Release and Sessions with the Authors:

https://discord.bpbonline.com

CHAPTER 5

Creational Design Patterns

Introduction

Within this chapter, the spotlight turns toward **creational design patterns** and passive constructs for object creation. These patterns are a category of design patterns in software engineering that deal specifically with the process of creating objects.

Creational design patterns provide solutions for creating objects in a way that is flexible, efficient, and promotes code reusability. By abstracting the instantiation process, they hide the complexities of object creation from the client code, enabling developers to focus on the overall structure and behavior of the application.

These patterns address various object creation scenarios. For example, the **singleton pattern** ensures a single instance of a class, while the **factory method pattern** provides a way to create objects without specifying their exact class. Similarly, the **abstract factory pattern** is used to create families of related objects, the **builder pattern** constructs complex objects step by step, and the **prototype pattern** copies existing objects.

By applying creational design patterns, developers can make their code more modular, maintainable, and adaptable to changing requirements. Each pattern serves a specific purpose and optimizes object creation in different scenarios. Collectively, these patterns enhance the overall design and efficiency of software systems.

Structure

The chapter covers the following topics:

- Creational design patterns
- Singleton pattern
- Factory method pattern
- Builder pattern
- Abstract factory pattern
- Prototype pattern

Objectives

By the end of this chapter, readers will gain a comprehensive understanding of creational design patterns and their application in Salesforce Apex development. These patterns provide effective strategies for object creation, addressing challenges related to flexibility, scalability, and maintainability. This chapter equips readers with the knowledge to implement the creational design patterns like singleton pattern, factory method pattern, builder pattern, abstract factory pattern, prototype pattern.

Creational design patterns

Creational design patterns are a subset of design patterns in software engineering that focus on the process of object creation. They provide ways to create objects while hiding the creation logic, making the system more flexible, efficient, and easy to maintain. Creational design patterns abstract the instantiation process, decoupling the client code from the specifics of how objects are created.

Following is an introduction to the key concepts and common creational design patterns:

- **Object creation challenges:** In software development, creating objects can be complex due to factors like configuration, initialization, and resource management. Directly instantiating objects in client code can lead to tight coupling and inflexibility.

- **Goals of creational design patterns**:

  o **Promote flexibility:** Allow the system to evolve without changing existing code.

  o **Encapsulate object creation**: Hide the details of object creation from the client code.

  o **Improve code maintainability**: Make it easier to modify or extend the object creation process.

- **Common creational design patterns**:

  - **Singleton pattern:** Ensures that a class has only one instance and provides a global point of access to it. It is used when exactly one object is needed to coordinate actions across a system.

  - **Factory method pattern**: Defines an interface for creating an object but let's subclasses alter the type of objects that will be created. It is used when a class cannot anticipate the type of objects it needs to create.

  - **Abstract factory pattern**: Provides an interface for creating families of related or dependent objects without specifying their concrete classes. It is used when a system needs to be independent of how its objects are created, composed, and represented.

  - **Builder pattern**: Separates the construction of a complex object from its representation. It allows you to create an object step by step and is often used for creating complex objects with many optional components.

  - **Prototype pattern**: Creates new objects by copying an existing object, known as the prototype. It is used when the cost of creating an object is more expensive or complex than copying an existing one.

- **Choosing the right creational pattern:** The choice of which creational design pattern to use depends on the specific requirements and constraints of your application. Consider factors such as the complexity of object creation, the need for flexibility, and resource efficiency when selecting a pattern.

Following figure illustrates the types of creational design patterns:

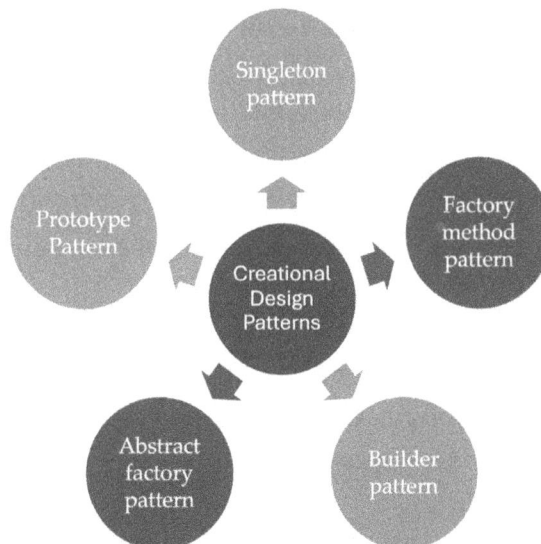

Figure 5.1: Creational design patterns

Overall, creational design patterns provide a toolbox of techniques for managing object creation, allowing you to design more flexible, maintainable, and efficient software systems. Each pattern addresses different challenges related to object creation, and their application depends on the specific context and requirements of your project.

Singleton pattern

The singleton Pattern is a creational design pattern that ensures a class has only one instance and provides a global point of access to that instance. This pattern is particularly useful in Salesforce Apex for managing shared resources, controlling access to critical components, and maintaining a single point of control across your application. In this section, we will explore the singleton pattern in-depth, and its benefits, and provide practical examples of its implementation in Salesforce Apex.

Understanding singleton pattern

At its core, the singleton pattern enforces the following key principles:

- **Single instance**: It ensures that a class has only one instance throughout the lifetime of an application.

- **Global access**: It provides a global point of access to that single instance.

Benefits of using singleton pattern

Implementing the singleton pattern in Salesforce Apex offers the following advantages:

- **Resource management:** It allows efficient management of shared resources, such as database connections, web service clients, or configuration settings.

- **Global state**: It maintains a consistent global state, ensuring that changes made to the singleton are visible across the application.

- **Reduced memory usage**: Since there is only one instance, memory usage is minimized, especially when dealing with resource-intensive components.

- **Consistency**: It ensures that the behavior of the singleton remains consistent, preventing unexpected changes or conflicts.

Implementing singleton pattern in Salesforce Apex

Following is an example of implementing the singleton pattern in Salesforce Apex:

```
public class PreInitializedSingleton {

    // Private static final instance created at the time of class loading
    private static final PreInitializedSingleton instance = new
```

```
PreInitializedSingleton();

    // Private constructor to prevent external instantiation
    private PreInitializedSingleton() {
        // Initialization logic if needed
    }

    // Public method to access the single instance
    public static PreInitializedSingleton getInstance() {
        return instance;
    }

    // Add other methods and properties as needed
    public void performAction() {
        System.debug('Pre-initialized Singleton is performing an action.');
    }
}
```

In this example, we created a **PreInitializedSingleton** class that follows the singleton pattern. We have a private static final variable instance that holds the single instance of the class, which is initialized at the time of class loading. The construction of the class is marked as private to prevent external instantiation. We provide a public static method **getInstance()** to allow access to the single instance of the class. Since the instance is already created during class loading, the **getInstance()** method simply returns this pre-initialized instance. Using the singleton.

Now, you can use the **PreInitializedSingleton** class to access the single instance, as follows:

```
PreInitializedSingleton singleton1 = PreInitializedSingleton.getInstance();
PreInitializedSingleton singleton2 = PreInitializedSingleton.getInstance();

System.assertEquals(singleton1, singleton2, 'Pre-initialized Singleton
instances should be the same.');

singleton1.performAction(); // Outputs: Pre-initialized Singleton is
performing an action
```

In this example, the **PreInitializedSingleton** class ensures that the same instance is used every time the **getInstance()** method is called. This is achieved through pre-initialization, where the instance is created at the time of class loading and stored in a static variable. When you call **getInstance()**, the pre-created instance is returned.

This guarantees that singleton1 and singleton2 refer to the exact same instance, as verified by the assertion. The **performAction()** method demonstrates how you can invoke behavior on the shared instance, maintaining consistency and control over a single, shared resource throughout your application.

Practical implementation example of singleton pattern

The singleton pattern is widely used in software design to ensure a single instance of a class is created and accessed globally.

The following practical examples demonstrate its implementation in different scenarios for Salesforce Apex:

Example 1: Centralized logging with singleton pattern

A real-world example of the singleton pattern in Salesforce Apex can be seen when dealing with a central logging service. Imagine you want to create a logging mechanism that records important events, errors, and messages in your Salesforce application. Using the singleton pattern ensures that you have a single point of access to your logging service throughout the application, making it easy to manage and control the logging behavior.

Following is how you can implement a singleton Logger in Salesforce Apex:

```apex
public class Logger {

    // Private static instance variable to hold the single instance
    private static Logger instance;

    // Private constructor to prevent external instantiation
    private Logger() {
        // Initialization code here (e.g., setting up log file)
    }

    // Public method to access the single instance
    public static Logger getInstance() {
        if (instance == null) {
            // Create the instance if it doesn't exist
            instance = new Logger();
        }
        return instance;
    }

    // Method to log messages
```

```
    public void log(String message) {
        // Actual logging implementation (e.g., writing to a log file or
sending to an external system)
        System.debug('Log: ' + message);
    }
}
```

In this example:

- The **Logger** class follows the singleton Pattern. It has a private static **instance** variable to hold the single instance of the class, a private constructor to prevent external instantiation, and a public **getInstance()** method to access the single instance.

- The **log(String message)** method represents the functionality of the logger. In a real-world scenario, this method might perform actions like writing log entries to a file, sending log data to a central server, or even publishing log messages to a chat system.

Now, you can use the **Logger** class to log messages from various parts of your Salesforce application, as follows:

```
Logger logger = Logger.getInstance();
logger.log('User logged in: ' + UserInfo.getUserId());
logger.log('Error occurred: ' + exception.getMessage());
```

By using the singleton Logger, you ensure that there is only one instance of the logger throughout your Salesforce application. This prevents the need to initialize and configure the logger in multiple places and provides a centralized point for managing and controlling your logging behavior.

Example 2: Global configuration management with singleton pattern

Another real-world example of using the singleton pattern in Salesforce Apex can be seen when managing a global configuration object. This configuration object stores settings or parameters that are shared across different parts of an application. By using the singleton pattern, you can ensure that there's only one instance of the configuration object throughout the application, and it provides a single point of access to retrieve and modify configuration settings.

Following is a simplified example of a singleton pattern implementation for a global configuration object in Salesforce Apex:

```
public class AppConfig {

    // Private static instance variable to hold the single instance
    private static AppConfig instance;
```

```apex
// Configuration settings
private Map<String, String> settings;

// Private constructor to prevent external instantiation
private AppConfig() {
    // Initialize the configuration settings
    settings = new Map<String, String>();
}

// Public method to access the single instance
public static AppConfig getInstance() {
    if (instance == null) {
        // Create the instance if it doesn't exist
        instance = new AppConfig();
    }
    return instance;
}

// Methods to get and set configuration settings
public String getSetting(String key) {
    return settings.get(key);
}

public void setSetting(String key, String value) {
    settings.put(key, value);
}
}
```

In this example:

- **AppConfig** is a class that follows the singleton pattern to manage a global configuration object.

- It has a private static variable **instance** to hold the single instance of **AppConfig**.

- The constructor is marked as private to prevent external instantiation, ensuring that no other code can create additional instances.

- The **getInstance()** method provides the global access point to retrieve the single instance of **AppConfig**. If the instance does not exist, it is created.

- **AppConfig** includes methods to get and set configuration settings. These settings are stored in a **Map** in this example, but in a real-world scenario, you might retrieve settings from custom metadata or a custom object.

Usage of the singleton pattern for the **AppConfig** is as follows:

```
// Access the configuration settings
AppConfig config = AppConfig.getInstance();
config.setSetting('api_key', 'my_api_key');
config.setSetting('log_level', 'DEBUG');


// Retrieve and use configuration settings
String apiKey = config.getSetting('api_key');
String logLevel = config.getSetting('log_level');


System.debug('API Key: ' + apiKey);
System.debug('Log Level: ' + logLevel);
```

By using the singleton pattern, you ensure that there is only one instance of **AppConfig** shared across your Salesforce application, making it a reliable and centralized way to manage configuration settings that are used by various components and classes.

Summary: The singleton pattern is a valuable tool in Salesforce Apex development for managing shared resources and maintaining a single point of control. By understanding and implementing this pattern effectively, you can enhance the efficiency and consistency of your Apex code, ultimately leading to a more robust and maintainable application.

Factory method pattern

Factory method pattern is a creational design pattern that provides an interface for creating objects but let subclasses decide which class to instantiate. It is particularly useful in Salesforce Apex when you need to create objects of different types based on specific conditions or configurations. In this section, we will explore the factory method pattern, and its benefits, and provide practical examples of its implementation in Salesforce Apex.

Understanding factory method pattern

Factory method pattern abstracts the process of object creation and allows it to be determined by subclasses. It promotes loose coupling between the client code and the concrete classes, making it easier to add new types of objects without modifying existing code.

Benefits of using factory method pattern

Implementing the Factory method pattern in Salesforce Apex offers the following advantages:

- **Flexibility:** It allows for dynamic object creation based on conditions or parameters, making the system more adaptable to changes.

- **Encapsulation**: The creation logic is encapsulated within the factory classes, which simplifies client code and reduces dependencies on concrete implementations.

- **Extensibility**: Adding new object types or variants is straightforward by creating new factory classes or extending existing ones.

- **Testing**: It facilitates easier testing by allowing you to replace concrete objects with mock objects during unit testing.

Implementing factory method pattern

Let us explore an example of implementing the factory method pattern in Salesforce Apex. We will create a simple factory that generates different types of **Shape** objects, as follows:

```
public abstract class Shape {
    public abstract void draw();
}

public class Circle extends Shape {
    public override void draw() {
        System.debug('Drawing a circle.');
    }
}

public class Square extends Shape {
    public override void draw() {
        System.debug('Drawing a square.');
    }
}

public abstract class ShapeFactory {
    public abstract Shape createShape();
}

public class CircleFactory extends ShapeFactory {
    public override Shape createShape() {
```

```
        return new Circle();
    }
}


public class SquareFactory extends ShapeFactory {
    public override Shape createShape() {
        return new Square();
    }
}
```

In this example:

- We have a base class **Shape** with two concrete subclasses, **Circle** and **Square**, representing different types of shapes.

- We define an abstract class **ShapeFactory** with an abstract method **createShape().** Subclasses of **ShapeFactory** will provide the implementation for creating specific shapes.

- Two concrete factory classes, **CircleFactory** and **SquareFactory**, extend **ShapeFactory** and implement the **createShape()** method to produce instances of **Circle** and **Square**, respectively.

Using the factory method

Now, you can use the factory method pattern to create objects, as follows:

```
ShapeFactory factory1 = new CircleFactory();
Shape circle = factory1.createShape();
circle.draw(); // Outputs: Drawing a circle.

ShapeFactory factory2 = new SquareFactory();
Shape square = factory2.createShape();
square.draw(); // Outputs: Drawing a square.
```

By using factory classes and the factory method pattern, you can dynamically create objects of different types without directly instantiating them in client code. This promotes code reusability, extensibility, and maintainability, allowing you to add new shape types or factories without modifying existing code.

Practical implementation example of factory method pattern

Following examples demonstrate how the factory method pattern can be practically implemented in Salesforce Apex, showcasing its adaptability across different scenarios.

Example 1: Factory method for data source connectors

A real-world example of using the factory method pattern in Salesforce Apex can be seen when dealing with different types of data sources or connectors. Imagine you have an application that needs to fetch data from various external sources, such as databases, REST APIs, or external services. Using the factory method pattern, you can create a factory for each type of data source to abstract the instantiation of data connectors.

Following is a simplified example:

```
// Interface for data connectors
public interface DataConnector {
    void connect();
    void fetchData();
    void disconnect();
}


// Concrete implementation for a database connector
public class DatabaseConnector implements DataConnector {
    public void connect() {
        // Logic to connect to the database
    }

    public void fetchData() {
        // Logic to fetch data from the database
    }

    public void disconnect() {
        // Logic to disconnect from the database
    }
}


// Concrete implementation for a REST API connector
public class RestApiConnector implements DataConnector {
    public void connect() {
        // Logic to establish a REST API connection
    }

    public void fetchData() {
        // Logic to fetch data from the REST API
```

```
    }

    public void disconnect() {
        // Logic to close the REST API connection
    }
}


// Data Connector Factory interface
public interface DataConnectorFactory {
    DataConnector createConnector();
}


// Factory for creating DatabaseConnectors
public class DatabaseConnectorFactory implements DataConnectorFactory {
    public DataConnector createConnector() {
        return new DatabaseConnector();
    }
}


// Factory for creating RestApiConnectors
public class RestApiConnectorFactory implements DataConnectorFactory {
    public DataConnector createConnector() {
        return new RestApiConnector();
    }
}
```

In this example:

- We have an interface, **DataConnector** that defines the methods common to all data connectors, including connecting, fetching data, and disconnecting.

- Two concrete implementations, **DatabaseConnector** and **RestApiConnector**, represent connectors for a database and a REST API, respectively.

- We define a **DataConnectorFactory** interface with a method **createConnector()**. Implementations of this interface will create instances of specific data connectors.

- Two concrete factory classes, **DatabaseConnectorFactory** and **RestApiConnectorFactory**, implement the **DataConnectorFactory** interface. Each factory is responsible for creating a specific type of data connector.

Now, you can use the factory method pattern to create data connectors dynamically, as follows:

```
DataConnectorFactory databaseFactory = new DatabaseConnectorFactory();
DataConnector databaseConnector = databaseFactory.createConnector();

DataConnectorFactory restApiFactory = new RestApiConnectorFactory();
DataConnector restApiConnector = restApiFactory.createConnector();

// Use the connectors
databaseConnector.connect();
databaseConnector.fetchData();
databaseConnector.disconnect();

restApiConnector.connect();
restApiConnector.fetchData();
restApiConnector.disconnect();
```

By using the factory method pattern, you can create data connectors of different types without needing to know their concrete implementations. This abstraction makes it easier to switch between data sources, add new data connectors, and maintain a consistent interface for interacting with them.

Example 2: Custom object record creation framework

Another real-world example of using the factory method pattern in Salesforce Apex can be found in the context of a custom object record creation framework. In Salesforce, organizations often have custom objects to store specific types of data, and these objects might have different record-creation requirements. By using the factory method pattern, you can create a set of record factories, each tailored to create records for a specific custom object type.

Following is an example:

```
// Interface for record creation
public interface RecordCreator {
    void createRecord(Map<String, Object> fields);
}

// Concrete implementation for creating Contact records
public class ContactRecordCreator implements RecordCreator {
    public void createRecord(Map<String, Object> fields) {
        // Logic to create a Contact record with the provided fields
        Contact newContact = new Contact();
        newContact.FirstName = (String)fields.get('FirstName');
```

```
            newContact.LastName = (String)fields.get('LastName');
            newContact.Email = (String)fields.get('Email');
            insert newContact;
    }
}


// Concrete implementation for creating Account records
public class AccountRecordCreator implements RecordCreator {
    public void createRecord(Map<String, Object> fields) {
        // Logic to create an Account record with the provided fields
        Account newAccount = new Account();
        newAccount.Name = (String)fields.get('Name');
        newAccount.Phone = (String)fields.get('Phone');
        insert newAccount;
    }
}


// Record Creator Factory interface
public interface RecordCreatorFactory {
    RecordCreator createRecordCreator();
}


// Factory for creating ContactRecordCreators
public class ContactRecordCreatorFactory implements RecordCreatorFactory {
    public RecordCreator createRecordCreator() {
        return new ContactRecordCreator();
    }
}


// Factory for creating AccountRecordCreators
public class AccountRecordCreatorFactory implements RecordCreatorFactory {
    public RecordCreator createRecordCreator() {
        return new AccountRecordCreator();
    }
}
```

In this example:

- We have an interface **RecordCreator** that defines a method **createRecord()** for creating records.

- Two concrete implementations, **ContactRecordCreator** and **AccountRecordCreator**, represent record creators for Contact and Account custom objects, respectively.

- We define a **RecordCreatorFactory** interface with a method **createRecordCreator()**. Implementations of this interface will create instances of specific record creator types.

- Two concrete factory classes, **ContactRecordCreatorFactory** and **AccountRecordCreatorFactory**, implement the **RecordCreatorFactory** interface. Each factory is responsible for creating instances of a specific record creator type.

Now, you can use the factory method pattern to create and insert records dynamically based on the custom object type, as follows:

```
RecordCreatorFactory contactFactory = new ContactRecordCreatorFactory();
RecordCreator contactRecordCreator = contactFactory.createRecordCreator();

Map<String, Object> contactFields = new Map<String, Object>{
    'FirstName' => 'Chamil',
    'LastName' => 'Madusanka',
    'Email' => 'chamil.madusanka@gmail.com'
};

contactRecordCreator.createRecord(contactFields);

RecordCreatorFactory accountFactory = new AccountRecordCreatorFactory();
RecordCreator accountRecordCreator = accountFactory.createRecordCreator();

Map<String, Object> accountFields = new Map<String, Object>{
    'Name' => 'Acme Inc',
    'Phone' => '123-456-7890'
};

accountRecordCreator.createRecord(accountFields);
```

By using the factory method pattern, you can create and insert records for different custom objects without needing to know the specific logic for each object type. This abstraction simplifies the record creation process, makes it easier to add new custom objects, and maintains a consistent interface for creating records in your Salesforce application.

Summary: The factory method pattern is a valuable tool in Salesforce Apex for flexible and extensible object creation. By employing this pattern effectively, you can simplify your code, reduce dependencies on concrete classes, and make your application more adaptable to changes in object creation requirements.

Builder pattern

The builder pattern is a creational design pattern that provides a way to construct complex objects step by step. It separates the construction of an object from its representation, allowing the same construction process to create different representations. In Salesforce Apex, this pattern is valuable when dealing with objects that have multiple optional parameters or configurations. This section explores the builder pattern, its benefits, and provides practical examples of its implementation in Salesforce Apex.

Understanding builder pattern

The builder pattern is especially useful when an object has numerous optional attributes, making it impractical to have a constructor with a long parameter list or multiple constructors with different combinations of parameters. Instead, it provides a dedicated builder class to construct an object with the desired configuration.

Benefits of using builder pattern

Implementing the builder pattern in Salesforce Apex offers the following advantages:

- **Flexibility**: It allows for the step-by-step construction of complex objects, providing fine-grained control over their configuration.
- **Readability**: Code using the builder is more self-explanatory, as each method invocation represents a configuration step.
- **Immutability**: Builders often produce immutable objects, ensuring that the constructed object cannot be modified after creation.
- **Default values**: Builders can provide default values for optional parameters, simplifying object creation.

Implementing builder pattern

Let us explore an example of implementing the builder pattern in Salesforce Apex. We will create a builder for constructing a **Product** object, which has several optional attributes, as follows:

```
public class Product {
    private String name;
    private Double price;
    private String description;
    private Integer stock;
```

```
    private Product(ProductBuilder builder) {
        this.name = builder.name;
        this.price = builder.price;
        this.description = builder.description;
        this.stock = builder.stock;
    }

    public static class ProductBuilder {
        private String name;
        private Double price;
        private String description;
        private Integer stock;

        public ProductBuilder(String name, Double price) {
            this.name = name;
            this.price = price;
        }

        public ProductBuilder setDescription(String description) {
            this.description = description;
            return this;
        }

        public ProductBuilder setStock(Integer stock) {
            this.stock = stock;
            return this;
        }

        public Product build() {
            return new Product(this);
        }
    }
}
```

In this example:

- We have a **Product** class with several optional attributes (name, price, description, and stock).

- We define a nested **ProductBuilder** class responsible for constructing **Product** objects.

- The builder provides methods to set optional attributes and a **build()** method to create the **Product** instance with the specified configuration.

Using builder pattern

Now, you can use the builder to create **Product** objects, as follows:

```
Product.ProductBuilder builder = new Product.ProductBuilder('Widget',
19.99);
builder.setDescription('A high-quality widget');
builder.setStock(100);


Product widget = builder.build();
```

By using the builder pattern, you can construct product objects with various configurations without dealing with a long constructor parameter list. This enhances code readability and maintainability, especially when dealing with complex objects.

Practical implementation example of builder pattern

The builder pattern provides a structured approach to constructing complex objects step-by-step.

Following are practical implementation examples demonstrating how this pattern simplifies object creation while ensuring flexibility and maintainability:

Example 1: Dynamic SOQL query builder

A real-world example of the builder pattern in Salesforce Apex can be seen when creating dynamic SOQL queries. In Salesforce, you often need to build queries with dynamic filtering conditions based on user input or other runtime factors. The builder pattern can be applied to create a query builder that simplifies the construction of dynamic SOQL queries.

Following is a simplified example:

```
public class DynamicQuery {
    private String objectName;
    private List<String> selectedFields;
    private List<String> filters;

    private DynamicQuery(QueryBuilder builder) {
        this.objectName = builder.objectName;
```

```
            this.selectedFields = builder.selectedFields;
            this.filters = builder.filters;
        }


    public static class QueryBuilder {
        private String objectName;
        private List<String> selectedFields;
        private List<String> filters;

        public QueryBuilder(String objectName) {
            this.objectName = objectName;
            this.selectedFields = new List<String>();
            this.filters = new List<String>();
        }

        public QueryBuilder selectFields(List<String> fields) {
            this.selectedFields.addAll(fields);
            return this;
        }

        public QueryBuilder addFilter(String filter) {
            this.filters.add(filter);
            return this;
        }

        public DynamicQuery build() {
            return new DynamicQuery(this);
        }
    }

    public String generateQuery() {
        String fields = String.join(selectedFields, ', ');
        String whereClause = filters.isEmpty() ? '' : ' WHERE ' + String.
join(filters, ' AND ');
        return 'SELECT ' + fields + ' FROM ' + objectName + whereClause;
    }
}
```

In this example:

- We have a **DynamicQuery** class that represents a dynamic SOQL query with an object name, selected fields, and filtering conditions.

- We define a nested **QueryBuilder** class responsible for constructing **DynamicQuery** instances.

- The builder provides methods to select fields, add filters, and a **build()** method to create the **DynamicQuery** instance with the specified configuration.

- The **generateQuery()** method generates the final SOQL query based on the builder's configuration.

Now, you can use the builder pattern to create dynamic queries, as follows:

```
DynamicQuery.QueryBuilder queryBuilder = new DynamicQuery.
QueryBuilder('Account');
queryBuilder.selectFields(new List<String>{'Name', 'Industry'});
queryBuilder.addFilter('Industry = \'Technology\'');
queryBuilder.addFilter('AnnualRevenue > 1000000');


DynamicQuery dynamicQuery = queryBuilder.build();
String soqlQuery = dynamicQuery.generateQuery();


// The generated SOQL query can be used for database operations
System.debug('Generated SOQL Query: ' + soqlQuery);
```

By using the builder pattern, you can dynamically construct complex SOQL queries with various selected fields and filtering conditions. This abstraction simplifies query construction, improves code readability, and allows for flexible customization of queries based on runtime conditions.

Example 2: Email message builder

Another real-world example of the builder pattern in Salesforce Apex can be found when constructing complex email messages. In many Salesforce applications, you may need to send email notifications with different components such as subject, body, attachments, and recipients. The builder pattern can be applied to create an email builder that simplifies the construction of email messages with varying components.

Following is a simplified example:

```
public class EmailMessage {
    private String subject;
    private String body;
    private List<String> recipients;
```

```
private List<String> attachments;

private EmailMessage(EmailBuilder builder) {
    this.subject = builder.subject;
    this.body = builder.body;
    this.recipients = builder.recipients;
    this.attachments = builder.attachments;
}

public static class EmailBuilder {
    private String subject;
    private String body;
    private List<String> recipients;
    private List<String> attachments;

    public EmailBuilder(String subject, String body) {
        this.subject = subject;
        this.body = body;
        this.recipients = new List<String>();
        this.attachments = new List<String>();
    }

    public EmailBuilder addRecipient(String recipient) {
        this.recipients.add(recipient);
        return this;
    }

    public EmailBuilder addAttachment(String attachment) {
        this.attachments.add(attachment);
        return this;
    }

    public EmailMessage build() {
        return new EmailMessage(this);
    }
}

public void sendEmail() {
```

```
        // Logic to send the email using Salesforce's email service
        Messaging.SingleEmailMessage email = new Messaging.
SingleEmailMessage();
        email.setSubject(subject);
        email.setPlainTextBody(body);
        email.setToAddresses(recipients);
        // Attachments logic here...

        Messaging.sendEmail(new List<Messaging.Email> { email });
    }
}
```

In this example:

- We have an **EmailMessage** class that represents an email message with a subject, body, recipients, and attachments.

- We define a nested **EmailBuilder** class responsible for constructing **EmailMessage** instances.

- The builder provides methods to add recipients, add attachments, and a **build()** method to create the **EmailMessage** instance with the specified configuration.

- The **sendEmail()** method sends the constructed email using Salesforce's email service, and you can extend it to handle attachments.

Now, you can use the builder pattern to create and send emails with varying components, as follows:

```
EmailMessage.EmailBuilder emailBuilder = new EmailMessage.
EmailBuilder('Important Update', 'Hello, please see the attached document
for an important update.');
emailBuilder.addRecipient('recipient1@example.com');
emailBuilder.addRecipient('recipient2@example.com');
emailBuilder.addAttachment('AttachmentFile.pdf');

EmailMessage emailMessage = emailBuilder.build();
emailMessage.sendEmail();
```

By using the builder pattern, you can construct email messages with different components in a flexible and readable way. This abstraction simplifies email construction, improves code readability, and allows for the creation of emails with varying components based on different use cases in your Salesforce application.

Summary: The builder pattern is a powerful tool in Salesforce Apex for constructing complex objects with multiple optional attributes. It promotes flexibility, readability, and immutability in your code. By employing this pattern effectively, you can simplify object creation and provide a more intuitive interface for configuring objects, making your codebase more maintainable and adaptable.

Abstract factory pattern

The abstract factory pattern is a creational design pattern that provides an interface for creating families of related or dependent objects without specifying their concrete classes. In Salesforce Apex, this pattern is valuable when you need to create objects that belong to different but related families or when you want to ensure that the created objects are compatible with each other. This section explores the abstract factory pattern, its benefits, and provides practical examples of its implementation in Salesforce Apex.

Understanding abstract factory pattern

The abstract factory pattern is a part of the **Gang of Four (GoF)** design patterns and is classified under creational patterns. It abstracts the process of creating multiple related objects and ensures that the created objects are compatible with each other. It defines a family of factory methods, each responsible for creating a different type of object. Clients use the factory interface to create objects without knowing their concrete classes.

Benefits of using abstract factory pattern

Implementing the abstract factory pattern in Salesforce Apex offers the following advantages:

- **Abstraction**: It abstracts the creation of complex objects and their compatibility, making the code more flexible and maintainable.

- **Consistency**: It ensures that objects created by a factory are compatible with each other, reducing the risk of runtime errors.

- **Scalability**: It makes it easier to add new families of objects without modifying existing client code.

- **Encapsulation**: It encapsulates the object creation process, keeping it hidden from the client code.

Implementing abstract factory pattern

Let us dive into an example of implementing the abstract factory pattern in Salesforce Apex. We will create an abstract factory for creating payment processors and their corresponding validators, as follows:

```
// Abstract Payment Processor
public interface PaymentProcessor {
```

```java
    void processPayment();
}


// Concrete Credit Card Payment Processor
public class CreditCardPaymentProcessor implements PaymentProcessor {
    public void processPayment() {
        System.debug('Processing credit card payment...');
    }
}


// Concrete PayPal Payment Processor
public class PayPalPaymentProcessor implements PaymentProcessor {
    public void processPayment() {
        System.debug('Processing PayPal payment...');
    }
}


// Abstract Payment Validator
public interface PaymentValidator {
    Boolean validatePayment();
}


// Concrete Credit Card Payment Validator
public class CreditCardPaymentValidator implements PaymentValidator {
    public Boolean validatePayment() {
        System.debug('Validating credit card payment...');
        // Validation logic here...
        return true;
    }
}


// Concrete PayPal Payment Validator
public class PayPalPaymentValidator implements PaymentValidator {
    public Boolean validatePayment() {
        System.debug('Validating PayPal payment...');
        // Validation logic here...
        return true;
    }
}
```

```
}

// Abstract Payment Factory
public interface PaymentFactory {
    PaymentProcessor createPaymentProcessor();
    PaymentValidator createPaymentValidator();
}
```

In this example:

- We have an abstract **PaymentProcessor** and an **AbstractPayment** validator.

- Concrete implementations, such as **CreditCardPaymentProcessor**, **PayPalPaymentProcessor**, **CreditCardPaymentValidator**, and **PayPalPaymentValidator**, belong to different but related families of objects.

- We define an abstract **PaymentFactory** interface with factory methods for creating **PaymentProcessor** and **PaymentValidator** objects.

Now, you can create concrete factories for each family of payment processors and validators, as follows:

```
// Concrete Credit Card Payment Factory
public class CreditCardPaymentFactory implements PaymentFactory {
    public PaymentProcessor createPaymentProcessor() {
        return new CreditCardPaymentProcessor();
    }

    public PaymentValidator createPaymentValidator() {
        return new CreditCardPaymentValidator();
    }
}

// Concrete PayPal Payment Factory
public class PayPalPaymentFactory implements PaymentFactory {
    public PaymentProcessor createPaymentProcessor() {
        return new PayPalPaymentProcessor();
    }

    public PaymentValidator createPaymentValidator() {
        return new PayPalPaymentValidator();
    }
}
```

By using the abstract factory pattern, you can create families of related objects (payment processors and validators) without specifying their concrete classes. Clients can use the abstract factory interface to create payment processors and validators that are guaranteed to be compatible with each other.

Using abstract factory pattern

Now, you can use the abstract factory to create payment processors and validators, as follows:

```
PaymentFactory creditCardFactory = new CreditCardPaymentFactory();
PaymentProcessor creditCardProcessor = creditCardFactory.
createPaymentProcessor();
PaymentValidator creditCardValidator = creditCardFactory.
createPaymentValidator();

creditCardProcessor.processPayment();
Boolean isValidCreditCardPayment = creditCardValidator.validatePayment();

PaymentFactory paypalFactory = new PayPalPaymentFactory();
PaymentProcessor paypalProcessor = paypalFactory.createPaymentProcessor();
PaymentValidator paypalValidator = paypalFactory.createPaymentValidator();

paypalProcessor.processPayment();
Boolean isValidPayPalPayment = paypalValidator.validatePayment();
```

By using the abstract factory pattern, you can create payment processors and validators that are guaranteed to be compatible with each other. This abstraction simplifies the creation of related objects and ensures their consistency, making your code more robust and maintainable.

Practical implementation example of abstract factory pattern

The abstract factory pattern is a powerful design pattern in Salesforce Apex that allows developers to create families of related objects without specifying their concrete classes. It ensures consistency and modularity while enabling flexibility to support new object families. Following are practical examples that demonstrate the application of the abstract factory pattern in Salesforce Apex:

Example 1: Document generation using abstract factory

A real-world example of the abstract factory pattern in Salesforce Apex can be found when dealing with multiple document generation providers. In Salesforce, you may need to generate various types of documents, such as PDFs, Word documents, or Excel spreadsheets, depending on user preferences or business requirements. Each document type might have a different generation process or service. Implementing the abstract factory pattern can help create a unified interface for generating different types of documents while allowing specific implementations for each document generator.

Following is a simplified example:

```
// Abstract Document Generator interface
public interface DocumentGenerator {
    void generateDocument(String documentData);
}


// Concrete PDF Document Generator
public class PdfDocumentGenerator implements DocumentGenerator {
    public void generateDocument(String documentData) {
        // Logic to generate a PDF document
        System.debug('Generating PDF document with data: ' + documentData);
    }
}


// Concrete Word Document Generator
public class WordDocumentGenerator implements DocumentGenerator {
    public void generateDocument(String documentData) {
        // Logic to generate a Word document
        System.debug('Generating Word document with data: ' +
documentData);
    }
}


// Abstract Document Generator Factory
public interface DocumentGeneratorFactory {
    DocumentGenerator createDocumentGenerator();
}


// Concrete PDF Document Generator Factory
public class PdfDocumentGeneratorFactory implements
DocumentGeneratorFactory {
    public DocumentGenerator createDocumentGenerator() {
        return new PdfDocumentGenerator();
```

```
    }
}


// Concrete Word Document Generator Factory
public class WordDocumentGeneratorFactory implements
DocumentGeneratorFactory {
    public DocumentGenerator createDocumentGenerator() {
        return new WordDocumentGenerator();
    }
}
```

In this example:

- We have an abstract **DocumentGenerator** interface that defines a common method **generateDocument** for generating documents.

- Concrete implementations like **PdfDocumentGenerator** and **WordDocumentGenerator** represent different document generation services with their specific logic.

- We define an abstract **DocumentGeneratorFactory** interface with a factory method **createDocumentGenerator** for creating **DocumentGenerator** instances.

- Concrete factory classes like **PdfDocumentGeneratorFactory** and **WordDocumentGeneratorFactory** implement the **DocumentGeneratorFactory** interface and provide specific implementations for creating document generators.

Now, you can use the abstract factory pattern to create and generate different types of documents in a unified way, as follows:

```
DocumentGeneratorFactory pdfFactory = new PdfDocumentGeneratorFactory();
DocumentGenerator pdfDocumentGenerator = pdfFactory.
createDocumentGenerator();
pdfDocumentGenerator.generateDocument("PDF Document Data");


DocumentGeneratorFactory wordFactory = new WordDocumentGeneratorFactory();
DocumentGenerator wordDocumentGenerator = wordFactory.
createDocumentGenerator();
wordDocumentGenerator.generateDocument("Word Document Data");
```

By using the abstract factory pattern, you can create document generators for different document types and generate documents through a common interface. This abstraction simplifies the document generation process, allows you to switch between document types seamlessly, and ensures consistency in your Salesforce application's codebase when dealing with various document generation providers.

Example 2: Authentication management with abstract factory

A real-world example of the abstract factory pattern in Salesforce Apex can be found when dealing with multiple authentication providers for user login. In Salesforce, you may need to support various authentication methods, such as username or password, **Single Sign-On (SSO)**, or **Multi-Factor Authentication (MFA)**. Each authentication method has its own set of protocols and logic. Implementing the abstract factory pattern can help create a unified interface for user authentication while allowing specific implementations for each authentication provider.

Following is a simplified example:

```apex
// Abstract Authentication Provider interface
public interface AuthenticationProvider {
    Boolean authenticate(String username, String password);
}


// Concrete Username/Password Authentication Provider
public class UsernamePasswordAuthProvider implements AuthenticationProvider
{
    public Boolean authenticate(String username, String password) {
        // Logic to authenticate using username and password
        System.debug('Authenticating using username/password for user: ' +
username);
        // Authentication logic here...
        return true;
    }
}


// Concrete Single Sign-On (SSO) Authentication Provider
public class SSOAuthProvider implements AuthenticationProvider {
    public Boolean authenticate(String username, String password) {
        // Logic to authenticate using SSO
        System.debug('Authenticating using SSO for user: ' + username);
        // Authentication logic here...
        return true;
    }
}


// Abstract Authentication Provider Factory interface
public interface AuthProviderFactory {
```

```
    AuthenticationProvider createAuthProvider();
}


// Concrete Username/Password Authentication Provider Factory
public class UsernamePasswordAuthProviderFactory implements
AuthProviderFactory {
    public AuthenticationProvider createAuthProvider() {
        return new UsernamePasswordAuthProvider();
    }
}


// Concrete Single Sign-On (SSO) Authentication Provider Factory
public class SSOAuthProviderFactory implements AuthProviderFactory {
    public AuthenticationProvider createAuthProvider() {
        return new SSOAuthProvider();
    }
}
```

In this example:

- We have an abstract **AuthenticationProvider** interface that defines a common method to **authenticate** for user authentication.

- Concrete implementations like **UsernamePasswordAuthProvider** and **SSOAuthProvider** represent different authentication providers with their specific logic.

- We define an abstract **AuthProviderFactory** interface with a factory method **createAuthProvider()** for creating **AuthenticationProvider** instances.

- Concrete factory classes like **UsernamePasswordAuthProviderFactory** and **SSOAuthProviderFactory** implement the **AuthProviderFactory** interface and provide specific implementations for creating authentication providers.

Now, you can use the abstract factory pattern to authenticate users through different authentication methods in a unified way, as follows:

```
AuthProviderFactory usernamePasswordFactory = new
UsernamePasswordAuthProviderFactory();
AuthenticationProvider usernamePasswordAuthProvider =
usernamePasswordFactory.createAuthProvider();
Boolean isAuthenticatedUsingUP = usernamePasswordAuthProvider.
authenticate('user', 'password');
```

```
AuthProviderFactory ssoFactory = new SSOAuthProviderFactory();
AuthenticationProvider ssoAuthProvider = ssoFactory.createAuthProvider();
Boolean isAuthenticatedUsingSSO = ssoAuthProvider.authenticate('user',
'ssoToken');
```

By using the abstract factory pattern, you can authenticate users using different authentication providers while interacting with them through a common interface. This abstraction simplifies the authentication process, allows you to switch between authentication methods seamlessly, and ensures consistency in your Salesforce application's codebase when dealing with various authentication providers.

Summary: The abstract factory pattern is a powerful tool in Salesforce Apex for creating families of related objects with guaranteed compatibility. It promotes abstraction, consistency, and scalability in your code. By employing this pattern effectively, you can simplify object creation, ensure compatibility among objects, and accommodate new families of objects with ease in your Salesforce application.

Prototype pattern

The prototype pattern is a creational design pattern that allows you to create new objects by copying an existing object, known as a prototype. This pattern is particularly useful when you need to create objects with the same initial state but want to avoid the overhead of creating them from scratch. In Salesforce Apex, where you often work with complex data structures and records, the prototype pattern can help you efficiently clone objects and records.

Understanding prototype pattern

The prototype pattern is based on the concept of a prototype, which is an existing object used as a template for creating new objects. Instead of creating objects through constructors or factories, you simply clone the prototype, which initializes the new object with the same state as the original.

In Salesforce Apex, this pattern can be applied to custom objects, SObject records, or any complex data structure that you want to replicate without creating a new instance manually.

Using prototype pattern

Following are some scenarios where the prototype pattern can be beneficial in Salesforce Apex:

- **Creating duplicate records**: When you need to create multiple records that share the same initial field values, such as when copying records from one object to another.

- **Efficient object creation**: To avoid the overhead of initializing objects with complex configurations repeatedly, you can clone an existing object instead.

- **Dynamic object generation**: When the exact type of object to be created is determined at runtime based on user input or other conditions.

Benefits of prototype pattern

The prototype pattern in Salesforce Apex offers the following advantages:

- **Efficiency**: It reduces the overhead of creating objects with complex configurations repeatedly.

- **Flexibility**: You can clone objects with slight variations, making it easy to adapt prototypes to specific use cases.

- **Dynamic object creation**: You can create objects dynamically based on runtime conditions.

- **Avoid constructor overload**: It helps avoid constructor overloading when you have multiple ways to initialize an object.

- **Consistency**: Ensures that cloned objects have consistent initial states.

Considerations

When using the prototype pattern in Salesforce Apex, consider the following:

- **Immutability**: If the objects you are cloning are mutable (can be modified after creation), ensure that you handle state changes appropriately to avoid unintended side effects.

- **Deep versus shallow cloning**: Depending on your requirements, you may need to implement deep cloning (cloning nested objects) or shallow cloning (cloning only the top-level object).

- **Prototype management**: Be mindful of managing your prototype objects, especially in situations where they may change over time.

- **Testing**: Ensure that you thoroughly test your cloned objects to verify that their states and behaviors match your expectations.

Let us explore an example of using the prototype pattern to clone Salesforce SObject records. Suppose you have a custom object called **Custom_Object__c**, and you want to create a new record based on an existing record, as follows:

```
public class SObjectPrototypePatternExample {

    public static Custom_Object__c cloneCustomObjectRecord(Custom_Object__c
prototypeRecord) {
```

```
        // Clone the prototype record
        Custom_Object__c clonedRecord = prototypeRecord.clone(false, true,
false, false);

        // Optionally modify some fields in the cloned record
        clonedRecord.Name = 'Cloned Record';
        // Modify other fields as needed

        return clonedRecord;
    }

    public static void main(String[] args) {
        // Retrieve an existing Custom_Object__c record (the prototype)
        Custom_Object__c prototypeRecord = [SELECT Id, Name, Field1__c,
Field2__c FROM Custom_Object__c WHERE Id = 'a0123456789ABCDE'];

        // Clone the prototype to create a new record
        Custom_Object__c clonedRecord =
cloneCustomObjectRecord(prototypeRecord);

        // Insert the cloned record into the database
        insert clonedRecord;

        System.debug('Cloned record ID: ' + clonedRecord.Id);
    }
}
```

In this example:

- We define a **cloneCustomObjectRecord** method that takes a prototype **Custom_ Object__c** record as input and returns a cloned record with the same field values. You can optionally modify specific fields in the cloned record before returning it.
- In the main method, we retrieve an existing **Custom_Object__c** record as the prototype.
- We use the **cloneCustomObjectRecord** method to clone the prototype and insert the cloned record into the database.

Practical implementation example of prototype pattern

The prototype pattern is a creational design pattern that allows you to create new objects by copying existing ones, offering an efficient way to handle object creation for scenarios where similar objects need to be instantiated repeatedly.

Following are some practical examples demonstrating the prototype pattern in Salesforce Apex:

Example 1: Cloning product records for variations

A real-world example of the prototype pattern in Salesforce Apex can be found in the context of creating custom record clones. Let us consider a scenario where you have a custom object called **Product__c**, and you need to create duplicate product records with slight variations, such as different prices or attributes. Using the prototype pattern, you can efficiently clone records to create new variations.

Following is an example:

```
public class ProductPrototypeExample {

    public static Product__c cloneProductWithVariation(Product__c
prototypeProduct, Decimal newPrice, String newDescription) {
        // Clone the prototype product
        Product__c clonedProduct = prototypeProduct.clone(false, true,
false, false);

        // Modify fields to create a variation
        clonedProduct.Price__c = newPrice;
        clonedProduct.Description__c = newDescription;

        return clonedProduct;
    }

    public static void main(String[] args) {
        // Retrieve an existing Product__c record (the prototype)
        Product__c prototypeProduct = [SELECT Id, Name, Price__c,
Description__c FROM Product__c WHERE Id = 'a0123456789ABCDE'];

        // Clone the prototype to create a product variation
        Product__c productVariation =
cloneProductWithVariation(prototypeProduct, 99.99, 'Special Edition
Product');

        // Insert the cloned product variation into the database
        insert productVariation;

        System.debug('Cloned product ID: ' + productVariation.Id);
    }
}
```

In this example:

- We have a **ProductPrototypeExample** class with a **cloneProductWithVariation** method that takes a prototype **Product__c** record, a new price, and a new description as input. It returns a cloned product with modified fields to create a variation.

- In the main method, we retrieve an existing **Product__c** record as the prototype.

- We use the **cloneProductWithVariation** method to clone the prototype and create a product variation with a different price and description.

- Finally, we insert the cloned product variation into the database.

This example demonstrates how the prototype pattern can be applied in Salesforce Apex to efficiently create variations of records based on a prototype. It allows you to avoid redundant field assignments and ensures that the new records maintain consistent field configurations while accommodating slight modifications as needed.

Example 2: Cloning report templates for customization

Another real-world example of the prototype pattern in Salesforce Apex can be found in the context of creating and managing templates for reports or documents. Let us say you have a scenario where you need to generate various reports with similar structures but different data sources or content. Using the prototype pattern, you can efficiently clone report templates to create new reports with slight variations.

Following is an example:

```
public class ReportPrototypeExample {

    public abstract class ReportTemplate implements Cloneable {
        public String title;
        public String header;
        public abstract void generateReport();

        // Define the clone method for prototypes
        public ReportTemplate clone() {
            try {
                return (ReportTemplate) super.clone();
            } catch (CloneNotSupportedException e) {
                return null;
            }
        }
    }
}
```

```
public class SalesReport extends ReportTemplate {
    public override void generateReport() {
        // Generate a sales report based on the template
        System.debug('Generating Sales Report: ' + title);
        System.debug('Header: ' + header);
        // Add report generation logic here...
    }
}

public class ExpenseReport extends ReportTemplate {
    public override void generateReport() {
        // Generate an expense report based on the template
        System.debug('Generating Expense Report: ' + title);
        System.debug('Header: ' + header);
        // Add report generation logic here...
    }
}

public static void main(String[] args) {
    ReportPrototypeExample example = new ReportPrototypeExample();

    // Create a prototype SalesReport template
    ReportTemplate salesReportTemplate = example.new SalesReport();
    salesReportTemplate.title = "Q4 Sales Report";
    salesReportTemplate.header = "Sales Data for Q4";

    // Clone the SalesReport template to create a new report
    ReportTemplate newSalesReport = salesReportTemplate.clone();
    newSalesReport.generateReport();

    // Create a prototype ExpenseReport template
    ReportTemplate expenseReportTemplate = example.new ExpenseReport();
    expenseReportTemplate.title = "Yearly Expense Report";
    expenseReportTemplate.header = "Expense Data for the Year";

    // Clone the ExpenseReport template to create a new report
```

```
        ReportTemplate newExpenseReport = expenseReportTemplate.clone();
        newExpenseReport.generateReport();
    }
}
```

In this example:

- We have a **ReportPrototypeExample** class that defines an abstract **ReportTemplate** class. This abstract class serves as the prototype for report templates and includes fields for the report title and header, as well as an abstract method **generateReport** to generate the report content.

- Concrete report templates, such as **SalesReport** and **ExpenseReport**, extend the **ReportTemplate** class and provide their implementations for the **generateReport** method.

- We implement the Cloneable interface in the **ReportTemplate** class to enable the cloning of report templates.

- In the main method, we create prototype report templates for a sales report and an expense report, set their titles and headers, and then clone these templates to generate new reports.

The prototype pattern allows you to efficiently create variations of reports based on prototype templates. This can be particularly useful when you have a dynamic reporting system with various report types and content structures, as it promotes code reusability and maintainability while accommodating slight modifications for each report.

Summary: The prototype pattern in Salesforce Apex can be a powerful tool for efficient object creation and management, especially when dealing with complex data structures and records. It simplifies the process of creating new objects based on existing ones, promoting code reusability and maintainability.

Conclusion

In this chapter, we explored the world of **creational design patterns**, a vital aspect of software engineering that focuses on abstracting and streamlining the process of object creation. These patterns play a pivotal role in enhancing the flexibility, scalability, and maintainability of applications by decoupling the object creation process from client code. We discussed the singleton pattern, which ensures a single instance of a class for shared resource management, and the factory method pattern, which allows for dynamic object creation by delegating instantiation to subclasses. The builder pattern demonstrated how complex objects can be constructed step by step, while the abstract factory pattern highlighted its ability to create families of related objects with consistent interfaces. The Prototype pattern provided an efficient mechanism for cloning objects, avoiding the overhead of creating them from scratch.

By understanding and implementing these patterns, developers can design software systems that adapt to evolving requirements while maintaining clean, reusable, and modular codebases. These patterns not only address specific challenges but also empower developers to create solutions that balance efficiency and flexibility.

In the next chapter, readers will build on this foundation to explore strategies for organizing and integrating components into robust and maintainable system architectures.

Points to remember

- Creational design patterns simplify the object instantiation process by decoupling it from client code, promoting flexibility and maintainability.

- Key creational design patterns include singleton, factory method, builder, abstract factory, and prototype, each addressing specific object creation challenges.

- The singleton pattern ensures a class has only one instance, offering benefits like efficient resource management, consistent global state, and reduced memory usage.

- The factory method pattern allows dynamic object creation by delegating the instantiation process to subclasses, reducing dependencies on concrete classes.

- The builder pattern is used for constructing complex objects step-by-step, offering better readability and handling of objects with multiple optional attributes.

- The abstract Factory pattern provides an interface for creating families of related objects, ensuring compatibility and supporting extensibility without altering existing code.

- The prototype pattern focuses on creating new objects by cloning existing ones, improving efficiency and enabling dynamic object creation with consistent configurations.

- Creational design patterns promote modularity and reusability in code by abstracting object creation and supporting diverse requirements and configurations.

- Real-world applications of these patterns include logging services, payment gateways, dynamic SOQL query generation, email creation, and cloning Salesforce SObject records.

- These patterns enhance maintainability, scalability, and efficiency in software systems by addressing common object creation challenges and offering flexible solutions.

Questions

1. What are creational design patterns, and why are they important in software development?

2. Explain the purpose and benefits of using the singleton pattern.

3. How does the factory method pattern promote loose coupling between classes?

4. What problem does the builder pattern solve, and when would you use it?

5. Why is the abstract factory pattern preferred for creating families of related objects?

6. Differentiate between shallow and deep cloning in the context of the prototype pattern.

7. Which creational design pattern would you use if you need to ensure that only one instance of a configuration object is used throughout your application?

8. How does the use of creational design patterns improve code maintainability and scalability?

9. Which design pattern (singleton, factory, builder, abstract factory, or prototype) do you think is most useful in Salesforce Apex development? Explain your answer with an example.

10. Discuss a real-world project where you would apply the prototype pattern. How would it simplify the task of object creation?

11. In what scenarios would you use the abstract factory pattern over the factory method pattern?

12. What are the potential drawbacks or limitations of using the singleton pattern in a multi-threaded environment?

13. Discuss how the builder pattern improves the readability of object creation, especially when dealing with objects that have multiple optional attributes.

14. What are some best practices to consider when implementing the Prototype pattern to ensure correct and efficient object cloning?

15. If you had to create a flexible framework for payment processing in Salesforce, which design pattern(s) would you combine to ensure scalability, flexibility, and maintainability?

16. Write a simple implementation of the singleton pattern in Salesforce Apex.

17. Create an example where the factory method pattern is used to create data connectors for REST and SOAP APIs.

18. Build a dynamic SOQL query generator using the builder pattern.

19. Write an abstract factory that produces two types of payment gateways: PayPal and Stripe.

20. Show how to use the prototype pattern to clone an SObject record in Salesforce Apex.

CHAPTER 6

Structural Design Patterns

Introduction

In this chapter, the focus now shifts to structural design patterns, passive constructs that optimize the composition of objects. Structural design patterns are a category of design patterns in software engineering that focus on the composition of classes or objects to form larger structures. They provide solutions for organizing and managing the relationships between these structures, ultimately improving the flexibility and scalability of software systems.

Structural patterns aim to define how different components and objects can work together to create more complex systems. These patterns promote the use of clear, well-defined interfaces, enabling systems that are easy to understand, maintain, and extend. By focusing on object composition and interaction, structural patterns abstract the underlying complexities and promote modular software design.

This chapter explores various structural design patterns, such as the adapter pattern, which makes incompatible interfaces work together, the decorator pattern, which adds functionality to objects dynamically, and the facade pattern, which provides a simplified interface to a complex system. It also covers the composite pattern, which treats individual objects and compositions uniformly, the bridge pattern, which separates an object's abstraction from its implementation, and the flyweight pattern, which treats individual objects and compositions uniformly while optimizing memory usage through shared instances.

Structural patterns address design challenges related to object composition, interface definition, and system scalability. By abstracting the composition and interaction of objects, they hide the intricacies of how components are interconnected from the client code. Ultimately, these patterns improve the organization and maintainability of software systems.

Structure

The chapter covers the following topics:

- Structural design patterns
- Adapter pattern
- Decorator pattern
- Facade pattern
- Composite pattern
- Bridge pattern
- Flyweight pattern

Objectives

By the end of this chapter, readers will develop a comprehensive understanding of structural design patterns and their applications in software engineering. Readers will gain insights into patterns like adapter, decorator, facade, composite, bridge, and flyweight, learning how these patterns enhance the organization, scalability, and maintainability of software systems. By the end of the chapter, readers will be able to implement each pattern, understand the benefits they offer, and identify practical scenarios where these patterns can be applied. The chapter emphasizes both theoretical and practical aspects, including real-world examples, to ensure a well-rounded grasp of how these patterns contribute to building robust and efficient software architectures. This knowledge will empower readers to apply structural patterns effectively in their projects, addressing complex design challenges with confidence.

Structural design patterns

Structural design patterns are a fundamental category of design patterns in software engineering that focus on the arrangement and composition of classes or objects to create larger, more complex structures. These patterns provide solutions for organizing and managing the relationships between software components, emphasizing the interaction between objects and classes. The primary goal of structural design patterns is to facilitate the construction of flexible, scalable, and maintainable software systems.

In essence, structural design patterns help you design software architectures that are easier to understand, modify, and extend. They abstract the complexities of how different components and objects collaborate and interact, making it easier for developers to work with the software.

Following are the key characteristics and purposes of structural design patterns:

- **Composition**: They deal with how classes and objects are composed to form larger structures. This involves defining relationships, such as aggregations or hierarchies, between components.

- **Reusability**: Structural patterns promote code reusability by encouraging the creation of well-defined and reusable building blocks that can be used in various parts of the software.

- **Flexibility**: They enhance the flexibility of software systems by allowing components to be replaced or extended without affecting the overall system architecture.

- **Encapsulation**: These patterns often enforce encapsulation, ensuring that the internal details of a component or object are hidden from the rest of the system.

- **Complexity management**: They assist in managing complexity in software design by providing clear guidelines for organizing code and handling intricate relationships between objects.

Following figure illustrates the common types of structural design patterns:

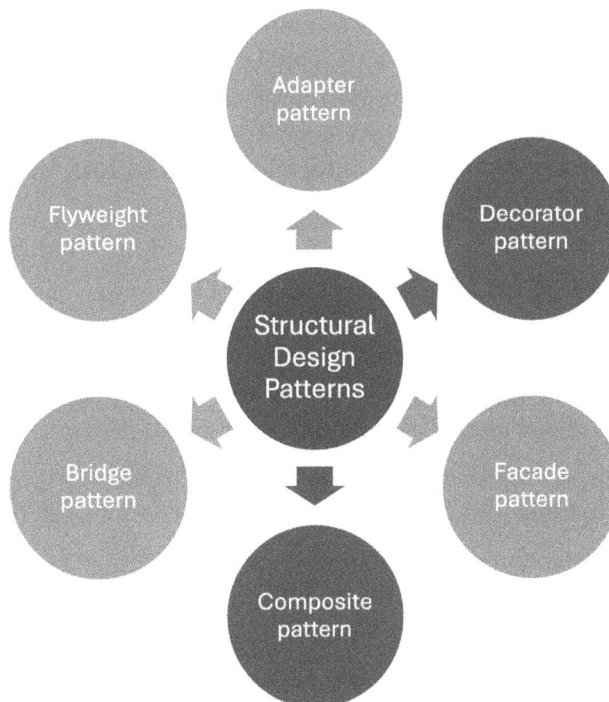

Figure 6.1: *Structural design patterns*

- **Adapter pattern**: Allows incompatible interfaces to work together by providing a wrapper or adapter that translates one interface into another.

- **Bridge pattern**: Separates an object's abstraction from its implementation, enabling it to vary independently.

- **Composite pattern**: Composes objects into tree structures to represent part-whole hierarchies. It allows clients to treat individual objects and compositions of objects uniformly.

- **Decorator pattern**: Dynamically adds responsibilities to objects without altering their code. It is used for adding features or behaviors to objects at runtime.

- **Facade pattern**: Provides a simplified interface to a complex system, making it easier for clients to interact with the system.

- **Flyweight pattern**: Minimizes memory usage or computational expenses by sharing as much as possible with related objects.

These structural design patterns play a crucial role in the design and architecture of software systems. By using them appropriately, software developers can build systems that are not only robust and scalable but also maintainable and adaptable to changing requirements.

Adapter pattern

The adapter pattern is a structural design pattern that allows objects with incompatible interfaces to work together. It acts as a bridge between two incompatible interfaces, making them compatible without changing their source code. In Salesforce Apex, the adapter pattern is valuable when you need to integrate or collaborate with external systems, libraries, or classes that have different interfaces.

Understanding adapter pattern

The adapter pattern involves three main components, as follows:

- **Target**: This is the interface or class that your client code expects to work with. It defines the methods and behaviors that your code relies on.

- **Adaptee**: This is the existing class or system that you want to integrate with but has an incompatible interface. It is the class you cannot modify directly.

- **Adapter**: The adapter is a class that implements the Target interface while internally delegating the actual work to the adaptee. It acts as a translator between the two interfaces.

The adapter pattern allows you to wrap the adaptee with an adapter, making it looks like a target to the client code. This enables seamless interaction between the client code and the adaptee, even though they have different interfaces.

Using adapter pattern

You should consider using the adapter pattern in Salesforce Apex under the following circumstances:

- **Third-party integrations:** When integrating with external systems or libraries that have different interfaces from your codebase.

- **Legacy code**: When you need to work with legacy code that cannot be modified directly but must interact with your new code.

- **Versioning**: When dealing with changes in interfaces, you want to isolate the impact of those changes.

Salesforce REST API adapter

Let us explore an example of the adapter pattern in the context of integrating with the Salesforce REST API. Suppose you have an existing class **LegacyDataService** that interacts with your legacy data storage system, and you want to adapt it to work with Salesforce REST API without modifying **LegacyDataService**.

Following is the code:

```
// Target Interface
public interface DataService {
    List<String> fetchData();
}


// Adaptee (Legacy Data Service)
public class LegacyDataService {
    public List<String> retrieveDataFromLegacySystem() {
        // Logic to fetch data from legacy system
        return new List<String>{'Legacy Data 1', 'Legacy Data 2'};
    }
}


// Adapter for Salesforce REST API
public class SalesforceRestApiAdapter implements DataService {
    private String apiEndpoint = 'https://yourinstance.salesforce.com/
services/data/v57.0/query/?q=SELECT+Name+FROM+Account';
    private String accessToken;

    public SalesforceRestApiAdapter(String accessToken) {
        this.accessToken = accessToken;
```

```
    }

    public List<String> fetchData() {
        List<String> apiData = new List<String>();

        try {
            HttpRequest request = new HttpRequest();
            request.setEndpoint(apiEndpoint);
            request.setMethod('GET');
            request.setHeader('Authorization', 'Bearer ' + accessToken);
            request.setHeader('Content-Type', 'application/json');

            Http http = new Http();
            HttpResponse response = http.send(request);

            if (response.getStatusCode() == 200) {
                // Parse JSON response
                Map<String, Object> responseBody = (Map<String, Object>)
JSON.deserializeUntyped(response.getBody());
                List<Object> records = (List<Object>) responseBody.
get('records');

                for (Object record : records) {
                    Map<String, Object> recordMap = (Map<String, Object>)
record;

                    apiData.add((String) recordMap.get('Name'));
                }
            } else {
                System.debug('Error: ' + response.getStatus());
            }
        } catch (Exception e) {
            System.debug('Exception while calling Salesforce REST API: ' +
e.getMessage());
        }

        return apiData;
    }
}
```

In this example:

- We have a **DataService** interface representing the target interface that our client code expects.

- The **LegacyDataService** class represents the adaptee, an existing class with a different interface.

- The **SalesforceRestApiAdapter** class implements the **DataService** interface, acting as an adapter for the Salesforce REST API. It delegates the call to **LegacyDataService**, adapting the data format if necessary. With the adapter in place, client code can seamlessly use the **DataService** interface to interact with both the legacy data service and the Salesforce REST API.

Benefits of adapter pattern

The adapter pattern offers several advantages in Salesforce Apex, as follows:

- **Flexibility**: It allows you to work with different systems or libraries, even if their interfaces are incompatible.

- **Maintainability**: It keeps the adapted code separate from the client code, making it easier to maintain and update.

- **Reusability**: Adapters can be reused for various clients and adaptees.

- **Versioning**: It isolates changes in the adaptee's interface, minimizing the impact on client code.

Practical implementation example of adapter pattern

The **adapter pattern** is a structural design pattern that enables incompatible interfaces to work together by acting as a bridge between them. This pattern is particularly useful in Salesforce Apex when integrating with external systems, legacy services, or third-party APIs that do not match the expected interface of the consuming application. By implementing an adapter, we can standardize communication between different systems without modifying their original implementations.

Following are some practical examples demonstrating the **adapter pattern** in Salesforce Apex:

Example 1: Integrating PayPal with Salesforce using the adapter pattern

A real-world example of the adapter pattern in Salesforce Apex can be found when integrating with external payment gateways that have different APIs and data formats. Let us consider adapting an external payment gateway, such as PayPal, to work with your Salesforce application.

The following steps demonstrate how the adapter pattern can be implemented in Salesforce Apex to integrate with external systems like payment gateways. This example illustrates adapting an external payment gateway, such as PayPal, to work seamlessly with Salesforce while conforming to its interface expectations.

1. **Define the target interface (PaymentService):**

```
public interface PaymentService {
    Boolean processPayment(String paymentDetails);
}
```

2. **Identify the adaptee (External Payment Gateway API):** Suppose you have an external payment gateway, like PayPal, that requires a specific API call and data format for processing payments.

3. **Create the adapter class (PayPalPaymentAdapter):** Create an adapter class that implements the **PaymentService** interface and communicates with the PayPal API. The adapter translates the Salesforce payment details into the required format for the PayPal API, as follows:

```
public class PayPalPaymentAdapter implements PaymentService {
    private PayPalApi paypalApi;

    public PayPalPaymentAdapter() {
        this.paypalApi = new PayPalApi(); // Assume you have a
PayPal API client
    }

    public Boolean processPayment(String paymentDetails) {
        // Adapt the payment details and call the PayPal API
        String adaptedPaymentDetails =
adaptToPayPalFormat(paymentDetails);
        Boolean paymentResult = paypalApi.
processPayment(adaptedPaymentDetails);

        return paymentResult;
    }

    // Method to adapt payment details to PayPal format
    private String adaptToPayPalFormat(String paymentDetails) {
        // Simple transformation example: Convert orderId to
transactionId
        return paymentDetails.replace('"orderId"',
'"transactionId"');
    }
}
```

4. **Adapt the adaptee (PayPalPaymentAdapter):** In this example, the adaptation involves converting Salesforce payment details into the format expected by the PayPal API.

5. **Client code**: Now, you can use the **PaymentService** interface in your client code to process payments, and the **PayPalPaymentAdapter** will handle the communication with the PayPal API, as follows:

```
PaymentService paymentService = new PayPalPaymentAdapter();

String paymentDetails = "{ \"amount\": 100.00, \"currency\":
\"USD\", \"orderId\": \"12345\" }";
Boolean paymentResult = paymentService.
processPayment(paymentDetails);

if (paymentResult) {
    System.debug('Payment successful.');
} else {
    System.debug('Payment failed.');
}
```

In this example:

*   The client code interacts with the **PaymentService** interface, which has a compatible method for processing payments.

*   We create an instance of the **PayPalPaymentAdapter**, which internally adapts the Salesforce payment details and communicates with the PayPal API.

*   The **PayPalPaymentAdapter** handles the complexity of adapting data formats and making the API call, allowing your Salesforce application to process payments using the adapted interface.

This demonstrates how the adapter pattern can be used in Salesforce Apex to integrate with external payment gateways and adapt their APIs and data formats to meet the requirements of your Salesforce application. It enhances flexibility and allows you to work with external services efficiently.

Example 2: Adapting email formats for external service integration in Salesforce

Another practical example of the adapter pattern in Salesforce Apex could involve integrating with an external email service provider that expects data in a specific format, while your Salesforce application uses a different format for sending emails.

When integrating Salesforce applications with external systems, ensuring compatibility between different interfaces is crucial. The adapter pattern provides an elegant solution to bridge the gap between incompatible interfaces by converting one interface into another without altering the existing code.

The following steps outline how the adapter pattern can be applied to enable Salesforce Apex to integrate seamlessly with an external email service API, ensuring a smooth exchange of data in the required format:

1. **Define the target interface (EmailService):**

   ```
   public interface EmailService {
       Boolean sendEmail(EmailMessage email);
   }
   ```

2. **Identify the Adaptee (External Email Service API):** Suppose you want to integrate with an external email service provider that expects email data in JSON format, as follows:

   ```
   {
       "to": "recipient@example.com",
       "subject": "Test Email",
       "body": "This is a test email."
   }
   ```

3. **Create the adapter class (EmailServiceAdapter):** Develop an adapter class that implements the **EmailService** interface and communicates with the external email service API. The adapter transforms the **EmailMessage** object from Salesforce into the required JSON format for the external service, as follows:

   ```
   public class EmailServiceAdapter implements EmailService {
       private String externalApiEndpoint;

       public EmailServiceAdapter(String externalApiEndpoint) {
           this.externalApiEndpoint = externalApiEndpoint;
       }

       public Boolean sendEmail(EmailMessage email) {
           // Convert the EmailMessage object to JSON format expected
       by the external service
           String jsonPayload = convertEmailToJson(email);

           // Send the JSON payload to the external email service API
           Boolean result = sendToExternalService(externalApiEndpoint,
       jsonPayload);

           return result;
       }
   ```

```
    // Convert EmailMessage object to JSON format (not shown in
detail here)
    private String convertEmailToJson(EmailMessage email) {
        // Implement JSON conversion logic here
    }


    // Send JSON payload to external email service API (not shown in
detail here)
    private Boolean sendToExternalService(String endpoint, String
payload) {
        // Implement HTTP callout logic here
    }
}
```

4. **Adapt the adaptee (EmailServiceAdapter):** In this example, the adaptation involves converting the **EmailMessage** object from Salesforce into the JSON format expected by the external email service API.

5. **Client code:** Now, you can use the **EmailService** interface in your client code to send emails, and the **EmailServiceAdapter** will handle the communication with the external API, as follows:

```
String externalApiEndpoint = 'https://external-email-service.com/
send';

EmailService emailService = new
EmailServiceAdapter(externalApiEndpoint);

EmailMessage email = new EmailMessage(
    to = 'recipient@example.com',
    subject = 'Test Email',
    body = 'This is a test email.'
);

Boolean success = emailService.sendEmail(email);
if (success) {
    System.debug('Email sent successfully.');
} else {
    System.debug('Failed to send email.');
}
```

In this example:

- The client code interacts with the `EmailService` interface, which has a compatible method for sending emails.

- We create an instance of the `EmailServiceAdapter`, passing the external API endpoint as an argument to the constructor.

- The `EmailServiceAdapter` internally adapts the `EmailMessage` object from Salesforce into the JSON format expected by the external email service API, enabling seamless integration.

This demonstrates how the adapter pattern can be employed in Salesforce Apex to integrate with external services and adapt their interfaces and data formats to meet the requirements of your Salesforce application. It enhances flexibility and facilitates efficient communication with external systems.

Summary: By using the adapter pattern, you can achieve seamless integration and collaboration between components with disparate interfaces, enhancing the modularity and flexibility of your Salesforce Apex applications.

Decorator pattern

The decorator pattern is a structural design pattern that allows behavior to be added to individual objects dynamically, without affecting the behavior of other objects from the same class. It is useful when you need to extend the functionality of objects in a flexible and reusable way. Decorator pattern involves adding new functionality to objects dynamically by placing them inside special wrapper objects known as decorators. These decorators contain the same interface as the original object they are wrapping, allowing them to be used interchangeably.

Understanding decorator pattern

In the decorator pattern, there are several key components, as follows:

- **Component**: It is the base interface or abstract class that defines the methods that can be decorated.

- **Concrete component**: It is the actual object that implements the component interface.

- **Decorator**: This is the abstract class that implements the component interface and maintains a reference to a component object. It acts as a base class for concrete decorators.

- **Concrete decorator**: This is the class that extends the decorator class and adds new functionality to the component object.

Using decorator pattern

The decorator pattern is best used in the following scenarios:

- **Adding functionality dynamically**: When you need to add new behavior or responsibilities to objects dynamically at runtime without affecting other objects of the same class.

- **Avoiding subclass proliferation**: Instead of creating multiple subclasses to add different combinations of behavior, the decorator pattern allows you to compose objects with different combinations of decorators.

- **Closed for modification, open for extension**: When you want to adhere to the open/closed principle, which states that classes should be open for extension but closed for modification. The decorator pattern allows you to extend the behavior of objects without modifying their existing code.

- **Flexibility and reusability**: When you need a flexible and reusable way to add or remove functionality to objects. Decorators can be combined in various ways to create different combinations of behavior, promoting code reuse.

- **Enhancing Single Responsibility principle**: By separating concerns into individual decorators, each decorator can focus on a Single Responsibility, making the codebase more modular and maintainable.

- **Transparent to client code**: When you want client code to remain unaware of the specific implementation details of decorators. Clients interact with objects through their common interface, allowing for seamless integration of decorators.

Overall, the decorator pattern is suitable for situations where you anticipate the need to add or modify the behavior of objects dynamically while keeping the codebase flexible, reusable, and maintainable.

Logging decorator

Let us consider a scenario where you have a base interface **Logger** and a concrete implementation **ConsoleLogger** that logs messages to the console. You want to add additional functionality to log messages to a file without modifying the existing **ConsoleLogger** class.

Implementation:

```
// Step 1: Define the Component interface
public interface Logger {
    void log(String message);
}


// Step 2: Implement the Concrete Component
```

```
public class ConsoleLogger implements Logger {
    public void log(String message) {
        System.debug('Console: ' + message);
    }
}

// Step 3: Implement the Decorator
public abstract class LoggerDecorator implements Logger {
    protected Logger logger;

    public LoggerDecorator(Logger logger) {
        this.logger = logger;
    }

    public void log(String message) {
        logger.log(message);
    }
}

// Step 4: Implement the Concrete Decorator
public class FileLoggerDecorator extends LoggerDecorator {
    public FileLoggerDecorator(Logger logger) {
        super(logger);
    }

    public void log(String message) {
        super.log(message);
        logToFile(message);
    }

    private void logToFile(String message) {
        // Logic to log message to a file
        System.debug('File: ' + message);
    }
}
```

Usage:

```
// Usage Example
Logger consoleLogger = new ConsoleLogger();
Logger fileLogger = new FileLoggerDecorator(consoleLogger);
```

```
consoleLogger.log('Message logged to console');
// Output: Console: Message logged to console

fileLogger.log('Message logged to file');
// Output: Console: Message logged to file
//         File: Message logged to file
```

Layered decorator

Layered decorators in the decorator pattern allow multiple decorators to be stacked on top of one another, progressively extending the behavior of an object in a flexible and modular way. This approach is particularly useful when different functionalities need to be dynamically added without modifying the existing code.

Following are the steps for working of layered decorators:

1. **Base component:** Defines the core functionality.

2. **Concrete component:** Implements the base component.

3. **Decorator:** Implements the same interface as the base component and wraps another component.

4. **Layering decorators:** Each decorator wraps the previous one, adding new behavior.

Example of layered decorators in action:

Consider an **OrderProcessor** system where decorators dynamically add behavior such as **logging, discount application,** and **tax calculation** without altering the base class.

Following are the steps:

1. **Base interface**

   ```
   public interface OrderProcessor {
       void processOrder();
   }
   ```

2. **Concrete component**

   ```
   public class BasicOrderProcessor implements OrderProcessor {
       public void processOrder() {
           System.debug('Processing basic order.');
       }
   }
   ```

3. **Abstract decorator**

```apex
public abstract class OrderProcessorDecorator implements
OrderProcessor {
    protected OrderProcessor wrappedProcessor;

    public OrderProcessorDecorator(OrderProcessor processor) {
        this.wrappedProcessor = processor;
    }

    public void processOrder() {
        wrappedProcessor.processOrder();
    }
}
```

4. **Concrete decorators**

```apex
public class LoggingDecorator extends OrderProcessorDecorator {
    public LoggingDecorator(OrderProcessor processor) {
        super(processor);
    }

    public void processOrder() {
        System.debug('Logging order details...');
        super.processOrder();
    }
}

public class DiscountDecorator extends OrderProcessorDecorator {
    public DiscountDecorator(OrderProcessor processor) {
        super(processor);
    }

    public void processOrder() {
        System.debug('Applying discount...');
        super.processOrder();
    }
}

public class TaxDecorator extends OrderProcessorDecorator {
```

```
    public TaxDecorator(OrderProcessor processor) {
        super(processor);
    }

    public void processOrder() {
        System.debug('Calculating tax...');
        super.processOrder();
    }
}
```

5. **Applying layered decorators**

```
public class OrderProcessingTest {
    public static void executeOrderProcessing() {
        OrderProcessor orderProcessor = new BasicOrderProcessor();

        // Layering multiple decorators
        orderProcessor = new LoggingDecorator(orderProcessor);
        orderProcessor = new DiscountDecorator(orderProcessor);
        orderProcessor = new TaxDecorator(orderProcessor);

        orderProcessor.processOrder();
    }
}
```

6. **Expected debug log output**

```
Logging order details...
Applying discount...
Calculating tax...
Processing basic order.
```

Benefits of decorator pattern

The following are the benefits of the decorator pattern:

- **Flexible**: Decorators can be combined in various ways to extend the behavior of objects dynamically.

- **Reusable**: Decorators can be reused across different objects that share the same interface.

- **Open/closed principle**: Allows for extending functionality without modifying existing code, adhering to the open/closed principle.

Key benefits of using layered decorators in Apex are as follows:

- **Modular and reusable:** Each decorator is independent and can be applied dynamically.

- **Flexible composition:** Decorators can be stacked in different orders to create customized behavior.

- **Adheres to open/closed principle:** New features are added without modifying existing classes.

- **Dynamic behavior customization:** The order of execution can be modified at runtime.

Practical implementation example of decorator pattern

The decorator pattern is a flexible structural design pattern that allows dynamic extension of object behavior without modifying existing code by wrapping objects with additional functionality.

The following are examples demonstrating how this pattern can be effectively implemented in real-world scenarios:

Example 1: Enhancing report generation with the decorator pattern in Salesforce:

A real-world example of the decorator pattern in Salesforce Apex could involve building a system for generating reports with various formatting options. Let us consider a scenario where you have a base report generator that produces basic text reports, and you want to enhance it with additional formatting options such as HTML formatting and PDF generation without modifying the existing code.

The following steps illustrate how to enhance report generation in Salesforce Apex using the decorator pattern. This approach allows for the dynamic addition of new formatting options to a base report generator without altering its existing code structure:

1. **Define the component interface (ReportGenerator):**

```
public interface ReportGenerator {
    String generateReport(List<String> data);
}
```

2. **Implement the concrete component (TextReportGenerator):**

```
public class TextReportGenerator implements ReportGenerator {
    public String generateReport(List<String> data) {
        // Generate basic text report
        return String.join(data, '\n');
    }
}
```

3. **Implement the decorator (ReportDecorator):**

```
public abstract class ReportDecorator implements ReportGenerator {
    protected ReportGenerator reportGenerator;

    public ReportDecorator(ReportGenerator reportGenerator) {
        this.reportGenerator = reportGenerator;
    }

    public String generateReport(List<String> data) {
        return reportGenerator.generateReport(data);
    }
}
```

4. **Implement concrete decorators (HtmlReportDecorator and PdfReportDecorator):**

```
public class HtmlReportDecorator extends ReportDecorator {
    public HtmlReportDecorator(ReportGenerator reportGenerator) {
        super(reportGenerator);
    }

    public String generateReport(List<String> data) {
        String textReport = super.generateReport(data);
        // Add HTML formatting to the text report
        return '<html><body><pre>' + textReport + '</pre></body></
html>';
    }
}

public class PdfReportDecorator extends ReportDecorator {
    public PdfReportDecorator(ReportGenerator reportGenerator) {
        super(reportGenerator);
    }

    public String generateReport(List<String> data) {
        String textReport = super.generateReport(data);
        // Convert text report to PDF format
        return 'PDF: ' + textReport;
    }
}
```

5. **Usage**:

```
// Create a base text report generator
ReportGenerator textReportGenerator = new TextReportGenerator();

// Wrap the text report generator with decorators
ReportGenerator htmlReportGenerator = new
HtmlReportDecorator(textReportGenerator);
ReportGenerator pdfReportGenerator = new
PdfReportDecorator(textReportGenerator);

// Generate reports
List<String> data = new List<String>{'Data 1', 'Data 2', 'Data 3'};

String textReport = textReportGenerator.generateReport(data);
String htmlReport = htmlReportGenerator.generateReport(data);
String pdfReport = pdfReportGenerator.generateReport(data);

// Output reports
System.debug('Text Report:\n' + textReport);
System.debug('HTML Report:\n' + htmlReport);
System.debug('PDF Report:\n' + pdfReport);
```

Following is the explanation:

- The **TextReportGenerator** class implements the basic report generation functionality.

- The **ReportDecorator** abstract class serves as the base class for all decorators, implementing the **ReportGenerator** interface.

- Concrete decorators (**HtmlReportDecorator** and **PdfReportDecorator**) extend the **ReportDecorator** class and add HTML formatting and PDF generation capabilities, respectively.

- In the usage example, we create instances of the base text report generator and wrap them with decorators to add additional functionality.

- Each decorator dynamically enhances the behavior of the underlying report generator without modifying its code.

This example demonstrates how the decorator pattern can be used in Salesforce Apex to dynamically add functionality to objects while adhering to the open/closed principle, promoting code reusability and maintainability.

Example 2: Multi-channel notification system with the decorator pattern

Another real-world scenario where the decorator pattern can be applied in Salesforce *i* Apex is in the context of a messaging system that sends notifications to users through various channels such as email, SMS, and push notifications. Each notification may require different formatting or additional information depending on the channel. Following are the steps:

1. **Define the component interface (NotificationSender):**

```
public interface NotificationSender {
    void sendNotification(String recipient, String message);
}
```

2. **Implement the concrete component (EmailNotificationSender, SMSNotificationSender, PushNotificationSender):**

```
public class EmailNotificationSender implements NotificationSender {
    public void send notification(String recipient, String message) {
        System.debug('Email sent to ' + recipient + ': ' + message);
    }
}


public class SMSNotificationSender implements NotificationSender {
    public void sendNotification(String recipient, String message) {
        System.debug('SMS sent to ' + recipient + ': ' + message);
    }
}


public class PushNotificationSender implements NotificationSender {
    public void sendNotification(String recipient, String message) {
        System.debug('Push Notification sent to ' + recipient + ': '
+ message);
    }
}
```

3. **Implement the decorator (NotificationDecorator):**

```
public abstract class NotificationDecorator implements
NotificationSender {
    protected NotificationSender notificationSender;

    public NotificationDecorator(NotificationSender notificationSender)
    {
```

```
            this.notificationSender = notificationSender;
        }

        public void sendNotification(String recipient, String message) {
            notificationSender.sendNotification(recipient, message);
        }
    }
```

4. **Implement concrete decorators (HtmlNotificationDecorator, ShortenUrlNotificationDecorator):**

```
// Add HTML Formatting
public class HtmlNotificationDecorator extends NotificationDecorator {
    public HtmlNotificationDecorator(NotificationSender
notificationSender) {
        super(notificationSender);
    }

    public void sendNotification(String recipient, String message) {
        String htmlMessage = "<html><body>" + message + "</body></
html>";
        System.debug('Applying HTML Formatting');
        super.sendNotification(recipient, htmlMessage);
    }
}


// Shorten URLs
public class ShortenUrlNotificationDecorator extends
NotificationDecorator {
    public ShortenUrlNotificationDecorator(NotificationSender
notificationSender) {
        super(notificationSender);
    }

    public void sendNotification(String recipient, String message) {
        String shortenedMessage = message.replace('example.com',
'exmpl.com');
        System.debug('Shortening URLs');
        super.sendNotification(recipient, shortenedMessage);
    }
```

```
}
//Add Priority Tag
public class PriorityNotificationDecorator extends
NotificationDecorator {
    public PriorityNotificationDecorator(NotificationSender
notificationSender) {
        super(notificationSender);
    }

    public void sendNotification(String recipient, String message) {
        String priorityMessage = "[PRIORITY] " + message;
        System.debug('Marking as High Priority');
        super.sendNotification(recipient, priorityMessage);
    }
}
```

5. **Usage by applying decorators in different sequences**: By changing the order of decorators, we achieve different behaviors dynamically:

```
// Base Email Notification Sender
NotificationSender emailSender = new EmailNotificationSender();

// Apply decorators in different sequences
NotificationSender htmlEmailSender = new
HtmlNotificationDecorator(emailSender);
NotificationSender shortenedHtmlEmailSender = new
ShortenUrlNotificationDecorator(htmlEmailSender);
NotificationSender priorityShortenedHtmlEmailSender = new
PriorityNotificationDecorator(shortenedHtmlEmailSender);

// Another sequence - First priority, then shorten URLs, then HTML
NotificationSender priorityFirstEmailSender = new
HtmlNotificationDecorator(
    new ShortenUrlNotificationDecorator(
        new PriorityNotificationDecorator(emailSender)
    )
);

// Sending Notifications
String recipient = 'user@example.com';
```

```
String message = 'Important update, visit example.com';

System.debug('--- Sending Standard Email ---');
emailSender.sendNotification(recipient, message);

System.debug('--- Sending HTML Email ---');
htmlEmailSender.sendNotification(recipient, message);

System.debug('--- Sending Shortened & HTML Email ---');
shortenedHtmlEmailSender.sendNotification(recipient, message);

System.debug('--- Sending Priority, Shortened, & HTML Email ---');
priorityShortenedHtmlEmailSender.sendNotification(recipient,
message);

System.debug('--- Sending Priority First, Then Shortened, Then HTML
Email ---');
priorityFirstEmailSender.sendNotification(recipient, message);
```

The following is the explanation:

- We define a **NotificationSender** interface and implement concrete sender classes for different notification channels (Email, SMS, and Push Notifications).

- The **NotificationDecorator** abstract class serves as the base class for all decorators, implementing the **NotificationSender** interface and allowing additional behaviors to be layered dynamically.

- Concrete decorators (**HtmlNotificationDecorator**, **ShortenUrlNotificationDecorator**, **PriorityNotificationDecorator**) extend the NotificationDecorator class to modify notification behavior. The **HtmlNotificationDecorator** adds HTML formatting, **ShortenUrlNotificationDecorator** replaces long URLs with shortened versions, and **PriorityNotificationDecorator** marks messages as high priority.

- The modified implementation highlights the flexibility of decorators by allowing them to be applied in different sequences, leading to varied notification behaviors.

- In the usage example, we create instances of the base email notification sender and apply decorators in different orders, such as:
    - Wrapping the base sender with **HtmlNotificationDecorator** first, then **ShortenUrlNotificationDecorator**, and finally **PriorityNotificationDecorator**.

o Changing the order to apply **PriorityNotificationDecorator** first, followed by **ShortenUrlNotificationDecorator** and **HtmlNotificationDecorator**, demonstrates how the sequence impacts the final output.

- Each decorator dynamically enhances the behavior of the notification sender without modifying its existing code, ensuring that the solution adheres to the open/closed principle.

- This approach provides maximum flexibility, making it easy to extend notification functionalities dynamically while keeping the core notification logic clean and maintainable.

By structuring the decorators in different orders, developers can achieve varied behaviors dynamically, making the pattern highly effective in real-world Salesforce Apex applications.

Summary: The decorator pattern provides an elegant solution for extending the functionality of objects dynamically in a flexible and reusable manner. By using decorators, you can easily add new behavior to objects without altering their existing code, promoting maintainability and extensibility in your Salesforce Apex applications.

Facade pattern

The facade pattern is a structural design pattern that provides a simplified interface to a complex system, hiding its internal complexities from clients. It acts as a single-entry point to various subsystems, making it easier to use and reducing dependencies.

Understanding facade pattern

In software development, complex systems often consist of multiple subsystems, each with its own set of interfaces and interactions. The facade pattern simplifies the usage of such systems by providing a unified interface that encapsulates the interactions with these subsystems. It acts as a facade, shielding clients from the complexities of the underlying system.

Following are the key components of façade patterns:

- **Facade**: This is the main class that clients interact with. It provides a simplified interface to access the functionalities of the underlying subsystems. The facade delegates client requests to appropriate subsystem objects.

- **Subsystem**: These are the individual components or systems that make up the complex system. Each subsystem has its own set of functionalities and interactions. The facade coordinates interactions with these subsystems on behalf of the client.

Following is how it works:

- Clients interact with the facade, unaware of the complexities of the underlying subsystems.

- The facade acts as a mediator between the client and the subsystems, handling requests and delegating them to the appropriate subsystem objects.

- Internally, the façade orchestrates the interactions with multiple subsystems to fulfill client requests.

- By encapsulating the complexities of the underlying system, the facade simplifies usage and reduces dependencies between clients and subsystems.

Using facade pattern

The facade pattern is beneficial in the following scenarios:

- **Complex systems:** When dealing with complex systems consisting of multiple subsystems, each with its own set of interactions.

- **Simplified interface:** When you want to provide a simplified and intuitive interface to clients, hiding the complexities of the underlying system.

- **Reducing dependencies:** When you want to reduce the dependencies between clients and subsystems, allowing for easier maintenance and changes.

Following is an example:

Consider a scenario where you have a complex order processing system in Salesforce Apex. The system involves interacting with multiple subsystems such as inventory management, billing, and shipping. Instead of exposing the intricacies of each subsystem to clients, you can create a facade that provides a simplified interface for placing orders, as follows:

```
public class OrderFacade {
    public static void placeOrder(OrderDetails orderDetails) {
        InventoryManager.checkAvailability(orderDetails);
        BillingSystem.processPayment(orderDetails);
        ShippingManager.shipOrder(orderDetails);
    }
}
```

In this example, The **OrderFacade** class acts as a facade, providing a single method **placeOrder** to clients. Internally, the facade coordinates the interactions with multiple subsystems (**InventoryManager**, **BillingSystem**, **ShippingManager**) to fulfill the order.

Benefits of facade pattern

Following are the benefits of using Façade pattern in your code based on the requirement:

- **Simplified usage**: Facade provides a simple and intuitive interface for clients, abstracting away the complexities of the underlying system.

- **Reduced complexity**: Clients interact with the facade, which handles the interactions with subsystems internally, reducing complexity and cognitive load.

- **Improved maintainability**: Changes to the subsystems can be made without affecting clients, as long as the facade interface remains unchanged. This promotes easier maintenance and extensibility of the system.

Practical implementation example of facade pattern

The following examples demonstrate how the facade pattern can be practically implemented to simplify complex system interactions by providing a unified interface. This pattern helps improve usability and maintainability while shielding clients from underlying system complexities.

Example 1: Simplifying external CRM integration using the facade pattern

In a Salesforce Apex context, let us consider a scenario where you have a complex integration with an external **customer relationship management (CRM)** system. This integration involves multiple steps such as authentication, data retrieval, data manipulation, and error handling. Instead of exposing the intricacies of each step to the client code, you can implement a facade to provide a simplified interface for interacting with the CRM system, as follows:

```
// Extends the Apex Exception class
public class CRMIntegrationException extends Exception {
    public CRMIntegrationException(String message) {
        super(message);
    }
}


public class SalesforceCRMIntegrationFacade {
    public static void syncContactsWithCRM(List<Contact> contacts) {
        try {
            SalesforceCRMService.authenticate(); // Step 1: Authenticate
with CRM. SalesforceCRMService is a placeholder for this example
            List<CRMContact> crmContacts = SalesforceCRMService.
retrieveContacts(); // Step 2: Retrieve CRM contacts
            List<CRMContact> updatedCRMContacts = SalesforceCRMService.
updateContacts(contacts); // Step 3: Update CRM contacts
            SalesforceCRMService.logSyncSuccess(updatedCRMContacts); //
Step 4: Log successful synchronization
        } catch (CRMIntegrationException e) {
```

```
        SalesforceCRMService.logSyncFailure(e.getMessage()); // Step 5:
Log synchronization failure
        throw e; // Rethrow the exception for handling at higher levels
    }
  }
}
```

In this example:

- The **SalesforceCRMIntegrationFacade** class acts as a facade, providing a single method **syncContactsWithCRM** for synchronizing Salesforce contacts with the CRM system.

- Internally, the facade coordinates the interactions with the CRM system by calling methods from the **SalesforceCRMService** class.

- The **SalesforceCRMService** class encapsulates the implementation details of interacting with the CRM system, including authentication, data retrieval, data manipulation, and error handling.

Usage:

```
List<Contact> contactsToSync = [SELECT Id, Name, Email FROM Contact
WHERE LastModifiedDate >= LAST_N_DAYS:7];

SalesforceCRMIntegrationFacade.syncContactsWithCRM(contactsToSync);
```

This real-world example demonstrates how the facade pattern can be applied in Salesforce Apex to simplify the integration with complex external systems, providing a unified interface for client code while encapsulating the complexities of the underlying implementation.

Example 2: Streamlined report generation and export using the facade pattern:

Let us consider another scenario in a Salesforce Apex application where you have a complex process for generating reports from multiple data sources and then exporting them in various formats like PDF, Excel, and CSV. Implementing this process directly in client code would involve handling interactions with different data sources and managing the export functionalities separately. Instead, you can use the facade pattern to simplify this process by providing a single interface for generating and exporting reports, as follows:

```
public class ReportGenerationFacade {

    public static Blob generateAndExportReport(String reportName,
List<String> dataSources, String exportFormat) {
        // Generate report data from multiple data sources
        List<String> reportData = generateReportData(dataSources);

        // Export report data in the specified format
```

```
        Blob exportedReport = exportReport(reportData, exportFormat);

        return exportedReport;
    }

    private static List<String> generateReportData(List<String>
dataSources) {
        List<String> reportData = new List<String>();
        // Logic to fetch and process data from multiple data sources
        // Add processed data to reportData list
        return reportData;
    }

    private static Blob exportReport(List<String> reportData, String
exportFormat) {
        Blob exportedReport;
        if (exportFormat == 'PDF') {
            // Logic to export report data as PDF
        } else if (exportFormat == 'Excel') {
            // Logic to export report data as Excel
        } else if (exportFormat == 'CSV') {
            // Logic to export report data as CSV
        }
        return exportedReport;
    }
}
```

In this example:

- The **ReportGenerationFacade** class acts as a facade, providing a single method **generateAndExportReport** for generating and exporting reports.

- Internally, the facade coordinates the interactions with multiple data sources and handles the export functionalities based on the specified format.

- Client code interacts with the facade by providing parameters such as report name, data sources, and export format.

Usage:

```
        List<String> dataSources = new List<String>{'DataSource1',
        'DataSource2'};
        Blob exportedReport = ReportGenerationFacade.
        generateAndExportReport('SalesReport', dataSources, 'PDF');
```

This real-world example illustrates how the facade pattern can be applied in Salesforce Apex to simplify complex processes, providing a unified interface for client code while encapsulating the complexities of the underlying implementation.

Summary: The composite pattern provides a way to represent part-whole hierarchies in a unified manner, making it easier to work with complex structures of objects. It promotes code reusability, flexibility, and maintainability in Salesforce Apex applications.

Composite pattern

The composite pattern is a structural design pattern that allows you to compose objects into tree-like structures to represent part-whole hierarchies. It enables clients to treat individual objects and compositions of objects uniformly. In Salesforce Apex, the composite pattern can be useful when dealing with hierarchical data structures or when you want to apply operations uniformly across individual objects and collections of objects.

Understanding composite pattern

Following are the key components of composite patterns:

- **Component**: This is the common interface or abstract class that defines the common operations for both individual objects and compositions of objects. It allows clients to treat individual objects and composite objects uniformly.

- **Composite**: This represents the composite objects that contain other components, forming a tree-like structure. A composite object can contain zero or more child components, which can be either individual objects or other composite objects.

Following is how it works:

- The component interface defines operations that are common to both individual objects and compositions of objects.

- The composite class represents composite objects and implements the component interface. It contains a collection of child components and provides methods to add, remove, and access these child components.

- Individual objects, also known as leaf nodes, implement the component interface directly. They represent the building blocks of the composite structure.

- Clients interact with the composite structure through the component interface, treating individual objects and compositions of objects uniformly.

Using composite pattern

The composite pattern is suitable in the following scenarios:

- When you have a hierarchical structure of objects, and you want to treat individual objects and compositions of objects uniformly.

- When you want to apply operations recursively across the entire hierarchy of objects.

Following is an example:

Let us consider a scenario where you must represent an organizational hierarchy of departments and employees. Each department can contain sub-departments and/ or employees. We will implement the composite pattern to represent this hierarchy, as follows:

```
// Component interface
public interface OrganizationalUnit {
    void display();
}


public class Company {
    private List<Department> departments;

    // Constructor to initialize the department list
    public Company() {
        this.departments = new List<Department>();
    }

    // Method to add a department to the company
    public void add(Department dept) {
        if (dept != null) {
            departments.add(dept);
            System.debug('Department added: ' + dept.getDepartmentName());
        } else {
            System.debug('Cannot add a null department.');
        }
    }

    // Method to get all departments
    public List<Department> getDepartments() {
        return departments;
    }
}


// Composite class representing departments
```

```
public class Department implements OrganizationalUnit {
    private String name;
    private List<OrganizationalUnit> children;

    public Department(String name) {
        this.name = name;
        this.children = new List<OrganizationalUnit>();
    }

    public void add(OrganizationalUnit unit) {
        children.add(unit);
    }

    public void display() {
        System.debug('Department: ' + name);
        for(OrganizationalUnit unit : children) {
            unit.display();
        }
    }
}


// Leaf class representing employees
public class Employee implements OrganizationalUnit {
    private String name;

    public Employee(String name) {
        this.name = name;
    }

    public void display() {
        System.debug('Employee: ' + name);
    }
}
```

Usage:

```
// Create departments
Department salesDept = new Department('Sales');
Department marketingDept = new Department('Marketing');
```

```
// Create employees
Employee emp1 = new Employee('John Doe');
Employee emp2 = new Employee('Jane Smith');

// Add employees to departments
salesDept.add(emp1);
marketingDept.add(emp2);

// Add departments to company
Company company = new Company();
company.add(salesDept);
company.add(marketingDept);

// Retrieve and display departments
for (Department dept : company.getDepartments()) {
        System.debug('Department: ' + dept.getDepartmentName());
}
```

Benefits of composite pattern

Following are the benefits of composite pattern:

- **Uniformity**: Clients can treat individual objects and compositions of objects uniformly through a common interface.

- **Flexibility**: You can compose complex hierarchies by combining simple components.

- **Simplified client code**: Clients interact with the composite structure without needing to know the internal structure of individual objects.

Practical implementation example of composite pattern

The composite pattern is highly effective in scenarios where objects need to be treated uniformly, regardless of whether they are individual elements or compositions of other objects.

Following are practical examples of how the composite pattern can be implemented in Apex:

Example 1: Hierarchical product catalog management using composite pattern:

In a Salesforce Apex context, let us consider a scenario where you have a hierarchical structure of products within a product catalog. Each product can be either a simple product or a composite product, which is a collection of multiple sub-products. We will use the composite pattern to represent this hierarchical structure and calculate the total price of the products in the catalog, as follows:

```
// Component interface representing products
public interface Product {
    Decimal getPrice();
}


// Leaf class representing simple products
public class SimpleProduct implements Product {
    private String name;
    private Decimal price;

    public SimpleProduct(String name, Decimal price) {
        this.name = name;
        this.price = price;
    }

    public Decimal getPrice() {
        return price;
    }
}


// Composite class representing composite products (collections of sub-products)
public class CompositeProduct implements Product {
    private String name;
    private List<Product> products;

    public CompositeProduct(String name) {
        this.name = name;
        this.products = new List<Product>();
    }

    public void addProduct(Product product) {
        products.add(product);
    }
```

```
    public void removeProduct(Product product) {
        products.remove(product);
    }

    public Decimal getPrice() {
        Decimal totalPrice = 0;
        for(Product product : products) {
            totalPrice += product.getPrice();
        }
        return totalPrice;
    }
}
```

Usage:

```
// Create simple products
Product laptop = new SimpleProduct('Laptop', 1000);
Product mouse = new SimpleProduct('Mouse', 20);

// Create composite product (laptop bundle)
CompositeProduct laptopBundle = new CompositeProduct('Laptop Bundle');
laptopBundle.addProduct(laptop);
laptopBundle.addProduct(mouse);

// Calculate total price of the laptop bundle
Decimal totalPrice = laptopBundle.getPrice();
System.debug('Total Price of Laptop Bundle: $' + totalPrice);
```

This real-world example demonstrates how the composite pattern can be applied in Salesforce Apex to represent hierarchical structures and calculate aggregate properties across the hierarchy. It promotes code reusability, flexibility, and maintainability in managing complex object structures.

Example 2: Hierarchical document management system using composite pattern:

In a Salesforce Apex scenario, let us consider another situation where you need to represent a document management system with a hierarchical structure of folders and files. Each folder can contain subfolders and files, and files can be of different types such as text files, images, or documents. We will use the composite pattern to represent this hierarchical structure and calculate the total size of all files in the system, as follows:

```
// Component interface representing documents
public interface Document {
```

```apex
        Integer getSize();
}


// Leaf class representing files
public class File implements Document {
    private String name;
    private Integer size;

    public File(String name, Integer size) {
        this.name = name;
        this.size = size;
    }

    public Integer getSize() {
        return size;
    }
}


// Composite class representing folders (collections of subfolders and/or
files)
public class Folder implements Document {
    private String name;
    private List<Document> contents;

    public Folder(String name) {
        this.name = name;
        this.contents = new List<Document>();
    }

    public void addDocument(Document document) {
        contents.add(document);
    }

    public void removeDocument(Document document) {
        contents.remove(document);
    }

    public Integer getSize() {
        Integer totalSize = 0;
```

```
        for(Document doc : contents) {
            totalSize += doc.getSize();
        }
        return totalSize;
    }
}
```

Usage:
```
// Create files
Document file1 = new File('Document.txt', 100);
Document file2 = new File('Image.jpg', 200);

// Create folders
Folder folder1 = new Folder('Folder A');
folder1.addDocument(file1);
Folder folder2 = new Folder('Folder B');
folder2.addDocument(file2);

// Create nested folders
Folder rootFolder = new Folder('Root');
rootFolder.addDocument(folder1);
rootFolder.addDocument(folder2);

// Calculate total size of all documents in the system
Integer totalSize = rootFolder.getSize();
System.debug('Total Size of Documents: ' + totalSize + ' bytes');
```

This real-world example demonstrates how the composite pattern can be applied in Salesforce Apex to represent hierarchical structures and perform operations across the entire hierarchy. It promotes code reusability, flexibility, and maintainability in managing complex object structures.

Summary: The composite pattern provides a way to represent part-whole hierarchies in a unified manner, making it easier to work with complex structures of objects. It promotes code reusability, flexibility, and maintainability in software systems.

Bridge pattern

The bridge pattern is a structural design pattern that decouples an abstraction from its implementation so that the two can vary independently. It allows you to separate the abstraction (an interface or abstract class) from its implementation (concrete classes), thereby enabling changes in one to not affect the other. In Salesforce Apex, the bridge pattern can be useful when you want to separate an abstraction from its implementation and provide different implementations without affecting client code.

Understanding bridge pattern

At the core of the bridge pattern are two main components as follows:

- **Abstraction**: This represents the high-level interface or abstract class that defines the operations that clients can perform. It contains a reference to an implementation object and delegates the actual implementation to it.

- **Implementor**: This represents the interface or abstract class that defines the methods for implementing the operations defined by the abstraction. Concrete implementations of the implementor interface provide different implementations of these methods.

Following is how it works:

- The abstraction interface defines high-level operations that are implemented by **ConcreteAbstraction** classes.

- The **Implementor** interface defines low-level operations that are implemented by **ConcreteImplementor** classes.

- Abstraction classes maintain a reference to an **Implementor** object and delegate operations to it.

- **ConcreteImplementor** classes provide different implementations of low-level operations.

- Clients interact with abstraction objects without needing to know the details of the implementation.

Using bridge pattern

The bridge pattern is suitable in the following scenarios:

- When you want to separate an abstraction from its implementation so that they can vary independently.

- When you want to avoid a permanent binding between an abstraction and its implementation, allowing them to change dynamically.

Following is an example:

Consider a scenario where you have a shape abstraction representing different geometric shapes (such as circles and squares) and you want to provide different drawing implementations (such as drawing on a canvas or printing to a printer). We will use the bridge pattern to decouple the shape abstraction from its drawing implementation, as follows:

```
// Implementor interface
public interface DrawingAPI {
    void drawCircle(Integer x, Integer y, Integer radius);
    void drawSquare(Integer x, Integer y, Integer side);
}


// ConcreteImplementorA class
public class DrawingCanvas implements DrawingAPI {
    public void drawCircle(Integer x, Integer y, Integer radius) {
        System.debug('Drawing circle on canvas at (' + x + ',' + y + ')
with radius ' + radius);
    }

    public void drawSquare(Integer x, Integer y, Integer side) {
        System.debug('Drawing square on canvas at (' + x + ',' + y + ')
with side ' + side);
    }
}


// ConcreteImplementorB class
public class DrawingPrinter implements DrawingAPI {
    public void drawCircle(Integer x, Integer y, Integer radius) {
        System.debug('Printing circle at (' + x + ',' + y + ') with radius
' + radius);
    }

    public void drawSquare(Integer x, Integer y, Integer side) {
        System.debug('Printing square at (' + x + ',' + y + ') with side '
+ side);
    }
}


// Abstraction interface
public interface Shape {
    void draw();
}


// RefinedAbstraction class
```

```
public class Circle implements Shape {
    private Integer x, y, radius;
    private DrawingAPI drawingAPI;

    public Circle(Integer x, Integer y, Integer radius, DrawingAPI
drawingAPI) {
        this.x = x;
        this.y = y;
        this.radius = radius;
        this.drawingAPI = drawingAPI;
    }

    public void draw() {
        drawingAPI.drawCircle(x, y, radius);
    }
}


// RefinedAbstraction class
public class Square implements Shape {
    private Integer x, y, side;
    private DrawingAPI drawingAPI;

    public Square(Integer x, Integer y, Integer side, DrawingAPI
drawingAPI) {
        this.x = x;
        this.y = y;
        this.side = side;
        this.drawingAPI = drawingAPI;
    }

    public void draw() {
        drawingAPI.drawSquare(x, y, side);
    }
}
```

Usage:
```
// Create drawing implementations
DrawingAPI canvasAPI = new DrawingCanvas();
```

```
DrawingAPI printerAPI = new DrawingPrinter();

// Create shapes and associate them with drawing implementations
Shape circleOnCanvas = new Circle(10, 20, 30, canvasAPI);
Shape squareOnPrinter = new Square(5, 5, 50, printerAPI);

// Draw shapes
circleOnCanvas.draw();
squareOnPrinter.draw();
```

Benefits of bridge pattern

Following are the benefits of bridge pattern:

- **Decoupling**: The bridge pattern decouples the abstraction from its implementation, allowing them to vary independently.

- **Flexibility**: You can change or extend the abstraction and implementation independently without affecting each other or client code.

- **Separation of concerns:** The bridge pattern separates the abstraction from its implementation, promoting a cleaner and more modular design.

Practical implementation example of bridge pattern

The bridge pattern in Salesforce Apex is particularly useful when you want to separate the abstraction of functionality from its implementation, allowing independent evolution of both.

Following are practical examples to illustrate its application:

Example 1: Payment gateway integration using the bridge pattern:

In a Salesforce Apex scenario, let us consider a situation where you need to integrate with different payment gateways to process payments. Each payment gateway may have its own implementation details and API. We will use the bridge pattern to decouple the payment processing abstraction from its various implementations, allowing you to switch between different payment gateways without modifying client code, as follows:

```
// Implementor interface
public interface PaymentGateway {
    void processPayment(Integer amount);
}

// ConcreteImplementorA class
```

```
public class PayPalGateway implements PaymentGateway {
    public void processPayment(Integer amount) {
        System.debug('Processing payment of $' + amount + ' using PayPal');
        // Actual PayPal payment processing logic here
    }
}


// ConcreteImplementorB class
public class StripeGateway implements PaymentGateway {
    public void processPayment(Integer amount) {
        System.debug('Processing payment of $' + amount + ' using Stripe');
        // Actual Stripe payment processing logic here
    }
}


// Abstraction interface
public interface PaymentProcessor {
    void processPayment(Integer amount);
}


// RefinedAbstraction class
public class OnlinePaymentProcessor implements PaymentProcessor {
    private PaymentGateway gateway;

    public OnlinePaymentProcessor(PaymentGateway gateway) {
        this.gateway = gateway;
    }

    public void processPayment(Integer amount) {
        gateway.processPayment(amount);
    }
}
```

Usage:

```
// Create payment gateway implementations
PaymentGateway paypal = new PayPalGateway();
PaymentGateway stripe = new StripeGateway();
```

```
// Create payment processors associated with payment gateways
PaymentProcessor paypalProcessor = new OnlinePaymentProcessor(paypal);
PaymentProcessor stripeProcessor = new OnlinePaymentProcessor(stripe);

// Process payments using different payment processors
paypalProcessor.processPayment(100);
stripeProcessor.processPayment(150);
```

Output:
```
Processing payment of $100 using PayPal
Processing payment of $150 using Stripe
```

In this example:

- **PaymentGateway** represents the implementor interface, defining a method for processing payments.

- **PayPalGateway** and **StripeGateway** are concrete implementor classes providing different implementations of payment processing logic.

- **PaymentProcessor** represents the abstraction interface, defining the **processPayment()** method.

- **OnlinePaymentProcessor** is a refined abstraction class associating payment processing with a specific payment gateway implementation.

- Client code interacts with payment processors through the abstraction interface without needing to know the details of payment gateway implementations.

This real-world example demonstrates how bridge pattern can be applied in Salesforce Apex to decouple the abstraction of payment processing from its various implementations, providing flexibility and extensibility in integrating with different payment gateways.

Example 2: Multi-channel notification system using the bridge pattern:

In a Salesforce Apex context, let us consider another scenario where you need to send notifications through different channels such as email, SMS, and push notifications. Each channel may have its own implementation details and API. We will use the bridge pattern to decouple the notification abstraction from its various implementations, allowing you to switch between different notification channels without modifying client code, as follows:

```
// Implementor interface
public interface NotificationSender {
    void sendNotification(String recipient, String message);
}


// ConcreteImplementorA class
```

```
public class EmailSender implements NotificationSender {
    public void sendNotification(String recipient, String message) {
        System.debug('Sending email to ' + recipient + ': ' + message);
        // Actual email sending logic here
    }
}


// ConcreteImplementorB class
public class SMSSender implements NotificationSender {
    public void sendNotification(String recipient, String message) {
        System.debug('Sending SMS to ' + recipient + ': ' + message);
        // Actual SMS sending logic here
    }
}


// Abstraction interface
public interface NotificationService {
    void sendNotification(String recipient, String message);
}


// RefinedAbstraction class
public class ChannelNotificationService implements NotificationService {
    private NotificationSender sender;

    public ChannelNotificationService(NotificationSender sender) {
        this.sender = sender;
    }

    public void sendNotification(String recipient, String message) {
        sender.sendNotification(recipient, message);
    }
}
```

Usage:

```
// Create notification sender implementations
NotificationSender emailSender = new EmailSender();
NotificationSender smsSender = new SMSSender();
```

```
// Create notification services associated with notification senders
NotificationService emailService = new
ChannelNotificationService(emailSender);
NotificationService smsService = new ChannelNotificationService(smsSender);

// Send notifications using different notification services
emailService.sendNotification('example@example.com', 'Hello via Email');
smsService.sendNotification('1234567890', 'Hello via SMS');
```

Output:

```
Sending email to example@example.com: Hello via Email
Sending SMS to 1234567890: Hello via SMS
```

In this example:

- **NotificationSender** represents the implementor interface, defining a method for sending notifications.

- **EmailSender** and **SMSSender** are concrete implementor classes providing different implementations of notification-sending logic.

- **NotificationService** represents the abstraction interface, defining the **sendNotification()** method.

- **ChannelNotificationService** is a refined abstraction class associating notification sending with a specific notification sender implementation.

- Client code interacts with notification services through the abstraction interface without needing to know the details of notification sender implementations.

This real-world example demonstrates how the bridge pattern can be applied in Salesforce Apex to decouple the abstraction of notification sending from its various implementations, providing flexibility and extensibility in sending notifications through different channels.

Summary: The bridge pattern provides a way to decouple an abstraction from its implementation, allowing them to vary independently. It promotes flexibility, extensibility, and separation of concerns in Salesforce Apex applications.

Flyweight pattern

The flyweight pattern is a structural design pattern that allows you to share objects to support large numbers of fine-grained objects efficiently. It achieves this by sharing objects that are common across multiple contexts, instead of creating new instances each time. In Salesforce Apex, the flyweight pattern can be useful when you have a large number of similar objects that share a common state, and you want to reduce memory usage and improve performance by sharing that common state.

Understanding flyweight pattern

The key concept of the flyweight pattern revolves around the idea of separating intrinsic state from extrinsic state and sharing as much state as possible among multiple objects to conserve memory and improve performance.

Following are the key concepts of the flyweight pattern:

- **Intrinsic state**: This is the part of the object's state that can be shared among multiple instances of the flyweight object. It remains constant and immutable across different contexts. By extracting and sharing intrinsic state, the flyweight pattern aims to minimize memory usage by avoiding redundant data.

- **Extrinsic state:** This is the part of the object's state that varies based on the context in which the object is used. Extrinsic state is not shared among flyweight objects and is provided by client objects when interacting with flyweight instances. By separating intrinsic state from extrinsic state, the flyweight pattern ensures that the shared state remains consistent while allowing flexibility for context-specific customization.

- **Flyweight objects:** These are the objects that represent the shared state and contain only intrinsic state. Flyweight objects are lightweight and immutable, making them safe to share among multiple clients. They do not store any context-specific information and rely on extrinsic state provided by client objects during runtime.

- **Flyweight factory:** This is responsible for creating and managing flyweight objects. The factory maintains a pool of flyweight objects and provides an interface for clients to access and retrieve shared instances. The factory ensures that clients receive existing flyweight instances when they request them, minimizing the creation of redundant objects.

By understanding and implementing these key concepts, the flyweight pattern enables efficient usage of resources by maximizing object sharing, thus optimizing memory usage and improving performance in applications where objects exhibit significant redundancy in their state.

Following is how it works:

- The flyweight factory creates and manages a pool of flyweight objects.

- Clients request flyweight objects from the factory.

- Flyweight objects store the intrinsic state and receive the extrinsic state from clients when needed.

- If a requested flyweight object already exists in the pool, the factory returns the existing instance; otherwise, it creates a new instance.

- Clients interact with flyweight objects through the factory without needing to create or manage them directly.

Using flyweight pattern

The flyweight pattern is suitable in the following scenarios:

- When you have many fine-grained objects that share a common state.
- When you want to reduce memory usage and improve performance by sharing a common state among multiple objects.

In Salesforce Apex, the flyweight pattern can be beneficial in scenarios where you need to manage many fine-grained objects with shared state efficiently.

Following are some situations where you may consider using the flyweight pattern in Apex:

- **Large volume of data**: In Salesforce applications, you may encounter situations where you need to process a large volume of data, such as records retrieved from queries or external sources. If these data objects share common characteristics or state, you can use the flyweight pattern to reduce memory usage by sharing the common state among multiple instances.

- **Custom metadata processing**: Salesforce provides custom metadata types for storing application configuration data. If your application uses custom metadata extensively and many metadata records share common attributes or settings, you can implement the flyweight pattern to optimize memory usage and improve performance when working with metadata records.

- **Bulk processing operations**: When performing bulk processing operations, such as data transformations or calculations on large datasets, memory efficiency becomes crucial. By using the flyweight pattern, you can minimize the memory footprint of your Apex code by sharing common state among objects, thus improving the scalability and performance of bulk processing operations.

- **Integration with external systems**: In Salesforce integrations with external systems, you may need to handle large volumes of data or responses from external APIs. If the data objects received from external systems have common attributes or properties, you can apply the flyweight pattern to reduce memory consumption and optimize resource usage during integration processing.

- **Reusable service components**: When designing reusable service components or utilities that are used across multiple parts of your Salesforce application, consider implementing the flyweight pattern to share a common state among instances of these components. This approach promotes memory efficiency and code reuse, leading to better overall application design.

Overall, the flyweight pattern can be useful in Salesforce Apex development when dealing with large volumes of data, custom metadata processing, bulk processing operations, integration with external systems, or building reusable service components. By leveraging the flyweight pattern, you can optimize memory usage, improve performance, and enhance the scalability of your Apex code in various scenarios.

Following is an example:

Consider a scenario where you are developing a game application where you need to render many trees on a game map. Each tree object has common properties such as type, (for example, oak, pine) and texture, which can be shared among multiple tree instances. We will use the flyweight pattern to share common properties among tree instances to reduce memory usage and improve performance, as follows:

```
// Flyweight interface
public interface Tree {
    void render(int x, int y);
}


// Concrete flyweight class representing a tree type
public class TreeType implements Tree {
    private String type;
    private String texture;

    public TreeType(String type, String texture) {
        this.type = type;
        this.texture = texture;
    }

    public void render(int x, int y) {
        System.debug('Rendering ' + type + ' tree with texture ' + texture
+ ' at position (' + x + ', ' + y + ')');
        // Actual rendering logic here
    }
}


// Flyweight factory class
public class TreeFactory {
    private static Map<String, TreeType> treeTypes = new Map<String,
TreeType>();

    public static TreeType getTreeType(String type, String texture) {
        String key = type + '-' + texture;
        if (!treeTypes.containsKey(key)) {
            treeTypes.put(key, new TreeType(type, texture));
        }
        return treeTypes.get(key);
```

```
        }
}


// Client class
public class GameMap {
    private List<Tree> trees = new List<Tree>();

    public void addTree(int x, int y, String type, String texture) {
        TreeType treeType = TreeFactory.getTreeType(type, texture);
        Tree tree = new TreeImpl(treeType, x, y);
        trees.add(tree);
    }

    public void render() {
        for (Tree tree : trees) {
            tree.render(tree.getX(), tree.getY());
        }
    }
}


// Concrete flyweight implementation class
public class TreeImpl implements Tree {
    private TreeType type;
    private int x;
    private int y;

    public TreeImpl(TreeType type, int x, int y) {
        this.type = type;
        this.x = x;
        this.y = y;
    }

    public void render(int x, int y) {
        type.render(x, y);
    }

    public int getX() {
        return x;
    }
```

```
    public int getY() {
        return y;
    }
}
```

Usage:

```
// Create a game map
GameMap map = new GameMap();

// Add trees to the game map
map.addTree(10, 20, 'oak', 'green');
map.addTree(30, 40, 'pine', 'brown');
map.addTree(50, 60, 'oak', 'green');

// Render the game map
map.render();
```

In this example:

- We have the tree interface representing the flyweight object behavior.
- The **TreeType** class is a concrete flyweight representing a tree type with common properties like type and texture.
- The **TreeFactory** class manages the creation and sharing of flyweight objects (tree types).
- The **GameMap** class is the client that adds trees to the game map and renders them.
- The **TreeImpl** class is the concrete flyweight implementation representing individual tree instances on the map.

This implementation demonstrates how the flyweight pattern can be used to share common properties among tree instances in a game map scenario, reducing memory usage and improving performance. Each tree instance only stores its position, while the shared properties (type and texture) are stored and managed by flyweight objects created by the factory.

Benefits of flyweight pattern

Following are the benefits of flyweight pattern:

- **Memory efficiency**: By sharing a common state among multiple objects, the flyweight pattern reduces memory usage, especially when dealing with a large number of similar objects.

- **Performance improvement**: Sharing a common state among objects can lead to performance improvements, as it reduces the overhead of creating and managing multiple instances of similar objects.

- **Simplicity**: The flyweight pattern simplifies the design by separating the intrinsic state (shared) from the extrinsic state (context-dependent), making it easier to manage objects.

Practical implementation example of flyweight pattern

To understand the flyweight pattern in action, consider the following scenarios where it optimizes memory usage by sharing common state among objects:

Example 1: E-Commerce product configuration optimization:

One real-world example of the flyweight pattern in Salesforce Apex is the management of product configurations in an e-commerce application. Let us consider a scenario where the e-commerce platform offers a wide range of products with various configurations, such as size, color, and material. Instead of creating separate instances for each product configuration, we can use the flyweight pattern to share common properties among similar product configurations, reducing memory usage and improving performance, as follows:

```
// Flyweight interface representing product configurations
public interface ProductConfiguration {
    void displayConfiguration();
}


// Concrete flyweight class representing a product configuration
public class ConcreteProductConfiguration implements ProductConfiguration {
    private String productId;
    private String size;
    private String color;
    private String material;

    public ConcreteProductConfiguration(String productId, String size,
String color, String material) {
        this.productId = productId;
        this.size = size;
        this.color = color;
        this.material = material;
    }

    public void displayConfiguration() {
```

```
        System.debug('Product Configuration - Product ID: ' + productId + ',
Size: ' + size + ', Color: ' + color + ', Material: ' + material);
        // Additional configuration display logic
    }
}


// Flyweight factory class for managing product configurations
public class ProductConfigurationFactory {
    private static Map<String, ProductConfiguration> configurations = new
Map<String, ProductConfiguration>();

    public static ProductConfiguration getProductConfiguration(String
productId, String size, String color, String material) {
        String key = productId + '-' + size + '-' + color + '-' + material;
        if (!configurations.containsKey(key)) {
            configurations.put(key, new
ConcreteProductConfiguration(productId, size, color, material));
        }
        return configurations.get(key);
    }
}


// Client class for using product configurations
public class ECommerceApplication {
    public static void main(String[] args) {
        // Example usage
        ProductConfiguration config1 = ProductConfigurationFactory.
getProductConfiguration('123', 'Large', 'Red', 'Cotton');
        ProductConfiguration config2 = ProductConfigurationFactory.
getProductConfiguration('123', 'Large', 'Red', 'Cotton');

        // Both configurations share the same instance
        System.assertEquals(config1, config2);

        // Display product configurations
        config1.displayConfiguration();
        config2.displayConfiguration();
    }
}
```

In this example:

- The **ProductConfiguration** interface represents the flyweight object behavior for product configurations.

- The **ConcreteProductConfiguration** class is a concrete flyweight representing a specific product configuration with properties like product ID, size, color, and material.

- The **ProductConfigurationFactory** class manages the creation and sharing of product configuration flyweight objects.

- The **ECommerceApplication** class is the client that uses product configurations.

By using the flyweight pattern, the e-commerce application can efficiently manage and display product configurations without creating redundant instances for similar configurations. This reduces memory usage and improves performance, especially when dealing with many product variations.

Example 2: Case management system optimization:

In a Salesforce Apex application, a real-world example of the flyweight pattern could be in a case management system where you need to handle a large number of case records, each with common attributes such as status, priority, and case owner. Instead of creating separate instances for each case record, you can use the flyweight pattern to share these common attributes among multiple case instances to reduce memory usage and improve performance, as follows:

```
// Flyweight interface representing case details
public interface CaseDetails {
    void displayDetails();
}


// Concrete flyweight class representing case details
public class ConcreteCaseDetails implements CaseDetails {
    private String status;
    private String priority;
    private String owner;

    public ConcreteCaseDetails(String status, String priority, String
owner) {
        this.status = status;
        this.priority = priority;
        this.owner = owner;
    }
```

```
    public void displayDetails() {
        System.debug('Case Details - Status: ' + status + ', Priority: ' +
priority + ', Owner: ' + owner);
        // Additional details display logic
    }
}


// Flyweight factory class for managing case details
public class CaseDetailsFactory {
    private static Map<String, CaseDetails> caseDetailsMap = new
Map<String, CaseDetails>();

    public static CaseDetails getCaseDetails(String status, String
priority, String owner) {
        String key = status + '-' + priority + '-' + owner;
        if (!caseDetailsMap.containsKey(key)) {
            caseDetailsMap.put(key, new ConcreteCaseDetails(status,
priority, owner));
        }
        return caseDetailsMap.get(key);
    }
}


// Client class for using case details
public class CaseManagementSystem {
    public static void main(String[] args) {
        // Example usage
        CaseDetails case1 = CaseDetailsFactory.getCaseDetails('Open',
'High', 'John Doe');
        CaseDetails case2 = CaseDetailsFactory.getCaseDetails('Open',
'Medium', 'Jane Smith');

        // Both cases share the same instance for the same combination of
status, priority, and owner
        System.assertEquals(case1, case2);

        // Display case details
```

```
        case1.displayDetails();
        case2.displayDetails();
    }
}
```

In this example:

- The **CaseDetails** interface represents the flyweight object behavior for case details.

- The **ConcreteCaseDetails** class is a concrete flyweight representing case details with properties like status, priority, and owner.

- The **CaseDetailsFactory** class manages the creation and sharing of case details flyweight objects based on a combination of status, priority, and owner.

- The **CaseManagementSystem** class is the client that uses case details.

By utilizing the flyweight pattern, the case management system can efficiently manage and display case details without creating redundant instances for cases with the same combination of status, priority, and owner. This optimization reduces memory usage and improves performance, especially when dealing with a large volume of case records in the system.

Summary: The flyweight pattern provides a way to share common state among multiple fine-grained objects efficiently, reducing memory usage and improving performance in Salesforce Apex applications.

Conclusion

This chapter explored the realm of structural design patterns, which play a pivotal role in optimizing the composition and relationships of classes and objects in software systems. Structural patterns such as adapter, decorator, facade, composite, bridge, and flyweight provide versatile solutions to common design challenges, enabling developers to create scalable, maintainable, and flexible architectures. Each pattern was discussed in detail, including its definition, key concepts, benefits, implementation steps, and real-world applications in contexts like Salesforce Apex and other software scenarios.

By applying structural design patterns, developers can streamline the integration of disparate systems, simplify complex interactions, enhance reusability, and optimize memory usage. These patterns encourage cleaner code, reduce dependencies, and promote separation of concerns, making them essential tools for crafting efficient software solutions. The examples and explanations in this chapter are designed to help readers understand when and how to use each pattern effectively.

In the next chapter, we will emphasize the interaction and communication between objects. These patterns will further enrich your toolkit, enabling you to design systems that are not only structurally sound but also behaviorally efficient. With a solid grasp of structural patterns, readers are well-prepared to tackle the dynamic challenges of software development.

Points to remember

- Structural design patterns focus on the composition of classes and objects to form larger systems, simplifying relationships and interactions between components.

- Key structural design patterns include adapter, decorator, facade, composite, bridge, and flyweight, each solving specific structural challenges in software design.

- The adapter pattern enables incompatible interfaces to work together by translating one interface into another, facilitating seamless integration with legacy systems or third-party APIs.

- The decorator pattern dynamically adds new functionality to objects without modifying their code, promoting flexibility and avoiding subclass proliferation.

- The facade pattern provides a simplified interface to complex systems, reducing client complexity and improving maintainability by decoupling subsystems.

- The composite pattern organizes objects into tree-like structures, allowing clients to treat individual objects and groups of objects uniformly, simplifying hierarchical management.

- The bridge pattern decouples an abstraction from its implementation, allowing them to evolve independently and promoting flexibility and extensibility.

- The flyweight pattern optimizes memory usage by sharing common states across objects, improving performance and reducing resource consumption in systems with large datasets.

- Structural design patterns promote flexibility, reusability, and scalability by abstracting composition and enhancing interactions between system components.

- Real-world applications of these patterns include integrating payment gateways, enhancing notification systems, organizing organizational hierarchies, and optimizing memory usage in large-scale applications.

- By addressing common structural challenges, these patterns help developers create robust, maintainable, and efficient software architectures.

Questions

1. What are the primary goals of structural design patterns?

2. How does the adapter pattern simplify integration with legacy systems?

3. What are the advantages of using the decorator pattern over inheritance for adding functionality?

4. How does the facade pattern reduce the complexity of interacting with subsystems?

5. Why is the composite pattern particularly useful for hierarchical structures?

6. What is the main advantage of the bridge pattern in terms of abstraction and implementation?

7. Which design pattern allows objects with incompatible interfaces to work together?

8. Which design pattern helps you add new responsibilities to objects dynamically?

9. Which design pattern helps to decouple abstraction from implementation?

10. What design pattern provides a single-entry point to a complex subsystem?

11. What is the primary goal of the flyweight pattern?

12. How does the flyweight pattern improve memory efficiency in applications?

13. Can you provide a real-world example of the facade pattern in Salesforce Apex?

Join our book's Discord space

Join the book's Discord Workspace for Latest updates, Offers, Tech happenings around the world, New Release and Sessions with the Authors:

https://discord.bpbonline.com

CHAPTER 7

Behavioral Design Patterns

Introduction

This chapter focuses on behavioral design patterns, which passively regulates communication between objects. Behavioral design patterns are a category of design patterns in software engineering that focus on the interaction and communication between objects. These patterns provide solutions for organizing and managing the responsibilities and algorithms of objects, facilitating flexible and efficient communication among them. Behavioral patterns abstract the flow of control and communication, allowing objects to collaborate decoupled and reusable, promoting code maintainability and scalability. Behavioral patterns are particularly useful when dealing with complex systems where objects need to communicate, coordinate, and collaborate effectively to achieve certain behaviors and functionalities. They help improve the flexibility, modifiability, and extensibility of the software by promoting loose coupling and separation of concerns. These patterns address various ways of design patterns, such as defining a dependency between objects (observer pattern), defining a family of algorithms and making them interchangeable (strategy pattern), Turning a request into a standalone object (command pattern), passing a request along a chain of handlers (chain of responsibility pattern), allowing an object to change its behavior when its internal state changes (state pattern), provides a way to access elements of an aggregate object (such as a list or collection) sequentially without exposing the underlying representation of that object (iterator pattern).

You will gain a profound understanding of these behavioral design patterns and their applications in Apex development, enabling more dynamic and adaptable software architectures.

Structure

The chapter covers the following topics:

- Behavioral design patterns
- Observer pattern
- Strategy pattern
- Command pattern
- Chain of responsibility pattern
- State pattern
- Iterator pattern

Objectives

By the end of this chapter, readers will gain a comprehensive understanding of behavioral design patterns, which focus on the interaction and communication between objects in software systems. The chapter explores six key patterns that is, observer, strategy, command, chain of responsibility, state, and iterator—each addressing specific challenges in organizing and managing object behavior. Readers will learn the principles behind these patterns, their implementation techniques, and real-world applications within Salesforce Apex development. This knowledge will empower readers to design more modular, flexible, and scalable systems, ensuring effective communication among objects while maintaining loose coupling and separation of concerns. By mastering these patterns, readers will be equipped to handle complex workflows, enhance code reusability, and build dynamic systems capable of adapting to changing requirements with minimal disruption.

Behavioral design patterns

Behavioral design patterns are a set of design patterns in software engineering that deal with the interaction and communication between objects. These patterns focus on defining algorithms and assigning responsibilities among objects to promote flexibility, efficiency, and reusability in the codebase.

The key characteristics of behavioral design patterns are as follows:

- **Encapsulating behavior**: Behavioral patterns focus on encapsulating behavior and algorithms, allowing objects to interact with each other in a decoupled manner.

This encapsulation promotes code reusability and maintainability by isolating the implementation details of behavior within specific objects.

- **Flexibility and adaptability**: These patterns promote flexibility and adaptability in software systems by allowing behavior to vary independently from the objects that use it. By encapsulating behavior in separate objects, systems become more adaptable to changes, as behavior can be modified or replaced without affecting the rest of the system.

- **Facilitating communication**: Behavioral patterns define standardized interaction protocols, ensuring clear and consistent communication between objects. This reduces ambiguity in object collaboration and makes the system more predictable. By establishing a structured way for objects to interact, these patterns prevent tightly coupled dependencies that can hinder code evolution.

- **Managing complex control flows**: They simplify intricate interactions by providing structured mechanisms for coordinating behavior, improving maintainability. Instead of relying on ad-hoc solutions, behavioral patterns introduce well-defined roles for objects, ensuring that logic remains clear and scalable. This is especially useful in systems with multiple interdependent components that need to function cohesively.

- **Promoting loose coupling**: By decoupling request senders from receivers, these patterns enhance flexibility, making systems easier to modify and maintain. Changes in one component do not necessitate changes in dependent components, reducing the risk of unintended side effects. This separation also enables testing individual components in isolation, improving debugging and testability.

- **Encouraging separation of concerns**: They separate behavior implementation from the objects using it, leading to better organization and modularity in the codebase. This enables developers to modify behavior without altering the core structure of objects, supporting cleaner and more reusable designs. Additionally, separation fosters a more maintainable architecture by preventing business logic from being scattered across different layers.

- **Enhancing extensibility and scalability**: Encapsulating behavior allows systems to evolve with minimal impact, making it easier to add, modify, or replace functionality over time. New features can be introduced by extending existing behavior rather than modifying core components, reducing technical debt. This makes the system more adaptable to future changes, whether it's business logic updates or integration with external services.

Some common examples of behavioral design patterns are shown in *Figure 7.1*:

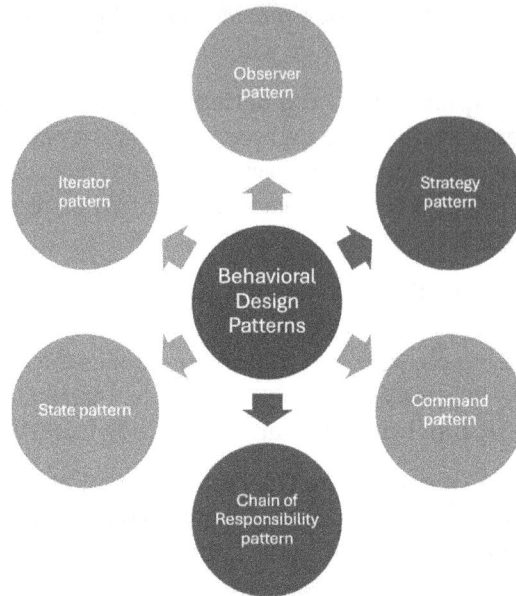

Figure 7.1: *Behavioral design patterns*

- **Observer pattern**: Defines one-to-many dependency between objects, so that when one object changes state, all its dependents are notified and updated automatically.

- **Strategy pattern**: Defines a family of algorithms, encapsulates each one, and makes them interchangeable. It allows the algorithm to vary independently from clients that use it.

- **Command pattern**: Encapsulates a request as an object, thereby allowing parameterization of clients with queues, requests, and operations.

- **Iterator pattern**: Provides a way to access the elements of an aggregate object sequentially without exposing its underlying representation.

- **Chain of responsibility pattern**: Decouples the sender of a request from its receiver by allowing multiple objects to handle the request, forming a chain.

- **State pattern**: Allows an object to alter its behavior when its internal state changes. The object appears to change its class.

These patterns, among others, help design more modular, maintainable, and scalable software systems by promoting better organization, flexibility, and reusability of code.

Observer pattern

The observer pattern is a behavioral design pattern where an object, known as the subject, maintains a list of its dependents, called observers, and notifies them of any changes in state, typically by calling one of their methods. This pattern is useful when you have one-to-many dependency between objects, and you want to ensure that all dependent objects are updated automatically when the state of the subject changes.

Understanding observer pattern

The observer pattern consists of several key components, as follows:

- **Subject**: The subject is the object that maintains a list of observers and notifies them of any changes in its state. It provides methods to register, unregister, and notify observers.

- **Observer**: The observer is the interface or abstract class that defines the method(s) that the subject calls to notify it of changes. Observers implement this interface and register themselves with the subject to receive notifications.

- **Concrete subject**: The concrete subject is a subclass of the subject that contains the actual implementation of the subject interface. It maintains the state of interest and notifies observers when this state changes.

- **Concrete observer**: The concrete observer is a subclass of the observer interface that contains the actual implementation of the update method. Multiple concrete observers can be registered with a subject to receive notifications.

Following is how it works:

- **Registration**: Observers register themselves with the subject to receive notifications when changes occur.

- **Notification**: When the state of the subject changes, it notifies all registered observers by calling their update method.

- **Update**: Each observer implements the update method to respond to changes in the subject's state. This method typically receives information about the change so that the observer can update itself accordingly.

Using observer pattern

The observer pattern is particularly useful in scenarios where you have one-to-many relationship between objects, and changes in one object need to be propagated to multiple other objects.

Following are some specific situations where the observer pattern is commonly employed:

- **Event handling**: When you need to implement event-driven systems, such as **graphical user interfaces (GUIs)** or asynchronous processing, the observer pattern is invaluable. It allows components to register as observers for specific events and react accordingly when those events occur.

- **Model-View-Controller (MVC) architecture**: In MVC architecture, the observer pattern is frequently used to maintain synchronization between the model (data) and the view (user interface). Views register themselves as observers of model objects, ensuring that they are updated whenever the underlying data changes.

- **Distributed systems**: The observer pattern enables communication between distributed components in distributed systems. Changes in one part of the system can be observed by other parts, facilitating coordination and synchronization across the distributed environment.

- **Publish-subscribe mechanisms**: The observer pattern forms the foundation of publish-subscribe systems where, publishers broadcast messages or events to multiple subscribers. This pattern is commonly used in messaging systems, event-driven architectures, and real-time data processing.

- **Logging and monitoring**: Observer pattern is suitable for implementing logging and monitoring functionalities where multiple observers must react to changes or events in the system's state. Observers can monitor specific components or log relevant information when certain conditions are met.

- **Dynamic configuration updates**: In systems where configurations can change dynamically, the observer pattern can notify interested components about changes in configuration parameters. This allows components to adapt their behavior dynamically based on the updated configuration.

Overall, the observer pattern is beneficial in scenarios where you need to establish loose coupling between the subject (the object being observed) and its observers. It promotes scalability, modularity, and maintainability by allowing objects to react dynamically to changes without tight coupling between them.

Stock market application

Let us consider an example where we have a stock market application that tracks the prices of various stocks. We want to notify investors whenever the price of a stock changes. We can use the observer pattern to implement this functionality, as follows:

```
// Observer interface
public interface StockObserver {
    void update(String stockName, Decimal price);
}


// Subject class
public class StockMarket {
    private Map<String, Decimal> prices = new Map<String, Decimal>();
    private List<StockObserver> observers = new List<StockObserver>();

    public void registerObserver(StockObserver observer) {
```

```
            observers.add(observer);
    }


    public void removeObserver(StockObserver observer) {
        observers.remove(observer);
    }


    public void setPrice(String stockName, Decimal price) {
        prices.put(stockName, price);
        notifyObservers(stockName, price);
    }


    private void notifyObservers(String stockName, Decimal price) {
        for (StockObserver observer : observers) {
            observer.update(stockName, price);
        }
    }
}


// Concrete Observer class
public class Investor implements StockObserver {
    private String name;

    public Investor(String name) {
        this.name = name;
    }

    public void update(String stockName, Decimal price) {
        System.debug(name + ": Price of " + stockName + " is now " +
price);
    }
}


// Usage
StockMarket market = new StockMarket();
Investor investor1 = new Investor('John');
Investor investor2 = new Investor('Jane');
```

```
market.registerObserver(investor1);
market.registerObserver(investor2);

market.setPrice('AAPL', 150.0);
market.setPrice('GOOG', 2000.0);
```

In this example:

- **StockMarket** is the subject class that maintains a list of observers and notifies them when the price of a stock changes.

- **StockObserver** is the observer interface that defines the update method.

- **Investor** is a concrete observer that implements the update method to receive notifications of stock price changes.

When the price of a stock changes, the **StockMarket** class notifies all registered observers by calling their update method.

Benefits of observer pattern

By using the observer pattern, you can gain the following benefits:

- **Loose coupling**: The observer pattern promotes loose coupling between subjects and observers, allowing them to vary independently of each other.

- **Flexibility**: Because observers are separate from the subject, you can easily add or remove observers without modifying the subject.

- **Reusability**: Observers can be reused across different subjects, promoting code reusability.

- **Scalability**: The observer pattern scales well to systems with multiple subjects and observers, making it suitable for large, complex systems.

Practical implementation example of an observer pattern

To understand the observer pattern in action, consider the following scenarios where it optimizes memory usage by sharing common state among objects.

Example 1: Real-time messaging notification system

Let us consider a scenario where we have a notification system for a messaging application. Whenever a new message is received, we want to notify multiple observers, such as user interfaces displaying messages in real-time, notification services, and logging systems. We can use the observer pattern to implement this functionality in Salesforce Apex, as follows:

```java
// Message class representing a simple message structure
public class Message {
    private String content;
    // Constructor to initialize the message with content
    public Message(String content) {
        this.content = content;
    }

    // Getter method to retrieve the message content
    public String getContent() {
        return content;
    }
}


// Observer interface
public interface MessageObserver {
    // Method to notify observers when a new message is received
    void notifyNewMessage(Message message);
}

// Subject class
public class MessageService {
    private List<MessageObserver> observers = new List<MessageObserver>();

    // Registers a new observer to receive message updates
    public void registerObserver(MessageObserver observer) {
        observers.add(observer);
    }

    // Removes an existing observer from the notification list
    public void removeObserver(MessageObserver observer) {
        observers.remove(observer);
    }

    // Processes an incoming message and notifies observers
    public void receiveMessage(Message message) {
        // Process the received message
```

```
        // (e.g., store it in a database, apply filters, etc.)
        // ...

        // Notify all registered observers about the new message
        notifyObservers(message);
    }

    // Notifies all registered observers about the received message
    private void notifyObservers(Message message) {
        for (MessageObserver observer : observers) {
            observer.notifyNewMessage(message);
        }
    }
}


// Concrete Observer class - UI component
public class MessageUI implements MessageObserver {
    // Notifies the UI component about the new message
    public void notifyNewMessage(Message message) {
        // Update UI to display the new message
        System.debug('New message received: ' + message.getContent());
    }
}


// Concrete Observer class - Notification service
public class NotificationService implements MessageObserver {
    // Notifies the notification service about the new message
    public void notifyNewMessage(Message message) {
        // Send notification to users
            System.debug('Notification sent for new message: ' + message.
getContent());
    }
        }

// Usage
MessageService messageService = new MessageService();
MessageObserver uiObserver = new MessageUI();
MessageObserver notificationObserver = new NotificationService();
```

```
// Register observers with the message service
messageService.registerObserver(uiObserver);
messageService.registerObserver(notificationObserver);

// Simulate receiving a new message
Message newMessage = new Message('Hello, world!');
messageService.receiveMessage(newMessage);
```

In this example:

- **MessageService** is the subject class that maintains a list of observers and notifies them when a new message is received.

- **MessageObserver** is the observer interface that defines the **notifyNewMessage** method.

- **MessageUI** and **NotificationService** are concrete observer classes that implement the **notifyNewMessage** method to respond to new messages.

When a new message is received, the **MessageService** class notifies all registered observers by calling their **notifyNewMessage** method. This allows the UI component and notification service to react to the new message accordingly.

This example demonstrates how the observer pattern can be used in Salesforce Apex to implement a notification system that notifies multiple observers of changes in the state of a subject.

Example 2: Order processing notification system

Let us consider a scenario where we have an e-commerce platform, and we want to implement a notification system for order processing. Whenever a new order is placed, we want to notify multiple observers, such as email notifications, SMS notifications, and order tracking systems. We can use the observer pattern to implement this functionality in Salesforce Apex, as follows:

```
// Order class representing a customer's purchase order
public class Order {
    private String orderNumber;
    private String customerName;
    private List<String> orderItems;
    private Decimal totalAmount;
    private String orderStatus;

    // Constructor to initialize an order
    public Order(String orderNumber, String customerName, List<String>
```

```
orderItems, Decimal totalAmount, String orderStatus) {
        this.orderNumber = orderNumber;
        this.customerName = customerName;
        this.orderItems = orderItems;
        this.totalAmount = totalAmount;
        this.orderStatus = orderStatus;
    }

    // Getter methods
    public String getOrderNumber() {
        return orderNumber;
    }

    public String getCustomerName() {
        return customerName;
    }

    public List<String> getOrderItems() {
        return orderItems;
    }

    public Decimal getTotalAmount() {
        return totalAmount;
    }

    public String getOrderStatus() {
        return orderStatus;
    }

    // Setter method for updating order status
    public void setOrderStatus(String orderStatus) {
        this.orderStatus = orderStatus;
    }
}

// Observer interface
public interface OrderObserver {
```

```
        void notifyNewOrder(Order order);
}


// Subject class
public class OrderService {
    private List<OrderObserver> observers = new List<OrderObserver>();

    public void registerObserver(OrderObserver observer) {
        observers.add(observer);
    }

    public void removeObserver(OrderObserver observer) {
        observers.remove(observer);
    }

    public void placeOrder(Order order) {
        // Process the order
        // ...

        // Notify observers of the new order
        notifyObservers(order);
    }

    private void notifyObservers(Order order) {
        for (OrderObserver observer : observers) {
            observer.notifyNewOrder(order);
        }
    }
}


// Concrete Observer class - Email notification
public class EmailNotification implements OrderObserver {
    public void notifyNewOrder(Order order) {
        // Send email notification for the new order
        System.debug('Email notification sent for new order: ' + order.
getOrderNumber());
    }
```

```
}

// Concrete Observer class - SMS notification
public class SmsNotification implements OrderObserver {
    public void notifyNewOrder(Order order) {
        // Send SMS notification for the new order
        System.debug('SMS notification sent for new order: ' + order.
getOrderNumber());
    }
}


// Usage
OrderService orderService = new OrderService();
OrderObserver emailObserver = new EmailNotification();
OrderObserver smsObserver = new SmsNotification();

// Register observers with the order service
orderService.registerObserver(emailObserver);
orderService.registerObserver(smsObserver);

// Simulate placing a new order
Order newOrder = new Order('12345', 100.00);
orderService.placeOrder(newOrder);
```

In this example:

- **OrderService** is the subject class that maintains a list of observers and notifies them when a new order is placed.

- **OrderObserver** is the observer interface that defines the **notifyNewOrder** method.

- **EmailNotification** and **SmsNotification** are concrete observer classes that implement the **notifyNewOrder** method to send email and SMS notifications for new orders, respectively.

When a new order is placed, the **OrderService** class notifies all registered observers by calling their **notifyNewOrder** method. This allows the email and SMS notification services to send notifications for the new order.

This example demonstrates how the observer pattern can be used in Salesforce Apex to implement a notification system for order processing, where multiple observers are notified of changes in the state of a subject.

Summary: The observer pattern is a powerful tool for implementing communication and coordination between objects in a decoupled and flexible manner. It promotes loose coupling, reusability, and scalability, making it a valuable pattern in software design.

Strategy pattern

The strategy pattern is a behavioral design pattern that enables an algorithm to be selected at runtime from a family of algorithms. It defines a family of algorithms, encapsulates each algorithm, and makes them interchangeable. This pattern allows the algorithm to vary independently of the clients that use it.

Understanding strategy pattern

Strategy pattern consists of several key components, as follows:

- **Context**: The context is the class that contains a reference to the strategy interface and is responsible for invoking the strategy algorithm. It does not implement the algorithm itself but delegates it to the strategy interface.

- **Strategy**: The strategy is an interface or abstract class that defines the algorithm to be used. Each concrete strategy implements this interface, providing its own implementation of the algorithm.

- **Concrete strategies**: Concrete strategies are the actual implementations of the algorithm defined by the strategy interface. These classes encapsulate the algorithm and provide specific behavior.

Following is how it works:

- The client interacts with the context class, unaware of the specific algorithm being used.

- The context class delegates the algorithm implementation to the strategy interface.

- Different concrete strategies implement the strategy interface with their unique algorithm implementations.

- At runtime, the context class can switch between different strategies, allowing the client to choose the appropriate algorithm dynamically.

Using strategy pattern

The strategy pattern is best suited for scenarios where you need to dynamically select an algorithm from a family of algorithms at runtime.

Following are some situations where the strategy pattern is commonly used:

- **Multiple algorithms:** When you have multiple algorithms that can be used interchangeably for a specific task, such as sorting, searching, or processing data.

- **Dynamic behavior:** When the behavior of an object needs to vary based on different conditions or requirements, and you want to encapsulate these behaviors in separate classes.

- **Algorithm abstraction:** When you want to define a set of algorithms independently of the code that uses them, allowing for easy swapping of algorithms without modifying the client code.

- **Reducing conditional statements**: When your code contains multiple conditional statements to select different algorithms, and you want to eliminate these conditionals to improve code readability and maintainability.

- **Promoting reusability**: When you want to encapsulate algorithms in separate classes to promote code reusability and facilitate testing and maintenance.

- **Open/closed principle**: When you want to design your code following the open/closed principle, allowing it to be open for extension (by adding new algorithms) but closed for modification (existing code remains unchanged).

Sorting algorithms

Consider a scenario where you have a sorting utility in a Salesforce Apex application, and you want to provide flexibility in choosing different sorting algorithms. You can apply the strategy pattern to encapsulate each sorting algorithm and make them interchangeable, as follows:

```
// Strategy interface
public interface SortingStrategy {
    List<Integer> sort(List<Integer> numbers);
}


// Concrete strategies
public class BubbleSort implements SortingStrategy {
    public List<Integer> sort(List<Integer> numbers) {
        // Implement Bubble Sort algorithm
        return numbers;
    }
}

public class QuickSort implements SortingStrategy {
    public List<Integer> sort(List<Integer> numbers) {
        // Implement Quick Sort algorithm
        return numbers;
    }
```

```
}

// Context class
public class SortUtility {
    private SortingStrategy strategy;

    public SortUtility(SortingStrategy strategy) {
        this.strategy = strategy;
    }

    public void setStrategy(SortingStrategy strategy) {
        this.strategy = strategy;
    }

    public List<Integer> sortNumbers(List<Integer> numbers) {
        return strategy.sort(numbers);
    }
}


// Usage
SortUtility utility = new SortUtility(new BubbleSort());
List<Integer> sortedNumbers = utility.sortNumbers(numbers);
```

In this example:

- **SortingStrategy** is the strategy interface that defines the sort method.

- **BubbleSort** and **QuickSort** are concrete strategies that implement the **SortingStrategy** interface with their sorting algorithms.

- **SortUtility** is the context class that contains a reference to the current sorting strategy and delegates the sorting operation to the strategy object.

By using the strategy pattern, you can easily switch between different sorting algorithms at runtime without modifying the client code. This promotes flexibility, extensibility, and maintainability in your application.

Benefits of strategy pattern

The strategy pattern offers several benefits that contribute to the flexibility, maintainability, and extensibility of software systems, as follows:

- **Encapsulation**: Each algorithm is encapsulated within its own class, promoting better organization of code and reducing code duplication. This encapsulation also isolates the algorithm's implementation details from the rest of the system.

- **Flexibility**: Clients can easily switch between different algorithms at runtime without modifying the context or client code. This flexibility allows for dynamic behavior selection based on runtime conditions or user preferences.

- **Extensibility**: New algorithms can be added to the system without affecting existing code. Since each algorithm is encapsulated within its own class, adding a new algorithm involves creating a new concrete strategy class and registering it with the context.

- **Maintainability**: The strategy pattern promotes code maintainability by decoupling the algorithm implementation from the client code. Changes to one algorithm do not affect other algorithms or the client code, making it easier to modify and maintain the system.

- **Testability**: Since each algorithm is encapsulated within its own class, it becomes easier to test individual algorithms in isolation. This promotes unit testing and ensures that changes to one algorithm do not inadvertently affect the behavior of other algorithms.

- **Promotes code reusability**: The strategy pattern promotes code reusability by allowing algorithms to be reused across different contexts or applications. Once an algorithm is implemented, it can be used in multiple scenarios without modification.

- **Supports design principles**: The strategy pattern aligns with various design principles such as the **Single Responsibility Principle (SRP)** and the **open/closed principle (OCP).** It promotes separation of concerns by encapsulating algorithms in separate classes and allows for system extension without modifying existing code.

Overall, the strategy pattern enhances software design by providing a flexible and maintainable approach to handling algorithmic variations in a system. It promotes clean code architecture, promotes code reuse, and facilitates system evolution over time.

Practical implementation example of a strategy pattern

The strategy pattern enables the selection of an algorithm's behavior at runtime. It provides a flexible way to define a family of algorithms, encapsulate each one, and make them interchangeable without altering the codebase.

Following are practical examples of how the strategy pattern can be implemented in Apex:

Example 1: Dynamic shipping cost calculation

Let us consider a scenario where we have a shipping calculation module in an e-commerce application. The shipping cost calculation may vary based on factors such as the shipping method, destination, and package dimensions. We can apply the strategy pattern to encapsulate different shipping calculation algorithms and allow the client to dynamically select the appropriate algorithm based on user preferences or system requirements, as follows:

```
// Strategy interface
public interface ShippingCalculationStrategy {
    Decimal calculateShippingCost(ShippingDetails details);
}


// Concrete strategies
public class StandardShippingStrategy implements
ShippingCalculationStrategy {
    public Decimal calculateShippingCost(ShippingDetails details) {
        // Implement standard shipping cost calculation
        return details.getWeight() * 0.5; // Example calculation based on
weight
    }
}


public class ExpressShippingStrategy implements ShippingCalculationStrategy
{
    public Decimal calculateShippingCost(ShippingDetails details) {
        // Implement express shipping cost calculation
        return (details.getWeight() * 1.5) + 10; // Example calculation
based on weight and fixed fee
    }
}


// Context class
public class ShippingCalculator {
    private ShippingCalculationStrategy strategy;

    public ShippingCalculator(ShippingCalculationStrategy strategy) {
        this.strategy = strategy;
    }

    public void setStrategy(ShippingCalculationStrategy strategy) {
        this.strategy = strategy;
    }

    public Decimal calculateShippingCost(ShippingDetails details) {
        return strategy.calculateShippingCost(details);
```

```
        }
}
```

```
// Client code
ShippingDetails details = new ShippingDetails(5); // Example: package
weighs 5 lbs
ShippingCalculator calculator = new ShippingCalculator(new
ExpressShippingStrategy());

Decimal shippingCost = calculator.calculateShippingCost(details);
System.debug('Shipping cost: $' + shippingCost);
```

In this example:

- **ShippingCalculationStrategy** is the strategy interface that defines the **calculateShippingCost** method.

- **StandardShippingStrategy** and **ExpressShippingStrategy** are concrete strategies that implement the **ShippingCalculationStrategy** interface with their respective shipping cost calculation algorithms.

- **ShippingCalculator** is the context class that contains a reference to the current shipping calculation strategy and delegates the calculation to the strategy object.

- The client code creates a **ShippingCalculator** object with a specific strategy, for example, express shipping and uses it to calculate the shipping cost based on the provided shipping details.

By using the strategy pattern, we can easily switch between different shipping calculation algorithms for example, standard shipping, express shipping, without modifying the client code. This promotes flexibility and maintainability in the shipping calculation module.

Example 2: Flexible payment processing

Let us consider another scenario where we have a payment processing system that needs to handle different payment methods such as credit card, PayPal, and bank transfer. Each payment method requires its own processing logic for charging the customer. We can use the strategy pattern to encapsulate the payment processing algorithms and allow the client to dynamically select the desired payment method, as follows:

```
// Strategy interface
public interface PaymentStrategy {
    Boolean processPayment(Decimal amount);
}

// Concrete strategies
```

```
public class CreditCardPaymentStrategy implements PaymentStrategy {
    public Boolean processPayment(Decimal amount) {
        // Implement credit card payment processing logic
        System.debug('Processing credit card payment for amount: $' +
amount);
        // Logic for charging the credit card
        return true; // Payment processed successfully
    }
}


public class PayPalPaymentStrategy implements PaymentStrategy {
    public Boolean processPayment(Decimal amount) {
        // Implement PayPal payment processing logic
        System.debug('Processing PayPal payment for amount: $' + amount);
        // Logic for processing payment via PayPal
        return true; // Payment processed successfully
    }
}


public class BankTransferPaymentStrategy implements PaymentStrategy {
    public Boolean processPayment(Decimal amount) {
        // Implement bank transfer payment processing logic
        System.debug('Processing bank transfer payment for amount: $' +
amount);
        // Logic for processing payment via bank transfer
        return true; // Payment processed successfully
    }
}


// Context class
public class PaymentProcessor {
    private PaymentStrategy strategy;

    public PaymentProcessor(PaymentStrategy strategy) {
        this.strategy = strategy;
    }

    public void setStrategy(PaymentStrategy strategy) {
```

```
        this.strategy = strategy;
    }


    public Boolean processPayment(Decimal amount) {
        return strategy.processPayment(amount);
    }
}


// Client code
Decimal paymentAmount = 100.00;
PaymentProcessor processor = new PaymentProcessor(new
CreditCardPaymentStrategy());
Boolean paymentProcessed = processor.processPayment(paymentAmount);


if (paymentProcessed) {
    System.debug('Payment processed successfully.');
} else {
    System.debug('Payment processing failed.');
}
```

In this example:

- **PaymentStrategy** is the strategy interface that defines the **processPayment** method.

- **CreditCardPaymentStrategy**, **PayPalPaymentStrategy**, and **BankTransferPaymentStrategy** are concrete strategies that implement the **PaymentStrategy** interface with their respective payment processing logic.

- **PaymentProcessor** is the context class that contains a reference to the current payment processing strategy and delegates the payment processing to the strategy object.

- The client code creates a **PaymentProcessor** object with a specific strategy for example, credit card payment, and uses it to process the payment amount.

By using the strategy pattern, we can easily switch between different payment processing methods for example, credit card, PayPal, bank transfer, without modifying the client code. This promotes flexibility and maintainability in the payment processing system.

Command pattern

The command pattern is a behavioral design pattern that encapsulates a request as an object, thereby allowing for parameterization of clients with queues, requests, and operations.

It allows you to decouple the sender of a request from the receiver by encapsulating a request as an object, thereby parameterizing clients with queues, requests, and operations. This enables clients to issue requests without knowing the requesting operation or the receiver's identity, promoting loose coupling and separation of concerns.

Understanding command pattern

The command pattern consists of several key components, as follows:

- **Command**: Represents an abstract command interface with an execute method that encapsulates the request to be performed. Concrete command classes implement this interface and provide specific implementations of the execute method.

- **Invoker**: Invokes commands without knowing the details of the command or the receiver. It holds a reference to the command object and invokes its execute method when necessary.

- **Receiver**: Performs the actual work associated with a command. It is responsible for carrying out the requested action.

- **Client**: Creates and configures command objects and sets their receivers. It passes command objects to invokers to execute the requests.

Following is how it works:

- The client creates concrete command objects and configures them with receivers.

- The client passes these command objects to the invoker.

- The invoker holds a reference to the command object and invoke its execute method when needed.

- The command object delegates the request to the receiver, which performs the actual work associated with the command.

Using command pattern

The command pattern is particularly useful in the following scenarios:

- **Decoupling invoker and receiver**: Use the command pattern to decouple the object that invokes a request (the invoker) from the object that performs the request (the receiver). This decoupling allows you to parameterize objects with queues, requests, and operations, making them independent.

- **Supporting undo operations**: Use the command pattern when supporting undoable operations. Command objects can encapsulate both the action and its inverse, allowing you to easily execute undo operations by invoking the inverse command.

- **Logging and auditing**: Use the command pattern when you need to log requests for auditing purposes or to support the replaying of requests. Command objects can encapsulate all the information needed to perform a request, making it easy to log and replay requests later.

- **Implementing queues and transactions**: Use the command pattern when you need to implement queues of requests or transactions. Command objects can be queued up and executed one by one, allowing you to control the order of execution and ensure that all commands are executed atomically.

- **Dynamic behavior selection:** Use the command pattern when you need to dynamically select the behavior of an object at runtime. By encapsulating different behaviors as command objects, you can easily switch between behaviors by changing the command object associated with the object.

Home automation command implementation

Consider a remote control for home devices, such as lights and fans. Each button on the remote control represents a command for example, turn on or off light, increase or decrease fan speed. We can use the command pattern to encapsulate these commands as objects and execute them when the corresponding button is pressed, as follows:

```
// Command interface
public interface Command {
    void execute();
}


// Concrete command classes
public class LightOnCommand implements Command {
    private Light light;

    public LightOnCommand(Light light) {
        this.light = light;
    }

    public void execute() {
        light.turnOn();
    }
}

public class LightOffCommand implements Command {
    private Light light;

    public LightOffCommand(Light light) {
```

```
            this.light = light;
    }

    public void execute() {
        light.turnOff();
    }
}

// Receiver class
public class Light {
    public void turnOn() {
        System.debug('Light turned on');
    }

    public void turnOff() {
        System.debug('Light turned off');
    }
}

// Invoker class
public class RemoteControl {
    private Command command;

    public void setCommand(Command command) {
        this.command = command;
    }

    public void pressButton() {
        command.execute();
    }
}

// Client code
Light light = new Light();
Command lightOnCommand = new LightOnCommand(light);
Command lightOffCommand = new LightOffCommand(light);
```

```
RemoteControl remote = new RemoteControl();
remote.setCommand(lightOnCommand);
remote.pressButton(); // Turns on the light

remote.setCommand(lightOffCommand);
remote.pressButton(); // Turns off the light
```

In this example:

- **Command** is the command interface with the execute method. **LightOnCommand** and **LightOffCommand** are concrete command classes that implement the Command interface and encapsulate the commands to turn the light on and off.

- Light is the receiver class that performs the actual work of turning the light on and off.

- **RemoteControl** is the invoker class that holds a reference to the command object and invoke its execute method when a button is pressed.

By using the command pattern, we achieve loose coupling between the sender of a request (invoker) and the receiver, allowing for extensibility and flexibility in managing requests and operations. Additionally, it enables support for undo operations and facilitates logging and auditing of commands.

Benefits of command pattern

The command pattern offers several benefits in software design, as follows:

- **Decoupling**: It decouples the sender of a request (the client or invoker) from the receiver (the object that performs the request), promoting loose coupling between objects. This decoupling allows for more flexible and maintainable code, as changes to one object do not necessarily require changes to other objects.

- **Flexibility**: By encapsulating requests as objects, the command pattern allows for the parametrization of clients with different commands. This makes it easy to switch between commands at runtime, allowing for dynamic behavior and configuration.

- **Undo operations**: The command pattern supports undoable operations by encapsulating both the action and its inverse within command objects. This makes it easy to implement undo functionality in applications where users need to reverse their actions.

- **Transaction management**: Command objects can be queued up and executed one by one, making it easy to implement transactions. If an error occurs during the execution of a command, the entire transaction can be rolled back by undoing the executed commands.

- **Logging and auditing**: Command objects encapsulate all the information needed to perform a request, making it easy to log requests for auditing purposes. This allows developers to track and analyze user actions, troubleshoot issues, and replay requests for testing and debugging purposes.

- **Dynamic behavior selection**: The command pattern allows for dynamic behavior selection at runtime by encapsulating different behaviors as command objects. This makes it easy to switch between behaviors by changing the command object associated with an object, without modifying its code.

Practical implementation example of a command pattern

The comman pattern enables the selection of an algorithm's behavior at runtime. It provides a flexible way to define a family of algorithms, encapsulate each one, and make them interchangeable without altering the codebase.

Following are practical examples of how the command pattern can be implemented in Apex:

Example 1: Task management system command implementation

Let us consider a scenario where we have a task management system where users can create, update, and delete tasks. We will use the command pattern to encapsulate these operations as command objects, allowing us to decouple the invoker for example, UI controller from the receiver for example, task service, and support undo functionality, as follows:

```
// Command interface
public interface TaskCommand {
    void execute();
}


// Concrete command classes
public class CreateTaskCommand implements TaskCommand {
    private TaskService taskService;
    private String taskName;

    public CreateTaskCommand(TaskService taskService, String taskName) {
        this.taskService = taskService;
        this.taskName = taskName;
    }

    public void execute() {
```

```
        taskService.createTask(taskName);
    }
}


public class UpdateTaskCommand implements TaskCommand {
    private TaskService taskService;
    private Task task;
    private String newTaskName;

    public UpdateTaskCommand(TaskService taskService, Task task, String
newTaskName) {
        this.taskService = taskService;
        this.task = task;
        this.newTaskName = newTaskName;
    }

    public void execute() {
        taskService.updateTask(task, newTaskName);
    }
}

public class DeleteTaskCommand implements TaskCommand {
    private TaskService taskService;
    private Task task;

    public DeleteTaskCommand(TaskService taskService, Task task) {
        this.taskService = taskService;
        this.task = task;
    }

    public void execute() {
        taskService.deleteTask(task);
    }
}

// Receiver class
public class TaskService {
```

```java
    public void createTask(String taskName) {
        // Logic to create a new task
    }

    public void updateTask(Task task, String newTaskName) {
        // Logic to update an existing task
    }

    public void deleteTask(Task task) {
        // Logic to delete an existing task
    }
}

// Task class
public class Task {
    // Properties of a task
}

// Invoker class
public class TaskController {
    public void executeCommand(TaskCommand command) {
        command.execute();
    }
}

// Client code
TaskService taskService = new TaskService();
TaskController taskController = new TaskController();

// Create a new task
TaskCommand createTaskCommand = new CreateTaskCommand(taskService, "New
Task");
taskController.executeCommand(createTaskCommand);

// Update an existing task
Task existingTask = new Task(/* task details */);
TaskCommand updateTaskCommand = new UpdateTaskCommand(taskService,
existingTask, "Updated Task Name");
```

```
taskController.executeCommand(updateTaskCommand);
```

```
// Delete an existing task
TaskCommand deleteTaskCommand = new DeleteTaskCommand(taskService,
existingTask);
taskController.executeCommand(deleteTaskCommand);
```

In this example:

- **TaskCommand** is the command interface with the execute method.

- **CreateTaskCommand**, **UpdateTaskCommand**, and **DeleteTaskCommand** are concrete command classes that implement the **TaskCommand** interface and encapsulate the logic for creating, updating, and deleting tasks.

- **TaskService** is the receiver class that performs the actual work of task management. **TaskController** is the invoker class that holds a reference to the command object and invoke its execute method when a task operation needs to be performed.

- The client code creates different command objects for creating, updating, and deleting tasks, and passes them to the **TaskController** for execution.

By using the command pattern, we achieve loose coupling between the sender of a request (the **TaskController**) and the receiver (the **TaskService**), allowing for extensibility and flexibility in managing tasks. It also facilitates the implementation of undo operations and supports logging and auditing of task operations.

Example 2: Banking transactions command implementation

Let us consider a scenario where we have another simple banking application that allows users to perform various transactions, such as depositing funds, withdrawing funds, and transferring funds between accounts. We will use the command pattern to implement these transactions as command objects, which can be queued up and executed by an invoker, as follows:

```
// Command interface
public interface TransactionCommand {
    void execute();
}
```

```
// Concrete command classes
public class DepositCommand implements TransactionCommand {
    private Account account;
    private Decimal amount;

    public DepositCommand(Account account, Decimal amount) {
```

```
            this.account = account;
            this.amount = amount;
        }


        public void execute() {
            account.deposit(amount);
        }
}


public class WithdrawCommand implements TransactionCommand {
        private Account account;
        private Decimal amount;

        public WithdrawCommand(Account account, Decimal amount) {
            this.account = account;
            this.amount = amount;
        }


        public void execute() {
            account.withdraw(amount);
        }
}


public class TransferCommand implements TransactionCommand {
        private Account sourceAccount;
        private Account destinationAccount;
        private Decimal amount;

        public TransferCommand(Account sourceAccount, Account
destinationAccount, Decimal amount) {
            this.sourceAccount = sourceAccount;
            this.destinationAccount = destinationAccount;
            this.amount = amount;
        }


        public void execute() {
            sourceAccount.withdraw(amount);
```

```
            destinationAccount.deposit(amount);
    }
}

// Receiver class
public class Account {
    private Decimal balance;

    public Account(Decimal initialBalance) {
        this.balance = initialBalance;
    }

    public void deposit(Decimal amount) {
        balance += amount;
    }

    public void withdraw(Decimal amount) {
        balance -= amount;
    }

    public Decimal getBalance() {
        return balance;
    }
}

// Invoker class
public class TransactionProcessor {
    public void processTransaction(TransactionCommand command) {
        command.execute();
    }
}

// Client code
Account sourceAccount = new Account(1000.00);
Account destinationAccount = new Account(500.00);

TransactionCommand depositCommand = new DepositCommand(sourceAccount,
```

```
500.00);
TransactionCommand withdrawCommand = new WithdrawCommand(sourceAccount,
200.00);
TransactionCommand transferCommand = new TransferCommand(sourceAccount,
destinationAccount, 300.00);

TransactionProcessor processor = new TransactionProcessor();

processor.processTransaction(depositCommand); // Deposits $500 into source
account
processor.processTransaction(withdrawCommand); // Withdraws $200 from
source account
processor.processTransaction(transferCommand); // Transfers $300 from
source account to destination account

System.debug('Source Account Balance: $' + sourceAccount.getBalance()); //
Output: $1000 - $500 + $200 - $300 = $400
System.debug('Destination Account Balance: $' + destinationAccount.
getBalance()); // Output: $500 + $300 = $800
```

In this example:

- **TransactionCommand** is the command interface with the execute method.

- **DepositCommand**, **WithdrawCommand**, and **TransferCommand** are concrete command classes that implement the **TransactionCommand** interface and encapsulate the logic for depositing funds, withdrawing funds, and transferring funds between accounts.

- Account is the receiver class that performs the actual work of depositing and withdrawing funds.

- **TransactionProcessor** is the invoker class that holds a reference to the command object and invoke its execute method when a transaction needs to be processed.

- The client code creates different command objects for depositing, withdrawing, and transferring funds, and passes them to the **TransactionProcessor** for execution.

By using the command pattern, we achieve loose coupling between the sender of a request (the client) and the receiver (the **Account** class), allowing for extensibility and flexibility in managing transactions. It also facilitates the implementation of undo operations and supports logging and auditing of transactions.

Chain of responsibility pattern

The chain of responsibility pattern is a behavioral design pattern that allows multiple objects to handle a request without the sender needing to know which object will ultimately process the request. Each handler in the chain either processes the request or passes it to the next handler in the chain. This pattern promotes loose coupling between senders and receivers of a request and enables flexibility in handling requests.

Understanding chain of responsibility pattern

The chain of responsibility pattern consists of several key components, as follows:

- **Handler interface**: Defines an interface for handling requests and optionally includes a reference to the next handler in the chain.

- **Concrete Handlers**: Implement the handler interface and contain the logic for processing requests. Each handler decides whether to handle the request or pass it to the next handler in the chain.

- **Client**: Initiates requests and passes them to the first handler in the chain.

The following is how it works:

- The client sends a request to the first handler in the chain.

- Each handler in the chain evaluates whether it can handle the request.

- If it can, it processes the request, otherwise, it passes the request to the next handler in the chain.

- The process continues until a handler successfully handles the request or until the end of the chain is reached.

Using chain of responsibility pattern

The chain of responsibility pattern is best suited for scenarios where you have multiple objects that can handle a request, and the sender of the request does not need to know which object will ultimately process it.

Following are some situations where you might consider using the chain of responsibility pattern:

- **Multiple handlers**: When you have a request that can be handled by one or more objects, and you want to avoid coupling the sender of the request to specific handler objects.

- **Dynamic handler chain**: When the composition of the handler chain may vary at runtime, allowing you to add or remove handlers without modifying the client code.

- **Sequential processing**: When you need to process a request through a series of steps, with each step potentially handled by a different object in the chain.

- **Fallback mechanism**: When you want to provide a fallback mechanism where if one handler cannot handle the request, it is automatically passed to the next handler in the chain.

- **Error handling**: When you want to implement error handling or exception propagation in a hierarchical manner, with each handler responsible for handling specific types of errors.

Overall, the chain of responsibility pattern is useful when you want to promote flexibility, extensibility, and maintainability by decoupling the sender of a request from its receivers, allowing for dynamic handling of requests in a hierarchical manner.

Implementation of approval handlers in a procurement workflow

Imagine a scenario where a series of approval processes must be applied to a purchase order in a procurement system. Each approval level has a different threshold, and the order must be approved by the appropriate authority based on its total amount. We can implement the chain of responsibility pattern to create a chain of approval handlers, each responsible for approving orders within a specific threshold. If an order amount exceeds a handler's threshold, it passes the order to the next handler in the chain until the order is approved, as follows:

```
// Handler Interface
public interface ApprovalHandler {
    void handleApproval(Order order);
    void setNextHandler(ApprovalHandler nextHandler);
}


// Concrete Handlers

public class JuniorApprover implements ApprovalHandler {
    private Decimal threshold;
    private ApprovalHandler nextHandler;

    public JuniorApprover(Decimal threshold) {
        this.threshold = threshold;
    }
```

```
    public void handleApproval(Order order) {
        if (order.getAmount() <= threshold) {
            // Logic to approve the order
        } else if (nextHandler != null) {
            nextHandler.handleApproval(order);
        }
    }

    public void setNextHandler(ApprovalHandler nextHandler) {
        this.nextHandler = nextHandler;
    }
}

public class SeniorApprover implements ApprovalHandler {
    private Decimal threshold;
    private ApprovalHandler nextHandler;

    public SeniorApprover(Decimal threshold) {
        this.threshold = threshold;
    }

    public void handleApproval(Order order) {
        if (order.getAmount() <= threshold) {
            // Logic to approve the order
        } else if (nextHandler != null) {
            nextHandler.handleApproval(order);
        }
    }

    public void setNextHandler(ApprovalHandler nextHandler) {
        this.nextHandler = nextHandler;
    }
}

// Client
public class OrderApprovalProcessor {
    private ApprovalHandler firstHandler;
```

```
   public OrderApprovalProcessor(ApprovalHandler firstHandler) {
      this.firstHandler = firstHandler;
   }

   public void processOrder(Order order) {
      firstHandler.handleApproval(order);
   }
}
```

In this example:

- **JuniorApprover** and **SeniorApprover** are concrete handlers responsible for approving orders below their respective thresholds.

- If an order exceeds a handler's threshold, it passes to the next handler in the chain until it's approved or rejected.

- The **OrderApprovalProcessor** acts as the client, initiating the approval process by passing the order to the first handler in the chain.

Benefits of chain of responsibility pattern

The chain of responsibility pattern offers several benefits, making it a valuable tool in software development, as follows:

- **Loose coupling**: The pattern promotes loose coupling between the sender of a request and its receivers. The sender does not need to know which object will handle the request, and the receivers are unaware of the sender, allowing for easier maintenance and changes.

- **Flexibility**: The chain can be easily modified at runtime by adding, removing, or reordering handlers without affecting the client code. This flexibility enables dynamic behavior and adapts to changing requirements.

- **Scalability**: As new handlers can be added to the chain without modifying existing code, the pattern scales well with increasing complexity. It accommodates a growing number of responsibilities and handlers while maintaining clarity and manageability.

- **Responsibility decoupling**: Each handler in the chain has a Single Responsibility, focusing on handling a specific type of request. This promotes the SRP and enhances code clarity, modularity, and reusability.

- **Fallback mechanism**: The pattern allows for the implementation of fallback mechanisms where if one handler cannot handle a request, it automatically passes the request to the next handler in the chain. This ensures that requests are processed effectively, even if specific handlers fail.

- **Hierarchical processing**: The pattern facilitates the hierarchical processing of requests, where requests can be handled at different levels of abstraction or by different types of handlers. This enables complex processing workflows and supports layered architectures.

- **Enhanced maintainability**: By encapsulating request-handling logic within individual handlers and organizing them in a chain, the pattern improves code maintainability. Changes to one handler typically have minimal impact on other parts of the system, reducing the risk of unintended side effects.

Overall, the chain of responsibility pattern promotes modularity, extensibility, and maintainability by decoupling components, enabling dynamic behavior, and facilitating scalable and hierarchical request processing.

Practical implementation example of chain of responsibility pattern

The chain of responsibility pattern is ideal for scenarios where multiple handlers are responsible for processing a request in a sequence.

Following are practical examples that demonstrate its implementation:

Example 1: Multi-level logging system in Salesforce

Let us consider a real-world scenario where the chain of responsibility pattern can be applied in Salesforce Apex: a logging system in an application.

In an application, various events, errors, and debug messages need to be logged to different destinations, such as files, databases, or external services. Each log message may have different severity levels, and the logging process may involve multiple steps, such as formatting, filtering, and storing the logs, as follows:

- **Handler interface:**

```
public interface LoggerHandler {
    void logMessage(LogMessage message);
    void setNextHandler(LoggerHandler nextHandler);
}
```

- **Concrete handlers:**

```
public class FileLoggerHandler implements LoggerHandler {
    private LoggerHandler nextHandler;

    public void logMessage(LogMessage message) {
        if (message.getLevel() == LogLevel.DEBUG || message.
getLevel() == LogLevel.INFO) {
```

```
        // Log the message to a file
    } else if (nextHandler != null) {
        nextHandler.logMessage(message);
    }
}

    public void setNextHandler(LoggerHandler nextHandler) {
        this.nextHandler = nextHandler;
    }
}

public class DatabaseLoggerHandler implements LoggerHandler {
    private LoggerHandler nextHandler;

    public void logMessage(LogMessage message) {
        if (message.getLevel() == LogLevel.WARNING || message.
getLevel() == LogLevel.ERROR) {
            // Log the message to a database
        } else if (nextHandler != null) {
            nextHandler.logMessage(message);
        }
    }

    public void setNextHandler(LoggerHandler nextHandler) {
        this.nextHandler = nextHandler;
    }
}

// Additional handlers for other logging destinations (e.g.,
external service)
```

- **Client:**

```
public class Logger {
    private LoggerHandler firstHandler;

    public Logger(LoggerHandler firstHandler) {
        this.firstHandler = firstHandler;
    }
```

```
        public void log(LogMessage message) {
            firstHandler.logMessage(message);
        }
    }
```

- **Usage:**

```
// Create handlers
LoggerHandler fileLoggerHandler = new FileLoggerHandler();
LoggerHandler databaseLoggerHandler = new DatabaseLoggerHandler();

// Chain the handlers
fileLoggerHandler.setNextHandler(databaseLoggerHandler);

// Create logger and log message
Logger logger = new Logger(fileLoggerHandler);
LogMessage message = new LogMessage("Error occurred", LogLevel.
ERROR);
logger.log(message);
```

In this example:

- Each concrete handler for example, **FileLoggerHandler**, **DatabaseLoggerHandler** implements the **LoggerHandler** interface and contains logic to log messages to specific destinations based on their severity levels.

- Handlers are chained together based on the order of their priority.

- The **Logger** class acts as the client, initiating the logging process and passing the log message to the first handler in the chain.

By using the chain of responsibility pattern, the logging system can dynamically route log messages to different handlers based on their severity levels, promoting flexibility and scalability in the logging workflow.

Example 2:

Let us consider another real-world scenario where the chain of responsibility pattern can be applied in Salesforce Apex, that is, a message processing system in a messaging application. In a messaging application, incoming messages need to be processed and routed to different handlers based on their content and type. Each handler performs specific actions on the message, such as filtering, encryption, or forwarding, before passing it to the next handler in the chain, as follows:

- **Handler interface:**

```
public interface MessageHandler {
    void handleMessage(Message message);
    void setNextHandler(MessageHandler nextHandler);
}
```

- **Concrete handler:**

```
public class FilterHandler implements MessageHandler {
    private MessageHandler nextHandler;

    public void handleMessage(Message message) {
        // Filter the message based on predefined criteria
        if (message.containsSensitiveContent()) {
            // Handle sensitive content
        } else if (nextHandler != null) {
            nextHandler.handleMessage(message);
        }
    }

    public void setNextHandler(MessageHandler nextHandler) {
        this.nextHandler = nextHandler;
    }
}

public class EncryptionHandler implements MessageHandler {
    private MessageHandler nextHandler;

    public void handleMessage(Message message) {
        // Encrypt the message content
        // Pass the encrypted message to the next handler
        if (nextHandler != null) {
            nextHandler.handleMessage(encryptedMessage);
        }
    }

    public void setNextHandler(MessageHandler nextHandler) {
        this.nextHandler = nextHandler;
    }
```

```
        }

        // Additional handlers for other message processing tasks (e.g.,
        forwarding)
```

- **Client:**

```
public class MessageProcessor {
    private MessageHandler firstHandler;

    public MessageProcessor(MessageHandler firstHandler) {
        this.firstHandler = firstHandler;
    }

    public void processMessage(Message message) {
        firstHandler.handleMessage(message);
    }
}
```

- **Usage:**

```
// Create handlers
MessageHandler filterHandler = new FilterHandler();
MessageHandler encryptionHandler = new EncryptionHandler();

// Chain the handlers
filterHandler.setNextHandler(encryptionHandler);

// Create processor and process message
MessageProcessor processor = new MessageProcessor(filterHandler);
processor.processMessage(message);
```

In this example:

- Each concrete handler for example, (**FilterHandler**, **EncryptionHandler**) implements the **MessageHandler** interface and contains logic to process the message based on specific criteria.

- Handlers are chained together based on the order of their priority.

- The **MessageProcessor** class acts as the client, initiating the message processing and passing the message to the first handler in the chain.

By using the chain of responsibility pattern, the messaging application can dynamically route messages to different handlers, each responsible for a specific processing task, promoting flexibility and scalability in the message processing workflow.

State pattern

The state pattern is a behavioral design pattern that allows an object to change its behavior when its internal state changes. This pattern is particularly useful when an object's behavior depends on its state and needs to switch between different behaviors dynamically during runtime. At the core of the state pattern is the concept of encapsulating each state of an object into a separate class, where each class represents a specific state and implements the same interface. This allows the object to delegate state-specific behavior to the corresponding state object, making the behavior modular and easier to maintain.

Understanding state pattern

The state pattern consists of several key components, as follows:

- **Context**: The object whose behavior changes based on its internal state. It maintains a reference to the current state object.

- **State**: An interface or abstract class that defines a common interface for all concrete state classes. It declares methods for handling state-specific behavior.

- **Concrete state**: Each concrete state class represents a specific state of the context object. It implements the state interface and provides its implementation for state-specific behavior.

Following is how it works:

- The context object delegates state-specific behavior to the current state object.

- When the internal state of the context object changes, it switches to a different concrete state class.

- Each concrete state class encapsulates the behavior associated with a specific state, making the context object behave differently based on its current state.

Using state pattern

The state pattern is particularly useful in situations where the behavior of an object varies based on its internal state and must change dynamically during runtime.

Following are some scenarios where you might consider using the state pattern:

- **Objects with multiple states**: When an object can exist in different states, each requiring different behavior, the state pattern helps manage these transitions efficiently.

- **Complex conditional logic**: If your codebase contains numerous conditional statements that depend on the object's state, using the state pattern can simplify and modularize the code, making it easier to understand and maintain.

- **Dynamic behavior changes**: When the behavior of an object needs to change dynamically at runtime based on internal or external factors, the state pattern provides a flexible solution.

- **Promoting modularity and extensibility**: By encapsulating state-specific behavior into separate classes, the state pattern promotes modularity, allowing you to add or modify states and behaviors independently without affecting other parts of the codebase.

- **State transitions**: When objects undergo complex state transitions with specific conditions or rules, the state pattern helps manage these transitions and ensures that each state's responsibilities are clearly defined.

Overall, consider using the state pattern when you need to model objects with multiple states and behaviors that change dynamically, and when you want to improve code modularity, flexibility, and maintainability.

Traffic light system modeled using state pattern

Let us consider a traffic light control system where the behavior of a traffic light for example, red, yellow, green, changes based on its current state. We can use the state pattern to model this system, as follows:

- **State interface**:

```
public interface TrafficLightState {
    void handleRequest(TrafficLight light);
}
```

- **Concrete state classes**:

```
public class RedState implements TrafficLightState {
    public void handleRequest(TrafficLight light) {
        // Change state to yellow
        light.setState(new YellowState());
    }
}

public class YellowState implements TrafficLightState {
    public void handleRequest(TrafficLight light) {
        // Change state to green
        light.setState(new GreenState());
    }
}
```

```
public class GreenState implements TrafficLightState {
    public void handleRequest(TrafficLight light) {
        // Change state to red
        light.setState(new RedState());
    }
}
```

- **Context class (traffic light):**

```
public class TrafficLight {
    private TrafficLightState state;

    public TrafficLight() {
        this.state = new RedState(); // Initial state is red
    }

    public void setState(TrafficLightState state) {
        this.state = state;
    }

    public void handleRequest() {
        state.handleRequest(this);
    }
}
```

- **Usage:**

```
// Create a traffic light
TrafficLight trafficLight = new TrafficLight();

// Simulate traffic light transitions
trafficLight.handleRequest(); // Red to Yellow
trafficLight.handleRequest(); // Yellow to Green
trafficLight.handleRequest(); // Green to Red
```

In this example:

- Each concrete state class for example, **RedState**, **YellowState**, **GreenState** represents a specific state of the traffic light and implements the **TrafficLightState** interface.

- The **TrafficLight** class acts as the context class and maintains a reference to the current state. It delegates state-specific behavior to the corresponding state object.

- The **handleRequest** method of the context class triggers a state transition based on its current state, demonstrating how the behavior changes dynamically.

By using the state pattern, the traffic light control system can switch between different states for example, red, yellow, green, seamlessly and adapt its behavior based on its current state, promoting modularity and maintainability.

Benefits of state pattern

The state pattern offers several benefits that contribute to the design and maintainability of software systems, as follows:

- **Modularity**: The pattern promotes modularity by encapsulating the behavior associated with each state into separate classes. Each state class is responsible for managing its own behavior, leading to a cleaner and more organized code.

- **Flexibility**: By allowing objects to change their behavior dynamically at runtime, the state pattern offers flexibility in adapting to different scenarios or requirements. It enables objects to transition between states seamlessly without altering their interface or causing disruption.

- **Simplicity**: The state pattern simplifies complex conditional logic that depends on the object's state. Instead of having large switches or if-else statements to handle different states, the pattern decomposes the logic into smaller, more manageable pieces, making the code easier to understand and maintain.

- **Scalability**: As the number of states and behaviors increases, the state pattern scales well without introducing complexity. New states can be added, or existing states modified independently, allowing for incremental changes and enhancements to the system.

- **Reusable states**: Since each state is encapsulated within its own class, states can be reused across different contexts or objects within the system. This promotes code reuse and reduces duplication, leading to more efficient development and maintenance.

- **Separation of concerns**: The state pattern promotes the separation of concerns by separating the behavior associated with each state from the core logic of the context object. This separation enhances code clarity, making it easier to reason about and test.

Overall, the state pattern facilitates the design of flexible, modular, and maintainable software systems by providing a structured approach to managing object behavior based on internal state changes.

Practical implementation example of a state pattern

The state pattern is often employed in situations where an object's behavior changes based on its internal state.

Following are examples that demonstrate its practical application:

Example 1: Order fulfillment workflow in e-commerce

Let us consider a real-world scenario where the state pattern can be applied in an e-commerce application for managing the order fulfillment process. In an e-commerce platform, orders can have different states such as **pending, processing, shipped, delivered,** and **cancelled.** Each state requires different behavior, such as updating inventory, sending notifications, and tracking shipments. By applying the state pattern, we can model the order fulfillment process efficiently, as follows:

- **State interface:**

```java
public interface OrderState {
    void process(Order order);
    void cancel(Order order);
    // Additional methods for state-specific behavior
}
```

- **Concrete state classes:**

```java
public class PendingState implements OrderState {
    public void process(Order order) {
        // Update inventory, send confirmation email, etc.
        order.setState(new ProcessingState());
    }

    public void cancel(Order order) {
        // Handle cancellation logic
        order.setState(new CancelledState());
    }
}

public class ProcessingState implements OrderState {
    public void process(Order order) {
        // Additional processing logic (e.g., prepare for shipment)
        order.setState(new ShippedState());
    }

    public void cancel(Order order) {
        // Handle cancellation logic
        order.setState(new CancelledState());
    }
```

```
}

// Similar classes for ShippedState, DeliveredState, and
CancelledState
```

- **Context class (order):**

```
public class Order {
    private OrderState state;

    public Order() {
        this.state = new PendingState(); // Initial state is Pending
    }

    public void setState(OrderState state) {
        this.state = state;
    }

    public void process() {
        state.process(this);
    }

    public void cancel() {
        state.cancel(this);
    }
}
```

- **Usage:**

```
// Create an order
Order order = new Order();

// Process the order
order.process();

// Cancel the order
order.cancel();
```

In this example:

- Each concrete state class for example, **PendingState**, **ProcessingState** represents a specific state of the order and implements the **OrderState** interface.

- The **Order** class acts as the context class and maintains a reference to the current state. It delegates state-specific behavior to the corresponding state object.

- Methods like **process()** and **cancel()** trigger state transitions based on the current state of the order, demonstrating how the behavior changes dynamically.

By using the state pattern, the e-commerce application can manage the order fulfillment process efficiently, handling state transitions and state-specific behavior in a structured and modular way.

Example 2: Task lifecycle management in task management systems

Let us consider a real-world example where the state pattern can be applied in a task management system where tasks can have different states such as **open**, **in progress**, **completed**, and **cancelled**. In a task management system, tasks go through various states during their lifecycle. Each state requires different actions to be performed, such as assigning tasks to users, updating progress, and notifying stakeholders. By applying the state pattern, we can model the behavior of tasks efficiently, as follows:

- **State interface:**

```
public interface TaskState {
    void assign(Task task, User assignedTo);
    void start(Task task);
    void complete(Task task);
    void cancel(Task task);
}
```

- **Concrete state classes:**

```
public class OpenState implements TaskState {
    public void assign(Task task, User assignedTo) {
        // Assign the task to a user
        task.setAssignedTo(assignedTo);
        task.setState(new InProgressState());
    }

    public void start(Task task) {
        // Cannot start an open task
        System.debug('Cannot start an open task');
    }

    public void complete(Task task) {
        // Cannot complete an open task
```

```
            System.debug('Cannot complete an open task');
        }

        public void cancel(Task task) {
            // Cancel the task
            task.setState(new CancelledState());
        }
    }

    public class InProgressState implements TaskState {
        public void assign(Task task, User assignedTo) {
            // Cannot reassign an in-progress task
            System.debug('Cannot reassign an in-progress task');
        }

        public void start(Task task) {
            // Task is already in progress
            System.debug('Task is already in progress');
        }

        public void complete(Task task) {
            // Complete the task
            task.setState(new CompletedState());
        }

        public void cancel(Task task) {
            // Cancel the task
            task.setState(new CancelledState());
        }
    }

    // Similar classes for CompletedState and CancelledState
```

- **Context class (task):**

```
    public class Task {
        private TaskState state;
        private User assignedTo;
```

```
    public Task() {
        this.state = new OpenState(); // Initial state is Open
    }

    public void setState(TaskState state) {
        this.state = state;
    }

    public void assign(User assignedTo) {
        state.assign(this, assignedTo);
    }

    public void start() {
        state.start(this);
    }

    public void complete() {
        state.complete(this);
    }

    public void cancel() {
        state.cancel(this);
    }

    // Getters and setters for other attributes
}
```

- **Usage:**

```
// Create a new task
Task task = new Task();

// Assign the task
task.assign(currentUser);

// Start the task
task.start();

// Complete the task
```

```
task.complete();

// Cancel the task
task.cancel();
```

In this example:

- Each concrete state class for example, **OpenState**, **InProgressState** represents a specific state of the task and implements the **TaskState** interface.

- The **Task** class acts as the context class and maintains a reference to the current state. It delegates state-specific behavior to the corresponding state object.

- Methods like **assign()**, **start()**, **complete()**, and **cancel()** trigger state transitions based on the current state of the task, demonstrating how the behavior changes dynamically.

By using the state pattern, the task management system can manage the lifecycle of tasks efficiently, handling state transitions and state-specific behavior in a structured and modular way.

Iterator pattern

The iterator pattern is a behavioral design pattern that provides a way to access elements of an aggregate object, such as a list, collection, or array, sequentially without exposing the underlying representation of that object. It decouples the traversal algorithm from the aggregate object, allowing the same traversal logic to work with different types of collections.

Understanding iterator pattern

The iterator pattern consists of several key components, as follows:

- **Iterator interface**: Defines methods for traversing elements in the collection, such as **next()**, **hasNext()**, etc.

- **Concrete iterator**: Implements the iterator interface and keeps track of the current position in the collection.

- **Aggregate interface**: Defines methods for creating iterators, such as **createIterator()**.

- **Concrete aggregate**: Implements the aggregate interface and provides the concrete implementation for creating iterators.

Following is how it works:

- The client requests an iterator from the aggregate object.

- The aggregate object creates and returns a concrete iterator that provides methods to traverse the collection.

- The client uses the iterator to sequentially access elements in the collection without knowing its internal structure.

Using iterator pattern

The iterator pattern is useful in various scenarios where you must traverse a collection's elements without exposing its internal representation.

Following are some situations where you may consider using the iterator pattern:

- **Encapsulating collection traversal**: Use the iterator pattern to encapsulate a collection's traversal logic within an iterator object. This allows you to hide the details of collection traversal from the client code, promoting encapsulation and abstraction.

- **Uniform traversal interface:** Use it to provide a uniform way to iterate over different types of collections, such as lists, sets, maps, or custom collections. By defining a common iterator interface, you can ensure that client code can traverse any collection using the same set of methods.

- **Decoupling collection and traversal logic**: Use the iterator pattern to decouple the traversal algorithm from the underlying collection implementation. This separation of concerns allows you to modify or replace the traversal algorithm without affecting the collection or client code.

- **Flexibility and reusability**: Use it to improve the flexibility and reusability of traversal logic. With the iterator pattern, you can easily add new traversal algorithms or modify existing ones without modifying the client code. Additionally, the same iterator implementation can be reused with different collections.

- **Support for multiple iterators**: Use it when you need to support multiple iterators for the same collection, each with its own traversal state. The iterator pattern allows you to create multiple independent iterators that can traverse the collection concurrently without interfering with each other.

- **Simplifying client code**: Use it to simplify client code by providing a higher-level abstraction for iterating over collections. Clients can focus on using iterators to access collection elements without worrying about the specific details of collection traversal.

Overall, the iterator pattern is a powerful tool for managing the traversal of collections in a flexible, reusable, and decoupled manner. It promotes encapsulation, abstraction, and separation of concerns, making it easier to work with collections in complex software systems.

Task management system using iterator pattern

Consider a scenario where you have a list of tasks in a task management system, and you want to iterate over them to perform certain operations. By implementing the iterator pattern, you can create a generic iterator interface and concrete iterators to traverse the list of tasks without exposing its internal structure to the client, as follows:

```
// Task class representing a task in the task management system
public class Task {
    public String name { get; private set; }

    public Task(String name) {
        this.name = name;
    }
}


// Iterator interface defining methods for iterating over tasks
public interface TaskIterator {
    Boolean hasNext();
    Task next();
}


// Concrete iterator implementation for iterating over a list of tasks
public class TaskListIterator implements TaskIterator {
    private List<Task> tasks;
    private Integer position;

    public TaskListIterator(List<Task> tasks) {
        this.tasks = tasks;
        this.position = 0;
    }

    public Boolean hasNext() {
        return position < tasks.size();
    }

    public Task next() {
        if (hasNext()) {
            Task task = tasks[position];
```

```
                position++;
                return task;
            }
            return null;
        }
    }


    // Aggregate interface defining method to create an iterator
    public interface TaskAggregate {
        TaskIterator createIterator();
    }


    // Concrete aggregate implementation representing a list of tasks
    public class TaskList implements TaskAggregate {
        private List<Task> tasks;

        public TaskList() {
            tasks = new List<Task>();
        }

        public void addTask(Task task) {
            tasks.add(task);
        }

        public TaskIterator createIterator() {
            return new TaskListIterator(tasks);
        }
    }


    // Client code using the iterator to iterate over tasks
    public class Client {
        public void iterateTasks(TaskAggregate taskAggregate) {
            TaskIterator iterator = taskAggregate.createIterator();
            while (iterator.hasNext()) {
                Task task = iterator.next();
                System.debug('Task Name: ' + task.name);
            }
```

```
        }
}

// Usage
TaskList taskList = new TaskList();
taskList.addTask(new Task('Task 1'));
taskList.addTask(new Task('Task 2'));
taskList.addTask(new Task('Task 3'));

Client client = new Client();
client.iterateTasks(taskList);
```

In this example:

- The **Task** class represents a task in the task management system.

- The **TaskIterator** interface defines methods for iterating over tasks, including **hasNext()** and **next()**.

- The **TaskListIterator** class is a concrete iterator implementation for iterating over a list of tasks.

- The **TaskList** class represents a list of tasks and implements the **TaskAggregate** interface to create an iterator.

- The **Client** class demonstrates how to use the iterator to iterate over tasks in the task list.

- Finally, in the usage section, we create a **TaskList**, add tasks to it, and use the client to iterate over the tasks.

Benefits of iterator pattern

The iterator pattern offers several benefits that contribute to improved code structure, flexibility, and maintainability, as follows:

- **Encapsulation of traversal logic**: The iterator pattern encapsulates the logic for traversing a collection within the iterator object. This encapsulation hides the details of collection traversal from the client code, promoting a cleaner and more modular design.

- **Uniform traversal interface**: By defining a common iterator interface, the Iterator Pattern provides a uniform way to iterate over different types of collections. This allows client code to iterate over collections using a consistent set of methods, regardless of the underlying collection implementation.

- **Decoupling of collection and traversal logic**: The iterator pattern decouples the traversal algorithm from the underlying collection implementation. This separation of concerns enables you to modify or replace the traversal algorithm without affecting the collection or client code, promoting code maintainability and flexibility.

- **Flexibility and reusability**: The iterator pattern improves the flexibility and reusability of traversal logic. You can easily add new traversal algorithms or modify existing ones without modifying the client code. Additionally, the same iterator implementation can be reused with different collections, reducing code duplication and promoting code reuse.

- **Support for multiple iterators**: The iterator pattern supports multiple iterators for the same collection, each with its own traversal state. This allows for concurrent traversal of the collection by multiple iterators without interference, providing greater flexibility in managing traversal operations.

- **Simplified client code**: The iterator pattern simplifies client code by providing a higher-level abstraction for iterating over collections. Clients can focus on using iterators to access collection elements without worrying about the specific details of collection traversal, leading to cleaner and more readable code.

Overall, the iterator pattern enhances code structure, flexibility, and maintainability by encapsulating traversal logic, providing a uniform traversal interface, decoupling collection and traversal logic, promoting code reuse, supporting multiple iterators, and simplifying client code. These benefits make it a valuable pattern for managing the traversal of collections in software systems.

Practical implementation example of iterator pattern

Iterator pattern is a behavioral design pattern that provides a standard way to traverse elements of a collection without exposing its underlying structure.

Following examples demonstrate its application in real-world scenarios:

Example 1: Employee records iterator implementation

Let us consider a real-world scenario where the iterator pattern can be applied in Apex. Imagine you have a custom object called **Employee__c**, and you want to iterate over a list of employee records to perform certain operations, such as updating their information or calculating their salaries. You can use the iterator pattern to encapsulate the traversal logic and provide a uniform way to iterate over the employee records, as follows:

```
// Define the Employee class representing an employee record
public class Employee {
    public String name { get; private set; }
    public Decimal salary { get; private set; }

    public Employee(String name, Decimal salary) {
```

```
            this.name = name;
            this.salary = salary;
    }
}


// Define the Iterator interface for iterating over employee records
public interface EmployeeIterator {
    Boolean hasNext();
    Employee next();
}


// Define the Concrete Iterator implementation for iterating over a list of
employee records
public class EmployeeListIterator implements EmployeeIterator {
    private List<Employee> employees;
    private Integer position;

    public EmployeeListIterator(List<Employee> employees) {
        this.employees = employees;
        this.position = 0;
    }

    public Boolean hasNext() {
        return position < employees.size();
    }

    public Employee next() {
        if (hasNext()) {
            Employee employee = employees[position];
            position++;
            return employee;
        }
        return null;
    }
}


// Define the Aggregate interface for creating an iterator
public interface EmployeeAggregate {
    EmployeeIterator createIterator();
```

```
}

// Define the Concrete Aggregate implementation representing a list of
employee records
public class EmployeeList implements EmployeeAggregate {
    private List<Employee> employees;

    public EmployeeList() {
        employees = new List<Employee>();
    }

    public void addEmployee(Employee employee) {
        employees.add(employee);
    }

    public EmployeeIterator createIterator() {
        return new EmployeeListIterator(employees);
    }
}

// Define the Client class using the iterator to iterate over employee
records
public class EmployeeProcessor {
    public void processEmployees(EmployeeAggregate employeeAggregate) {
        EmployeeIterator iterator = employeeAggregate.createIterator();
        while (iterator.hasNext()) {
            Employee employee = iterator.next();
            // Perform operations on employee record, such as updating
information or calculating salary
            System.debug('Processing Employee: ' + employee.name);
        }
    }
}

// Usage
EmployeeList employeeList = new EmployeeList();
employeeList.addEmployee(new Employee('John Doe', 5000));
employeeList.addEmployee(new Employee('Jane Smith', 6000));
employeeList.addEmployee(new Employee('Mike Johnson', 5500));
```

```
EmployeeProcessor employeeProcessor = new EmployeeProcessor();
employeeProcessor.processEmployees(employeeList);
```

In this example:

- The **Employee** class represents an employee record with attributes like name and salary.

- The **EmployeeIterator** interface defines methods for iterating over employee records, such as **hasNext()** and **next()**.

- The **EmployeeListIterator** class is a concrete iterator implementation for iterating over a list of employee records.

- The **EmployeeList** class represents a list of employee records and implements the **EmployeeAggregate** interface to create an iterator.

- The **EmployeeProcessor** class demonstrates how to use the iterator to iterate over employee records and perform operations on each record.

- Finally, in the usage section, we create an **EmployeeList**, add employee records to it, and use the **EmployeeProcessor** to process the employee records.

Example 2: Invoice processing with iterator pattern

Let us consider another scenario where you have a custom object called **Invoice__c**, and you want to iterate over a list of invoices to calculate the total amount and perform certain operations.

Following is how you can implement the iterator pattern in Apex:

```
// Define the Invoice class representing an invoice record
public class Invoice {
    public Decimal amount { get; private set; }

    public Invoice(Decimal amount) {
        this.amount = amount;
    }
}


// Define the Iterator interface for iterating over invoice records
public interface InvoiceIterator {
    Boolean hasNext();
    Invoice next();
}
```

```
// Define the Concrete Iterator implementation for iterating over a list of
invoice records
public class InvoiceListIterator implements InvoiceIterator {
    private List<Invoice> invoices;
    private Integer position;

    public InvoiceListIterator(List<Invoice> invoices) {
        this.invoices = invoices;
        this.position = 0;
    }

    public Boolean hasNext() {
        return position < invoices.size();
    }

    public Invoice next() {
        if (hasNext()) {
            Invoice invoice = invoices[position];
            position++;
            return invoice;
        }
        return null;
    }
}


// Define the Aggregate interface for creating an iterator
public interface InvoiceAggregate {
    InvoiceIterator createIterator();
}


// Define the Concrete Aggregate implementation representing a list of
invoice records
public class InvoiceList implements InvoiceAggregate {
    private List<Invoice> invoices;

    public InvoiceList() {
        invoices = new List<Invoice>();
    }
```

```
    public void addInvoice(Invoice invoice) {
        invoices.add(invoice);
    }

    public InvoiceIterator createIterator() {
        return new InvoiceListIterator(invoices);
    }
}

// Define the InvoiceProcessor class using the iterator to iterate over
invoice records
public class InvoiceProcessor {
    public Decimal calculateTotalAmount(InvoiceAggregate invoiceAggregate)
    {
        Decimal totalAmount = 0;
        InvoiceIterator iterator = invoiceAggregate.createIterator();
        while (iterator.hasNext()) {
            Invoice invoice = iterator.next();
            totalAmount += invoice.amount;
        }
        return totalAmount;
    }
}

// Usage
InvoiceList invoiceList = new InvoiceList();
invoiceList.addInvoice(new Invoice(100));
invoiceList.addInvoice(new Invoice(200));
invoiceList.addInvoice(new Invoice(300));

InvoiceProcessor invoiceProcessor = new InvoiceProcessor();
Decimal totalAmount = invoiceProcessor.calculateTotalAmount(invoiceList);
System.debug('Total Amount: ' + totalAmount);
```

In this example:

- The Invoice class represents an invoice record with an amount attribute.

- The **InvoiceIterator** interface defines methods for iterating over invoice records, such as **hasNext()** and **next()**.

- The **InvoiceListIterator** class is a concrete iterator implementation for iterating over a list of invoice records.

- The **InvoiceList** class represents a list of invoice records and implements the **InvoiceAggregate** interface to create an iterator.

- The **InvoiceProcessor** class demonstrates how to use the iterator to iterate over invoice records and calculate the total amount.

- Finally, in the usage section, we create an **InvoiceList**, add invoice records to it, and use the **InvoiceProcessor** to calculate the total amount of invoices.

Conclusion

In this chapter, we explored behavioral design patterns, which focus on object interaction and communication to build dynamic, adaptable, and scalable systems. These patterns enable developers to organize responsibilities among objects while maintaining loose coupling, separation of concerns, and flexibility. The observer pattern ensures seamless communication in one-to-many relationships, allowing dependent objects to stay updated on state changes. The strategy pattern promotes dynamic algorithm selection, offering reusability and adaptability. The command pattern simplifies request handling by encapsulating operations as objects, enabling features like undo functionality and dynamic behavior configuration. The chain of responsibility pattern decouples request senders and receivers, creating a flexible chain for request processing. The state pattern facilitates dynamic behavior changes by encapsulating states as distinct objects, simplifying complex conditional logic. The iterator pattern abstracts collection traversal, providing a clean and consistent mechanism for sequential access.

By understanding these patterns, developers can design robust solutions for real-world challenges, such as managing workflows, optimizing communication, and enhancing system scalability. These patterns empower developers to create modular, maintainable, and reusable code, laying a strong foundation for complex software architectures.

In the next chapter, we will discuss Apex specific design patterns, focusing on customization, bulkification strategies, and effective exception handling to further enhance development efficiency.

Points to remember

- Behavioral design patterns focus on object interaction and communication to promote flexibility, scalability, and reusability in software systems.

- These patterns help organize responsibilities among objects, maintain loose coupling, and ensure separation of concerns for better code modularity and maintainability.

- The observer pattern manages one-to-many dependencies, automatically notifying dependent objects of state changes and facilitating event-driven architectures.

- The strategy pattern allows dynamic selection of algorithms by encapsulating each one, making them interchangeable and promoting code reusability.

- The command pattern encapsulates requests as objects, enabling features such as undo operations, logging, and dynamic behavior customization.

- The chain of responsibility pattern decouples request senders from receivers, passing requests along a chain until they are handled, promoting scalability and flexibility.

- The state pattern enables objects to alter behavior dynamically based on their internal state, simplifying complex state management and conditional logic.

- The iterator pattern provides a consistent and abstract way to traverse elements of a collection sequentially without exposing its internal structure.

- These patterns enhance code clarity, support hierarchical workflows, and make it easier to manage complex interactions and state transitions in software systems.

- Real-world applications include event handling with the observer pattern, dynamic shipping calculations using the strategy pattern, and approval workflows with the chain of responsibility pattern.

- Behavioral patterns simplify system design by offering reusable solutions to common challenges, such as communication, state management, and traversal of collections.

By applying behavioral design patterns, developers can create robust, adaptable, and efficient systems tailored to dynamic and evolving requirements.

Questions

1. What are behavioral design patterns, and why are they important in software development?

2. List the benefits of using behavioral design patterns in Apex.

3. How does the observer pattern support one-to-many dependency management?

4. When should you use the strategy pattern instead of conditional statements?

5. Describe how the command pattern can simplify undo operations.

6. Explain how the chain of responsibility pattern enhances scalability in a system.

7. How does the state pattern improve modularity in handling object states?

8. What are the key benefits of the iterator pattern in collection management?

9. Provide a real-world example where the observer pattern can be used in Salesforce Apex.

10. Describe a scenario where the strategy pattern is better than hardcoding algorithms.

11. How would you implement the command pattern in a task management application?

12. Give an example of using the chain of responsibility pattern in an approval workflow.

13. Illustrate how the state pattern can model the behavior of an order fulfillment system.

14. Discuss how the iterator pattern simplifies traversal of custom objects like Employee__c or Invoice__c.

15. How would you ensure that the observer pattern is implemented efficiently in Salesforce?

16. What considerations should you keep in mind when applying the State Pattern in dynamic workflows?

17. Describe how the command pattern supports logging and auditing in Salesforce applications.

Join our book's Discord space

Join the book's Discord Workspace for Latest updates, Offers, Tech happenings around the world, New Release and Sessions with the Authors:

https://discord.bpbonline.com

CHAPTER 8
Apex Specific Patterns

Introduction

This chapter delves into specialized design patterns tailored specifically for Salesforce Apex development. These patterns offer solutions to common challenges and scenarios encountered in Salesforce development, providing strategies for organizing, optimizing, and enhancing Apex codebases. Apex specific patterns focuses on leveraging the unique features and capabilities of the Salesforce platform to build robust, scalable, and maintainable applications.

In this chapter, we will explore a range of patterns designed to address specific needs and requirements of Salesforce development projects. From managing configuration settings with custom settings to implementing efficient trigger logic with the trigger and handler pattern, each pattern offers practical guidance and best practices for tackling common development tasks in Salesforce.

Developers can elevate their skills and approach to building Salesforce solutions by understanding and applying these Apex specific patterns. These patterns empower developers to write cleaner, more efficient code, leverage platform features effectively, and adhere to best practices for Apex development. Whether you are a seasoned Salesforce developer or starting with Apex, this chapter provides invaluable insights and strategies for optimizing your development workflow and building high-quality Salesforce applications.

Structure

The chapter covers the following topics:

- Apex specific patterns
- Trigger and handler pattern
- Bulkification strategies
- Exception management patterns

Objectives

By the end of this chapter, readers will gain a deep understanding of Apex specific design patterns and their practical applications within the Salesforce ecosystem. The chapter delves into areas such as custom settings for managing configuration data, the trigger and handler pattern for separating trigger logic from business logic, and bulkification strategies for handling large data volumes efficiently. Additionally, readers will explore exception management patterns to handle and report errors effectively, ensuring robust error-handling mechanisms in their applications. This comprehensive exploration equips developers with the knowledge and tools to enhance the quality, maintainability, and scalability of their Salesforce solutions. Whether optimizing configurations, streamlining trigger logic, or improving system performance through bulkification, this chapter provides actionable insights to elevate Salesforce development practices.

Apex specific patterns

In the realm of Salesforce development, Apex specific patterns are specialized solutions and best practices tailored for the unique environment of the Salesforce platform. These patterns address common challenges and requirements encountered when developing Apex code for customizations, integrations, and business logic implementation.

Understanding and applying Apex specific patterns can significantly enhance your Salesforce solutions' quality, performance, and maintainability. These patterns leverage the capabilities and limitations of the Apex programming language and the Salesforce platform to achieve efficient and effective development outcomes.

Custom settings for configuration management

Custom settings are a powerful feature in Salesforce for managing custom application settings and configuration data. They provide a convenient way to store and retrieve application settings without hardcoding values in Apex code.

Imagine custom settings as a set of knobs and dials that allow you to fine-tune your Salesforce application's behavior without modifying the underlying code. For example, you can use Custom settings to define thresholds, default values, or feature toggles that administrators or users can adjust without needing code changes.

Custom settings are custom objects in Salesforce that provide a convenient way to store and retrieve application settings. They are similar to custom objects but are specifically designed for storing configuration data.

Custom settings have several advantages over traditional approaches to configuration management, as follows:

- **Flexibility**: Custom settings can be easily modified through the Salesforce UI without requiring changes to code.

- **Global access**: Custom settings can be accessed globally, making them suitable for storing configuration data that needs to be shared across the organization.

- **Hierarchy custom settings**: Salesforce supports hierarchical custom settings, allowing you to define different levels of configuration data for different user profiles or record types.

- **Performance**: Custom settings are cached in memory, making them faster to access than querying custom objects or using static variables.

Types of custom settings

Salesforce supports two types of custom settings, as follows:

- **List custom settings**: List custom settings allow developers to define a list of custom records containing one or more fields. These settings are suitable for storing configuration data with a finite number of records, such as feature toggles or picklist values.

- **Hierarchy custom settings**: Hierarchy custom settings extend list custom settings by supporting hierarchy-based access. They allow developers to define different levels of configuration data for different user profiles or record types. Hierarchy custom settings are useful for defining organization-wide defaults that can be overridden at lower levels of the hierarchy.

Best practices for using custom settings

When leveraging custom settings for configuration management in Apex development, it is essential to follow best practices to ensure optimal performance and maintainability, as follows:

- **Use hierarchical custom settings**: Whenever possible, use hierarchy custom settings to define organization-wide defaults that can be overridden at lower levels of the hierarchy. This approach enables greater flexibility and customization.

- **Limit the number of records**: Avoid creating too many records in list custom settings, as each record consumes a small amount of storage space and contributes to the overall data storage limits. Keep the number of records manageable to avoid hitting storage limits.

- **Cache data**: Take advantage of the built-in caching mechanism for custom settings to improve performance and reduce the number of SOQL queries in your code. By caching custom settings data, you can minimize database access and enhance application responsiveness.

- **Secure access**: Ensure that access to custom settings is properly secured using Salesforce's built-in security features, such as profiles, permission sets, and field-level security. Restrict access to sensitive configuration data to authorized users and roles.

- **Document configuration**: Document the purpose and usage of each custom setting in your Salesforce application to facilitate maintenance and troubleshooting. Provide clear documentation to developers and administrators on how to configure and manage custom settings effectively.

Custom settings and design patterns

Custom setting usage can be enhanced by incorporating design patterns.

The following is how custom settings can be utilized in conjunction with various design patterns in Salesforce development:

- **Singleton pattern:** The singleton pattern ensures that a class has only one instance and provides a global point of access to it. Custom settings can be implemented as singletons to store global configuration data that is accessible throughout the application. By ensuring that only one instance of the configuration class is created, developers can centralize configuration management and avoid data duplication.

Example: Implementing global configuration settings, as follows:

```
public class GlobalConfigSettings {
    private static GlobalConfigSettings instance;
    public String apiUrl;
    public String apiKey;

    private GlobalConfigSettings() {
        // Load configuration from Custom Settings
        ConfigSettings__c settings = ConfigSettings__c.getInstance();
        apiUrl = settings.Api_URL__c;
        apiKey = settings.Api_Key__c;
    }
```

```
    public static GlobalConfigSettings getInstance() {
        if(instance == null) {
            instance = new GlobalConfigSettings();
        }
        return instance;
    }
}
```

In this example:

- We create a singleton class **GlobalConfigSettings** to manage global configuration settings.

- The class has private constructors to prevent direct instantiation and a static method **getInstance()**, to access the singleton instance. Custom settings are inherently cached by Salesforce, so using **getInstance()** avoids unnecessary SOQL queries.

- Configuration data is loaded from custom settings in the constructor, ensuring that there is only one instance of **GlobalConfigSettings** throughout the application.

- **Factory method pattern:** The factory method pattern defines an interface for creating objects but allows subclasses to alter the type of objects that will be created. Custom settings can serve as factory methods by defining different sets of configuration data for different scenarios or environments. Developers can create multiple instances of custom settings, each representing a specific configuration set, and use factory methods to dynamically retrieve the appropriate settings based on the application context.

  Example: Dynamically retrieving configuration settings based on environment:

```
public class ConfigSettingsFactory {
    public static ConfigSettings__c getConfigSettings() {
        if(Test.isRunningTest()) {
            return TestConfigSettings__c.getInstance();
        } else if(UserInfo.isSandboxUser()) {
            return SandboxConfigSettings__c.getInstance();
        } else {
            return ProductionConfigSettings__c.getInstance();
        }
    }
}
```

In this example:

- o The **ConfigSettingsFactory** class provides a factory method **getConfigSettings()** to dynamically retrieve configuration settings based on the execution environment.

- o Depending on whether the code is running in a test context, a sandbox environment, or a production environment, the appropriate custom setting instance (**TestConfigSettings__c**, **SandboxConfigSettings__c**, or **ProductionConfigSettings__c**) is returned.

- **Builder pattern:** The builder pattern separates the construction of a complex object from its representation, allowing the same construction process to create different representations. The builder pattern separates the construction of a complex object from its representation. Custom settings can follow this pattern by allowing developers to dynamically assemble configuration data based on specific requirements. By defining a flexible structure for custom settings and providing methods for building and configuring them, developers can create complex configuration objects with ease.

Example: Dynamically construct custom settings, as follows:

```
// Builder Class for ConfigSettings
public class ConfigSettingsBuilder {
    private ConfigSettings__c settings;

    // Constructor initializes a blank instance of ConfigSettings__c
    public ConfigSettingsBuilder() {
        settings = new ConfigSettings__c();
    }

    // Method to set the environment
    public ConfigSettingsBuilder setEnvironment(String environment) {
        settings.Environment__c = environment;
        return this;
    }

    // Method to set the API URL
    public ConfigSettingsBuilder setApiUrl(String apiUrl) {
        settings.Api_URL__c = apiUrl;
        return this;
    }
```

```
    // Method to set the API Key
    public ConfigSettingsBuilder setApiKey(String apiKey) {
        settings.Api_Key__c = apiKey;
        return this;
    }


    // Build method to return the configured settings object
    public ConfigSettings__c build() {
        return settings;
    }
}
```

Usage example: Dynamically building ConfigSettings

```
public class ConfigSettingsManager {
    public static ConfigSettings__c getSettings(String environment) {
        ConfigSettingsBuilder builder = new ConfigSettingsBuilder();

        if (environment == 'Sandbox') {
            return builder
                .setEnvironment('Sandbox')
                .setApiUrl('https://sandbox.api.com')
                .setApiKey('sandbox_api_key')
                .build();
        } else {
            return builder
                .setEnvironment('Production')
                .setApiUrl('https://api.com')
                .setApiKey('production_api_key')
                .build();
        }
    }
}
```

In this example:

o The **ConfigSettingsBuilder** allows setting individual fields (e.g., environment, API URL, API Key) incrementally.

o Each setter method returns the builder itself, enabling method chaining for more readable code.

- o The builder class handles the construction process, while the **ConfigSettingsManager** orchestrates how the builder is used for different environments.

- o Additional fields or configuration logic can easily be added without modifying the core structure of the builder.

- o The builder class can be reused in various contexts to create **ConfigSettings__c** objects with different configurations.

- **Abstract factory:** The abstract factory pattern provides an interface for creating families of related or dependent objects without specifying their concrete classes. Custom settings can embody the abstract factory pattern by grouping related configuration data under different settings. Each custom setting can represent a family of configurations, and developers can use abstract factories to create instances of these settings based on specific criteria or requirements.

Example: Creating families of related configuration settings:

```
// Abstract Factory Interface
public interface ConfigSettingsAbstractFactory {
    ConfigSettings__c createSettings();
    LoggingSettings__c createLoggingSettings();
}


// Concrete Factory for Sandbox Settings
public class SandboxConfigSettingsFactory implements
ConfigSettingsAbstractFactory {
    public ConfigSettings__c createSettings() {
        ConfigSettings__c settings = new ConfigSettings__c();
        settings.Environment__c = 'Sandbox';
        settings.Api_URL__c = 'https://sandbox.api.com';
        settings.Api_Key__c = 'sandbox_api_key';
        return settings;
    }

    public LoggingSettings__c createLoggingSettings() {
        LoggingSettings__c logSettings = new LoggingSettings__c();
        logSettings.LogLevel__c = 'DEBUG';
        return logSettings;
    }
}
```

```apex
// Concrete Factory for Production Settings
public class ProductionConfigSettingsFactory implements
ConfigSettingsAbstractFactory {
    public ConfigSettings__c createSettings() {
        ConfigSettings__c settings = new ConfigSettings__c();
        settings.Environment__c = 'Production';
        settings.Api_URL__c = 'https://api.com';
        settings.Api_Key__c = 'production_api_key';
        return settings;
    }

    public LoggingSettings__c createLoggingSettings() {
        LoggingSettings__c logSettings = new LoggingSettings__c();
        logSettings.LogLevel__c = 'ERROR';
        return logSettings;
    }
}


// Factory Producer to Get the Appropriate Factory
public class ConfigSettingsFactoryProducer {
    public static ConfigSettingsAbstractFactory getFactory(String
environment) {
        if (environment == 'Sandbox') {
            return new SandboxConfigSettingsFactory();
        } else {
            return new ProductionConfigSettingsFactory();
        }
    }
}
```

Usage example:

```apex
// Example of getting settings dynamically based on environment
public class ConfigManager {
    public static void configure(String environment) {
        ConfigSettingsAbstractFactory factory =
ConfigSettingsFactoryProducer.getFactory(environment);
```

```
                    ConfigSettings__c settings = factory.createSettings();
                    LoggingSettings__c logging = factory.
createLoggingSettings();

                    System.debug('Environment: ' + settings.Environment__c);
                    System.debug('API URL: ' + settings.Api_URL__c);
                    System.debug('Logging Level: ' + logging.LogLevel__c);
          }
}
```

In this example:

o   Abstract factory pattern provides an interface for creating families of related objects without specifying their concrete classes.

o   We define an abstract class **ConfigSettingsFactory** with two abstract method **createSettings()** and **createLoggingSettings()**.

o   Subclasses (**SandboxConfigSettingsFactory** and **ProductionConfigSettingsFactory**) implement this method to create instances of sandbox and production configuration settings, respectively. Each environment has its own settings family, making the pattern scalable for adding more configuration types (e.g., **SecuritySettings**, **DatabaseConfig**).

o   Factory producer (**ConfigSettingsFactoryProducer**) Serves as a central access point for retrieving the appropriate factory instance based on the environment.

o   New configuration families (e.g., **SecuritySettings**, **CacheSettings**) can be added without modifying the existing factories.

o   This allows for creating families of related configuration settings with consistent interfaces.

• **Prototype pattern:** The prototype pattern allows the creation of new objects by cloning (Custom settings are not directly cloneable at the record level unless they are hierarchical settings) an existing object, thus promoting efficiency and reusability. The prototype pattern allows the creation of new objects by cloning an existing object. Custom settings can act as prototypes, where a predefined set of configuration data serves as a template for creating new instances with slight variations. Developers can clone existing custom settings to create new configurations while maintaining consistency and reusability.

Example: Cloning existing configuration settings, as follows:

```
public class ConfigSettingsCloner {
    public static ConfigSettings__c cloneSettings(String
```

```
originalName) {
        // Retrieve the original Custom Setting record
        ConfigSettings__c originalSettings = [SELECT Name, Api_
URL__c, Api_Key__c

                                            FROM ConfigSettings__c
                                            WHERE Name =
:originalName

                                            LIMIT 1];


        // Create a new instance manually as direct cloning is not
supported
        ConfigSettings__c clonedSettings = new ConfigSettings__c();
        clonedSettings.Name = originalSettings.Name + '_Clone';
        clonedSettings.Api_URL__c = originalSettings.Api_URL__c;
        clonedSettings.Api_Key__c = originalSettings.Api_Key__c;


        // Insert the cloned custom setting record
        insert clonedSettings;
        return clonedSettings;

    }
}
```

In this example:

o The **ConfigSettingsCloner** class provides a method **cloneSettings(String originalName)** to clone existing configuration settings.

o The function retrieves an existing custom setting record. It copies its field values into a new instance, maintaining the original structure. Here, it's not used **clone()** directly because Salesforce custom settings do not support it at the database level.

o The new instance has a modified Name (_Clone appended) to differentiate it. Other configuration values are retained, ensuring a **consistent structure**.

o Prototype patterns usually involve deep copies (including references). Here, it manually copies primitive fields.

o This allows for creating new configuration settings based on existing ones with slight modifications.

Trigger and handler pattern

In Salesforce development, triggers are pieces of Apex code that execute before or after records are inserted, updated, or deleted in the database. While triggers provide powerful automation capabilities, they can quickly become complex and difficult to maintain as applications grow. The trigger and handler pattern is a design pattern commonly used to address these challenges by separating trigger logic from business logic and promoting code modularity and maintainability.

Understanding trigger and handler pattern

The trigger and handler pattern is a design pattern commonly used in Salesforce development to manage the logic executed in triggers. Triggers in Salesforce are pieces of Apex code that are executed before or after specific data manipulation events, such as insertion, updating, or deletion of records.

The Salesforce trigger and handler pattern architecture follows a top-down flow, where DML operations initiate a cascade of structured processes through trigger contexts, centralized handler classes, and specific business logic implementations. This architectural pattern ensures clean code organization, maintainable business logic, and proper separation of concerns in Salesforce development.

The following figure illustrates the Salesforce trigger-handler pattern architecture flow:

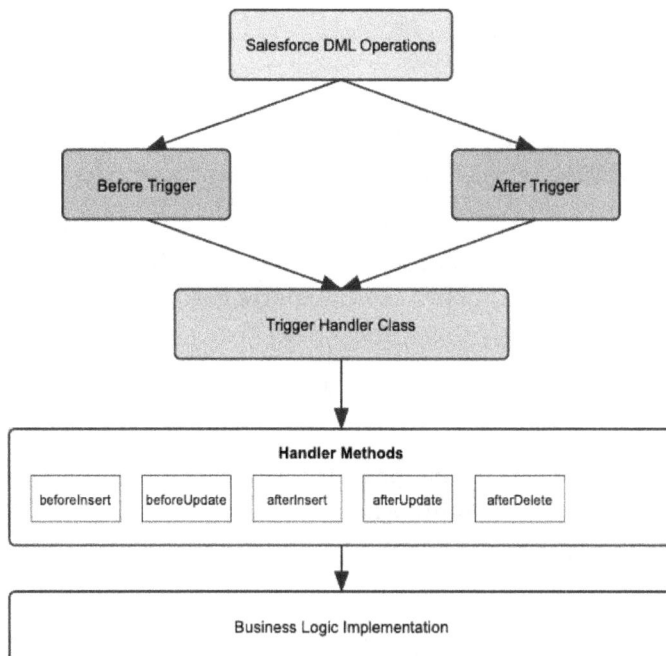

Figure 8.1: *Salesforce trigger-handler pattern architecture flow*

Figure 8.1 explains the following:

- **Top layer: DML operations**
  - This represents the entry point where any data changes occur in Salesforce
  - Could be insert, update, delete, or undelete operations
  - These operations can be triggered by users or system processes

- **Second layer: Trigger layer**
  - Shows two types of triggers that can intercept the DML operations:
  - Before triggers: Execute before the records are saved to the database
  - After triggers: Execute after the records are saved to the database
  - Both triggers act as interceptors but serve different purposes

- **Middle layer: Handler class**
  - This is the central processing unit of the pattern
  - Receives context from both before and after triggers
  - Acts as an orchestrator for all trigger-related operations
  - Provides a structured way to manage trigger logic

- **Fourth layer: Handler methods**
  - Shows specific methods for different trigger contexts:
  - beforeInsert: Logic before new records are created
  - beforeUpdate: Logic before existing records are modified
  - afterInsert: Logic after new records are created
  - afterUpdate: Logic after records are modified
  - afterDelete: Logic after records are deleted
  - Each method handles specific business requirements for its context

- **Bottom layer: Business logic implementation**
  - Where the actual business rules and logic are implemented
  - Contains the reusable code that performs specific operations
  - Separates the implementation details from the trigger handling logic

- **Flow direction (arrows):**
  - The arrows show how data and control flow from top to bottom
  - DML operations trigger both before and after events
  - These events are routed to the appropriate handler class

o   The handler class delegates to specific methods

o   Methods implement or call the necessary business logic

This architecture promotes the following:

- A clean separation of concerns
- Organized code structure
- Easier maintenance and updates
- Better testing capabilities
- Reusable business logic
- Scalable design for complex requirements

Following are the key components of trigger and handler pattern:

- **Trigger:**

  o   A trigger is an Apex code block that is executed in response to specific data manipulation events, such as before insert, after update, etc.

  o   Triggers act as entry points to your Apex logic and are responsible for intercepting data manipulation operations.

- **Handler classes:**

  o   Handler classes contain the actual business logic that needs to be executed when a trigger is fired.

  o   Each handler class is responsible for specific operations or business logic related to a particular object or trigger event. Handler classes encapsulate the logic related to trigger events, making the code more modular and easier to maintain.

- **Trigger context:**

  o   Trigger context variables provide information about the trigger execution context, such as the type of event, for example, before insert, after update, the records involved, and the old and new field values.

  o   Handler classes often use trigger context variables to access information about the trigger event and the records being processed.

Following are the advantages of trigger and handler pattern:

- **Modularity**:

  o   The trigger and handler pattern promotes modularity and code organization by separating trigger logic into handler classes.

  o   Each handler class can focus on a specific aspect of the trigger logic, making the code easier to understand and maintain.

- **Reusability**:
  - Handler classes can be reused across different triggers or trigger events, promoting code reuse and reducing duplication.
  - Common business logic can be encapsulated in reusable handler classes, leading to more efficient development.

- **Testability**:
  - Separating trigger logic into handler classes makes it easier to write unit tests for the business logic.
  - Handler classes can be tested independently of the trigger context, allowing for more comprehensive test coverage.

- **Scalability**:
  - The trigger and handler pattern provides a scalable approach to managing trigger logic, allowing developers to add or modify business logic without impacting existing code.
  - New handler classes can be added to accommodate additional requirements, making the codebase more flexible and adaptable.

Bulkification is a key reason for using the trigger and handler pattern in Salesforce development. Triggers in Salesforce can process one or multiple records at a time, making it crucial to handle bulk operations efficiently to avoid hitting governor limits. The trigger and handler pattern ensures that all records in a trigger execution are processed collectively rather than individually, reducing the number of SOQL queries, DML operations, and processing overhead.

By implementing a handler class, business logic is decoupled from the trigger, allowing reusable methods that batch-process records efficiently. This approach follows best practices by ensuring the following:

- Minimized SOQL and DML operations within loops
- Scalability to handle large data volumes
- Better testability and maintainability

Ultimately, bulkification in the trigger and handler pattern optimizes performance and ensures that triggers comply with Salesforce governor limits while maintaining clean, structured, and efficient code.

Implementation guidelines

It is crucial to follow certain best practices and guidelines to ensure effective implementation and maintainability of trigger-based operations in Salesforce.

These practices help in adhering to coding standards, promoting modularity, and reducing complexity, as follows:

- **Single Responsibility Principle (SRP):**
  - ○ Each handler class should have a Single Responsibility or reason to change, adhering to the SRP.
  - ○ Avoid implementing multiple unrelated functionalities within a single handler class.

- **Separation of concerns:**
  - ○ Keep trigger logic separate from business logic to maintain code clarity and organization.
  - ○ Avoid embedding complex business logic directly within trigger code.

- **Handler composition**
  - ○ Use multiple handler classes to handle different aspects of trigger logic, such as validation, data manipulation, and error handling.
  - ○ Compose handler classes in a way that promotes code reuse and modularity.

- **Trigger context management:**
  - ○ Use trigger context variables to access information about the trigger event and the records being processed.
  - ○ Avoid performing complex data manipulation operations directly within trigger code; delegate such operations to handler classes.

- **Maintain consistency**
  - ○ Adopt naming conventions and coding standards to ensure consistency across handler classes and triggers.

Practical implementation of trigger and handler pattern

Let us consider a scenario where we have a **Case** object with a trigger that executes before records are inserted. We will implement the trigger and handler pattern to handle various operations such as validation, assignment, and notification in separate handler classes, as follows:

```
// Trigger
trigger CaseTrigger on Case (before insert) {
    CaseTriggerHandler.handleBeforeInsert(Trigger.new);
}


// Handler Interface
```

```
public interface CaseTriggerHandler {
    void handleBeforeInsert(List<Case> newCases);
}


// Handler Class for Validation
public class CaseValidationHandler implements CaseTriggerHandler {
    public void handleBeforeInsert(List<Case> newCases) {
        // Perform validation logic
    }
}


// Handler Class for Assignment
public class CaseAssignmentHandler implements CaseTriggerHandler {
    public void handleBeforeInsert(List<Case> newCases) {
        // Perform assignment logic
    }
}


// Handler Class for Notification
public class CaseNotificationHandler implements CaseTriggerHandler {
    public void handleBeforeInsert(List<Case> newCases) {
        // Perform notification logic
    }
}
```

In this example, the trigger **CaseTrigger** delegates the before insert event to the **CaseTriggerHandler** interface, which is implemented by separate handler classes (**CaseValidationHandler**, **CaseAssignmentHandler**, **CaseNotificationHandler**). Each handler class encapsulates a specific aspect of the trigger logic, promoting separation of concerns and code maintainability.

Let us relate trigger and handler pattern to some common design principles and patterns, as follows:

- **Single Responsibility Principle (SRP):**
    - ○ **Relation**: Each handler class in the trigger and handler pattern focuses on a Single Responsibility, such as validation, assignment, or notification, aligning with the SRP.
    - ○ **Explanation**: By adhering to the SRP, each handler class becomes easier to understand, test, and maintain, leading to cleaner and more modular code.

- **Interface Segregation Principle (ISP):**

  - **Relation**: The trigger and handler pattern often utilizes interfaces to define contracts between trigger and handler classes, allowing clients to depend only on the methods they use.

  - **Explanation**: Following the ISP ensures that handler classes implement only the methods relevant to their specific responsibilities, preventing unnecessary dependencies and promoting flexibility.

- **Dependency Inversion Principle (DIP):**

  - **Relation**: In the trigger and handler pattern, trigger code depends on handler interfaces rather than concrete implementations, allowing for decoupling and inversion of control.

  - **Explanation**: By relying on abstractions (interfaces) rather than concrete implementations, the trigger and handler pattern adheres to the DIP, enabling easier maintenance, testing, and extension of the codebase.

- **Factory method pattern:**

  - **Relation**: In the trigger and handler pattern, the handler factory class acts as a factory that creates instances of handler classes based on trigger events.

  - **Explanation**: By employing a factory method, for example, `handleBeforeInsert`, to instantiate handler classes, the trigger and handler pattern follows the factory method pattern, promoting flexibility and extensibility in object creation.

- **Observer pattern:**

  - **Relation**: The trigger and handler pattern can be seen as an implementation of the observer pattern, where handler classes observe and react to changes in trigger events.

  - **Explanation**: By separating trigger logic into observable events (e.g., before insert, after update) and handling them in observer-like handler classes, the trigger and handler pattern exhibits characteristics of the observer pattern, promoting loose coupling and event-driven architecture.

- **Command pattern:**

  - **Relation**: Each handler class in the trigger and handler pattern encapsulates a command or action to be executed in response to trigger events.

  - **Explanation**: By encapsulating commands in handler classes and decoupling them from the trigger context, the trigger and handler pattern resembles the command pattern, promoting encapsulation, flexibility, and reusability of commands.

- **Composite pattern**:
    - **Relation**: In some implementations of the trigger and handler pattern, handler classes can be composed hierarchically to achieve complex trigger logic.

    - **Explanation**: By composing handler classes into a hierarchical structure, the trigger and handler pattern exhibits characteristics of the composite pattern, enabling the construction of complex trigger logic from simple building blocks.

The trigger and handler pattern is a powerful design pattern that enhances the maintainability, scalability, and testability of trigger logic in Salesforce applications. By separating trigger logic into handler classes, developers can achieve greater modularity, reusability, and flexibility, leading to more robust and maintainable codebases.

Bulkification strategies

Bulkification is a crucial aspect of Salesforce development, especially when dealing with large volumes of data. It refers to the practice of designing code to efficiently handle bulk data operations, such as inserting, updating, or deleting multiple records simultaneously. Effective Bulkification strategies help optimize performance, reduce resource consumption, and ensure the scalability of Apex code.

Understanding bulkification

In order to understand the bulkification, you need to understand the key aspects of bulkification.

Following are the key aspects of bulkification:

- **Efficient data processing:**
    - Bulkification involves processing data in batches or sets rather than processing individual records one at a time.

    - By operating on data in bulk, Apex code can significantly reduce the number of database operations, resulting in improved performance and reduced governor limit consumption.

- **Governor limits management**:
    - Salesforce enforces various governor limits to ensure fair resource allocation and prevent abuse of the platform.

    - Bulkification helps developers stay within these limits by minimizing the number of database operations, and reducing CPU time, heap size, and **Data Manipulation Language** (**DML**) statements used per transaction.

- **Scalability:**

  o Applications must be designed to handle increasing data volumes as the organization grows.

  o Bulkification ensures that Apex code can scale efficiently, allowing it to process large data sets without sacrificing performance or exceeding governor limits.

Design patterns for bulkification

Several design patterns and best practices can be applied to achieve bulkification in Salesforce Apex, as follows:

- **Bulk DML patterns:**

  o **Use bulk DML operations**: Instead of performing DML operations inside loops, leverage bulk DML methods like insert, update, and delete to process multiple records in a single transaction, as follows:

  ```
  // Example of bulk insert using List
  List<Account> newAccounts = new List<Account>();
  for (Integer i = 0; i < 200; i++) {
      newAccounts.add(new Account(Name='Test Account ' + i));
  }
  insert newAccounts;
  ```

  o **Aggregate data:** Aggregate data before performing DML operations to minimize the number of records processed. For instance, use SOQL queries with **GROUP BY** clauses to summarize data before updating or inserting records. Here is a sample code to aggregate data with SOQL.

  ```
  // Example of using aggregate queries with GROUP BY clause
  List<AggregateResult> aggResults = [SELECT Industry, COUNT(Id)
  FROM Account GROUP BY Industry];
  for (AggregateResult agg : aggResults) {
      System.debug('Industry: ' + agg.get('Industry') + ', Count:
  ' + agg.get('expr0'));
  }
  ```

- **Query optimization patterns:**

  o **Selective SOQL queries:** Design SOQL queries to retrieve only the necessary data, avoiding unnecessary fields or conditions. Utilize selective filters to limit the number of records returned. Selective SOQL queries help optimize Salesforce database performance by reducing the number of records retrieved, minimizing CPU time, and avoiding governor limits. Poorly optimized SOQL queries can lead to performance degradation, timeouts, and hitting row limits (e.g., "Too many query rows: 50001" error).

Following is a sample code to query optimization patterns:

```
// Retrieve Account records where Industry is 'Technology'
List<Account> techAccounts = [SELECT Id, Name, Industry FROM
Account WHERE Industry = 'Technology'];

// Iterate over the queried records and perform further
processing
for (Account acc : techAccounts) {
    System.debug('Account Name: ' + acc.Name + ', Industry: ' +
acc.Industry);
}
```

o **Use relationship queries:** Leverage relationship queries (parent-child queries) to fetch related records efficiently, reducing the need for subsequent queries or loops.

Following is a sample code to use relationship queries:

```
// Retrieve Opportunity Line Items associated with a specific
Opportunity
Id opportunityId = '006XXXXXXXXXXXXXXX'; // Specify Opportunity
Id
List<OpportunityLineItem> lineItems = [SELECT Id, Name FROM
OpportunityLineItem WHERE OpportunityId = :opportunityId];

// Iterate over the queried Opportunity Line Items and perform
further processing
for (OpportunityLineItem item : lineItems) {
    System.debug('Opportunity Line Item Name: ' + item.Name);
}
```

- **Handler patterns:**

  o **Trigger and handler pattern**: Implement the trigger and handler pattern to encapsulate bulk data processing logic in handler classes. Each handler class can handle a specific trigger event and process records in bulk, promoting code reuse and modularity.

  Following is a sample code to handle patterns:

```
// Example of Trigger and Handler Pattern
trigger AccountTrigger on Account (before insert) {
    // Instantiate handler class and delegate processing
    AccountTriggerHandler handler = new AccountTriggerHandler();
```

```
        handler.handleBeforeInsert(Trigger.new);
}


public class AccountTriggerHandler {
    public void handleBeforeInsert(List<Account> newAccounts) {
        // Logic to process new accounts goes here
    }
}
```

- **Service layer patterns**:

  o **Service layer:** Implement a service layer architecture to centralize bulk data operations and business logic. Service classes can handle complex data manipulation tasks, aggregate data, and perform bulk DML operations efficiently.

    Following is a simple service layer pattern for managing accounts in Salesforce. We will have a service class for CRUD operations on accounts, encapsulating the logic and making it reusable:

```
public with sharing class AccountService {

    // Method to create a new account
    public static void createAccount(String accName, String
accIndustry) {
        Account newAccount = new Account(Name = accName,
Industry = accIndustry);
        insert newAccount;
    }


    // Method to update an existing account
    public static void updateAccount(Id accId, String accName) {
        Account existingAccount = [SELECT Id, Name FROM Account
WHERE Id = :accId LIMIT 1];
        existingAccount.Name = accName;
        update existingAccount;
    }


    // Method to delete an existing account
    public static void deleteAccount(Id accId) {
        Account existingAccount = [SELECT Id FROM Account WHERE
Id = :accId LIMIT 1];
```

```
        delete existingAccount;
    }
}
```

Usage:

```
// Create a new account using the service layer pattern
AccountService.createAccount('Acme Inc.', 'Technology');


// Update an existing account using the service layer pattern
Id accountId = '001XXXXXXXXXXXXXXX'; // Specify Account Id
AccountService.updateAccount(accountId, 'New Acme Inc.');


// Delete an existing account using the service layer pattern
AccountService.deleteAccount(accountId);
```

- **Error handling patterns:**
    - **Bulk error handling**: Design error handling mechanisms to handle errors gracefully during bulk operations. Utilize try-catch blocks and bulkified error-handling techniques to identify and address errors without interrupting the entire transaction.

        Following is a sample code to error handling patterns:

        ```
        // Example of bulkified error handling with try-catch blocks
        try {
            insert newAccounts;
        } catch (DMLException e) {
            for (Integer i = 0; i < e.getNumDml(); i++) {
                // Handle individual errors
                System.debug('Error message: ' + e.getDmlMessage(i));
            }
        }
        ```

Best practices for bulkification

Bulkification is a critical aspect of Salesforce development, especially when dealing with large volumes of data.

Following are some best practices to ensure efficient bulk processing in Salesforce:

- **Use collections**: Instead of processing records individually, gather them into collections (lists, sets, or maps) and perform operations on these collections. This reduces the number of DML statements and SOQL queries executed, improving performance.

- **Bulk DML operations:** Utilize Salesforce's bulk DML operations (insert, update, delete, upsert) to process records in batches. Bulk DML allows you to handle up to 10,000 records in a single transaction, optimizing resource usage and reducing governor limit consumption.

- **Querying bulk data**: When querying records, use selective and efficient SOQL queries to retrieve only the necessary data. Avoid querying fields or records that are not needed for processing to minimize query execution time and reduce governor limits usage.

- **Avoid nested queries and loops**: Refrain from using nested queries or loops within loops, as they can lead to performance degradation and governor limit breaches, especially when dealing with large datasets. Instead, leverage relationship queries and bulk processing techniques.

- **Bulk Apex triggers**: Implement triggers to handle bulk data processing scenarios efficiently. Bulkify your trigger logic to handle multiple records in a single transaction, ensuring that trigger operations scale effectively with increasing data volumes.

- **Asynchronous processing**: Consider using asynchronous Apex (such as Batch Apex or Queueable Apex) for long-running or resource-intensive operations. Asynchronous processing allows you to split large jobs into manageable chunks and execute them asynchronously, preventing timeouts and governor limit exceptions.

- **Governor limits monitoring**: Monitor and analyze governor limit usage regularly, especially during bulk data processing operations. Implement logging and error handling mechanisms to capture and handle limit exceptions gracefully.

- **Testing bulk scenarios**: Thoroughly test your code for bulk data processing scenarios using Salesforce's bulk data load feature or custom test data generation. Ensure that your code performs optimally and remains within governor limits under various load conditions.

By adhering to these best practices, you can ensure efficient bulk processing in Salesforce, improve application performance, and prevent governor limit issues, ultimately enhancing the scalability and reliability of your Salesforce solutions.

Benefits of bulkification

There are main benefits of implementing bulkification, as follows:

- **Improved performance:**
  - Bulkification reduces the number of database operations and improves the overall performance of Apex code.
  - By processing data in bulk, transactions complete more quickly, leading to better user experience and higher productivity.

- **Optimized resource usage**:

    o Bulkification helps minimize resource consumption by reducing CPU time, heap size, and database round-trips.

    o Applications can operate efficiently within Salesforce governor limits, ensuring stability and reliability.

- **Scalability and flexibility**:

    o Bulkified code scales well with increasing data volumes and user loads.

    o Applications can accommodate growth and handle large data sets without sacrificing performance or exceeding limits.

Bulkification is a fundamental practice in Salesforce development, and mastering it is essential for building high-performing, scalable, and reliable applications on the Salesforce platform. By adopting bulkification strategies and best practices, developers can optimize the performance and efficiency of their Apex code while ensuring compliance with Salesforce governor limits.

Exception management patterns

Exception management patterns in Salesforce involve strategies for handling and managing exceptions, errors, and failures gracefully within your Apex code. These patterns aim to improve code reliability, maintainability, and user experience by implementing robust error-handling mechanisms.

Following are the key strategies to implement robust exception management patterns in your Apex codebase:

- **Exception handling strategy**:

    o Define a consistent exception-handling strategy across your Apex codebase to ensure uniformity and clarity.

    o Implement try-catch blocks to capture and handle exceptions gracefully, preventing unhandled exceptions from propagating to users.

    o Use meaningful error messages and logging to provide informative feedback to users and developers.

    ```
    try {
        // Code block where exception may occur
        Integer result = 10 / 0; // Division by zero will cause
    ArithmeticException
    } catch (Exception e) {
        // Exception handling logic
    ```

```
        System.debug('An error occurred: ' + e.getMessage());
    }
```

- **Custom exception classes**:

  - Define custom exception classes to encapsulate specific types of errors or exceptional conditions in your application.

  - Create a hierarchy of custom exception classes to categorize and organize exceptions based on their severity or type.

```
public class CustomException extends Exception {}

public class CustomValidationException extends CustomException
{}

try {
    if (condition) {
        throw new CustomValidationException('Validation
failed');
    }
} catch (CustomValidationException e) {
    System.debug('Custom validation error: ' + e.getMessage());
}
```

- **Error logging and monitoring**:

  - Implement error logging mechanisms to capture and record exceptions, errors, and debug information.

  - Utilize Salesforce's debug logs, platform event logs, or custom logging solutions to track and monitor application errors. Integrate logging with external monitoring tools or services for proactive error detection and troubleshooting.

```
try {
    // Code block
} catch (Exception e) {
    // Error logging
    System.debug('An error occurred: ' + e.getMessage());
    // Log error to custom object, platform event, or external
logging service
}
```

- **Retry and recovery mechanisms**:

    o Implement retry logic to automatically retry failed operations in case of transient errors or temporary failures.

    o Design recovery mechanisms to recover from errors and resume normal operation without user intervention. Use backoff strategies to prevent excessive retries and avoid overloading external systems.

```
Integer attempts = 0;
while (attempts < MAX_RETRIES) {
    try {
        // Code block
        break; // Exit loop if successful
    } catch (Exception e) {
        // Retry logic
        attempts++;
        if (attempts >= MAX_RETRIES) {
            // Recovery mechanism
            // Perform fallback operation or notify
administrators
        }
    }
}
```

- **Circuit breaker pattern**:

    o Implement the circuit breaker pattern to protect your application from cascading failures and excessive load during system outages or degraded performance.

    o Monitor external service dependencies and trip the circuit breaker to temporarily suspend requests when the service is unavailable or experiencing issues.

```
public class CircuitBreakerService {
    private static final Integer FAILURE_THRESHOLD = 3;
    private static final Integer RESET_TIMEOUT = 60000; // 60
seconds

    // Method to check if service is available
    public static Boolean isServiceAvailable() {
        CircuitBreaker__c cb = CircuitBreaker__c.
getInstance('ExternalService');
```

```
        if (cb == null) {
            cb = new CircuitBreaker__c(Name = 'ExternalService',
FailureCount__c = 0, LastFailureTime__c = null, IsOpen__c =
false);
            upsert cb;
        }

        // If circuit breaker is open, check if reset timeout
has passed
        if (cb.IsOpen__c && (System.now().getTime() -
cb.LastFailureTime__c.getTime()) < RESET_TIMEOUT) {
            return false; // Circuit breaker is still open
        }

        return true; // Service is available
    }

    // Method to execute service call with circuit breaker logic
    public static void executeWithCircuitBreaker() {
        if (isServiceAvailable()) {
            try {
                // Simulating an external service call
                callExternalService();

                // Reset failure count on successful call
                resetCircuitBreaker();
            } catch (Exception e) {
                // Increment failure count and possibly trip the
breaker
                handleFailure();
            }
        } else {
            System.debug('Circuit breaker is OPEN. Skipping
request.');
        }
    }

    // Simulated external service call
```

```
    private static void callExternalService() {
        // Simulating failure scenario
        if (Math.random() > 0.7) {
            throw new CalloutException('External service is
down');
        }
        System.debug('External service call successful');
    }


    // Reset circuit breaker on successful request
    private static void resetCircuitBreaker() {
        CircuitBreaker__c cb = CircuitBreaker__c.
getInstance('ExternalService');
        cb.FailureCount__c = 0;
        cb.IsOpen__c = false;
        cb.LastFailureTime__c = null;
        upsert cb;
    }


    // Handle failure and trip circuit breaker if threshold is
reached
    private static void handleFailure() {
        CircuitBreaker__c cb = CircuitBreaker__c.
getInstance('ExternalService');
        cb.FailureCount__c += 1;

        if (cb.FailureCount__c >= FAILURE_THRESHOLD) {
            cb.IsOpen__c = true;
            cb.LastFailureTime__c = System.now();
            System.debug('Circuit breaker TRIPPED!');
        } else {
            System.debug('Failure count increased: ' +
cb.FailureCount__c);
        }

        upsert cb;
    }
}
```

Example usage

```
CircuitBreakerService.executeWithCircuitBreaker();
```

In this example:

- o **Uses custom metadata (CircuitBreaker__c)**: Stores the state of the circuit breaker persistently.

- o **Tracks failure count**: If failures exceed **FAILURE_THRESHOLD**, the circuit breaker is tripped.

- o **Implements reset timeout**: The breaker re-attempts after **RESET_TIMEOUT** milliseconds.

- o **Handles service calls gracefully**: Calls external services only if the breaker is closed.

- o **Prevents overloading unavailable services**: Requests are skipped if the breaker is open.

- o This ensures that **unavailable services do not overload the system**, preventing cascading failures.

- **Idempotent operations**:

  - o Design Apex code to support idempotent operations, ensuring that the same operation can be safely retried without causing unintended side effects.

  - o Use unique identifiers or transactional semantics to detect and prevent duplicate operations during retries or recovery attempts.

    ```
    try {
        // Check if operation is idempotent
        if (!isOperationAlreadyPerformed()) {
            // Perform operation
        }
    } catch (Exception e) {
        // Handle exceptions
    }
    ```

- **Bulkification of error handling**:

  - o Bulkify error handling logic to efficiently process multiple errors or exceptions in bulk data processing scenarios.

  - o Aggregate error messages and responses to minimize overhead and improve performance during bulk operations.

    ```
    public class BulkAccountProcessor {

        public static void processAccounts(List<Account> accounts) {
    ```

```
        List<Account> accountsToUpdate = new List<Account>();
        Map<Id, String> errorMap = new Map<Id, String>();

        for (Account acc : accounts) {
            try {
                // Perform validation or business logic
                if (String.isEmpty(acc.Name)) {
                    throw new CustomException('Account Name
cannot be empty');
                }
                acc.Industry = 'Technology';   // Example update
                accountsToUpdate.add(acc);
            } catch (Exception e) {
                // Capture errors per record
                errorMap.put(acc.Id, 'Error processing Account '
+ acc.Name + ': ' + e.getMessage());
            }
        }

        // Perform bulk update only if there are valid records
        if (!accountsToUpdate.isEmpty()) {
            try {
                update accountsToUpdate;
            } catch (DmlException dmle) {
                // Capture DML-related bulk errors
                for (Integer i = 0; i < dmle.getNumDml(); i++) {
                    errorMap.put(accountsToUpdate[i].Id, 'DML
Error: ' + dmle.getDmlMessage(i));
                }
            }
        }

        // Log or return errors for reporting
        if (!errorMap.isEmpty()) {
            for (Id accId : errorMap.keySet()) {
                System.debug(errorMap.get(accId)); // Replace
with a proper logging mechanism
            }
```

```
            }
        }

        // Custom exception for validation
        public class CustomException extends Exception {}
    }
```

Example usage:

```
List<Account> accounts = [SELECT Id, Name FROM Account];
BulkAccountProcessor.processAccounts(accounts);
```

In this example:

o **Aggregates errors efficiently:** Uses a `Map<Id, String>` to store errors per record.

o **Bulk-safe processing:** Collects records before performing a single DML operation.

o **Handles record-level failures:** Skips invalid records without affecting valid ones.

o **Catches DML exceptions**: Captures partial failures when updating records in bulk.

o **Supports logging or reporting**: Errors can be logged or returned to the caller.

- **Testability and coverage**:

  o Implement unit tests to validate exception handling logic and ensure comprehensive test coverage for error scenarios.

  o Use mock objects and test data to simulate error conditions and verify the behavior of exception handling code.

```
@IsTest
public class ExceptionHandlingTest {
    @IsTest
    static void testExceptionHandling() {
        try {
            // Code block to test exception handling logic
        } catch (Exception e) {
            // Test assertion
            System.assertEquals('Expected exception message',
e.getMessage());
        }
    }
}
```

Conclusion

This chapter highlighted the critical importance of Apex specific patterns in Salesforce development and their role in building scalable, maintainable, and high-performing applications. By understanding and implementing these patterns, developers can enhance their ability to manage configurations with ease using custom settings, streamline trigger logic through the trigger and handler pattern, and ensure efficiency in data processing with bulkification strategies. Furthermore, robust exception management patterns allow developers to address errors gracefully, improving user experience and application reliability. Together, these patterns offer practical solutions to common development challenges and align with industry best practices for designing resilient Salesforce applications. As the Salesforce platform continues to evolve, mastering these patterns empowers developers to adapt to changing business needs, leverage platform features effectively, and deliver impactful solutions with confidence.

In the next chapter, the spotlight turns toward Architectural Patterns in Salesforce. It will cover the **Model-View-Controller (MVC)** pattern in Apex, Service layer pattern: Encapsulating business logic **Data Access Object (DAO)** pattern: Abstracting data access.

Points to remember

- Apex specific patterns leverage Salesforce's platform features to build scalable, robust, and maintainable applications.

- Custom settings provide a flexible approach to managing configuration data without hardcoding, with types such as list and hierarchy custom settings.

- The trigger and handler pattern separates trigger logic from business logic, promoting modularity and easier maintainability.

- Bulkification strategies are essential for handling large data volumes efficiently while adhering to Salesforce governor limits.

- Exception management patterns ensure reliable error handling through consistent strategies, custom exception classes, and logging mechanisms.

- Custom settings integrate well with design patterns like singleton, factory, builder, and prototype for dynamic and reusable configuration management.

- Bulkification emphasizes techniques like bulk DML operations, query optimization, and avoiding nested loops to ensure performance and scalability.

- Asynchronous processing, such as Batch Apex, helps manage large data operations without breaching governor limits.

- The circuit breaker pattern and idempotent operations enhance system resilience during service outages or retries.

- Thorough testing of bulkified code and exception handling ensures robust functionality and comprehensive error coverage.

Questions

1. What are the advantages of using Apex specific patterns in Salesforce development?

2. How do these patterns enhance scalability and maintainability?

3. What is the difference between list and hierarchy custom settings?

4. How does the singleton pattern integrate with custom settings?

5. How does the trigger and handler pattern promote modularity?

6. What principles and patterns align with this design approach?

7. Why is bulkification critical in Salesforce development?

8. How can asynchronous processing help in large data operations?

9. What is the role of custom exception classes in handling errors?

10. How do retry and recovery mechanisms improve system resilience?

11. How can the factory method pattern be used in dynamic configuration management?

12. What is the significance of the prototype pattern in custom settings?

13. Why is caching crucial when working with custom settings?

14. How can developers ensure proper testing of bulkified code and exception handling?

Join our book's Discord space

Join the book's Discord Workspace for Latest updates, Offers, Tech happenings around the world, New Release and Sessions with the Authors:

https://discord.bpbonline.com

CHAPTER 9

Architectural Patterns in Salesforce

Introduction

Architectural patterns in Salesforce delves into specialized design patterns tailored specifically for building robust and scalable applications on the Salesforce platform. These patterns offer solutions to common challenges and scenarios encountered in Salesforce development, providing strategies for organizing, optimizing, and enhancing the architecture of Salesforce solutions.

In this chapter, we explore a range of architectural patterns designed to address specific needs and requirements of Salesforce development projects. From structuring code with **Model-View-Controller (MVC)** to implementing **event-driven architectures (EDAs)** and microservices, each pattern offers practical guidance and best practices for designing scalable and maintainable solutions on the Salesforce platform.

Developers can elevate their skills and approach to building Salesforce solutions by understanding and applying these architectural patterns. These patterns empower developers to design architectures that are flexible, scalable, and aligned with best practices for Salesforce development. Whether you're a seasoned Salesforce architect or just starting with Salesforce development, this chapter provides invaluable insights and strategies for optimizing your architecture and building high-quality Salesforce applications.

Structure

The chapter covers the following topics:

- Architectural patterns
- Microservices architecture in Salesforce
- Serverless architecture in Salesforce

Objectives

By the end of this chapter, readers will understand architectural pattern areas namely, layered architecture, **Model-View-Controller (MVC)**, service layer pattern, **Domain-Driven Design (DDD)**, EDA, microservices architecture, and **Command Query Responsibility Segregation (CQRS)** in Salesforce

By the end of this chapter, readers will have a comprehensive understanding of the various architectural patterns applied in Salesforce development. The chapter explores how these patterns, such as layered architecture, MVC, service layer, DDD, EDA, microservices, and CQRS, contribute to designing scalable, maintainable, and efficient Salesforce solutions. It emphasizes the practical implementation of these patterns to address diverse business needs, enhance system performance, and streamline workflows. Readers will gain insights into how to apply these patterns to solve real-world challenges while aligning with Salesforce's best practices. Through this exploration, developers can elevate their ability to design robust, flexible applications that fully leverage the Salesforce platform's capabilities, ensuring that their solutions remain adaptable to evolving business requirements.

Architectural patterns

Architectural patterns are high-level design structures that solve recurring design problems in software architecture. They offer proven approaches for organizing and structuring software systems to address specific concerns such as scalability, maintainability, and performance. Architectural patterns guide the overall structure of an application, defining how various components interact with each other and how data flows within the system.

Architectural patterns provide a blueprint for designing software systems and help developers make informed decisions about the system's architecture. They encapsulate best practices, principles, and design decisions accumulated over time by experienced practitioners. By applying architectural patterns, developers can create robust, scalable, and maintainable software architectures that meet the system's requirements.

In Salesforce development, architectural patterns play a crucial role in designing solutions that align with best practices, maximize platform capabilities, and meet business requirements. This chapter explores several architectural patterns commonly used in Salesforce development, as follows:

- **Layered architecture**: Salesforce applications often follow a layered architecture, with distinct layers for presentation (Visualforce, Lightning Web Components), business logic (Apex classes and triggers), and data access (SOQL queries, DML operations).

- **Model-View-Controller (MVC):** The MVC pattern is inherent in Salesforce development, with Apex serving as the controller, Visualforce or Lightning components as the view, and Salesforce objects and database operations as the model.

- **service layer pattern:** Apex classes are often organized into service layers to encapsulate business logic and provide reusable functions for various components of the application.

- **Domain-Driven Design (DDD):** Salesforce applications can benefit from DDD principles by focusing on modeling the application domain and creating a shared understanding between domain experts and developers.

- **Event-driven architecture:** Salesforce supports event-driven development through triggers, platform events, and asynchronous processing mechanisms like Apex Queueable and Batchable interfaces. This enables the implementation of event-driven patterns for decoupling and scalability.

- **Microservices architecture**: While Salesforce is a monolithic platform, aspects of microservices architecture can be implemented using techniques such as integrating with external services via REST or SOAP APIs and leveraging platform events for asynchronous communication between services.

- **Serverless architecture:** With the serverless capabilities provided by Salesforce, developers can focus on writing code (Apex, Lightning components) without managing infrastructure. Features like Salesforce functions enable serverless execution of code in response to events.

- **CQRS:** While Salesforce does not inherently support CQRS, patterns resembling CQRS can be implemented by separating read and write operations using different models, for example, standard objects for data storage and custom objects for reporting.

These architectural patterns, among others, provide guidance and best practices for structuring Salesforce applications to ensure scalability, maintainability, and flexibility while leveraging the capabilities of the platform.

Layered architecture in Salesforce

Layered architecture is a common architectural pattern that divides an application into distinct layers, each responsible for a specific set of functionalities. In the context of Salesforce development, layered architecture can be implemented to organize and structure the application to promote scalability, maintainability, and flexibility.

Following figure and the description explains how layered architecture can be applied in Salesforce:

Salesforce Layered Architecture

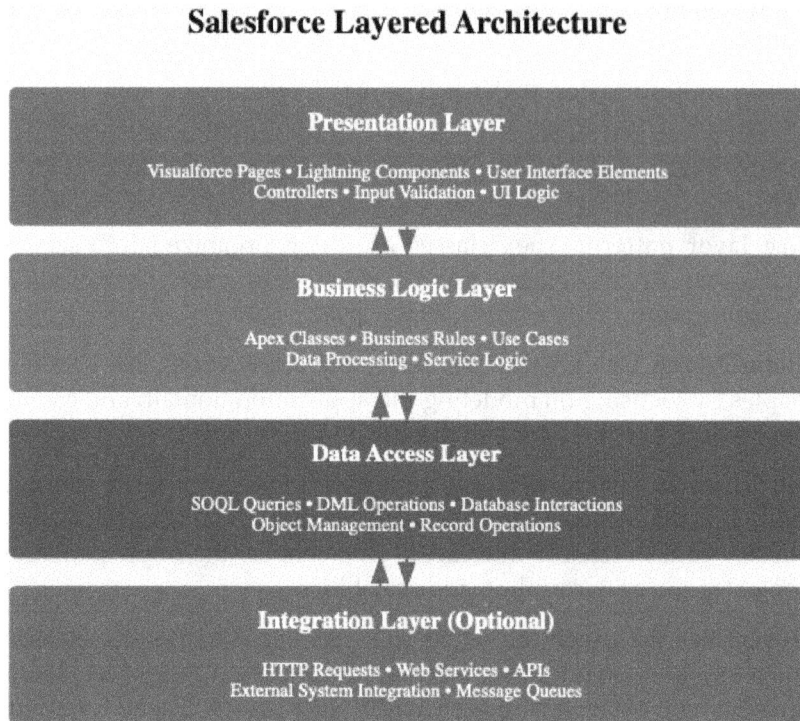

Presentation Layer

Visualforce Pages • Lightning Components • User Interface Elements
Controllers • Input Validation • UI Logic

Business Logic Layer

Apex Classes • Business Rules • Use Cases
Data Processing • Service Logic

Data Access Layer

SOQL Queries • DML Operations • Database Interactions
Object Management • Record Operations

Integration Layer (Optional)

HTTP Requests • Web Services • APIs
External System Integration • Message Queues

Figure 9.1: Salesforce layered architecture

- **Presentation layer:**
    - The presentation layer handles user interactions and renders the UI. In Salesforce, this layer typically consists of Visualforce pages, Lightning components, and other UI elements.
    - Visualforce pages or Lightning components capture user input and display data from the underlying layers.
    - Controllers or Apex classes in this layer handle user input, perform validation, and orchestrate interactions with other layers.

- **Business logic layer:**
    - The business logic layer contains the application's core business logic and rules. It encapsulates the logic that defines how the application processes and manipulates data.
    - In Salesforce, the business logic layer is implemented using Apex classes. These classes contain methods that implement the application's use cases, enforce business rules, and perform data processing tasks.

o The business logic layer should be independent of any specific data storage or UI concerns, promoting reusability and maintainability.

- **Data access layer:**

  o The data access layer is responsible for interacting with the data storage mechanisms, such as databases or external APIs, to retrieve and persist data.

  o In Salesforce, the Data Access Layer interacts with the Salesforce database using Apex **Data Manipulation Language (DML)** operations and **Salesforce Object Query Language (SOQL)** queries.

  o Apex classes in this layer encapsulate the logic for querying and manipulating Salesforce objects and records, abstracting the details of database interactions from the business logic layer.

- **Integration layer (optional):**

  o In some Salesforce applications, an integration layer may be added to facilitate communication with external systems or services.

  o This layer handles integration tasks such as making outbound HTTP requests, consuming web services, or implementing message queues.

  o Apex classes or triggers in this layer manage the integration logic and data exchange between Salesforce and external systems.

Using layered architecture

Layered architecture is a versatile architectural pattern that can be beneficial in various scenarios, particularly in complex software systems like those built on the Salesforce platform. Following are some situations where layered architecture is commonly used:

- **Large-scale applications**: Layered architecture is well-suited for large-scale applications with multiple components and functionalities. By organizing the application into distinct layers, developers can manage complexity more effectively and ensure that each layer focuses on a specific aspect of the system.

- **Modular development**: When a development team needs to work on different parts of an application simultaneously, Layered architecture allows for modular development. Each layer can be developed, tested, and deployed independently, enabling parallel development efforts and faster iteration cycles.

- **Maintainability**: Layered architecture promotes maintainability by enforcing separation of concerns. Changes or updates to one layer can be made without impacting other layers, making it easier to maintain and evolve the application over time. This is especially important in long-lived applications like those built on the Salesforce platform.

- **Scalability**: Layered architecture facilitates scalability by allowing for the horizontal scaling of individual layers. For example, if the data access layer becomes a bottleneck due to increased data volume or user load, it can be scaled independently of other layers to handle the increased demand.

- **Flexibility**: Layered architecture provides flexibility in adapting to changing requirements or technologies because each layer is loosely coupled with the others, components can be replaced or updated without affecting the overall architecture. This flexibility is essential in dynamic environments like Salesforce, where business needs and technologies may evolve rapidly.

- **Security**: Layered architecture supports security by enabling the implementation of security measures at each layer. For example, authentication and authorization logic can be enforced in the presentation layer, business logic layer, and data access layer to ensure that only authorized users have access to sensitive data and functionalities.

Implementing layered architecture in Salesforce

Implementing layered architecture in Salesforce involves organizing your codebase into separate layers, each responsible for specific functionalities and with clear boundaries between them.

Following is a high-level guide on how to implement layered architecture in Salesforce:

- **Identify layers:** Identify the different layers of your application. Common layers in Salesforce applications include the presentation layer (UI), service layer (Business logic), data access layer, and external integration layer.

- **Create separate modules:** Organize your code into separate modules or packages for each layer. This helps maintain clear separation of concerns and makes it easier to manage and scale your application.

- **Presentation layer:** The presentation layer contains the UI components of your application, such as Visualforce pages, Lightning components, or mobile app interfaces. Keep this layer focused on displaying information to users and capturing user input.

- **Service layer:** The service layer contains the business logic and application logic of your application. Create Apex classes to encapsulate business processes, calculations, validations, and other operations. These classes serve as intermediaries between the presentation layer and the data access layer.

- **Data access layer:** The data access layer is responsible for interacting with the database and external data sources. Use Apex classes to encapsulate data access logic, including SOQL queries, DML operations, and calls to external APIs. Separate data access logic from business logic to promote reusability and maintainability.

- **External integration layer:** If your application interacts with external systems or APIs, create a separate layer for handling these integrations. Use Apex classes or callouts to communicate with external systems and encapsulate integration logic within dedicated classes.

- **Define interfaces**: Define clear interfaces and contracts between layers to establish communication and define boundaries. This helps decouple layers and allows for easier testing and maintenance.

- **Enforce separation of concerns:** Ensure that each layer is responsible for a specific aspect of the application and does not encroach on the responsibilities of other layers. Avoid mixing presentation logic with business logic or data access logic.

- **Write unit tests:** Write unit tests for each layer of your application to ensure that individual components behave as expected. Test the interaction between layers using mocks or stubs to simulate dependencies.

- **Adhere to best practices:** Follow best practices for Apex development, such as writing modular, reusable code, using design patterns where appropriate, and adhering to Salesforce coding standards and guidelines.

By implementing layered architecture in Salesforce, you can achieve a modular, scalable, and maintainable application structure that supports flexibility, reusability, and easier maintenance and testing.

Benefits of layered architecture

The following are the benefits of layered architecture in Salesforce development:

- **Separation of concerns**: Each layer is responsible for a specific aspect of the application, which promotes modularity and makes the system easier to understand and maintain.

- **Scalability**: The modular structure allows for independent scaling of individual layers, enabling better performance and resource management.

- **Testability**: Layers can be tested independently, allowing for more comprehensive unit testing and easier identification of bugs or issues.

- **Flexibility**: Changes to one layer can be made without affecting other layers, providing flexibility in adapting to evolving requirements or technologies.

By following the principles of layered architecture, Salesforce developers can create well-structured and maintainable applications that meet the needs of their users and organizations.

Model view controller in Salesforce

MVC is a widely used architectural pattern that separates an application into three interconnected components: Model, View, and Controller. In Salesforce, MVC can be implemented to organize and structure Apex code for better maintainability and scalability. Following figure and the description explains the breakdown of each component in MVC as applied to Salesforce:

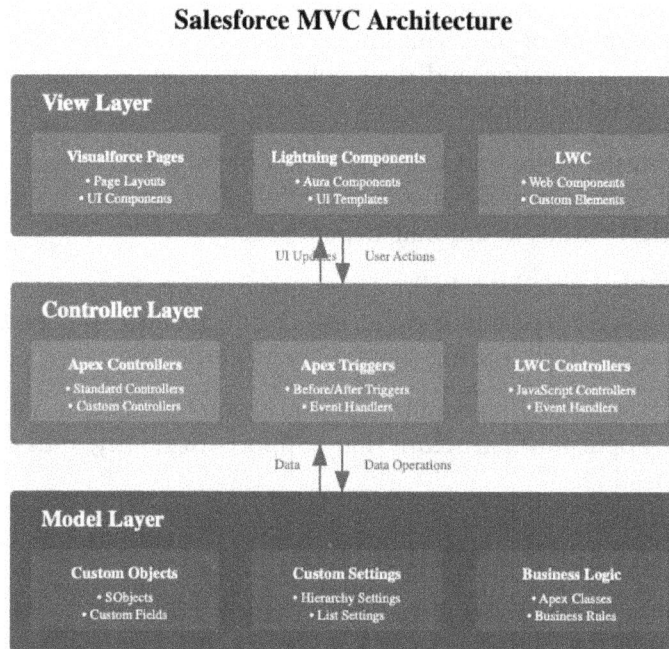

Figure 9.2: Salesforce MVC Architecture

- **Model**:
  - The model represents the data and business logic of the application. In Salesforce, the model corresponds to objects and classes responsible for data manipulation and business rules.
  - Examples of model components in Salesforce include custom objects & standard objects.

- **View**:
  - The view represents the UI of the application. It is responsible for presenting data to the user and capturing user input.
  - In Salesforce, Visualforce pages, Lightning components, and Lightning Web Components serve as the view layer. These components render the UI elements that users interact with.

- **Controller**:

  o The controller acts as an intermediary between the model and the view. It handles user input, processes requests, and updates the model accordingly.

  o In Salesforce, Apex controllers, Apex triggers, and Aura/LWC controllers serve as the controller layer. These controllers receive input from the view, interact with the model to retrieve or manipulate data, and update the view accordingly.

Using Model-View-Controller

MVC architecture is well-suited for various software development scenarios.

Following are some situations where use MVC architecture is particularly beneficial:

- **Web development**: MVC architecture is commonly used in web development frameworks like Ruby on Rails, Django, and ASP.NET MVC. It is suitable for building web applications that require a clear separation of concerns between the data (model), presentation (view), and user interaction (controller). Web applications with complex UIs, dynamic content, and frequent updates can benefit from the modular structure and maintainability offered by MVC.

- **Large-scale applications**: MVC architecture is ideal for large-scale applications with multiple developers working on different parts of the codebase. The separation of concerns provided by MVC allows teams to work on different components independently, reducing the risk of conflicts and making it easier to manage the development process.

- **Cross-platform development**: MVC architecture can be applied to develop cross-platform applications that need to run on different devices and platforms. By separating the business logic (model) from the UI (view), developers can create platform-agnostic code that can be reused across multiple platforms with minimal modifications.

- **Maintainable codebase**: MVC architecture promotes code modularity, making it easier to maintain and update the codebase over time. Changes to one component, for example, the model or view, can be made without affecting other components, reducing the risk of introducing bugs and speeding up the development process.

- **Testability**: MVC architecture enhances the testability of the codebase by allowing components to be tested independently. Developers can write unit tests, integration tests, and end-to-end tests for each component, ensuring that the application behaves as expected under various conditions.

Implementing MVC architecture in Salesforce

MVC architecture in Salesforce involves separating the application logic into three distinct components: the model, the view, and the controller.

Following is a guide on how to implement MVC architecture in Salesforce:

- **Model**: The model represents the data and business logic of your application. In Salesforce, the model is typically represented by Salesforce objects, for example, custom objects, standard objects and Apex classes that encapsulate business logic.

  Following is how you can implement the model:

  o Define Salesforce objects to represent your data entities. These objects will serve as the data model for your application.

  o Write Apex classes to encapsulate business logic, such as calculations, validations, and data manipulation operations.

  o These classes act as the backbone of your application's functionality. Ensure that the model layer focuses on data management and business rules, keeping it separate from the presentation layer and the UI.

- **View**: The view represents the UI components of your application. In Salesforce, the view is typically represented by Visualforce pages, Lightning components, or Lightning web components.

  Following is how you can implement the view:

  o Create Visualforce pages or Lightning components to render the UI elements, for example, forms, tables, buttons based on the data provided by the controller.

  o Use Visualforce markup or Lightning component markup to define the layout and appearance of the UI elements.

  o Ensure that the view layer is responsible for presenting data to users and capturing user input, without containing any business logic.

- **Controller**: The controller acts as an intermediary between the model and the view, handling user input, processing data, and coordinating interactions between the model and the view. In Salesforce, the controller is typically represented by Apex classes.

  Following is how you can implement the controller:

  o Write Apex classes to handle user interactions, such as submitting forms, clicking buttons, or making API requests.

  o Implement methods in Apex classes to interact with the model layer, fetching data from Salesforce objects, performing business logic operations, and updating records.

  o Ensure that the controller layer orchestrates the flow of data and actions between the model and the view, without containing any business logic or presentation logic.

- **Establish communication**: Use Apex properties, methods, and data binding techniques to establish communication between the model, the view, and the controller. Pass data between layers as needed to ensure seamless interaction and synchronization.

- **Adhere to MVC principles**: Follow the principles of MVC architecture, such as separation of concerns, modularity, and reusability. Keep each component (Model, View, Controller) focused on its specific responsibilities and avoid mixing presentation logic with business logic or data access logic.

- **Write unit tests**: Write unit tests for each component (Model, View, Controller) to ensure that they behave as expected and interact correctly with each other. Test the integration between components using mock objects or stubs to simulate dependencies.

By implementing MVC architecture in Salesforce, you can achieve a well-structured, modular, and maintainable application design that separates concerns, promotes code reusability, and facilitates easier maintenance and testing.

Benefits of Model-View-Controller

MVC architectural pattern offers several benefits that contribute to the development of scalable, maintainable, and robust software applications.

Following are some key advantages of using MVC:

- **Separation of concerns**: MVC separates the application into three distinct components, that is, model, view, and controller. This separation ensures that each component has a specific responsibility, making the codebase more modular and easier to understand. Developers can focus on implementing business logic (model), UI (view), and request handling (controller) separately, leading to cleaner and more maintainable code.

- **Modularity and reusability**: MVC promotes modularity by breaking down the application into smaller, reusable components. Each component can be developed independently and reused across different parts of the application or in other projects. This reduces redundancy, improves code organization, and speeds up development time.

- **Scalability**: MVC facilitates scalability by allowing developers to add new features or modify existing ones without affecting other parts of the application. As the application grows in complexity or user base, developers can easily extend or enhance specific components without rewriting the entire codebase. This makes it easier to accommodate changing requirements and scale the application as needed.

- **Maintainability**: MVC enhances maintainability by providing a clear separation between different layers of the application. Changes to one component (e.g., the model or view) can be made without impacting other components, reducing the risk of unintended side effects. This makes it easier to debug, test, and maintain the codebase over time, leading to fewer bugs and faster development cycles.

- **Testability**: MVC improves testability by decoupling components and reducing dependencies between them. Each component can be tested independently using unit tests, integration tests, or end-to-end tests, ensuring that it behaves as expected under various conditions. This enables developers to identify and fix issues early in the development process, resulting in higher software quality and reliability.

Service layer pattern in Salesforce

The service layer pattern in Salesforce is a design pattern that helps to organize and centralize business logic and data operations within an application. It encapsulates complex business logic into reusable services, providing an abstraction layer between the presentation layer (UI) and the data access layer (database operations).

The service layer pattern in Salesforce typically consists of the following components:

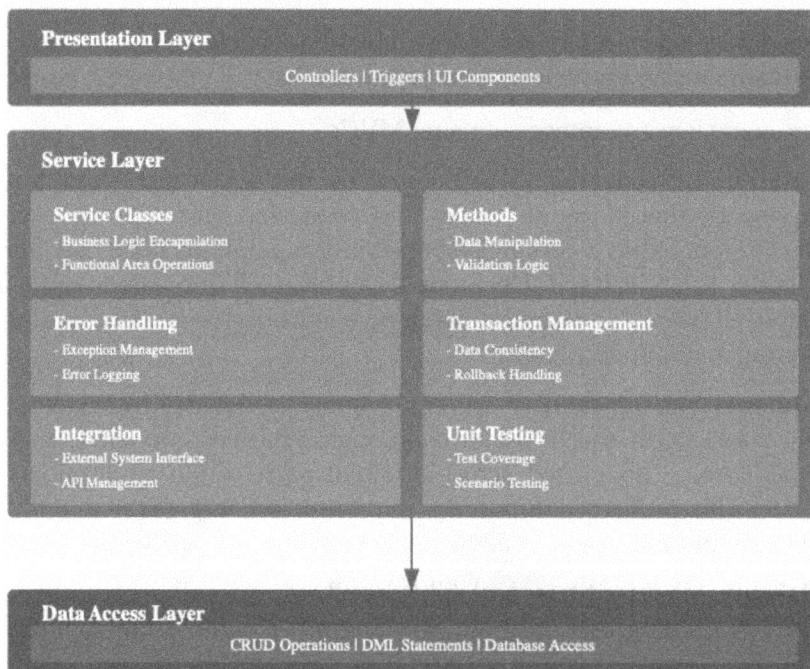

Figure 9.3: Service layer pattern in Salesforce

- **Service classes:** Apex classes encapsulate business logic and operations related to specific functional areas or entities within the application. Each service class represents a service layer responsible for performing related operations.

- **Methods**: Granular methods are defined within service classes to perform specific tasks or operations. These methods encapsulate business logic, data manipulation, validation, and other processing required by the application.

- **Data access:** Interaction with Salesforce database objects such as records, fields, and relationships to perform **Create, Read, Update, Delete (CRUD)** operations, using DML statements.

- **Business logic**: Implementation of business rules, calculations, validations, and other complex logic required by the application. This includes enforcing data integrity, applying security rules, and ensuring compliance with business requirements.

- **Error handling**: Handling exceptions and errors gracefully within the service layer, providing meaningful error messages to users and logging relevant information for troubleshooting purposes.

- **Transaction management**: Ensuring that operations are executed within appropriate transaction boundaries to maintain data consistency and integrity. This includes handling transactional behavior, rollbacks, and save points as needed.

- **Integration**: Interface with external systems or APIs if required, performing data exchange, synchronization, or integration tasks. This can include making outbound web service callouts, parsing responses, and handling asynchronous processing.

- **Dependency injection (optional):** Utilizing dependency injection techniques to inject dependencies into service classes, making them more modular, flexible, and testable. Dependencies can include other services, utility classes, or external resources.

- **Unit testing**: Writing unit tests for each service method to ensure that they behave as expected under various scenarios. This includes testing both positive and negative cases, boundary conditions, and error-handling paths.

- **Usage in controllers or triggers**: Invoking the service layer from Apex controllers, triggers, or other components to execute the encapsulated business logic. This promotes code reuse, reduces duplication, and maintains a clear separation of concerns between the presentation and business logic layers.

By structuring your Salesforce application using the service layer pattern and incorporating these components, you can achieve a more modular, maintainable, and scalable architecture. This approach promotes code organization, reusability, and testability, facilitating easier development, testing, and maintenance of your Salesforce applications.

Using service layer pattern

The service layer pattern is beneficial in various scenarios within Salesforce applications.

Following are some situations where, using the service layer pattern is advantageous:

- **Complex business logic**: When your Salesforce application involves complex business logic, calculations, validations, or workflows that span multiple objects or modules, the service layer pattern helps encapsulate and manage this logic effectively. By centralizing business logic within service classes, you can ensure consistency, maintainability, and reusability across your application.

- **Modularity and separation of concerns:** If you want to maintain a clear separation of concerns and avoid tightly coupling your business logic with other layers of your application (such as controllers or triggers), the service layer pattern provides a structured approach. It allows you to isolate business logic into dedicated service classes, promoting modularity, flexibility, and easier maintenance.

- **Code reusability and maintainability**: When you anticipate the need to reuse certain business logic across multiple components or scenarios within your application, the service layer pattern facilitates code reuse. By encapsulating common operations and functionalities within service methods, you can avoid duplicating code and promote maintainability by centralizing logic in one place.

- **Testing and testability**: If you value testability and want to write comprehensive unit tests for your Salesforce application, the service layer pattern is beneficial. It allows you to write focused unit tests for individual service methods, mock dependencies as needed, and validating the behavior of business logic in isolation. This promotes robust testing practices and helps identify and prevent regressions.

- **Transaction management**: When your application requires transactional integrity for complex operations involving multiple database transactions, the service layer pattern can help manage transactions effectively. Service methods can encapsulate transactional behavior, ensuring that operations are executed within appropriate transaction boundaries and providing error handling and rollback mechanisms when necessary.

- **Integration with external systems**: If your Salesforce application interacts with external systems or APIs, the service layer pattern facilitates integration tasks. Service methods can encapsulate integration logic, making outbound web service callouts, processing responses, and handling data exchange tasks in a structured manner. This promotes reusability and maintainability of integration code.

- **Scalability and performance**: When designing for scalability and performance, the service layer pattern can help optimize resource utilization and minimize overhead. By centralizing and optimizing business logic within service classes, you can improve code efficiency, reduce code duplication, and streamline application performance.

Implementing service layer pattern in Salesforce

Implementing the service layer pattern in Salesforce involves structuring your Apex code to encapsulate business logic within dedicated service classes.

Following are the steps on how to implement this pattern:

1. **Identify business logic**: Identify the business logic or operations that need to be encapsulated and managed within your Salesforce application. This may include operations such as data manipulation, calculations, validations, and integrations with external systems.

2. **Create service classes**: Create Apex classes to serve as service classes. These classes will contain methods that encapsulate specific business logic or operations. Each service class should focus on a specific domain or functionality within your application.

3. **Define service methods**: Within each service class, define methods to encapsulate individual business operations. These methods should have clear and descriptive names that reflect their purpose. Aim for granular methods that perform specific tasks to promote reusability and maintainability.

4. **Encapsulate logic**: Implement the business logic or operations within the service methods. This may involve querying and manipulating data, performing calculations, invoking external APIs, or orchestrating complex workflows. Keep the logic cohesive and organized within each method.

5. **Handle transactions**: Consider transaction management within your service methods, especially if they involve multiple database operations that need to be executed atomically. Use Salesforce's transaction control mechanisms such as `Database.insert`, `Database.update`, `Database.delete`, and `Database.rollback` to manage transactions effectively.

6. **Implement error handling**: Implement error handling within your service methods to handle exceptions and errors gracefully. Use try-catch blocks to catch and handle exceptions, and consider using custom exception classes or error messages to provide meaningful feedback to callers.

7. **Promote reusability**: Design your service methods to be reusable across different parts of your application. Avoid hardcoding values or assumptions that limit the flexibility and reusability of the methods. Instead, make use of parameters and configurable options to customize behavior as needed.

8. **Unit testing**: Write unit tests for your service methods to ensure they behave as expected under various conditions. Test both the positive and negative scenarios, including edge cases and error conditions. Use mocking frameworks like ApexMocks or Stub API to mock dependencies and isolate the code under test.

9. **Integration and callouts**: If your service methods interact with external systems or make callouts to web services, implement integration logic within the service classes. Consider using Apex HTTP classes or third-party libraries for making HTTP callouts, and handle response parsing and error handling within the service methods.

10. **Documentation and usage guidelines**: Document your service classes and methods to provide usage guidelines and information for developers consuming the service layer. Include descriptions of each method, expected inputs and outputs, error-handling strategies, and any other relevant details.

By following these steps, you can effectively implement the service layer pattern in Salesforce to encapsulate and manage your application's business logic in a structured and maintainable manner.

Benefits of service layer pattern

The service layer pattern offers several benefits when implemented in Salesforce or any software application, as follows:

- **Encapsulation of business logic:** Service layer classes encapsulate business logic, ensuring that it is centralized and easily accessible. This promotes code organization and maintainability by keeping related functionality grouped.

- **Modular design**: By breaking down business operations into separate service methods, the application becomes more modular. This modular design allows for easier comprehension, testing, and modification of individual functionalities without affecting other parts of the application.

- **Reusability:** Service layer methods are designed to be reusable across different components of the application. Once implemented, they can be invoked from various triggers, controllers, or other service methods, reducing redundancy, and promoting code reuse.

- **Separation of concerns**: The service layer pattern helps in separating concerns within the application. Business logic is separated from presentation logic (such as Visualforce pages or Lightning components) and data access logic (such as queries or DML operations), leading to cleaner and more maintainable code.

- **Transaction management**: Service layer methods can handle transactions effectively, ensuring that multiple database operations are executed atomically. This helps maintain data integrity and consistency by rolling back changes in case of errors or exceptions.

- **Promotes testability**: With business logic encapsulated within service methods, unit testing becomes more straightforward. Developers can write focused unit tests to verify the behavior of individual service methods, promoting code quality and reliability.

- **Improved error handling**: Service layer methods can implement robust error handling mechanisms, catching exceptions and errors at the appropriate level. This allows for graceful error recovery, logging, and providing meaningful feedback to users or calling components.

- **Facilitates integration**: Service layer classes can encapsulate integration logic with external systems or APIs. This abstraction simplifies the integration process, making it easier to modify or replace integration endpoints without affecting the rest of the application.

- **Scalability and flexibility**: A well-designed service layer promotes scalability and flexibility in the application architecture. As the application grows or requirements change, new service methods can be added or existing ones modified with minimal impact on other parts of the system.

Overall, the service layer pattern contributes to cleaner, more modular, and maintainable codebases in Salesforce applications, leading to improved developer productivity and enhanced application reliability.

Domain-Driven Design in Salesforce

Domain-Driven Design (**DDD**) is an approach to software development that emphasizes the importance of understanding the domain or problem space of an application and modeling it in code. While DDD principles can be applied to various software projects, including those built on the Salesforce platform, some adaptations may be necessary due to Salesforce's specific architecture and constraints.

In Salesforce, the domain typically revolves around the business processes and data model of the organization. DDD principles can help design a Salesforce solution that closely aligns with the business requirements and optimizes flexibility, maintainability, and scalability.

Following is how DDD concepts can be applied in Salesforce:

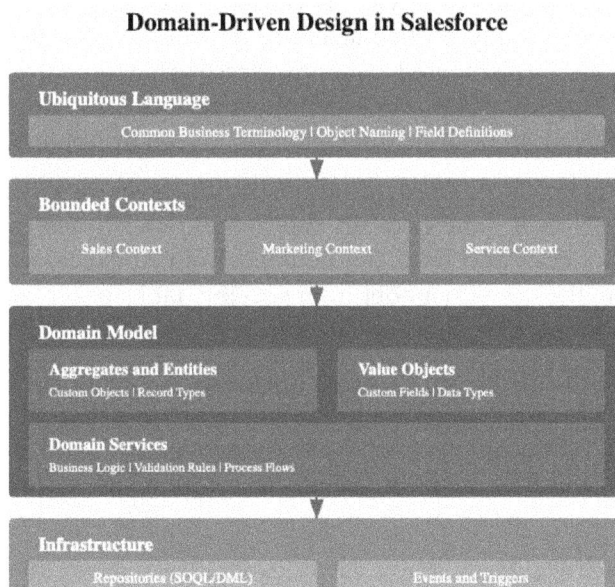

Figure 9.4: *Domain-Driven Design in Salesforce*

- **Ubiquitous language**: DDD encourages the use of a common, shared language between business stakeholders and developers to ensure clarity and alignment. In Salesforce, this involves using terminology that reflects the business domain when naming objects, fields, classes, and methods. By speaking the same language, everyone involved in the project can better understand and communicate about the solution.

- **Bounded contexts:** In DDD, bounded contexts define clear boundaries within which a particular model is valid and applicable. In Salesforce, bounded contexts can be represented by different modules, applications, or even Salesforce orgs, each focusing on a specific aspect of the business domain. For example, a Salesforce org might have separate bounded contexts for sales, marketing, and customer support, each with its own set of objects, processes, and rules.

- **Aggregates and entities:** DDD introduces the concept of aggregates, which are clusters of related objects treated as a single unit for data consistency and transactional integrity. In Salesforce, custom objects often represent aggregates, with child records (such as related list items) encapsulated within the parent object. Entities, on the other hand, represent individual domain objects with their own identity and lifecycle.

- **Value objects:** Value objects are immutable objects that represent attributes or characteristics of domain concepts. In Salesforce, value objects can be represented as custom data types, such as custom fields on objects or composite data structures returned by Apex methods. Using value objects can help in modeling complex domain concepts more accurately and efficiently.

- **Domain services:** Domain services encapsulate domain-specific logic that doesn't naturally belong to any particular entity or value object. In Salesforce, domain services can be implemented as Apex classes that operate on domain objects and enforce business rules. For example, a service class might handle complex validation logic or orchestrate interactions between multiple objects.

- **Repositories:** Repositories provide an abstraction layer for accessing and persisting domain objects in a data store. In Salesforce, repositories can be implemented using SOQL queries and DML operations within Apex classes. Repositories help in decoupling the domain model from specific data storage mechanisms, making the application more flexible and testable.

- **Event-driven architecture**: DDD encourages EDA, where domain events are used to communicate changes and trigger reactions across different parts of the system. In Salesforce, platform events or Apex triggers can be used to implement event-driven communication between Salesforce components or integrate with external systems.

Using Domain-Driven Design

The DDD is beneficial in various scenarios within Salesforce applications. Following are some situations where using the DDD is advantageous:

- **Complex business domains:** DDD is particularly beneficial when dealing with complex business domains where the requirements are not fully understood upfront or are subject to frequent changes. By focusing on the domain, DDD helps in modeling and managing the complexity inherent in such domains.

- **Large-scale applications:** For large-scale Salesforce applications with multiple modules, integrations, and business processes, DDD provides a structured approach to organizing and managing the complexity. It allows teams to break down the system into smaller, more manageable parts, each focusing on a specific aspect of the domain.

- **Collaborative development:** DDD promotes collaboration between business stakeholders and development teams by using a common, shared language to discuss and model the domain. This collaborative approach ensures that the resulting solution meets the needs of the business and reflects the domain accurately.

Implementing Domain-Driven Design in Salesforce

Implementing DDD in Salesforce involves several key steps to effectively model the domain, encapsulate business logic, and create a solution that closely aligns with the business requirements.

Following is a high-level overview of how to implement DDD principles in Salesforce:

- **Identify the core domain**: Start by identifying the core domain of your Salesforce application, the part of the business that provides the most value or differentiation. This could include areas such as sales, customer service, marketing, or custom business processes.

- **Understand the domain:** Work closely with business stakeholders to gain a deep understanding of the domain, including key concepts, rules, and processes. Use techniques such as domain modeling workshops, interviews, and documentation review to gather domain knowledge.

- **Model the domain:** Based on your understanding of the domain, create a domain model that accurately represents the key concepts, relationships, and rules. Use DDD concepts such as entities, value objects, aggregates, and bounded contexts to model the domain effectively.

- **Use ubiquitous language**: Establish a ubiquitous language, a common, shared vocabulary for discussing the domain between business stakeholders and development teams. Use the same terminology in code, documentation, and conversations to ensure clarity and alignment.

- **Encapsulate business logic**: Implement domain logic in Apex classes, methods, and triggers that are specific to the domain. Use domain services to encapsulate complex business rules and processes that don't naturally belong to any particular object. Aim for a clear separation of concerns and avoid mixing domain logic with infrastructure or presentation concerns.

- **Define aggregate roots**: Identify aggregate roots, top-level entities that serve as the entry points to the domain and ensure that all changes to related entities are made through the aggregate roots. Use aggregate design to maintain consistency and enforce transactional integrity within the domain.

- **Implement repositories**: Use repository patterns to encapsulate data access logic and provide a unified interface for interacting with domain objects. Implement custom repository classes in Apex to perform CRUD operations on Salesforce objects, using SOQL queries and DML operations as needed.

- **Apply event-driven architecture:** Leverage EDA to implement asynchronous communication and decouple Salesforce components or integrate with external systems. Use platform events, Apex triggers, or other mechanisms to publish and subscribe to domain events that signal changes and trigger reactions across different parts of the system.

- **Test domain logic**: Write comprehensive unit tests to validate the behavior of domain logic and ensure that it meets the expected requirements. Use test TDD practices to drive the design of domain classes and ensure test coverage for critical business rules and edge cases.

- **Iterate and refine**: Continuously iterate and refine your domain model and implementation based on feedback from stakeholders, changes in requirements, and lessons learned from implementation. Keep the domain model flexible and adaptable to accommodate future changes and evolving business needs.

By following these steps and principles, you can effectively implement DDD in Salesforce and create solutions that are closely aligned with the business domain, flexible, maintainable, and scalable.

Benefits of Domain-Driven Design

DDD offers several benefits when applied effectively in Salesforce development, as follows:

- **Alignment with business requirements**: DDD encourages close collaboration between business stakeholders and development teams, leading to a shared understanding of the domain and its requirements. By modeling the domain using a ubiquitous language and focusing on core business concepts, DDD ensures that the resulting solution closely aligns with the needs of the business.

- **Improved maintainability**: DDD promotes modular and well-structured code by encapsulating domain logic within domain objects and services. This modularization makes it easier to understand, modify, and extend the codebase over time, leading to improved maintainability and reduced technical debt.

- **Flexibility and adaptability**: DDD emphasizes the creation of a flexible and adaptable domain model that can evolve with changing business requirements. By using concepts such as aggregates, bounded contexts, and domain events, DDD enables developers to model complex domains in a way that accommodates future changes without extensive rework.

- **Clear separation of concerns**: DDD encourages a clear separation of concerns by dividing the application into distinct layers and components, each responsible for a specific aspect of the system. This separation makes the codebase easier to manage, test, and maintain, leading to improved overall quality and reliability.

- **Reduced complexity**: By focusing on the core domain and modeling complex business concepts using DDD patterns, DDD helps to reduce the overall complexity of the system. This simplification makes it easier for developers to reason about the code and reduces the risk of introducing errors or inconsistencies.

- **Increased collaboration**: DDD fosters collaboration between different roles within the development team, including developers, domain experts, and testers. By using a ubiquitous language and working closely together to refine the domain model, teams can ensure that the resulting solution meets the needs of all stakeholders and delivers maximum value.

- **Scalability and performance**: By designing the system around core business concepts and using DDD patterns such as aggregates and repositories, DDD enables developers to build scalable and performant solutions. This architectural approach allows for efficient data access, transaction management, and event processing, supporting the system's growth and scalability over time.

Overall, DDD offers numerous benefits for Salesforce development, including improved alignment with business requirements, enhanced maintainability and flexibility, clearer separation of concerns, reduced complexity, increased collaboration, and better scalability and performance. By embracing DDD principles and practices, organizations can create robust, adaptable, and business-focused solutions that drive value and innovation.

Event-driven architecture in Salesforce

EDA is an architectural pattern that emphasizes the production, detection, consumption, and reaction to events that occur within a system or between systems. In the context of Salesforce, EDA enables organizations to build scalable, decoupled, and responsive applications by leveraging events to trigger actions and drive business processes.

EDA is a software architecture paradigm where the flow of the system is driven by events. An event represents a significant occurrence or state change within the system and can be anything from a user action, system notification, or external stimulus. In an event-driven system, components communicate asynchronously through the exchange of events, enabling loose coupling, scalability, and responsiveness.

Following are the components of an EDA:

Event-Driven Architecture in Salesforce

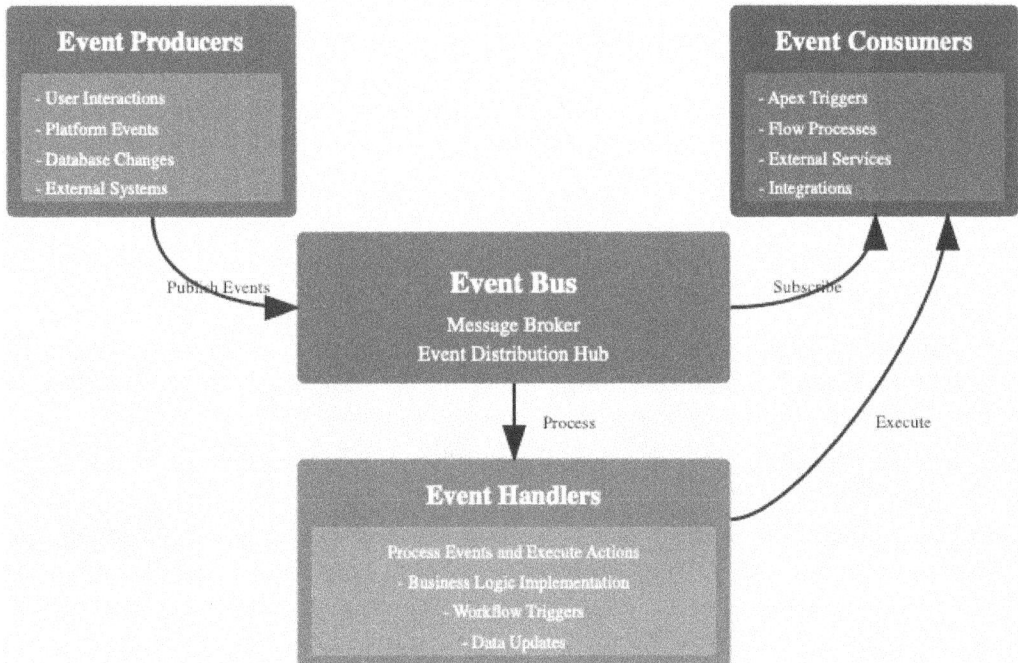

Figure 9.5: EDA in Salesforce

- **Event producers**: These are components or systems that generate events based on specific triggers or conditions. In Salesforce, event producers can include user interactions, platform events, database changes, or external integrations.

- **Event bus or message broker**: The event bus or message broker serves as the central hub for routing and distributing events to interested consumers. It decouples event producers from consumers and ensures reliable event delivery and processing.

- **Event consumers**: These are components or systems that subscribe to specific types of events and react accordingly. Event consumers can execute business logic, update data, trigger workflows, or send notifications based on received events.

- **Event handlers**: Event handlers are responsible for processing incoming events and executing the corresponding actions or workflows. They can be implemented as Apex triggers, process builder flows, Apex classes, or external services.

Using event-driven architecture

EDA is particularly suitable for scenarios where real-time responsiveness, scalability, flexibility, and integration are paramount.

Following are some situations where EDA is commonly used:

- **Real-time data processing**: When applications require immediate processing and response to events as they occur, such as processing user interactions, sensor data, or financial transactions in real time.

- **Scalable and distributed systems**: In environments where scalability and distribution are critical, EDA allows for the horizontal scaling of components and the distribution of workloads across multiple event consumers and handlers.

- **Complex workflows and business processes**: EDA is well-suited for orchestrating complex workflows and business processes that involve multiple steps, dependencies, and participants. Events serve as triggers for initiating workflow actions and coordinating interactions between different systems or components.

- **Integration and interoperability**: When integrating disparate systems, applications, or services, EDA provides a flexible and interoperable architecture for exchanging data, events, and notifications in real time. It facilitates seamless integration between systems with varying technologies, protocols, and communication patterns.

- **Event-driven automation**: In scenarios where automation is required to react to specific events or conditions, EDA enables the implementation of event-driven automation workflows, such as triggering alerts, notifications, or automated actions based on predefined rules or thresholds.

- **Asynchronous processing and offline capabilities**: For applications that require asynchronous processing of tasks or offline capabilities, EDA supports the execution of background tasks, batch processing, and offline synchronization by processing events asynchronously and queuing tasks for later execution.

- **Dynamic and adaptive systems**: In dynamic and adaptive environments where system requirements, configurations, or behaviors may change frequently, EDA promotes adaptability and agility by decoupling components and enabling dynamic reconfiguration or extension of functionality without disrupting the overall system architecture.

Overall, EDA is suitable for applications and systems that require real-time responsiveness, scalability, flexibility, and seamless integration with other systems or services. By leveraging events as the primary means of communication and coordination, EDA enables organizations to build agile, resilient, and future-proof solutions that can evolve and adapt to changing business needs and technological advancements.

Implementing event-driven architecture in Salesforce

Implementing EDA in Salesforce involves several key components and design considerations. Following is an overview of how to implement EDA in Salesforce:

- **Event objects:** Define custom objects to represent different types of events in your Salesforce org. These event objects should encapsulate relevant information about the event, such as its type, timestamp, source, and payload data.

- **Event publishers:** Identify the sources or triggers of events within your Salesforce org. These can include user interactions, data changes, platform events, or external integrations. Implement logic to publish events whenever these triggers occur. This logic can be implemented in Apex triggers, process builder flows, workflow rules, or external systems integrated with Salesforce.

- **Event consumers**: Designate Salesforce components or external systems as event consumers that subscribe to and process events. These consumers can include Apex triggers, workflows, process builder flows, Lightning components, external services, or third-party applications integrated with Salesforce.

- **Event processing logic:** Implement logic to process events when they are received by event consumers. This logic may involve querying related records, performing calculations, updating data, sending notifications, or invoking external services based on the event's type and payload. Ensure that event processing logic is efficient, scalable, and adheres to Salesforce best practices.

- **Event bus or messaging platform**: Consider using an event bus or messaging platform to facilitate event-driven communication between different Salesforce components or external systems. Platforms like Salesforce Platform Events, Salesforce Connect, or external messaging services, for example, Apache Kafka, AWS SNS/SQS, can be used to publish and subscribe to events asynchronously, ensuring reliable message delivery and scalability.

- **Error handling and retry mechanisms**: Implement error handling and retry mechanisms to handle exceptions and ensure message delivery in case of failures or network issues. Use Salesforce's native error handling features, such as Apex exception handling, platform event triggers, or asynchronous processing patterns, to manage errors and retries effectively.

- **Monitoring and analytics**: Set up monitoring and analytics tools to track event flows, performance metrics, and system health. Use Salesforce's built-in monitoring tools, for example, event monitoring, Salesforce optimizer or third-party monitoring solutions to monitor event-driven processes, identify bottlenecks, and optimize system performance.

- **Security and compliance**: Ensure that event-driven processes adhere to security and compliance requirements, such as data privacy regulations, for example, GDPR, CCPA, access controls, and audit trails. Implement security measures such as encryption, authentication, and authorization to protect sensitive data and prevent unauthorized access to event data.

Benefits of event-driven architecture

EDA offers several benefits that can enhance the scalability, responsiveness, and flexibility of applications built on the Salesforce platform.

Following are some key benefits of EDA:

- **Scalability**: EDA allows for decoupled, asynchronous communication between different components or services, enabling horizontal scalability. By distributing event processing across multiple nodes or services, organizations can handle increasing workloads and scale their applications more efficiently.

- **Real-time responsiveness**: Events are processed asynchronously, enabling near-real-time or real-time responsiveness to changes or events within the system. This ensures that critical business processes can be triggered and executed promptly, leading to faster decision-making and improved user experiences.

- **Loose coupling**: EDA promotes loose coupling between components, services, and systems by allowing them to communicate through events without direct dependencies. This decoupling enhances modularity, flexibility, and maintainability, making it easier to evolve and update individual components without affecting the entire system.

- **Flexibility and extensibility**: Events serve as a flexible and extensible mechanism for integrating disparate systems, services, or applications. Organizations can easily add new event sources, event consumers, or event types without modifying existing components, enabling agile development and seamless integration with third-party systems.

- **Fault tolerance and resilience**: Event-driven systems are inherently fault-tolerant and resilient to failures, as events can be queued, buffered, or retried in case of errors or network issues. This ensures reliable message delivery and prevents data loss, even in distributed or unreliable environments.

- **Event sourcing and auditing**: EDA facilitates event sourcing, where events serve as a source of truth for changes or transactions within the system. This allows organizations to track and audit data changes, maintain an immutable record of events, and reconstruct the state of the system at any point in time for compliance, auditing, or debugging purposes.

- **Decentralized architecture**: EDA enables decentralized architectures where components or services can communicate directly with each other through events, bypassing central orchestrators or intermediaries. This reduces bottlenecks, single points of failure, and dependencies on central components, leading to more resilient and distributed systems.

- **Event-driven insights:** By capturing and analyzing event data, organizations can gain valuable insights into system behavior, user interactions, and business processes. Event-driven analytics can help identify patterns, trends, and anomalies, enabling data-driven decision-making and continuous optimization of the system.

Overall, EDA offers a powerful paradigm for building modern, scalable, and responsive applications that can adapt to changing business requirements and evolving technology landscapes. By leveraging events as the primary means of communication, organizations can build flexible, loosely coupled systems that are well-suited for the dynamic and interconnected nature of today's digital ecosystems.

Microservices architecture in Salesforce

Microservices architecture is a design approach where an application is composed of multiple small, independent services, each focused on a specific business capability or function. In the context of Salesforce, adopting a microservices architecture involves breaking down a monolithic application into smaller, self-contained services that can be developed, deployed, and scaled independently.

Microservices architecture is composed of several key components, each playing a specific role in enabling the development, deployment, and operation of microservices-based applications.

Following are the main components of a microservices architecture:

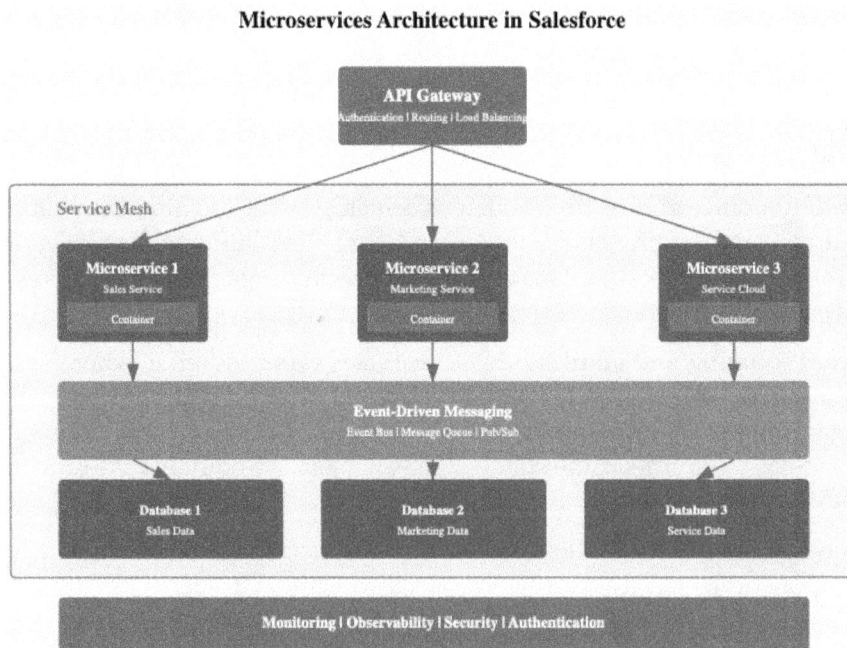

Figure 9.6: *Microservices architecture in Salesforce*

- **Microservices**: Microservices are the core building blocks of the architecture. Each microservice represents a small, independently deployable unit of functionality that is focused on a specific business capability. Microservices are designed to be loosely coupled, allowing them to be developed, deployed, and scaled independently.

- **Service discovery**: Service discovery is a mechanism that allows microservices to find and communicate with each other dynamically. In a microservices architecture, services may come and go frequently due to scaling, deployment, or failure, so a service discovery mechanism is essential for maintaining connectivity between services. Common service discovery solutions include DNS-based discovery, client-side discovery, and service registries.

- **API gateway**: The API gateway is a central entry point for client requests into the microservices architecture. It acts as a reverse proxy that routes requests to the appropriate microservices based on predefined rules or routes. The API gateway handles tasks such as authentication, authorization, rate limiting, and request routing, providing a unified interface for clients to interact with the microservices.

- **Service mesh**: A service mesh is a dedicated infrastructure layer for handling service-to-service communication within a microservices architecture. It provides features such as service discovery, load balancing, circuit breaking, and observability to improve the reliability and resilience of microservices-based applications. Service mesh solutions like Istio, Linkerd, and Envoy are commonly used in microservices architectures.

- **Containerization**: Containers are lightweight, portable units of software that encapsulate an application and its dependencies. Containerization technologies like Docker and Kubernetes are often used in microservices architectures to package, deploy, and manage microservices in isolated environments. Containers provide consistency across development, testing, and production environments, enabling seamless deployment and scaling of microservices.

- **Orchestration**: Orchestration tools are used to automate the deployment, scaling, and management of microservices and containers in a distributed environment. Orchestration platforms like Kubernetes, Docker Swarm, and Amazon ECS provide features such as scheduling, load balancing, service discovery, and health monitoring to streamline the operation of microservices-based applications.

- **Event-driven architecture**: EDA is a messaging pattern that enables asynchronous communication between microservices through events. In an EDA, microservices produce and consume events to trigger actions, share information, and maintain consistency across distributed systems. Event-driven messaging systems like Apache Kafka, RabbitMQ, and Amazon SQS are commonly used in microservices architectures.

- **Data management**: Data management is a critical aspect of microservices architecture, as each microservice may have its own database or data store. Common approaches to data management in microservices architectures include database per service, polyglot persistence, event sourcing, and CQRS. Data management solutions should prioritize data isolation, consistency, and scalability to support the needs of microservices-based applications.

- **Monitoring and observability**: Monitoring and observability tools are essential for gaining insights into the health, performance, and behavior of microservices-based applications. Monitoring solutions like Prometheus, Grafana, and Datadog provide real-time visibility into system metrics, while distributed tracing tools like Jaeger and Zipkin enable end-to-end visibility into request flows across microservices. Observability practices such as logging, tracing, and metrics collection help identify and troubleshoot issues in complex, distributed environments.

- **Security**: Security is a top priority in microservices architecture, as the distributed nature of microservices introduces new attack vectors and security challenges. Security measures such as authentication, authorization, encryption, and network segmentation should be implemented to protect sensitive data and resources. Security best practices should be followed throughout the development lifecycle, from design and implementation to deployment and operation. These are some of the key components of microservices architecture, each contributing to the overall flexibility, scalability, and resilience of modern software systems built on microservices principles.

Using microservices architecture

Microservices architecture is beneficial in certain scenarios where the complexity, scale, and requirements of the application warrant a more distributed and decoupled approach.

Following are some situations where microservices architecture may be appropriate:

- **Scalability**: When different components of the application have varying resource demands or need to scale independently, microservices architecture allows scaling only the necessary components. This is particularly useful for high-traffic applications or those with fluctuating workloads.

- **Complexity**: For large, complex applications with diverse functionalities, breaking them down into smaller, self-contained services makes it easier to manage and maintain. Each microservice can focus on a specific business capability or domain, reducing the system's overall complexity.

- **Technology heterogeneity**: Microservices architecture enables different technologies, programming languages, and frameworks for each microservice based on its requirements. This flexibility allows teams to choose the most suitable technology stack for each component, optimizing performance and productivity.

- **Continuous deployment**: Organizations that prioritize rapid development, testing, and deployment cycles can benefit from microservices architecture. Each microservice can be developed, tested, and deployed independently, enabling faster release cycles and minimizing the impact of changes on other parts of the application.

- **Resilience and fault isolation**: Microservices architecture promotes fault isolation, where failures in one microservice do not necessarily affect the entire application. This resilience allows organizations to maintain uptime and reliability even in the presence of failures or issues in individual components.

- **Team autonomy**: Microservices architecture aligns well with agile and DevOps practices, enabling cross-functional teams to take ownership of individual microservices. This autonomy fosters faster innovation, better collaboration, and improved time-to-market for new features and updates.

- **Polyglot persistence**: With microservices, each service can choose its own data storage technology based on specific requirements. This approach, known as polyglot persistence, allows organizations to use the most suitable database technology for each microservice, optimizing performance, scalability, and data management.

- **Domain-Driven Design:** Microservices architecture aligns well with the principles of DDD, where each microservice corresponds to a specific domain or subdomain within the application. This alignment facilitates better understanding of the business domain and enables more focused development efforts.

It is important to note that while microservices architecture offers many benefits, it also introduces complexities such as distributed system management, service orchestration, and inter-service communication. Organizations should carefully evaluate their requirements, technical capabilities, and organizational readiness before adopting microservices architecture.

Implementing microservices architecture in Salesforce

Implementing microservices architecture in Salesforce involves breaking down a monolithic application into smaller, independent services that can be developed, deployed, and scaled separately.

Following are the key steps to implement microservices architecture in Salesforce:

- **Identify service boundaries**: Analyze the existing monolithic application to identify distinct business capabilities or domains. Each of these capabilities will become a separate microservice. Consider factors such as data dependencies, functional boundaries, and scalability requirements when defining service boundaries.

- **Decompose the monolith**: Once you've identified service boundaries, refactor the monolithic application into individual microservices. This may involve extracting code, separating databases, and defining clear interfaces between services. Use tools and frameworks that support modular development and deployment.

- **Define service contracts**: Clearly define the interfaces and contracts between microservices to enable communication and integration. Use technologies such as RESTful APIs, GraphQL, or event-driven messaging for inter-service communication. Establish standards for data formats, protocols, and authentication mechanisms.

- **Choose deployment models**: Decide on the deployment models for your microservices. Salesforce provides various deployment options, including Heroku for custom applications, Salesforce Functions for serverless functions, and Salesforce Platform for low-code development. Choose the deployment model that best suits your requirements for scalability, flexibility, and resource management.

- **Implement Continuous Integration and Deployment (CI/CD):** Set up automated CI/CD pipelines to streamline the development, testing, and deployment of microservices. Use tools like Salesforce DX, Jenkins, or GitHub Actions to automate build, test, and deployment processes. Ensure that each microservice is independently deployable and tested in isolation.

- **Manage data consistency**: Implement data management strategies to ensure consistency and integrity across microservices. Use techniques such as event sourcing, distributed transactions, or eventual consistency patterns to manage data across multiple services. Leverage Salesforce features like Platform Events, **Change Data Capture (CDC)**, or External Objects for real-time data synchronization.

- **Monitor and manage services**: Implement monitoring, logging, and error handling mechanisms to track the health and performance of microservices. Use tools like Salesforce Event Monitoring, Health Check APIs, or third-party monitoring solutions to monitor service uptime, response times, and resource utilization. Implement resilience patterns such as circuit breakers, retries, and fallback mechanisms to handle failures gracefully.

- **Implement security measures**: Ensure that each microservice is secured against unauthorized access, data breaches, and other security threats. Implement authentication, authorization, and encryption mechanisms to protect sensitive data and resources. Use Salesforce Shield for data encryption, IAM for user authentication, and API security measures such as OAuth tokens or API keys.

- **Establish governance and compliance**: Define governance policies and compliance standards for microservices development and deployment. Ensure that microservices adhere to organizational guidelines, regulatory requirements, and industry best practices. Implement versioning, documentation, and change management processes to maintain service quality and reliability.

- **Evolve and iterate**: Continuously iterate and evolve your microservices architecture based on feedback, changing requirements, and emerging technologies. Monitor performance metrics, user feedback, and market trends to identify areas for improvement and innovation. Foster a culture of experimentation, learning, and adaptation to drive continuous improvement in your microservices ecosystem.

By following these steps, organizations can successfully implement microservices architecture in Salesforce, enabling greater agility, scalability, and innovation in application development and delivery.

Benefits of microservices architecture

Microservices architecture offers several benefits that make it an attractive choice for building modern, scalable, and resilient software systems.

Following are some of the key benefits of microservices architecture:

- **Scalability:** Microservices architecture enables horizontal scalability, allowing individual microservices to be scaled independently based on demand. This granular scalability ensures that resources are allocated efficiently and enables applications to handle varying workloads effectively.

- **Flexibility and agility**: Microservices promote flexibility and agility by decoupling the components of an application into small, autonomous services. Each microservice can be developed, deployed, and updated independently, enabling teams to innovate and release new features quickly without impacting other parts of the system.

- **Resilience and fault isolation**: Microservices architecture enhances resilience and fault isolation by isolating failures to individual services. If a microservice experiences a failure or becomes unresponsive, it does not affect the overall system, allowing other services to continue functioning without disruption.

- **Technology diversity**: Microservices architecture enables technology diversity, allowing teams to choose the most appropriate technology stack for each microservice based on its requirements. This flexibility allows organizations to leverage the strengths of different technologies and frameworks and adopt new technologies as needed.

- **Continuous Delivery and Deployment**: Microservices architecture facilitates continuous delivery and deployment practices, enabling automated testing, integration, and deployment of individual microservices. This streamlined workflow reduces time-to-market and enables organizations to deliver value to customers more frequently and reliably.

- **Improved maintainability**: Microservices architecture improves maintainability by reducing the complexity of individual services and making it easier to understand, modify, and refactor code. Each microservice has a well-defined scope and responsibility, making it simpler to manage and evolve over time.

- **Team autonomy:** Microservices architecture promotes team autonomy by enabling small, cross-functional teams to own and operate individual microservices. This decentralized approach empowers teams to make independent decisions, iterate quickly, and take ownership of the services they develop.

- **Scalable development**: Microservices architecture supports scalable development practices, allowing teams to work on different parts of the system concurrently without blocking dependencies. This parallel development approach accelerates the pace of development and fosters collaboration among teams.

- **Enhanced performance**: Microservices architecture can improve application performance by allowing services to be optimized independently for specific use cases or workloads. This optimization enables organizations to achieve better performance and responsiveness for critical functions or user interactions.

- **Easier integration and interoperability:** Microservices architecture simplifies integration and interoperability between systems by defining clear boundaries and APIs for communication between services. This modular approach facilitates integration with external systems, third-party services, and legacy applications, enabling organizations to build flexible and extensible solutions.

Overall, adopting microservices architecture in Salesforce can help organizations achieve greater agility, scalability, and resilience by breaking down monolithic applications into smaller, more manageable components. By embracing a modular, decentralized approach to application development, organizations can accelerate innovation, improve time-to-market, and deliver more responsive and scalable solutions to meet evolving business needs.

Serverless architecture in Salesforce

Serverless architecture is an approach where the responsibility for managing infrastructure and servers is shifted from the developer to the cloud provider. In a serverless model, developers can focus on writing code without worrying about provisioning, scaling, or managing servers. Instead, they can leverage cloud services, such as AWS Lambda, Azure Functions, or Google Cloud Functions, to execute code in response to events or triggers.

In the context of Salesforce, serverless architecture can be implemented using a combination of Salesforce's platform services and external serverless computing services.

Following is an overview of how serverless architecture can be applied in Salesforce:

Serverless Architecture in Salesforce

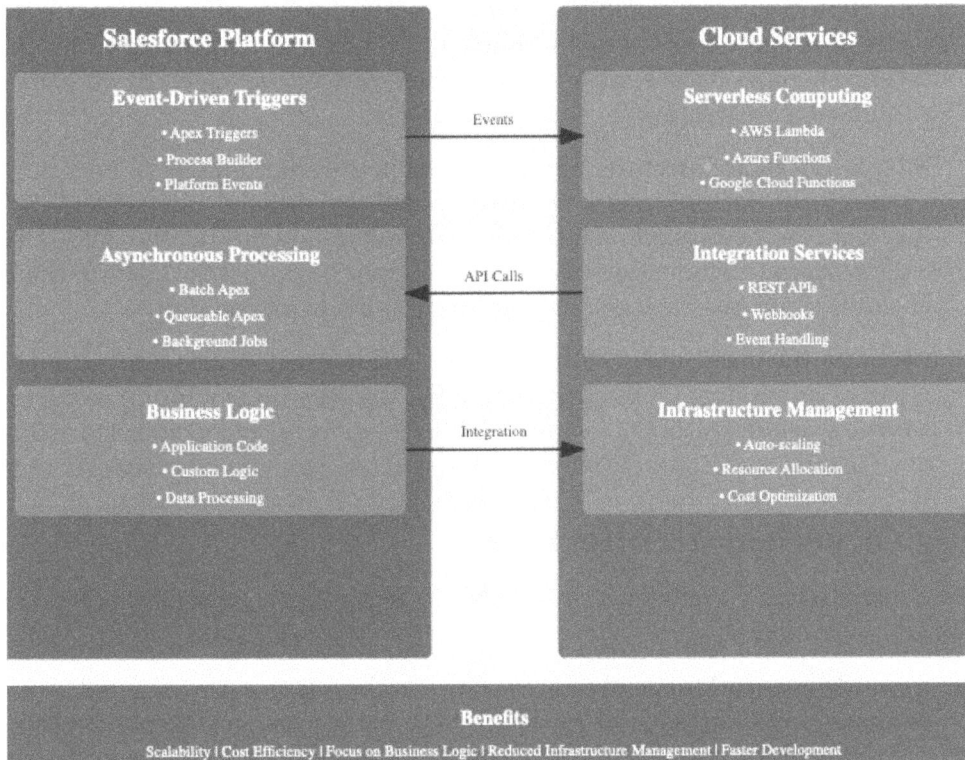

Figure 9.7: Serverless Architecture in Salesforce

- **Event-driven triggers**: Salesforce provides various event-driven triggers, such as Apex triggers, process builder, and platform events, which can be used to execute code in response to changes in Salesforce data or external events. Developers can write Apex code or use declarative tools to define the logic that should be executed when a specific event occurs.

- **External integration**: Salesforce can integrate with external serverless compute services, such as AWS Lambda or Azure Functions, using platform events, webhooks, or REST APIs. This allows developers to leverage the scalability and flexibility of serverless compute services to perform complex data processing, integrate with third-party systems, or execute long-running tasks asynchronously.

- **Asynchronous processing**: Serverless architecture is well-suited for handling asynchronous processing tasks, such as batch processing, data transformation, or background jobs. Developers can use Salesforce's asynchronous processing features, such as Batch Apex or Queueable Apex, in combination with external serverless compute services to offload long-running or resource-intensive tasks to the cloud.

- **Scalability and cost efficiency**: By leveraging serverless compute services, organizations can benefit from the scalability and cost efficiency offered by cloud providers. Serverless compute services automatically scale up or down based on demand, ensuring optimal resource utilization and cost savings. This allows organizations to handle spikes in workload without provisioning or managing additional infrastructure.

- **Microservices architecture**: Serverless architecture encourages a microservices approach, where applications are decomposed into smaller, independent services that can be developed, deployed, and scaled independently. This enables organizations to build modular and flexible applications that can adapt to changing business requirements and scale seamlessly as the workload grows.

- **Focus on business logic**: With serverless architecture, developers can focus on writing business logic and application code, rather than managing infrastructure or worrying about scalability and availability. This allows organizations to accelerate development cycles, iterate more quickly, and deliver value to customers faster.

Using serverless architecture

Serverless architecture is well-suited for various scenarios in the Salesforce ecosystem, as follows:

- **Event-driven workloads**: When you have workloads that are triggered by events or changes in data, such as processing incoming messages, responding to user actions, or executing background tasks in response to Salesforce events like record updates or platform events.

- **Asynchronous processing**: For tasks that can be performed asynchronously and don't require immediate user interaction, such as data processing, batch jobs, or long-running tasks that can be offloaded to serverless compute services.

- **Scalability and bursty workloads**: When you need to handle variable or unpredictable workloads that may experience spikes in traffic or processing demand. Serverless architecture automatically scales resources up or down based on demand, ensuring optimal performance and cost efficiency.

- **Microservices architecture**: In scenarios where you want to decompose monolithic applications into smaller, independent services that can be developed, deployed, and scaled independently. Serverless architecture enables a microservices approach, allowing you to build modular, flexible, and scalable applications.

- **Cost efficiency**: For organizations looking to optimize infrastructure costs by paying only for the resources consumed during execution, rather than provisioning and maintaining dedicated servers or virtual machines. Serverless compute services offer a pay-as-you-go pricing model, making them cost-effective for both small-scale and large-scale workloads.

- **Rapid prototyping and development**: When you need to quickly prototype, iterate, and deploy applications without the overhead of managing infrastructure or provisioning servers. Serverless architecture allows developers to focus on writing code and delivering value to customers faster, accelerating the development cycle.

Overall, serverless architecture is suitable for a wide range of use cases in the Salesforce ecosystem, offering scalability, flexibility, cost efficiency, and rapid development capabilities that can help organizations innovate and deliver value to their customers more effectively.

Implementing serverless architecture in Salesforce

Implementing serverless architecture in Salesforce involves leveraging various cloud services and features provided by the platform to build scalable, event-driven, and cost-effective solutions.

Following is a high-level overview of steps involved in implementing serverless architecture in Salesforce:

- **Identify use cases**: Determine which parts of your Salesforce solution could benefit from serverless architecture. Look for tasks or processes that can be executed asynchronously, triggered by events, or scaled dynamically based on demand.

- **Choose serverless services**: Salesforce provides several serverless services that you can use to build your architecture, as follows:

  o **Platform events:** Use platform events to publish and subscribe to events within Salesforce or integrate with external systems.

  o **Asynchronous apex**: Utilize Queueable Apex, Batch Apex, or Scheduled Apex for background processing and long-running tasks.

  o **External services**: Integrate with external serverless compute services such as AWS Lambda or Azure Functions using External Services and External Objects.

  o **Heroku functions**: Leverage Heroku Functions (powered by AWS Lambda) for building custom serverless functions and microservices outside of Salesforce.

- **Design event-driven workflows**: Design event-driven workflows using platform events to trigger serverless functions or Apex jobs in response to specific events or changes in Salesforce data. Define event publishers and subscribers to communicate asynchronously and decouple different parts of your architecture.

- **Develop serverless functions**: Write serverless functions using Apex, JavaScript (for Heroku functions), or any supported programming language for external services. Implement business logic, data processing, or integrations within these functions, keeping them lightweight, stateless, and idempotent.

- **Deploy and configure**: Deploy your serverless functions to the appropriate environment (Salesforce org, Heroku, or external cloud platform) and configure event triggers, subscriptions, and permissions as needed. Use Salesforce tools like Salesforce CLI, Apex code, or Heroku CLI for deployment and configuration.

- **Test and monitor**: Test your serverless architecture thoroughly to ensure reliability, scalability, and performance under different conditions. Monitor event processing, function executions, error rates, and resource utilization using Salesforce monitoring tools, logging, or external monitoring solutions.

- **Optimize and iterate**: Continuously optimize your serverless architecture for cost, performance, and reliability. Identify bottlenecks, optimize resource usage, implement caching strategies, and iterate on your design based on feedback and evolving requirements.

By following these steps and leveraging Salesforce's serverless capabilities, you can build scalable, event-driven, and cost-effective solutions that meet your organization's needs and drive innovation in your Salesforce environment.

Benefits of serverless architecture

Serverless architecture offers several benefits for organizations building applications on the Salesforce platform. Some of the key benefits are as follows:

- **Scalability:** Serverless architectures automatically scale up or down based on demand, allowing applications to handle varying workloads without manual intervention. This elasticity ensures optimal performance and responsiveness, even during peak usage periods.

- **Cost-effectiveness**: With serverless computing, organizations only pay for the resources consumed by their applications, rather than for idle server capacity. This pay-as-you-go model can lead to significant cost savings, especially for applications with fluctuating usage patterns.

- **Reduced operational complexity**: Serverless architectures abstract away the underlying infrastructure management, including provisioning, scaling, and maintenance tasks. This simplifies operational overhead, allowing developers to focus on writing code and delivering business value, rather than managing servers.

- **Faster time-to-market**: By leveraging pre-built serverless services and managed platforms, developers can accelerate the development and deployment of applications. This agility enables organizations to iterate quickly, respond to market changes, and deliver new features to users faster.

- **Increased resilience**: Serverless architectures often incorporate built-in fault tolerance and redundancy mechanisms, such as automatic retries, error handling, and geographic redundancy. These features enhance the resilience of applications, reducing the risk of downtime and data loss.

- **Improved scalability**: Serverless architectures often support event-driven, asynchronous processing models, allowing applications to handle bursts of traffic and process large volumes of data efficiently. This architectural flexibility enables organizations to build highly scalable and responsive systems.

- **Focus on business logic**: With serverless computing, developers can focus more on writing application code and implementing business logic, rather than managing infrastructure or worrying about scalability and availability. This enables teams to deliver value to customers more quickly and efficiently.

Overall, serverless architecture offers a compelling approach for building scalable, flexible, and cost-effective solutions in the Salesforce ecosystem. By leveraging Salesforce's platform services in combination with external serverless compute services, organizations can unlock new capabilities, improve developer productivity, and deliver innovative solutions to meet the evolving needs of their business.

Command Query Responsibility Segregation in Salesforce

CQRS is an architectural pattern that separates the responsibilities of handling commands (actions that change the state of the system) from handling queries (actions that retrieve data from the system). In Salesforce, CQRS can be implemented to improve the scalability, performance, and maintainability of applications.

In a CQRS architecture, there are several key components, as follows:

- **Command handlers**: Command handlers are responsible for executing commands received from clients or other parts of the system. They enforce business rules, perform validation, and orchestrate the execution of commands. Command handlers typically interact with domain objects to carry out the requested operations.

- **Command model**: The command model represents the data and behavior necessary to execute commands. It encapsulates the logic required to process commands and change the state of the system. The command model may include entities, value objects, aggregates, and domain services needed to fulfill command requests.

- **Command bus**: The command bus is a messaging mechanism that routes commands from clients or other parts of the system to the appropriate command handlers. It decouples the sender of a command from its receiver and allows for flexible routing and dispatching of commands based on their type or destination.

- **Event handlers**: Event handlers listen for events generated as a result of executing commands and update the read models or projections accordingly. Events represent facts or notifications about changes to the system's state and are typically stored in an event store or event log. Event handlers subscribe to specific events and update the query side of the system to reflect the changes.

- **Query handlers**: Query handlers are responsible for handling read operations and retrieving data from the system in response to queries. They fetch data from one or more data sources, such as databases, caches, or external services, and return the results to clients or other parts of the system.

- **Read models**: Read models represent denormalized or optimized views of the data tailored for specific query requirements. They are optimized for fast data retrieval and are often precomputed or materialized to improve query performance. Read models are typically updated asynchronously in response to events generated by command execution.

- **Command store:** The command store is a persistent storage mechanism that records the commands executed by the system. It serves as a log of all changes made to the system's state and provides a historical record of command execution for auditing, debugging, or replaying purposes.

- **Event store**: The event store is a persistent storage mechanism that stores the events generated as a result of executing commands. It acts as a durable log of all state changes in the system and enables event sourcing, replayability, and eventual consistency. Events stored in the event store can be used to rebuild or synchronize read models and recover the system's state.

Using CQRS

CQRS is particularly suitable for scenarios, as follows:

- **Complex domain logic**: When your domain logic involves complex business rules or workflows that require different processing paths for command execution and query retrieval.

- **Performance optimization**: When you need to optimize the performance of read and write operations independently. CQRS allows you to scale and optimize the read and write sides of your system separately to handle varying loads and requirements.

- **Scalability requirements**: When you anticipate high scalability requirements and want to distribute the workload across multiple components or services. CQRS enables horizontal scaling by decoupling command processing from query handling.

- **Reporting and analytics**: When you have diverse reporting and analytics needs that require tailored views of the data. CQRS allows you to create optimized read models or projections tailored for specific query requirements, improving query performance and flexibility.

- **Event-driven architecture**: When you want to embrace EDA principles and leverage events as a means of communication and synchronization between different parts of the system. CQRS often goes hand in hand with event sourcing, where events capture changes to the system's state and serve as the primary source of truth.

- **Domain-Driven Design (DDD)**: When your application follows DDD principles and you want to model your domain logic more accurately by separating command and query responsibilities. CQRS aligns well with the bounded context concept in DDD, allowing you to define clear boundaries and responsibilities within your domain model.

- **Regulatory compliance and auditing**: When you need to maintain a comprehensive audit trail of all changes made to the system's state for regulatory compliance or auditing purposes. CQRS, combined with event sourcing, provides a robust mechanism for recording and replaying commands and events, ensuring data integrity and accountability.

In summary, CQRS is a suitable architectural pattern for applications with complex domain logic, diverse scalability requirements, and a need for optimized query performance, event-driven communication, and comprehensive auditing capabilities. However, it may introduce additional complexity and overhead, so it's essential to evaluate whether the benefits outweigh the associated costs based on your specific requirements and constraints.

Implementing CQRS in Salesforce

Implementing CQRS in Salesforce involves several key steps to separate the command and query responsibilities within your application.

Following is a high-level overview of how you can implement CQRS in Salesforce:

- **Identify command and query responsibilities**: Start by identifying the command operations (write operations that modify the system's state) and query operations (read operations that retrieve data from the system) within your application. Commands typically include create, update, and delete operations, while queries involve retrieving data based on various criteria.

- **Define command handlers**: Create command handler classes responsible for processing command operations. Each command handler should encapsulate the logic for validating and executing a specific command. These handlers should enforce business rules, perform data validation, and update the system's state accordingly.

- **Implement command objects**: Define command objects that encapsulate the data and parameters required to execute a command operation. These command objects should represent the intent or action to be performed, including the necessary input data.

- **Create command processing logic**: Within the command handlers, implement the logic to process the command objects. This logic may involve data manipulation, invoking external services, performing calculations, and updating database records. Ensure that the command processing logic is modular, testable, and follows best practices for error handling and transaction management.

- **Design query handlers**: Similarly, create query handler classes responsible for processing query operations. Each query handler should encapsulate the logic for retrieving data based on specific criteria or requirements. These handlers should optimize query performance, handle filtering and sorting, and return the requested data in the desired format.

- **Define query objects**: Define query objects or **Data Transfer Objects** (**DTOs**) that represent the parameters and criteria for executing a query operation. These query objects should contain the necessary filters, fields, sorting instructions, and pagination parameters to fetch data from the system.

- **Implement query execution logic**: Within the query handlers, implement the logic to execute query operations using **Salesforce Object Query Language** (**SOQL**) or other data retrieval mechanisms. Apply appropriate query optimizations, such as selective filtering, relationship queries, and query batching, to enhance performance and minimize resource consumption.

- **Decouple command and query components**: Ensure that command and query components are decoupled to enforce separation of concerns. Avoid mixing command and query logic within the same classes or methods to maintain clarity and modularity. Use interfaces, dependency injection, or inversion of control techniques to facilitate loose coupling between components.

- **Test command and query operations**: Write comprehensive unit tests to validate the behavior of command and query handlers. Test command handlers to ensure they correctly process commands, enforce business rules, and update the system's state. Similarly, test query handlers to verify they retrieve the expected data and handle various query scenarios accurately.

- **Iterate and refine**: Continuously iterate on your implementation, gathering feedback, and refining your design based on evolving requirements and lessons learned. Pay attention to performance optimizations, scalability considerations, and maintainability improvements to ensure the long-term success of your CQRS implementation.

By following these steps, you can effectively implement CQRS in Salesforce to achieve separation of command and query responsibilities, improve modularity and testability, and optimize the performance and scalability of your application's data operations.

Benefits of CQRS

Implementing the CQRS pattern in Salesforce offers several benefits that can enhance the architecture, performance, and maintainability of your application.

Following are some key advantages of using CQRS:

- **Improved scalability**: CQRS allows you to scale command and query processing independently based on the specific requirements of your application. This scalability enables you to handle varying workloads more effectively, ensuring that write-heavy or read-heavy operations can be optimized separately.

- **Optimized performance**: By separating command and query responsibilities, CQRS enables you to optimize each aspect of your application's data operations independently. Command processing logic can focus on efficient data manipulation and validation, while query handling can be optimized for fast data retrieval and response times.

- **Enhanced flexibility**: CQRS promotes a more flexible architecture by decoupling the write and read sides of your application. This decoupling allows you to evolve and scale each aspect independently, making it easier to introduce new features, adjust data access patterns, or optimize performance without affecting other parts of the system.

- **Improved maintainability**: Separating command and query logic simplifies the design and maintenance of your application by reducing complexity and minimizing dependencies between components. This separation makes it easier to understand, modify, and extend the codebase, leading to improved maintainability and agility.

- **Better domain model alignment**: CQRS encourages a closer alignment between your application's domain model and its data access patterns. By modeling commands and queries based on domain concepts and business requirements, you can create a more cohesive and intuitive architecture that reflects the underlying domain logic more accurately.

- **Support for complex business logic**: CQRS provides a flexible foundation for implementing complex business logic and domain-specific operations. By encapsulating command processing logic within dedicated command handlers, you can enforce business rules, validations, and workflows more effectively, ensuring data integrity and consistency.

- **Optimized resource utilization**: Separating command and query processing allows you to allocate resources more efficiently based on the specific demands of each operation. This optimization can help reduce resource contention, improve throughput, and optimize resource consumption, leading to better overall performance and resource utilization.

- **Facilitates event sourcing**: CQRS is often used in conjunction with event sourcing, a pattern where changes to application state are captured as a series of domain events. This combination enables you to implement sophisticated EDAs that support auditability, replayability, and eventual consistency, providing additional benefits for certain use cases.

In summary, CQRS can be a valuable architectural pattern in Salesforce applications, especially in scenarios where you need to optimize performance, scalability, and maintainability by separating command and query responsibilities.

Conclusion

This chapter has provided an in-depth exploration of architectural patterns in Salesforce, demonstrating their critical role in building robust, scalable, and maintainable applications. By understanding the principles behind patterns like layered architecture, MVC, service layer, DDD, EDA, microservices, and CQRS, developers can approach complex challenges with structured and proven solutions. These patterns serve not only as tools to enhance application design but also as a means to align development with organizational goals and user needs. Through real-world applications and examples, the chapter highlights how these patterns can streamline processes, optimize performance, and improve flexibility. Whether it's handling complex business logic, integrating with external systems, or scaling to meet user demands, these patterns offer clear frameworks to guide development. As organizations increasingly rely on Salesforce to drive innovation and efficiency, mastering these architectural patterns equips developers to deliver solutions that are both impactful and future-proof.

In the next chapter, the spotlight turns toward integrating patterns in Apex Projects. It will cover combining different patterns to solve complex problems, case studies and real-world examples of pattern implementation, and considerations for selecting the right pattern for a specific scenario.

Points to remember

- Architectural patterns provide structured approaches to design scalable and maintainable Salesforce applications.

- Layered architecture separates concerns into presentation, business logic, and data access layers for modularity and maintainability.

- MVC helps organize applications into model, view, and controller components to streamline development and improve scalability.

- The service layer encapsulates business logic, promoting code reuse and separation of concerns.

- DDD focuses on aligning application architecture with the business domain, fostering better collaboration and flexibility.

- EDA uses triggers, platform events, and asynchronous processing to create decoupled and scalable systems.

- Microservices architecture breaks applications into small, independently deployable services for enhanced scalability and flexibility.

- Serverless architecture leverages event-driven and cloud-based resources to reduce operational complexity and improve cost-efficiency.

- CQRS separates read and write operations for optimized performance and better alignment with business processes.

- Each pattern supports Salesforce best practices, such as scalability, modularity, and testability, ensuring alignment with platform capabilities.

- Understanding when and how to apply these patterns is critical to designing effective and future-proof Salesforce solutions.

- Combining patterns can address complex requirements, balancing performance, flexibility, and maintainability.

Questions

1. What are architectural patterns, and why are they important in Salesforce development?

2. How does layered architecture enhance the maintainability and scalability of Salesforce applications?

3. What are the main components of the MVC pattern, and how do they apply to Salesforce development?

4. How does the service layer pattern contribute to code reuse and separation of concerns in Salesforce?

5. What is DDD, and how can it improve collaboration between developers and business stakeholders?

6. Explain how EDA enables decoupled and scalable Salesforce solutions.

7. What are the benefits and challenges of implementing microservices architecture in Salesforce?

8. How does serverless architecture reduce operational complexity while enhancing scalability and cost-efficiency?

9. Describe how CQRS separates command and query responsibilities and its benefits in Salesforce applications.

10. When should developers consider using a combination of architectural patterns in Salesforce projects?

11. What are the key considerations when choosing the right architectural pattern for a specific business scenario in Salesforce?

12. How do architectural patterns align with Salesforce best practices and platform capabilities?

Join our book's Discord space

Join the book's Discord Workspace for Latest updates, Offers, Tech happenings around the world, New Release and Sessions with the Authors:

https://discord.bpbonline.com

CHAPTER 10

Integrating Patterns in Apex Projects

Introduction

Integrating patterns in Apex projects delves into the critical process of seamlessly combining different design patterns to address complex challenges and scenarios encountered in Salesforce Apex development. These integrated patterns offer tailored solutions for organizing, optimizing, and enhancing the architecture of Apex projects, leading to more robust and scalable applications.

In this chapter, we will explore various aspects of integrating patterns in Apex projects, covering topics such as the importance of pattern integration, strategies for effectively combining different patterns, real-world case studies and examples showcasing successful pattern integration, and best practices and recommendations for implementing integrated patterns.

Developers can significantly enhance their skills and approach to building Apex solutions by understanding and applying these integrating patterns. By leveraging the synergies between different design patterns, developers can design architectures that are flexible, scalable, and aligned with best practices for Apex development. Whether you are an experienced Apex developer or just starting with Salesforce development, this chapter provides invaluable insights and strategies for optimizing your architecture and building high-quality Apex applications.

Structure

The chapter covers the following topics:

- Integrating patterns in Apex projects
- Importance of pattern integration
- Strategies for pattern integration

Objectives

By the end of this chapter, readers will gain a comprehensive understanding of integrating patterns in Apex projects, including the significance of combining multiple design patterns to address complex business and technical challenges. They will learn how to strategically select and implement patterns to create robust, scalable, and maintainable solutions tailored to Salesforce development needs. The chapter also equips readers with actionable insights into strategies for effective pattern integration, illustrated through case studies and real-world examples. Furthermore, readers will explore practical applications, understand the benefits of pattern integration, and identify common pitfalls with proven mitigation strategies. This knowledge will empower developers to enhance their architectural decisions, foster better collaboration within teams, and design solutions that adhere to industry best practices, ultimately driving project success.

Integrating patterns in Apex projects

In Salesforce development, integrating patterns is pivotal in solving complex problems and optimizing solutions. This chapter delves into the art of seamlessly blending different design patterns to address intricate challenges encountered in Apex projects. By combining various patterns, developers can enhance code modularity, maintainability, and scalability, thereby ensuring the success of their projects.

Integrating patterns in Apex projects refers to the process of combining multiple design patterns to address complex requirements and challenges encountered in Salesforce development. This approach involves leveraging the strengths of different patterns and integrating them seamlessly to create more robust, flexible, and scalable solutions. By combining patterns, developers can break down complex problems into smaller, more manageable pieces, allowing for better organization, modularity, and maintainability of the codebase.

Integrating patterns in Apex projects involves identifying the most suitable patterns for a given scenario, understanding how they can complement each other, and effectively combining them to achieve the desired outcome. This process requires careful planning, coordination, and consideration of factors such as system requirements, architecture, and performance constraints.

Overall, integrating patterns in Apex projects enables developers to build high-quality solutions that adhere to best practices, promote code reuse, and facilitate collaboration among team members. It empowers developers to design and implement robust, scalable applications that meet the evolving needs of Salesforce projects.

Importance of pattern integration

Integrating multiple design patterns in Salesforce Apex projects offers many benefits that significantly enhance the development process and the resulting solutions. One of the primary advantages is the ability to leverage the strengths of different patterns to create more robust and flexible solutions.

For example, combining the **Model-View-Controller (MVC)** pattern with the service layer pattern in Salesforce separates business logic from presentation and database layers, making the codebase more maintainable, reusable, and easier to test. Similarly, integrating the command pattern with the observer pattern can efficiently handle asynchronous processing in Salesforce using Queueable Apex, future methods, or Platform Events.

Furthermore, pattern integration in Apex promotes code reusability and modularity, allowing developers to encapsulate common functionalities into reusable components. This reduces redundancy and improves code organization. By reusing proven design patterns, developers can build upon existing Salesforce solutions without reinventing the wheel, leading to faster deployment cycles and better maintainability.

Additionally, integrating patterns ensures consistency and standardization across Salesforce projects. Following established design principles like the trigger and handler pattern, factory method, or singleton improves code readability and fosters better collaboration among developers working on Salesforce applications.

Combining patterns leads to robust solutions in Apex

Combining multiple design patterns in Apex enables developers to break down complex requirements into manageable components, ensuring each pattern addresses a specific concern while maintaining a scalable architecture.

For example, in Salesforce asynchronous processing, where background execution and event handling are necessary, combining the command pattern with the observer pattern ensures a scalable and decoupled approach.

This can be implemented using the following:

- Queueable Apex to queue commands asynchronously.
- Future methods for lightweight asynchronous execution.
- Platform Events to notify multiple subscribers about system-wide changes.

This decouples execution logic from event handling, improving maintainability and resilience in high-volume data processing scenarios.

Combining multiple design patterns in Apex projects leads to robust solutions by leveraging the strengths of each pattern to address different aspects of the problem at hand.

Following is an explanation of how this integration process contributes to the robustness of the solution:

- **Comprehensive problem-solving:** Each design pattern in Apex is designed to solve specific types of problems or address particular concern. By integrating multiple patterns, developers can tackle various aspects of a problem comprehensively. For example, combining singleton with factory method in Apex-managed caching improves performance and reduces repeated queries to the database.

- **Modular and reusable components**: Design patterns promote modularity and code reuse by encapsulating common functionalities into standalone components. When integrated, these modular components can be reused across different parts of the application, reducing duplication of code and promoting consistency. For example, integrating the command pattern with the observer pattern in Salesforce batch processing ensures that commands execute asynchronously using Queueable Apex while observers handle real-time monitoring of process completion.

- **Flexibility and adaptability**: Integrating multiple patterns provide flexibility in designing solutions that can adapt to changing Salesforce requirements or environments. Using the strategy pattern with the adapter pattern allows dynamic selection of API integrations in Salesforce External Services and Named Credentials, supporting multiple third-party systems without modifying core logic.

- **Improved maintainability and scalability**: Design patterns promote code maintainability by providing well-defined structures and conventions that make it easier to understand and modify the codebase. When integrated effectively, patterns enhance the maintainability of the solution by promoting clean, modular architectures that are easier to extend and refactor. For example, combining the decorator pattern with the facade pattern in Salesforce Lightning Components simplifies UI logic, ensuring consistent styling and behaviour across multiple components.

- **Enhanced performance and efficiency**: Integrating patterns can lead to improvements in performance and efficiency by optimizing critical areas of the application. For instance, integrating Flyweight with composite pattern enables efficient memory handling in bulk processing of hierarchical records, improving SOQL query performance and governor limit compliance.

Challenges and solutions of integrating patterns

While integrating patterns in Salesforce Apex development offers numerous benefits, it also presents certain challenges that developers must overcome.

The following are some common challenges of integrating patterns in Apex and strategies to address them:

- **Complexity:**
  - ○ **Challenge:** Integrating multiple patterns in Salesforce development can make the codebase complex and harder to debug and maintain.
  - ○ **Real-world Salesforce example:** A trigger and handler pattern combined with the command pattern for processing bulk records in Queueable Apex can introduce complexity if not structured properly.
  - ○ **Solution in Apex:**
    - ▪ Break down the integration into modular, reusable classes.
    - ▪ Use Custom Metadata to store configurations dynamically instead of hardcoding logic.
    - ▪ Maintain separate layers for triggers, handlers, and service classes to keep clean separation of concerns.
    - ▪ Document design decisions using ApexDoc or inline comments to explain interactions.

- **Conflicting patterns:**
  - ○ **Challenge:** Some patterns may have conflicting principles **that** make them difficult to integrate seamlessly.
  - ○ **Real-world Salesforce example:** Integrating the singleton pattern (which enforces a single instance) with the factory method pattern (which creates new instances) can lead to design conflicts.
  - ○ **Solution in Apex:**
    - ▪ Use lazy initialization in singleton pattern to allow controlled instantiation.
    - ▪ Modify the factory method pattern to reuse existing instances when necessary.
    - ▪ Follow Salesforce best practices like Apex Managed Sharing instead of using conflicting manual record ownership handling.

- **Performance overhead:**
  - ○ **Challenge:** Combining multiple design patterns can increase memory usage and slow execution times, which is a concern due to Salesforce Governor Limits.
  - ○ **Real-world Salesforce example:** A decorator pattern used for logging combined with the chain of responsibility pattern for workflow approvals may lead to unnecessary heap size growth.

- **Solution in Apex:**
  - Use Platform Events for asynchronous processing instead of synchronous logging to avoid CPU time overages.
  - Implement SOQL query optimization techniques, such as selective filtering and indexed fields, to improve performance.
  - Bulkify queries and use `Database.Stateful` Batch Apex where applicable.
  - Leverage Salesforce Cache (Platform Cache API) for frequently used data to reduce repeated queries.

- **Maintenance burden:**
  - **Challenge:** As the Salesforce org grows, maintaining pattern-integrated solutions becomes increasingly difficult.
  - **Real-world Salesforce example:** A facade pattern implemented for third-party API integrations may require frequent updates if the external API structure changes.
  - **Solution in Apex:**
    - Centralize API calls in a dedicated Apex class to prevent scattered updates.
    - Use Named Credentials and External Services instead of hardcoding API authentication details.
    - Implement unit tests with stub data (Mock Classes) to validate integrations proactively.
    - Automate deployments using Salesforce DevOps tools like Copado, Gearset, or SFDX CI/CD Pipelines.

- **Learning curve:**
  - **Challenge:** Understanding how multiple patterns interact in Salesforce can be challenging for new developers.
  - **Real-world Salesforce example:** A developer unfamiliar with the observer pattern may struggle with Platform Events and **Change Data Capture (CDC)** notifications.
  - **Solution in Apex:**
    - Encourage trailhead learning paths on Apex design patterns and asynchronous processing.
    - Use Apex debug logs and log inspector for analyzing event-driven interactions.
    - Promote code reviews and peer programming to share best practices.

- Maintain a shared knowledge base or wiki documenting pattern integration strategies.

Showcase examples of successful pattern integration

To illustrate the benefits and challenges of pattern integration, it is helpful to showcase real-world examples of successful implementations in Salesforce projects. These examples can highlight how different patterns were combined to address specific requirements and challenges, resulting in more robust and flexible solutions.

For instance, consider a Salesforce project that requires both batch processing and error handling. By integrating the strategy pattern for defining different processing strategies and the chain of responsibility pattern for handling errors cascadingly, developers can implement a scalable and fault-tolerant solution that meets the project's requirements.

Another example could involve integrating the decorator pattern for dynamically adding functionalities to objects with the observer pattern for asynchronously notifying subscribers of state changes. This combination enables developers to build highly customizable and reactive systems that can adapt to changing requirements and user interactions. By showcasing these examples, developers gain valuable insights into the practical applications of pattern integration and how it can be leveraged to solve real-world challenges in Salesforce development.

Following are some showcase examples of successful pattern integration in real-world Salesforce projects:

- **Trigger and handler pattern with service layer:** In Salesforce development, it is common to use the trigger and handler pattern to manage trigger logic and separate it from business logic. Additionally, integrating a service layer pattern can help encapsulate complex business logic and improve code maintainability. By combining these two patterns, developers can achieve a modular and scalable architecture for handling trigger operations. For example, the trigger handlers can delegate the execution of business logic to service classes, allowing for easier testing, reuse, and maintenance.

  o **Apex implementation example:** The following code snippets explain the Apex implementation example for the trigger & handler pattern with the service layer.

  Trigger:

```
trigger AccountTrigger on Account (before insert, before update)
{
    AccountTriggerHandler handler = new AccountTriggerHandler();
    handler.handleTrigger(Trigger.new, Trigger.oldMap, Trigger.
operationType);
}
```

Trigger Handler:

```
public class AccountTriggerHandler {
    public void handleTrigger(List<Account> newRecords, Map<Id,
Account> oldRecords, System.TriggerOperation operation) {
        if (operation == System.TriggerOperation.BEFORE_INSERT)
{

            AccountService.processNewAccounts(newRecords);
        }
    }
}
```

Service Layer:

```
public class AccountService {
    public static void processNewAccounts(List<Account>
accounts) {
        for (Account acc : accounts) {
            acc.Description = 'Processed by Service Layer';
        }
    }
}
```

- **MVC architecture with dependency injection**: Implementing the MVC architecture in Salesforce applications can promote code organization and separation of concerns. Integrating **Dependency Injection (DI)** allows for the inversion of control and facilitates the decoupling of components, making the codebase more flexible and testable. By combining MVC with DI, developers can build highly modular and extensible applications on the Salesforce platform. For instance, the controller layer can inject service dependencies into the view or model components, enabling seamless communication and collaboration between different layers of the application.

  o **Apex implementation example:** The following code snippets explain the Apex implementation example for the MVC architecture with DI:

  Service interface (Dependency)

```
public interface ContactService {
    List<Contact> getContactsByAccount(Id accountId);
}
```

  Concrete implementation:

```
public class ContactServiceImpl implements ContactService {
    public List<Contact> getContactsByAccount(Id accountId) {
```

```
        return [SELECT Id, Name, Email FROM Contact WHERE
AccountId = :accountId];
    }
}
```

Controller using DI:

```
public class ContactController {
    private ContactService contactService;

    public ContactController(ContactService service) {
        this.contactService = service;
    }

    public List<Contact> fetchContacts(Id accountId) {
        return contactService.getContactsByAccount(accountId);
    }
}
```

Usage:

```
ContactService service = new ContactServiceImpl();
ContactController controller = new ContactController(service);
List<Contact> contacts = controller.
fetchContacts('001XXXXXXXXXXXX');
```

- **Bulkification strategies with query optimization patterns:** Bulkification is essential for optimizing the performance of Salesforce applications, especially when dealing with large data volumes. By integrating bulkification strategies with query optimization patterns, developers can ensure efficient and scalable data access operations. For example, developers can leverage selective SOQL queries to retrieve only the necessary data, use relationship queries to fetch related records efficiently and implement query batching techniques to process large datasets in smaller chunks. This combination of strategies minimizes the number of SOQL queries executed and reduces the overall processing time, improving the application's performance and scalability.

  o **Apex implementation example:** The following code snippets explain the Apex implementation example for the bulkification strategies with query optimization patterns:

  Bulkified SOQL query:

```
public class AccountQueryService {
    public static List<Account> getAccountsByIndustry(Set<String>
industries) {
```

```
        return [SELECT Id, Name, Industry FROM Account WHERE
Industry IN :industries];
    }
}
```

Batch processing for large data sets:

```
public class AccountBatchProcessor implements Database.
Batchable<SObject> {
    public Database.QueryLocator start(Database.BatchableContext
context) {
        return Database.getQueryLocator('SELECT Id, Name FROM
Account');
    }

    public void execute(Database.BatchableContext context,
List<Account> scope) {
        for (Account acc : scope) {
            acc.Description = 'Processed in batch';
        }
        update scope;
    }

    public void finish(Database.BatchableContext context) {
        System.debug('Batch Job Completed');
    }
}
```

Trigger with bulkified query:

```
trigger ContactTrigger on Contact (before insert) {
    Set<String> industries = new Set<String>{'Technology',
'Finance'};
    List<Account> accounts = AccountQueryService.
getAccountsByIndustry(industries);
    System.debug('Fetched Accounts: ' + accounts.size());
}
```

- **Event-Driven Architecture with Microservices**: **Event-Driven Architecture (EDA)** enables loosely coupled communication between different components of a system, while microservices architecture promotes modularity and scalability by breaking down the application into smaller, independently deployable services. By integrating EDA with microservices, developers can build event-driven, distributed systems on the Salesforce platform. For instance, events triggered by changes in Salesforce data can be propagated to microservices through event streams, allowing for real-time processing and response. This integration enables a highly scalable and resilient architecture that can handle complex business requirements and adapt to changing needs over time.

- o **Apex implementation example:** The following code snippets explain the Apex implementation example for EDA with Microservices:

Publishing an event:

```
public class AccountEventPublisher {
    public static void publishAccountUpdate(Id accountId) {
        Account__e event = new Account__e(Account_Id__c =
accountId, Change_Type__c = 'Update');
        EventBus.publish(event);
    }
}
```

Trigger to publish events:

```
trigger AccountTrigger on Account (after update) {
    for (Account acc : Trigger.new) {
        AccountEventPublisher.publishAccountUpdate(acc.Id);
    }
}
```

Subscriber listening to the event:

```
public class AccountEventSubscriber {
    @InvocableMethod
    public static void handleEvent(List<Account__e> events) {
        for (Account__e evt : events) {
            System.debug('Received event for Account Id: ' +
evt.Account_Id__c);
        }
    }
}
```

Strategies for pattern integration

Strategies for pattern integration refer to the approaches and techniques used to combine multiple design patterns within a software architecture effectively. These strategies enable developers to create cohesive, robust, and flexible solutions by leveraging the strengths of various patterns and integrating them seamlessly.

Pattern integration strategies are as follows.

Pattern Integration Strategies in Salesforce

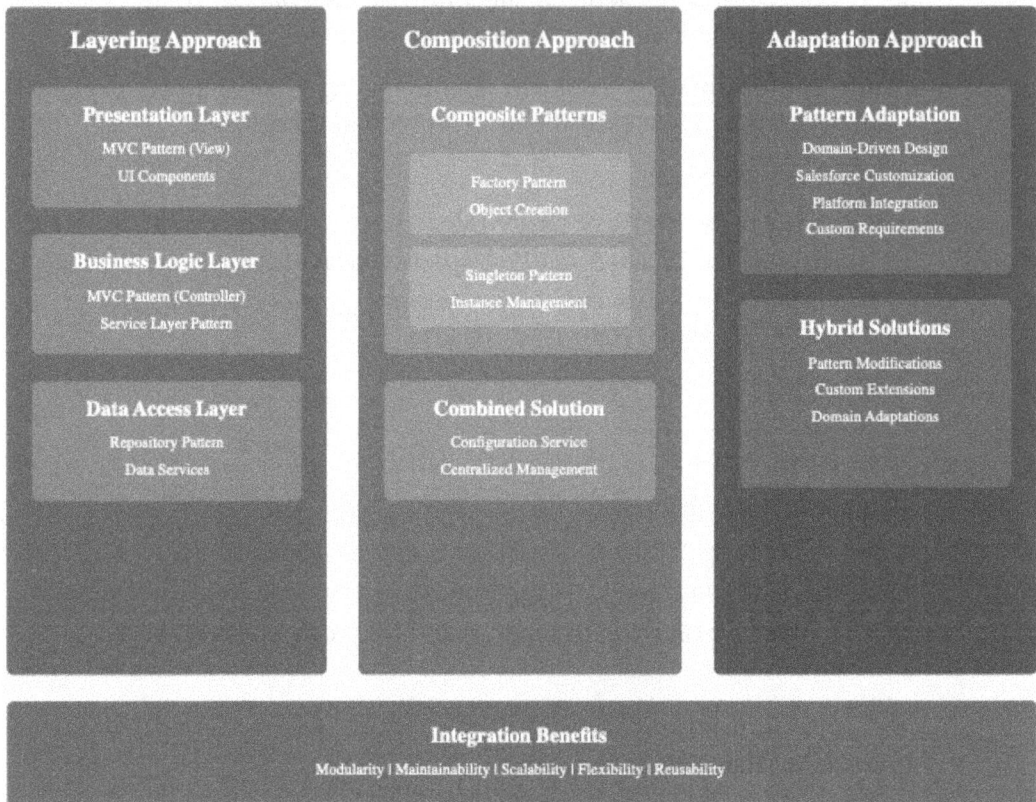

Figure 10.1: Pattern integration strategies

- **Layering approach**:

  o The layering approach involves organizing patterns into distinct layers, each responsible for a specific aspect of the application's architecture.

  o Common layers in Salesforce projects include presentation (UI), business logic, data access, and integration. Each layer encapsulates related functionality and interacts with adjacent layers through well-defined interfaces.

  o By adopting a layered architecture, developers can achieve better separation of concerns, making the codebase more modular, maintainable, and scalable.

  o **Example**: In a Salesforce project, the MVC pattern can be used to separate the presentation layer (View) from the business logic layer (Controller), while the service layer pattern encapsulates complex business logic and acts as an intermediary between the controller and data access layer.

- **Composition:**

  - The composition approach involves composing patterns together to form higher-level abstractions or composite patterns.

  - Composite patterns combine the strengths of multiple patterns to address specific architectural concerns or achieve desired functionality.

  - **Apex limitation considerations:** Unlike other languages, Apex does not support multiple inheritance, which limits the direct composition of behaviors from multiple classes. Instead, developers must rely on interfaces, DI, or service classes to compose functionalities effectively. This can lead to additional boilerplate code compared to languages that natively support mixins or multiple inheritance.

  - **Example**: In Salesforce, combining the factory method and singleton patterns can implement a centralized configuration service that dynamically creates and manages singleton instances of configuration objects.

- **Adaptation:**

  - The adaptation approach involves adapting or extending existing patterns to meet the unique requirements of a specific project or domain.

  - Adaptation may involve modifying pattern implementations, combining multiple patterns to form hybrid solutions, or introducing customizations to suit specific needs.

  - **Example**: In a Salesforce project, the **Domain-Driven Design (DDD)** pattern can be adapted to align with the platform's data model and architectural conventions, allowing developers to apply DDD principles effectively within the Salesforce ecosystem.

Role of architectural patterns in integrating patterns

Architectural patterns play a crucial role in integrating patterns effectively within Apex Salesforce projects. They provide a high-level blueprint for organizing the structure and behavior of the application, guiding the selection and integration of individual design patterns. Given Salesforce's multi-tenant architecture, governor limits, and best practices, architectural patterns help developers build scalable, maintainable, and efficient applications.

Following is how architectural patterns contribute to integrating patterns:

- **Framework for organization**: Architectural patterns establish a well-defined structure for organizing components in Apex projects, such as **Lightning Web Components (LWC),** Apex controllers, service layers, and integration layers. For example, using the MVC pattern, developers can separate business logic (Apex classes), presentation logic (LWC/Visualforce), and data access (SOQL/SOSL) queries) to maintain a structured application.

- **Encapsulation of concerns**: Salesforce applications often require complex business rules that interact with multiple objects and APIs. Patterns like service layer help encapsulate business logic within service classes, keeping it separate from triggers or controllers. This ensures that trigger handlers delegate business logic to services, enhancing modularity.

- **Facilitation of communication**: Many Salesforce applications involve asynchronous processing and event-driven communication. **Event-Driven Architecture (EDA)**, supported by Platform Events, CDC, and Asynchronous Apex (Queueable, Batch, Future methods), enables loosely coupled communication between system components. Integrating observer and command patterns within this architecture facilitates real-time updates and scalable processing.

- **Support for scalability and extensibility**: As Salesforce applications scale, maintaining performance under governor limits becomes crucial. Microservices-inspired architectures, where components interact using REST APIs, Named Credentials, and External Services, allow decoupling of functionalities. For example, integrating facade and factory patterns helps modularize external system integrations, improving extensibility.

- **Flexibility for variation**: Architectural patterns provide flexibility by allowing developers to integrate different design patterns based on project-specific needs. For example, the strategy pattern can be integrated with adapter to dynamically select different processing strategies based on Salesforce Custom Metadata Types, enabling dynamic business rule execution.

- **Alignment with best practices**: Architectural patterns embody best practices and proven solutions for common architectural challenges. Adhering to Salesforce best practices, such as Bulkification, Governor Limit Handling, and Security Enforcements (CRUD/FLS checks, sharing rules), architectural patterns ensure code consistency and maintainability. Unit of work and repository patterns facilitate optimized DML operations, preventing multiple redundant queries and ensuring transaction control.

- **Adherence to principles of separation of concerns**: Architectural patterns enforce the principles of separation of concerns, which are fundamental to effective pattern integration. Salesforce encourages a layered architecture, where patterns are modular and loosely coupled. For example, a combination of trigger handler pattern, service layer, and factory method ensures that Apex triggers remain lightweight, delegating logic to service classes for easy testing and reusability.

- **Guidance for pattern selection**: Architectural patterns help in selecting the right design patterns by considering Salesforce-specific constraints, such as governor limits and multi-threaded asynchronous execution limits. For instance, selecting Batch Apex for large-scale processing instead of future methods aligns with Salesforce's bulk processing capabilities.

Architectural patterns are a foundation for integrating design patterns within Apex projects by providing a structured framework, defining clear boundaries, facilitating communication, supporting scalability and extensibility, promoting best practices, and guiding pattern selection. By leveraging architectural patterns effectively, developers can create cohesive, well-structured systems that leverage the benefits of pattern integration to achieve their project goals.

Practical tips for identifying complementary patterns

Identifying complementary patterns is essential for successful pattern integration in Apex projects.

Following are some practical tips to help you identify patterns that work well together:

- **Understand project requirements**: Start by thoroughly understanding the requirements and constraints of your Apex project. Identify the key functionalities and architectural aspects that need to be addressed.

- **Analyze existing patterns**: Review existing design patterns and architectural decisions within your project. Identify patterns that are already being used and assess their effectiveness in addressing specific requirements.

- **Consider pattern interactions**: Analyze how different patterns interact with each other and their impact on the overall architecture. Look for patterns that complement each other in terms of functionality, responsibilities, and behavior.

- **Leverage pattern catalogs and references**: Refer to established pattern catalogs and literature to explore a wide range of design patterns. Use pattern references and documentation to understand the characteristics, strengths, and weaknesses of individual patterns.

- **Evaluate pattern suitability**: Evaluate the suitability of patterns based on the specific requirements and constraints of your project. Consider factors such as scalability, performance, maintainability, and ease of implementation.

- **Identify patterns with overlapping concerns**: Look for patterns that address overlapping concerns or responsibilities within the architecture. Identify opportunities to combine or integrate patterns to achieve a more cohesive and efficient design.

- **Seek input from peers and experts**: Collaborate with peers, colleagues, and domain experts to gather insights and perspectives on pattern selection. Solicit feedback and recommendations from experienced developers and architects.

- **Prototype and experiment**: Prototype different combinations of patterns to assess their feasibility and effectiveness. Experiment with alternative approaches and iterate on your design to find the best fit for your project.

- **Consider contextual factors**: Take into account contextual factors such as project timeline, team expertise, and technology stack. Choose patterns that align with the project's goals, constraints, and available resources.

- **Stay flexible and iterative**: Recognize that pattern selection is not a one-time decision but an iterative process. Stay flexible and open to revising your design based on evolving requirements and feedback.

By following these practical tips, you can effectively identify and integrate complementary patterns that enhance the architecture and design of your Apex projects.

Common pitfalls and mitigation strategies

When implementing architectural patterns in Salesforce or other Apex projects, developers often encounter common challenges. These pitfalls can hinder the effectiveness and maintainability of their solutions if not addressed proactively.

Following are some prevalent pitfalls and the corresponding mitigation strategies to ensure successful integration of patterns:

- **Overengineering:**
  - **Pitfall:** Avoid overcomplicating the architecture by incorporating unnecessary patterns or excessive abstraction layers.
  - **Mitigation**: Start with a minimalistic approach and gradually introduce patterns as the project evolves, focusing on solving immediate problems and addressing emerging requirements.

- **Tight coupling:**
  - **Pitfall:** Be cautious of tight coupling between patterns, which can hinder flexibility and make the system harder to maintain.
  - **Mitigation**: Use design principles such as Dependency Inversion and Interface Segregation to decouple components and promote loose coupling between patterns.

- **Lack of documentation:**
  - **Pitfall**: Inadequate documentation of pattern integrations can lead to confusion and misunderstanding among team members.
  - **Mitigation**: Document design decisions, architectural choices, and pattern integrations comprehensively, providing clear explanations and examples to guide developers and stakeholders.

By adopting these strategies and best practices, developers can effectively integrate patterns in Apex projects, creating robust, scalable, and maintainable solutions that meet the needs of the business and end users.

Practical applications of integrated patterns

In this section, we will delve into case studies and real-world examples that demonstrate the practical application of integrated patterns in Salesforce development. These examples will showcase how different patterns can be effectively combined to address complex challenges and optimize solutions. Through in-depth analysis and insights, we will explore the thought process behind selecting and implementing integrated patterns, as well as the impact they have on project outcomes.

The following are the case studies for integrated patterns:

- Optimizing data access using layered architecture and facade pattern in Salesforce

  - **Overview**: This case study focuses on a Salesforce project dealing with large data volumes and complex data access requirements. The project requires efficient data retrieval and processing mechanisms while ensuring that governor limits are not exceeded. Additionally, the application must support scalability and maintainability as business needs evolve.

  - **Challenges**: The project faces several challenges related to:

    - **Governor limits:** Salesforce imposes strict limits on SOQL queries, DML operations, and heap size, making it difficult to use traditional **Data Access Object (DAO)** patterns effectively.

    - **Complex data access logic:** The system requires multiple related records to be fetched and processed efficiently, leading to performance bottlenecks due to redundant queries.

    - **Handling large data volumes:** The application processes many records, which can result in query selectivity issues and long processing times.

    - **Need for modular and maintainable code:** The data access logic needs to be reusable, loosely coupled, and scalable to accommodate future changes.

  - **Solution**: To address these challenges, the project replaces the DAO pattern with the facade pattern, which provides a centralized interface for data access while ensuring optimal SOQL execution. Additionally, the solution integrates Asynchronous Apex mechanisms such as:

    - **Batch Apex:** To process large datasets efficiently without hitting governor limits.

    - **Queueable Apex:** For chaining asynchronous jobs and ensuring modular execution.

    - **Platform Events:** To enable EDA for real-time data updates across different system components.

By combining these patterns and techniques, the project ensures optimized data retrieval, maintainability, and scalability.

o **Implementation**:

o Facade pattern for data access:

- A Facade class is introduced to encapsulate SOQL queries and DML operations, ensuring that queries are optimized and reusable.

  The facade provides methods for retrieving, updating, and processing records while maintaining a single point of access for data operations.

o **Bulk processing with Batch Apex:**

- Instead of executing DML operations in a loop, Batch Apex is used to process large datasets in manageable chunks.

- The **start()**, **execute()**, and **finish()** methods allow processing millions of records asynchronously without exceeding governor limits.

o **Event-Driven Approach with Platform Events:**

- Platform Events are used to trigger data processing whenever new records are inserted.

- External systems can subscribe to these events, ensuring real-time data synchronization.

o **Queueable Apex for chained execution:**

- Queueable Apex is used for processing dependent tasks asynchronously, such as sending notifications after records are updated.

- It allows for dynamic execution flow by chaining multiple jobs together.

The following is the impact:

o **Improved performance:**

- The facade pattern ensures optimized SOQL queries by reducing redundant database calls.

- Asynchronous Apex mechanisms enable efficient bulk processing without hitting governor limits.

o **Scalability:**

- The system can handle large datasets with minimal impact on performance due to Batch Apex and Queueable Apex.

- New processing tasks can be added without disrupting existing workflows.

o **Maintainability and modularity:**

- The facade pattern encapsulates data access logic, reducing code duplication and improving reusability.

- Asynchronous Apex patterns promote decoupled and testable components.

o **Event-Driven Architecture:**

- Platform Events ensure real-time updates and loosely coupled integrations, allowing external systems to react to Salesforce data changes dynamically.

- Enhancing trigger logic using trigger handler pattern and service layer pattern

o **Overview:** This case study focuses on a Salesforce project that involves complex trigger logic and business process automation. The project requires an efficient way to manage trigger execution while ensuring maintainability, reusability, and scalability. Additionally, the system must support modular development to accommodate future business logic changes.

o **Challenges:** The project faces several challenges related to:

- **Trigger logic sprawl:** As the business logic grows, multiple triggers on the same object can lead to unstructured and unmanageable code.

- **Tight coupling:** Business logic embedded directly in triggers makes modifying or reusing without affecting existing functionality difficult.

- **Difficulty in unit testing:** Testing becomes complex due to the interdependencies between trigger logic and business rules.

- **Governor limits compliance:** Poorly designed triggers can lead to hitting Salesforce governor limits due to inefficient SOQL queries and DML operations within loops.

o **Solution:** To address these challenges, the project implements the trigger and handler pattern in conjunction with the service layer pattern. This combination helps structure trigger execution in a modular way, allowing for better organization, scalability, and reusability of trigger-related business logic. Additionally, the solution integrates Asynchronous Apex mechanisms, such as:

- **Queueable Apex:** For deferring time-consuming operations, such as sending notifications, ensuring efficient execution.

- **Future methods:** For handling external API calls asynchronously, avoiding transaction limits within trigger execution.

- **Platform events:** For enabling event-driven workflows that decouple trigger execution from dependent processes.

By leveraging these patterns and techniques, the project ensures modular trigger management while improving maintainability and compliance with Salesforce best practices.

○ **Implementation**:

Trigger and handler pattern for decoupling business logic:

- A single trigger per object approach is enforced to delegate logic execution to handler classes.

- A trigger handler class processes different trigger events (before insert, after update, etc.) and directs execution to appropriate service classes.

Service layer for business logic:

- The service layer encapsulates business logic in separate classes, ensuring modularity and testability.

- This separation allows business rules to be updated independently without modifying the trigger code.

Asynchronous processing with Queueable Apex:

- Queueable Apex is used for deferred execution of complex tasks, such as sending automated emails or logging audit trails.

- Chained Queueable jobs enable sequential processing without blocking trigger execution.

Future methods for external API calls:

- External API calls required within trigger execution (e.g., updating an external system) are processed asynchronously using Future methods.

- This ensures that API callouts do not interfere with DML operations.

Event-driven Architecture with Platform Events:

- Platform Events are published when key business events occur, such as opportunity stage changes or order fulfillment.

- External systems and internal Salesforce processes can subscribe to these events for real-time updates.

○ **Impact**:

Improved performance:

- The trigger handler pattern eliminates redundant logic execution, ensuring optimized trigger performance.

- Asynchronous processing mechanisms prevent trigger execution from hitting governor limits.

Scalability and extensibility:

- The service layer pattern allows new business rules to be added without modifying trigger logic.

- New trigger-based processes can be easily integrated using event-driven workflows.

Maintainability and modularity:

- The separation of concerns between triggers, handlers, and service classes promotes modular, testable, and reusable code.

- The event-driven approach enables loosely coupled integrations, improving overall system resilience.

Better compliance with Salesforce best practices:

- The solution avoids SOQL queries in loops, ensuring bulkification.

- DML operations are optimized to execute efficiently without violating governor limits.

- Scaling solutions using microservices architecture and serverless computing patterns in Salesforce

  o **Overview**: This case study focuses on a large-scale Salesforce project that requires high scalability, agility, and efficient resource management to handle diverse business processes. The project aims to break down monolithic architecture into independently deployable services, reducing complexity while improving flexibility in handling workloads.

  o **Challenges**: The project faces several challenges related to:

    - **Monolithic architecture constraints:** The existing monolithic design limits scalability and increases deployment complexity.

    - **Limited scalability:** A centralized system struggles to handle variable workloads, leading to performance bottlenecks.

    - **High infrastructure management costs:** Maintaining and provisioning dedicated servers increases operational expenses.

    - **Complex service deployment and updates:** Managing service dependencies and deploying new features without disrupting existing functionality is difficult.

  o **Solution**: To address these challenges, the project adopts a microservices architecture combined with serverless computing patterns. This approach modularizes the application into small, independent services that can be deployed and scaled dynamically. The solution also integrates Salesforce Functions and Platform Events to enhance event-driven communication and real-time data processing.

Additionally, **serverless platforms** such as **AWS Lambda** or **Salesforce Functions** are utilized to run business logic without provisioning or managing dedicated infrastructure.

o **Implementation**:

Microservices for business logic:

- Each **microservice** is designed to handle a **specific business capability**, ensuring modular development.
- Communication between services is facilitated through **RESTful APIs** or **message queues (e.g., AWS SQS or Salesforce Platform Events)**.

Serverless execution with Salesforce Functions:

- **Salesforce Functions** execute business logic in response to events, reducing the dependency on synchronous processing.
- This allows processing-intensive tasks to **scale dynamically** based on demand.

Event-Driven Processing with Platform Events:

- **Platform Events** enable **asynchronous** communication between Salesforce and external microservices, ensuring real-time updates.
- **Example**: When a **new order is placed**, an event is published, triggering multiple services such as inventory updates and shipping notifications.

Scalable processing with Asynchronous Apex:

- **Queueable Apex** is used for chaining background tasks without blocking synchronous operations.
- **Batch Apex** processes large data loads efficiently, ensuring smooth execution without exceeding **governor limits**.

o **Impact**: The integrated approach brings several key benefits:

Improved scalability:

- The system can dynamically scale services based on real-time demand.

- Serverless functions reduce unnecessary resource consumption when services are not in use.

Enhanced fault isolation and maintainability:

- Microservices operate independently, preventing failures in one service from affecting the entire system.

- Event-driven processing decouples dependencies, making system updates and feature enhancements easier.

Optimized infrastructure costs:

- Serverless execution eliminates the need for dedicated infrastructure, reducing operational costs.

- Pay-as-you-go models ensure that resources are used efficiently based on actual demand.

Better performance and responsiveness:

- Asynchronous processing enables Salesforce to handle high transaction loads without performance degradation.

- Event-driven microservices provide real-time processing and response mechanisms.

- Applying domain-driven design principles for complex business domains in Salesforce

  - **Overview**: This case study revolves around a Salesforce project that requires a structured approach to handling complex business logic, domain-specific rules, and evolving requirements. The project demands a solution that aligns technical implementations with business concepts to improve maintainability and collaboration.

  - **Challenges**: The project faces multiple challenges, including:

    - **Understanding and modeling complexity:** Mapping intricate business rules and workflows into a structured domain model.

    - **Ensuring alignment between business and technical teams:** Bridging the gap between domain experts and developers to maintain consistency.

    - **Scalability and maintainability:** Managing domain growth without introducing excessive complexity or technical debt.

  - **Solution**: By implementing DDD principles, the project adopts a domain-centric approach that emphasizes:

- **Modeling core domain concepts:** Identifying key business entities, their relationships, and behaviors.

- **Defining a ubiquitous language:** Establishing a shared vocabulary between business and technical stakeholders.

- **Designing a domain-driven architecture:** Structuring the application to reflect real-world business processes.

o **Implementation:**

- **Bounded contexts:** The system is divided into smaller, self-contained modules to prevent cross-domain dependencies.

- **Context mapping:** Relationships between different parts of the system are explicitly defined to manage dependencies and communication.

- **Strategic design:** Business logic is encapsulated within domain services, aggregates, and value objects, ensuring a clean separation of concerns.

o **Impact:**

- **Improved business-technology alignment:** Ensures that the technical implementation accurately represents business needs.

- **Enhanced code maintainability:** A well-defined domain model reduces complexity and improves code readability.

- **Scalability and adaptability:** The modular approach allows new business rules to be integrated without disrupting the existing system.

- Enhancing Integration with EDA and Command Query Responsibility Segregation

  o **Overview:** This case study focuses on a Salesforce project that requires seamless integration with multiple external systems while ensuring efficient real-time data processing and consistency. The project aims to build a responsive and scalable integration solution.

  o **Challenges:** The project encounters several key challenges, including:

    - **Data consistency issues:** Ensuring data remains synchronized across different systems in near real-time.

    - **Latency in processing:** Reducing delays in data updates and system responses.

    - **Complexity in system integration:** Managing interactions between disparate data sources and external services while minimizing system dependencies.

- o **Solution**: The project leverages EDA in conjunction with CQRS to:

  - **Enable asynchronous communication:** Events are used to trigger updates and propagate data changes across systems.

  - **Separate read and write operations:** CQRS ensures that data modifications (commands) and data retrieval (queries) are handled independently for improved efficiency.

  - **Ensure eventual consistency:** Systems achieve synchronization without requiring tight coupling, improving fault tolerance.

- o **Implementation**:

  - **Event-driven processing:** Salesforce **Platform Events** are used to asynchronously propagate changes, reducing direct dependencies between systems.

  - **CQRS for data segregation:** Commands (write operations) and queries (read operations) are handled separately to optimize database interactions and reduce contention.

  - **Asynchronous Apex for processing: Queueable Apex** and **Batch Apex** facilitate scalable and deferred execution of commands without impacting system performance.

- o **Impact**:

  - **Improved integration efficiency:** Asynchronous event-driven workflows minimize system delays and ensure smooth data propagation.

  - **Enhanced system scalability:** Decoupled components enable better load distribution, making the system more adaptable to business growth.

  - **Fault tolerance and reliability:** CQRS and EDA work together to improve resilience, ensuring that failures in one part of the system do not impact the entire architecture.

- Applying EDA for asynchronous processing

  - o **Overview**: This case study highlights the implementation of an EDA in a Salesforce project designed to manage background processing tasks efficiently while ensuring system responsiveness.

  - o **Challenges**: The project faces several challenges, including:

    - **High data processing volumes:** Handling large datasets asynchronously without impacting system performance.

- **System responsiveness:** Ensuring real-time user interactions remain unaffected by background operations.

- **Scalability:** Designing a solution that can adapt to increasing data loads and system demands.

o **Solution:** The team adopts an EDA combined with Salesforce Platform Events and Asynchronous Apex to:

- **Enable real-time event processing:** Events are published to trigger background tasks dynamically.

- **Optimize system performance:** Long-running operations are moved to asynchronous execution to prevent delays.

- **Decouple components:** Loose coupling between components allows flexible data handling and improved fault tolerance.

o **Implementation:**

- **Platform events for event-driven processing:** Events are published when key business processes require background execution.

- **Asynchronous Apex for background jobs:** Batch Apex processes large datasets, while Queueable Apex enables job chaining for complex workflows.

- **Event handlers for scalable processing:** Subscribers listen for events and execute necessary actions, ensuring seamless data flow across different system components.

o **Impact:**

- **Improved responsiveness:** Moves heavy processing tasks to the background, ensuring real-time operations remain unaffected.

- **Enhanced scalability:** The architecture dynamically scales to handle varying workloads efficiently.

- **Increased system reliability:** Decoupled event-driven processing enhances fault tolerance and ensures system stability.

- Implementing asynchronous processing with Platform Events

o **Overview:** This case study showcases the use of Platform Events in a Salesforce project to efficiently manage asynchronous data processing and automate event-driven workflows, ensuring seamless system interactions.

o **Challenges:** The project faces several key challenges, including:

- **Managing asynchronous workflows:** Handling background tasks such as large-scale data processing, notifications, and external system interactions.

- **Minimizing system load:** Ensuring that long-running processes do not impact user experience or slow down core transactions.

- **Ensuring event consistency:** Coordinating event-driven workflows to maintain data integrity across different components.

o **Solution**: The team implements Platform Events to create a scalable and decoupled EDA, allowing:

- **Separation of concerns:** Business logic is decoupled from real-time user interactions, ensuring a more responsive system.

- **Efficient event processing:** System components communicate asynchronously, reducing dependency on synchronous transactions.

- **Enhanced system performance:** Background processing tasks are triggered via events, ensuring minimal impact on primary system operations.

o **Implementation**:

- **Defining and publishing Platform Events:** Events are structured to encapsulate key data changes and are published asynchronously when critical business transactions occur.

- **Subscribing to events for background processing:** Event subscribers process the data independently, allowing tasks such as record updates, notifications, and external API calls to execute without user intervention.

- **Best practices in Event-Driven Design:** Strategies like event sequencing, fault tolerance, and replayability are applied to ensure event consistency and reliability.

o **Impact**:

- **Improved responsiveness:** Moves resource-intensive tasks to the background, preventing delays in primary system operations.

- **Scalability:** Allows the system to handle increasing workloads by leveraging event-driven execution instead of synchronous processing.

- **Reliability & decoupling:** Platform Events provide a loosely coupled architecture, ensuring modularity and ease of future enhancements.

- Implementing composite applications with LWC

o **Overview**: This case study highlights the development of modular and interactive user interfaces using LWC in Salesforce to create scalable and maintainable applications.

- o **Challenges**: The project encounters several key challenges, including:

  - ▪ **Managing UI complexity:** Building composite applications that consist of multiple interactive components working together seamlessly.

  - ▪ **Ensuring component reusability:** Creating UI elements that can be reused across different parts of the application to reduce redundancy.

  - ▪ **Facilitating efficient data communication:** Enabling smooth communication between components to maintain a consistent user experience.

- o **Solution**: The team leverages LWC to create a structured, component-based UI framework by:

  - ▪ **Encapsulating specific functionalities:** Breaking down complex UI requirements into smaller, self-contained components.

  - ▪ **Promoting code reusability and maintainability:** Ensuring each component can be independently developed and reused across multiple applications.

  - ▪ **Enhancing component communication:** Utilizing **Lightning Message Service (LMS)**, events, and APEX controllers for seamless data flow and interactivity.

- o **Implementation**:

  - ▪ **Structuring LWC-based composite applications:** Components are designed following a modular approach, ensuring separation of concerns and scalability.

  - ▪ **Defining parent-child component relationships:** Complex applications are broken down into parent and child LWCs, ensuring proper hierarchy and structured interactions.

  - ▪ **Using events and LMS for communication:** Implementing custom events, public properties, and LMS for efficient component interactions.

  - ▪ **Optimizing performance:** Adopting lazy loading, caching strategies, and imperative Apex calls to improve responsiveness and reduce processing overhead.

- o **Impact**:

  - ▪ **Enhanced user experience:** Provides a seamless, interactive, and modern UI experience across devices.

  - ▪ **Improved code maintainability:** The modular approach enables easier debugging, testing, and enhancements.

- **Greater flexibility and scalability:** The structured design allows the application to evolve with new features and integrations.

Best practices and recommendations

When integrating patterns into your Salesforce Apex projects, it's essential to follow best practices to ensure success.

Following are some key guidelines to consider:

- **Understand the problem domain:** Before integrating patterns, thoroughly understand the problem domain, including business requirements, technical constraints, and user needs. This understanding will guide the selection and implementation of appropriate patterns.

- **Choose patterns wisely**: Select patterns that align with the specific requirements and objectives of your project. Consider factors such as scalability, maintainability, performance, and complexity when choosing patterns for integration.

- **Start small**: Begin with small, manageable integrations of patterns before tackling larger, more complex implementations. Starting small allows you to experiment, learn, and iterate on your approach, minimizing the risk of errors and setbacks.

- **Focus on modularity**: Design patterns should promote modularity and encapsulation, enabling components to be developed, tested, and maintained independently. Strive to create loosely coupled, highly cohesive modules that can be easily integrated and modified as needed.

- **Follow design principles**: Adhere to design principles such as **Single Responsibility, Open/Closed, Liskov Substitution, Interface Segregation, Dependency Inversion (SOLID)** and **Don't Repeat Yourself (DRY)** when integrating patterns. These principles promote code clarity, flexibility, and maintainability.

- **Document patterns and integration points**: Document the patterns you're integrating, their responsibilities, and how they interact with other components in the system. Clear documentation helps ensure consistency and facilitates collaboration among team members.

- **Test extensively**: Thoroughly test your integrated patterns to verify their correctness, robustness, and performance. Implement unit tests, integration tests, and end-to-end tests to validate the behavior and interactions of integrated components.

- **Monitor and measure**: Continuously monitor and measure the performance and effectiveness of integrated patterns in real-world scenarios. Collect metrics such as response times, resource utilization, and user satisfaction to identify areas for improvement and optimization.

- **Foster collaboration**: Promote collaboration and communication among team members involved in integrating patterns. Encourage sharing of knowledge, experiences, and best practices to facilitate learning and continuous improvement.

- **Iterate and refactor**: Embrace an iterative approach to pattern integration, refining and optimizing your implementation over time based on feedback and lessons learned. Don't hesitate to refactor your code and architecture as needed to maintain alignment with evolving requirements and priorities.

By following these best practices and recommendations, you can effectively integrate patterns in your Apex projects, leading to more robust, maintainable, and scalable solutions.

Conclusion

Integrating patterns in Apex projects is a critical skill for developers seeking to solve complex challenges and design scalable, maintainable solutions in Salesforce development. This chapter provided an in-depth exploration of the importance of pattern integration, strategies for combining design patterns, and practical applications illustrated through case studies and real-world examples. By leveraging the strengths of multiple patterns, developers can create modular, reusable, and flexible architectures that align with best practices. Understanding the benefits and addressing the challenges of pattern integration enables teams to optimize their solutions while promoting code clarity and maintainability. By applying the lessons from this chapter, developers can design innovative solutions that not only meet current project demands but also remain adaptable to future requirements, ensuring long-term success and efficiency in Salesforce projects.

In the next chapter, the spotlight turns toward anti-patterns and pitfalls. It will cover common mistakes and anti-patterns to avoid in Apex development, how to refactor code to remove anti-patterns, and best practices for maintaining code quality over time.

Points to remember

- Integrating patterns in Apex projects involves combining multiple design patterns to address complex technical and business challenges.

- Pattern integration enhances code modularity, reusability, scalability, and maintainability, leading to more robust solutions.

- Key strategies for integration include layering, composition, and adaptation of design patterns based on project requirements.

- Leveraging architectural patterns provides a structured framework for organizing components and facilitates effective pattern integration.

- Pattern integration fosters consistency, promotes collaboration among team members, and aligns with industry best practices.

- Successful integration requires thorough documentation, extensive testing, and iterative refinement of patterns.

- Common pitfalls like overengineering, tight coupling, and inadequate documentation should be addressed with proactive strategies.

- Real-world examples and case studies illustrate how combining patterns like MVC, service layer, and EDA can optimize Salesforce solutions.

- Practical tips for identifying complementary patterns include analyzing project requirements, evaluating pattern interactions, and prototyping.

- Monitoring, measuring, and refining pattern integrations ensure long-term effectiveness and alignment with evolving project needs.

Questions

1. What does integrating patterns in Apex projects entail, and why is it important for Salesforce development?

2. How can combining multiple design patterns improve the scalability and maintainability of a Salesforce application?

3. What are some common strategies for integrating design patterns in Apex projects?

4. How do architectural patterns support the integration of multiple design patterns?

5. What are some of the challenges of integrating patterns, and how can developers mitigate them?

6. Can you explain how combining patterns like trigger and handler with the service layer enhances code organization?

7. What role do layering, composition, and adaptation play in pattern integration?

8. How can real-world examples help developers understand the practical application of pattern integration?

9. What best practices should developers follow to ensure successful integration of patterns in Salesforce projects?

10. Why is it important to document and test integrated patterns thoroughly, and how does this benefit the development process?

Join our book's Discord space

Join the book's Discord Workspace for Latest updates, Offers, Tech happenings around the world, New Release and Sessions with the Authors:

https://discord.bpbonline.com

CHAPTER 11

Anti-Patterns and Pitfalls in Apex Development

Introduction

Anti-patterns and pitfalls in Salesforce Development delves into the critical process of identifying and avoiding common mistakes and anti-patterns encountered in Salesforce Apex development. These anti-patterns can hinder the performance, scalability, and maintainability of Apex projects, making it essential for developers to be aware of them and know how to refactor code to remove them.

In this chapter, we will explore various aspects of anti-patterns and pitfalls in Salesforce development, covering topics such as common mistakes to avoid, techniques for refactoring code to eliminate anti-patterns, and best practices for maintaining code quality over time.

By understanding and avoiding these anti-patterns, developers can significantly improve the quality and efficiency of their Salesforce projects, leading to more robust, scalable, and maintainable applications. Whether you are a seasoned Salesforce developer or new to the platform, this chapter provides valuable insights and strategies for optimizing your development workflow and building high-quality Salesforce solutions.

Structure

The chapter covers the following topics:

- Anti-patterns and pitfalls
- Best practices for maintaining code quality

Objectives

By the end of this chapter, readers will have a deep understanding of anti-patterns and pitfalls in Apex development and their impact on code quality, performance, and maintainability. By the end of this chapter, readers will be able to identify and avoid common mistakes that can hinder the development process. Additionally, the chapter provides actionable techniques for refactoring code to eliminate anti-patterns, using real-world examples and best practices to guide readers toward writing more efficient and maintainable code. Readers will also learn about practices that ensure long-term code quality, enabling them to build scalable, robust Salesforce applications. Whether new to Salesforce or experienced in Apex development, readers will find valuable insights and strategies to optimize their coding practices and elevate the quality of their solutions.

Anti-patterns and pitfalls

Anti-patterns and pitfalls refer to common mistakes, poor practices, or design patterns that lead to suboptimal solutions, inefficiencies, or difficulties in software development. These anti-patterns and pitfalls can occur at various stages of the development lifecycle and may impact different aspects of the software, such as performance, maintainability, scalability, or reliability. Identifying and avoiding these anti-patterns is essential for maintaining code quality, enhancing productivity, and ensuring the success of software projects.

Apex development, like any programming endeavor, can be prone to common mistakes and anti-patterns that hinder code quality, performance, and maintainability.

SOQL queries inside loops

One of the most common mistakes in Apex development is performing SOQL queries inside loops. This can lead to hitting Salesforce governor limits and significantly impact performance, especially when dealing with large datasets. Instead, bulkify your code by querying outside of loops and leveraging collections to process data efficiently, as follows:

- **Excessive trigger logic:** Trigger logic is often essential for automating business processes in Salesforce. However, cramming too much logic into triggers can make them complex and difficult to maintain. Instead, consider using a trigger handler pattern to encapsulate logic outside of triggers, making it more modular and testable.

- **Ignoring governor limits:** Salesforce imposes various governor limits to ensure the stability and performance of its multi-tenant architecture. Ignoring these limits can lead to unexpected exceptions and degraded performance. Always design your code with governor limits in mind and implement strategies such as bulkification and query optimization to stay within limits.

- **Not using design patterns:** Failing to leverage design patterns like singleton, factory, or service layer can result in spaghetti code that's hard to understand, test, and maintain. Design patterns provide proven solutions to common problems and promote code reusability, scalability, and maintainability.

- **Hardcoding IDs and values**: Hardcoding record IDs, field names, or other values directly into your code can make it inflexible and error-prone. Instead, use custom settings, custom metadata, or hierarchical custom settings to store configurable data externally and make your code more dynamic and adaptable.

- **Lack of error handling**: Incomplete or inadequate error handling can lead to unexpected failures and poor user experiences. Always include comprehensive error handling mechanisms in your code to gracefully handle exceptions, log errors, and provide meaningful feedback to users.

- **Mixing business logic with presentation logic**: Mixing business logic with presentation logic in Apex classes or Visualforce pages can make your code tightly coupled and difficult to maintain. Follow the separation of concerns principle and keep your business logic separate from presentation logic to improve code readability and maintainability.

- **Ignoring test coverage**: Neglecting to write unit tests or failing to achieve sufficient test coverage can result in buggy code and deployment failures. Prioritize writing comprehensive unit tests for your Apex classes and triggers to ensure code reliability and facilitate continuous integration and deployment processes.

- **Overlooking security considerations**: Failing to implement proper security measures in your Apex code can expose sensitive data and make your Salesforce org vulnerable to security breaches. Always follow Salesforce security best practices, such as enforcing CRUD and FLS, using Shield Platform Encryption, and implementing secure coding practices.

- **Not optimizing for performance**: Overlooking security considerations in Apex code can expose sensitive data and make a Salesforce organization vulnerable to breaches. A common vulnerability is SOQL injection, which occurs when user inputs are directly concatenated into SOQL queries. This allows malicious users to manipulate query logic, potentially exposing sensitive information or disrupting functionality. SOQL injection typically arises from unsanitized inputs and improper handling of dynamic queries. To prevent this, developers should always use bind variables, which securely handle user inputs. For instance, instead of directly appending user inputs into a query, binding them ensures the input is safely processed, maintaining data integrity.

- Additionally, enforcing CRUD and **Field-Level Security** (**FLS**) is essential to ensure users only access data they are authorized to handle. By leveraging Salesforce's Schema methods, developers can confirm that users have the required permissions before performing operations on objects or fields. Secure coding practices, such as avoiding exposure of sensitive data in debug logs, implementing Shield Platform Encryption for data at rest, and restricting Apex class access through profiles and sharing settings, further bolster security. Validating and sanitizing both user inputs and outputs also helps mitigate risks like injection attacks and cross-site scripting in Visualforce or Lightning components.

- **Non-selective queries:** One of the lesser-known issues in Apex development is failing to optimize query selectivity. Salesforce uses a query optimizer to ensure queries run efficiently. However, if your query is not selective enough (e.g., it retrieves too many rows or has poorly filtered WHERE clauses), it can lead to non-selective query errors during operations like bulk DML or triggers. This can significantly affect performance and even block execution. We should regularly monitor the **query plan** to evaluate selectivity and use indexed fields.

- **Heap size limits**: Another common issue in Apex development is exceeding heap size limits, especially when working with large datasets or handling complex operations in-memory. Salesforce imposes a strict heap size limit (e.g., 6 MB for synchronous and 12 MB for asynchronous Apex). Exceeding this limit results in runtime exceptions and crashes. We should regularly monitor heap size consumption during development using debug logs and optimize data handling to stay within limits.

Following figure briefly illustrates Salesforce Development anti-patterns and best practices:

Common Anti-patterns and Best Practices

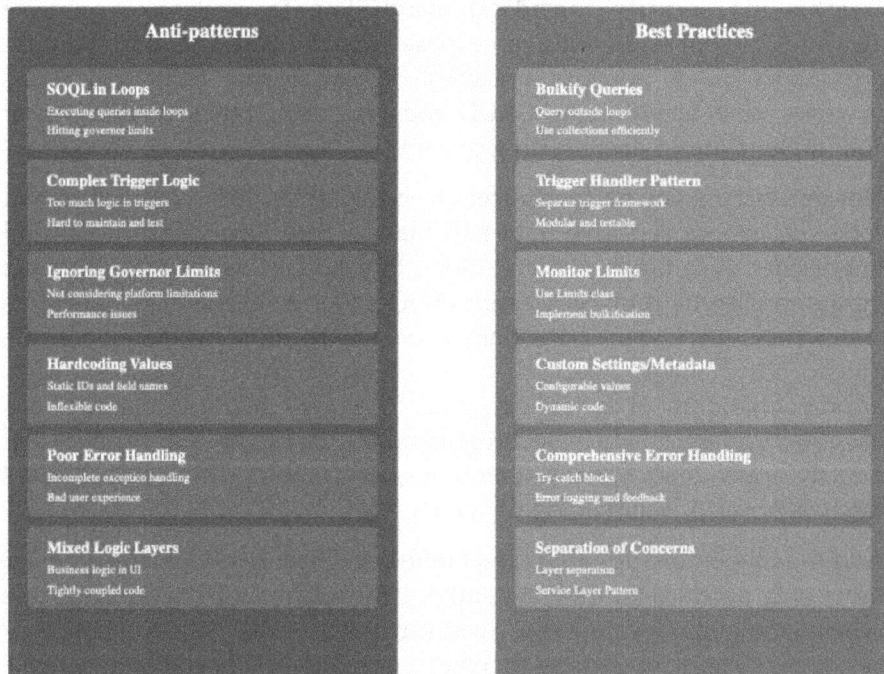

Anti-patterns	Best Practices
SOQL in Loops Executing queries inside loops Hitting governor limits	**Bulkify Queries** Query outside loops Use collections efficiently
Complex Trigger Logic Too much logic in triggers Hard to maintain and test	**Trigger Handler Pattern** Separate trigger framework Modular and testable
Ignoring Governor Limits Not considering platform limitations Performance issues	**Monitor Limits** Use Limits class Implement bulkification
Hardcoding Values Static IDs and field names Inflexible code	**Custom Settings/Metadata** Configurable values Dynamic code
Poor Error Handling Incomplete exception handling Bad user experience	**Comprehensive Error Handling** Try-catch blocks Error logging and feedback
Mixed Logic Layers Business logic in UI Tightly coupled code	**Separation of Concerns** Layer separation Service Layer Pattern

Best Practices for Salesforce Development

Figure 11.1: *Salesforce Development anti-patterns and best practices*

By being aware ofthese common mistakes and anti-patterns, developers can avoid pitfalls and write more robust, maintainable, and scalable Apex code in Salesforce.

Refactoring code to remove anti-patterns

Refactoring is the process of restructuring existing code without changing its external behavior to improve its readability, maintainability, and performance. When dealing with anti-patterns in Apex development, refactoring is often necessary to eliminate these pitfalls and ensure code quality. Tools such as Salesforce Health Check, Checkmarx, and PMD Apex provide valuable support in identifying and addressing vulnerabilities. By embedding these practices into development workflows, teams can enhance the security and resilience of their Salesforce applications.

Following are the ways on how to refactor code to remove anti-patterns effectively:

- **Identify anti-patterns**: The first step in refactoring code is identifying the anti-patterns in your codebase. Common anti-patterns include SOQL queries inside loops, excessive trigger logic, and hard-coded values. Use code reviews, static code analysis tools, and Salesforce best practices documentation to identify anti-patterns in your code.

- **Understand the anti-pattern:** Before refactoring, you must understand the root cause and implications of the anti-pattern you're dealing with. Determine why the anti-pattern exists and how it negatively impacts code quality, performance, or maintainability. This understanding will guide your refactoring efforts.

- **Break down large methods**: If you encounter methods with high cyclomatic complexity or excessive lines of code, break them down into smaller, more manageable methods. This improves code readability, testability, and maintainability by isolating specific functionality in cohesive units.

- **Extract business logic from triggers**: If you have triggers with complex business logic, consider refactoring this logic into separate Apex classes using the trigger handler pattern. This decouples business logic from trigger execution, making it easier to test, maintain, and reuse across different triggers.

- **Optimize queries and loops**: Address anti-patterns related to query performance by optimizing SOQL queries and eliminating queries inside loops. Use bulkification techniques to query data in bulk and leverage collections to process records efficiently, reducing the risk of hitting governor limits.

- **Replace hardcoded values with configurable options**: Remove hardcoded values from your code and replace them with configurable options stored in custom settings, custom metadata, or hierarchical custom settings. This makes your code more flexible and adaptable to changes in configuration requirements.

- **Implement error handling**: If your code lacks comprehensive error handling, refactor it to include error handling mechanisms such as try-catch blocks, custom exceptions, and error logging. Handle exceptions gracefully and provide meaningful error messages to users to improve the user experience.

- **Separate concerns:** Refactor code to adhere to the principle of separation of concerns by separating business logic from presentation logic, database access logic from application logic, and so on. This promotes code modularity, maintainability, and testability.

- **Optimize for performance**: Address performance-related anti-patterns by refactoring code to optimize resource utilization, minimize database queries, and reduce processing overhead. Implement caching, lazy loading, and asynchronous processing where appropriate to improve performance. Implementing asynchronous Apex mechanisms like **queueable**, **batch**, and **future methods** is essential to handle performance-intensive tasks effectively.

- **Test and validate changes**: After refactoring code to remove anti-patterns, thoroughly test and validate the changes to ensure that they haven't introduced regressions or unintended side effects. Write unit tests to cover refactored code and perform integration testing to verify correct behavior across the application.

By following these steps, you can effectively refactor code to remove anti-patterns and improve the overall quality, maintainability, and performance of your Apex codebase in Salesforce.

Enhancing Apex code maintainability through refactoring

The **OpportunityController** consists of four methods to fetch opportunities in different open statuses, update opportunities, and calculate revenue.

Original code:

```
public class OpportunityController {

    // Method to fetch open opportunities
    public List<Opportunity> getOpenOpportunities() {
        List<Opportunity> openOpportunities = new
List<Opportunity>();
        for(Opportunity opp : [SELECT Id, Name, StageName FROM
Opportunity WHERE IsClosed = false]) {
            openOpportunities.add(opp);
        }
        return openOpportunities;
    }
```

```
    // Method to fetch closed opportunities
    public List<Opportunity> getClosedOpportunities() {
        List<Opportunity> closedOpportunities = new
List<Opportunity>();
        for(Opportunity opp : [SELECT Id, Name, StageName FROM
Opportunity WHERE IsClosed = true]) {
            closedOpportunities.add(opp);
        }
        return closedOpportunities;
    }


    // Method to update opportunity stage
    public void updateOpportunityStage(Id opportunityId, String
newStage) {
        Opportunity opp = [SELECT Id, StageName FROM Opportunity
WHERE Id = :opportunityId];
        opp.StageName = newStage;
        update opp;
    }


    // Method to calculate opportunity revenue
    public Decimal calculateOpportunityRevenue(Id opportunityId) {
        Opportunity opp = [SELECT Id, Amount FROM Opportunity WHERE
Id = :opportunityId];
        return opp.Amount;
    }
}
```

Refactored code:

```
public class OpportunityController {

    // Method to fetch open opportunities
    public List<Opportunity> getOpenOpportunities() {
        try {
            return [SELECT Id, Name, StageName FROM Opportunity
WHERE IsClosed = false];
        } catch (Exception e) {
            System.debug('Error fetching open opportunities: ' +
e.getMessage());
            return new List<Opportunity>();
```

```
        }
    }

    // Method to fetch closed opportunities
    public List<Opportunity> getClosedOpportunities() {
        try {
            return [SELECT Id, Name, StageName FROM Opportunity
WHERE IsClosed = true];
        } catch (Exception e) {
            System.debug('Error fetching closed opportunities: ' +
e.getMessage());
            return new List<Opportunity>();
        }
    }

    // Method to update opportunity stage
    public void updateOpportunityStage(Id opportunityId, String
newStage) {
        try {
            if (opportunityId != null && newStage != null) {
                Opportunity opp = [SELECT Id, StageName FROM
Opportunity WHERE Id = :opportunityId];
                opp.StageName = newStage;
                update opp;
            } else {
                System.debug('Opportunity ID or new stage is null.
Cannot update.');
            }
        } catch (DmlException dmlEx) {
            System.debug('Error updating opportunity stage: ' +
dmlEx.getMessage());
        } catch (Exception e) {
            System.debug('Unexpected error updating opportunity
stage: ' + e.getMessage());
        }
    }

    // Method to calculate opportunity revenue
    public Decimal calculateOpportunityRevenue(Id opportunityId) {
        try {
```

```
            if (opportunityId != null) {
                Opportunity opp = [SELECT Amount FROM Opportunity
WHERE Id = :opportunityId];
                if (opp.Amount != null) {
                    return opp.Amount;
                } else {
                    System.debug('Opportunity Amount is null for Id:
' + opportunityId);
                    return 0; // Return 0 as a fallback value
                }
            } else {
                System.debug('Opportunity ID is null. Cannot
calculate revenue.');
                return 0; // Return 0 as a fallback value
            }
        } catch (QueryException queryEx) {
            System.debug('Error fetching opportunity for revenue
calculation: ' + queryEx.getMessage());
            return 0; // Return 0 as a fallback value
        } catch (Exception e) {
            System.debug('Unexpected error calculating revenue: ' +
e.getMessage());
            return 0; // Return 0 as a fallback value
        }
    }
}
```

Following is the explanation and points to refactor:

- **Single Responsibility Principle (SRP)**: The original **OpportunityController** class had multiple responsibilities, such as fetching open/closed opportunities, updating opportunity stage, and calculating opportunity revenue. We refactored it into the **OpportunityService** class, where each method now has a Single Responsibility.

- **Code duplication**: The original code had duplicate SOQL queries for fetching opportunities. Refactoring consolidated these queries into a single method, reducing code duplication and improving maintainability.

- **Query optimization**: Refactored methods use parameterized queries and bulkified DML operations for better performance and efficiency. You can use Set and Map to bulkyfy the code in many ways.

- **Improved naming conventions:** Renamed methods and classes to reflect their responsibilities more accurately (`getOpenOpportunities` | `getOpportunitiesByStatus`, `OpportunityController` | `OpportunityService`).

- **Encapsulation:** Encapsulated the opportunity object creation and update logic within the `OpportunityService`, promoting encapsulation and separation of concerns.

- **Testability:** The refactored code is more testable as each method has a clear purpose, making it easier to write unit tests and ensure code coverage.

- **Consistency:** The refactored code follows consistent coding standards and patterns, enhancing readability and making it easier for other developers to understand and maintain the codebase.

Refactoring account creation logic

Refactoring Apex code is a critical practice for ensuring robust, maintainable, and scalable solutions in Salesforce development. This example highlights how enhancements in error handling, modularity, and encapsulation can improve the account creation process in Apex.

Original code:

```
public class AccountController {


    public void createNewAccount(String name, String industry,
String billingCity) {
        Account acc = new Account();
        acc.Name = name;
        acc.Industry = industry;
        acc.BillingCity = billingCity;
        insert acc;
    }


}
```

Following is the explanation:

- **Lack of error handling:** The original code does not handle potential errors that may occur during the account creation process, such as validation rule failures or DML exceptions.

- **Tight coupling:** The method directly interacts with the account object and sets its fields, violating the principle of loose coupling and making the code less maintainable.

- **Scalability**: As the application grows, adding more functionality related to account creation, for example, setting additional fields, triggering workflows will result in further bloating of this method.

Refactored code:

```
public class AccountController {

    public void createNewAccount(AccountDTO accountDTO) {
        try {
            Account acc = new Account();
            acc.Name = accountDTO.getName();
            acc.Industry = accountDTO.getIndustry();
            acc.BillingCity = accountDTO.getBillingCity();
            insert acc;
        } catch(Exception e) {
            // Handle the exception appropriately, such as logging
    it or displaying an error message to the user.
            System.debug('Error occurred while creating account: ' +
    e.getMessage());
        }
    }

}
```

Following are the refactoring points:

- **Error handling**: Introduce error handling to catch and handle any exceptions that may occur during the account creation process.

- **Encapsulation**: Encapsulate account creation logic within a method that takes an **AccountDTO** parameter, promoting loose coupling and making the code more modular.

- **Separation of concerns**: Delegate the responsibility of setting account fields to the **AccountDTO** class, ensuring that the controller focuses on coordinating actions rather than data manipulation.

In this refactored code, we addressed the original code's shortcomings by introducing error handling, encapsulating account creation logic, and promoting separation of concerns. This makes the code more robust, maintainable, and scalable, facilitating future enhancements and modifications to the account creation process.

Optimizing order processing with refactored utility classes

Let us consider a real-world scenario where we have a utility class responsible for processing data related to orders in an e-commerce application. The original utility class might have some issues that need to be addressed through refactoring.

Original code:

```
public class OrderUtility {

    // Method to calculate total order amount
    public Decimal calculateOrderTotal(List<Order> orders) {
        Decimal totalAmount = 0;
        for(Order ord : orders) {
            totalAmount += ord.Amount__c;
        }
        return totalAmount;
    }

    // Method to check if an order is eligible for discount
    public Boolean isEligibleForDiscount(Order order) {
        return order.Amount__c >= 1000;
    }

    // Method to process order and apply discount
    public void processOrder(Order order) {
        if(isEligibleForDiscount(order)) {
            order.Discount__c = 0.1 * order.Amount__c;
        }
    }

}
```

Following is the explanation:

- **Single Responsibility Principle (SRP)**: The **OrderUtility** class violates the SRP by performing multiple tasks such as calculating order total, checking eligibility for discount, and processing orders. We can refactor it by separating these responsibilities into different classes.

- **Modularity**: The methods in the **OrderUtility** class are tightly coupled, making it difficult to test and maintain. We can refactor the code to make it more modular and loosely coupled.

- **Code duplication:** There is some duplication of code, such as calculating the total order amount in the **calculateOrderTotal** method and applying the discount in the **processOrder** method. We can refactor the code to eliminate duplication and improve code reuse.

Refactored code:

```
// Separate class for calculating order total
public class OrderTotalCalculator {
    public Decimal calculateOrderTotal(List<Order> orders) {
        Decimal totalAmount = 0;
        for (Order ord : orders) {
            totalAmount += ord.Amount__c;
        }
        return totalAmount;
    }
}


// Separate class for discount calculation
public class DiscountCalculator {
    public static final Decimal DISCOUNT_RATE = 0.1;

    public Boolean isEligibleForDiscount(Order order) {
        return order.Amount__c >= 1000;
    }

    public Decimal calculateDiscount(Order order) {
        if (isEligibleForDiscount(order)) {
            return DISCOUNT_RATE * order.Amount__c;
        }
        return 0;
    }
}


// Separate class for processing orders
public class OrderProcessor {
    public void processOrders(List<Order> orders) {
        DiscountCalculator discountCalculator = new
DiscountCalculator();
```

```
                    List<Order> ordersToUpdate = new List<Order>();

                    for (Order order : orders) {
                        if (discountCalculator.isEligibleForDiscount(order)) {
                            order.Discount__c = discountCalculator.
            calculateDiscount(order);
                            ordersToUpdate.add(order);
                        }
                    }

                    if (!ordersToUpdate.isEmpty()) {
                        update ordersToUpdate; // Single bulk update
                    }
                }
            }
```
}Following are the refactoring points:

- We have divided the original **OrderUtility** class into three separate classes: **OrderTotalCalculator**, **DiscountCalculator**, and **OrderProcessor**, each responsible for a single task.

- This separation adheres to the SRP, making the code more maintainable, testable, and flexible.

- The **DiscountCalculator** class now has a method **calculateDiscount** to calculate the discount amount based on the order amount and eligibility criteria.

- The **OrderProcessor** class utilizes the **DiscountCalculator** to calculate and apply discounts to orders.

By refactoring the original code, we've addressed the issues of SRP violation, modularity, and code duplication, resulting in cleaner, more maintainable code.

Best practices for maintaining code quality

Maintaining code quality over time is essential for the long-term success and sustainability of Salesforce projects. As applications evolve and requirements change, it is crucial to adopt best practices that ensure code remains clean, efficient, and easy to maintain.

Following are some best practices for maintaining code quality over time in Salesforce development:

- **Follow coding standards**: Adhere to coding standards and best practices established by Salesforce and your organization. Consistent coding conventions improve code readability, maintainability, and collaboration among team members. Document and enforce coding standards through code reviews, static code analysis tools, and developer training.

- **Write self-documenting code**: Write code that is self-explanatory and easy to understand without excessive comments. Use meaningful variable names, method names, and class names that accurately describe their purpose and functionality. Follow the principle of **code as documentation** to make your codebase more accessible to developers.

- **Refactor regularly:** Regularly refactor code to improve its structure, readability, and maintainability. Address code smells, anti-patterns, and technical debt to prevent them from accumulating over time. Refactoring should be an ongoing process integrated into your development workflow, rather than a one-time activity.

- **Test Driven Development (TDD):** Adopt TDD practices to ensure that your code is thoroughly tested and resilient to changes. Write unit tests before implementing new functionality to validate its behavior and detect regressions early. Aim for high test coverage while also validating CRUD, FLS, and sharing rules compliance to ensure secure and functional code.

- **Code reviews**: Conduct regular code reviews to evaluate code quality, adherence to best practices, and alignment with project requirements. Encourage constructive feedback and collaboration among team members during code reviews to identify areas for improvement and knowledge sharing. Leverage code review tools and checklists to streamline the review process.

- **Logging and monitoring**: Implement robust logging and monitoring mechanisms for debugging and tracking system behavior. Use `System.debug` for development purposes but avoid logging sensitive information. For production environments, consider using custom logging frameworks or the Salesforce Event Monitoring tool for detailed insights into performance, user activities, and errors.

- **Version control**: Use version control systems such as Git to track changes to your codebase and collaborate effectively with other developers. Follow branching and merging best practices to manage code changes, releases, and feature development in a controlled and organized manner. Ensure that all changes are accompanied by descriptive commit messages for traceability.

- **Documentation:** Maintain comprehensive documentation for your codebase, including high-level architecture diagrams, API documentation, and inline comments. Document design decisions, implementation details, and configuration settings to provide context for future development efforts and onboard new team members effectively.

- **Monitor and analyze:** Implement monitoring and analytics tools to track the health and performance of your Salesforce applications in real time. Monitor system metrics, user interactions, and error logs to identify potential issues, bottlenecks, and opportunities for optimization. Use this data to make informed decisions and prioritize areas for improvement.

- **Continual learning:** Stay updated on the latest Salesforce features, best practices, and industry trends through continuous learning and professional development. Attend conferences, webinars, and training sessions, participate in community forums, and engage with fellow developers to expand your knowledge and skills. By incorporating these best practices into your Salesforce development process, you can maintain code quality over time and ensure the long-term success of your projects.

Conclusion

In this chapter, we learned the significance of identifying and avoiding anti-patterns and pitfalls in Apex development to ensure code quality and maintainability. Anti-patterns, when left unchecked, can lead to suboptimal solutions, inefficiencies, and scalability issues that compromise the robustness of Salesforce applications. Through practical examples and refactoring techniques, we demonstrated how to address common anti-patterns like SOQL queries in loops, excessive trigger logic, and hard coding. By adopting best practices such as modular design, comprehensive testing, and separation of concerns, developers can mitigate these challenges and enhance code efficiency. This chapter emphasized the importance of adhering to Salesforce best practices, staying mindful of governor limits, and employing strategic refactoring to maintain an optimal codebase. With these strategies in place, developers are better equipped to create scalable, robust, and high-performing Apex solutions that meet business needs effectively.

In the next chapter, the spotlight turns toward future trends in Apex design patterns. It will cover exploring emerging patterns and practices in Apex development, integration of design patterns with new Salesforce features, and evolving challenges and opportunities in designing Apex applications.

Points to remember

- Anti-patterns are common mistakes or poor practices that negatively affect the performance, scalability, and maintainability of Apex code.

- Examples of anti-patterns include SOQL queries inside loops, excessive trigger logic, and hardcoded IDs or values.

- Refactoring is essential to address anti-patterns and involves restructuring code without changing its external behavior.

- Bulkifying SOQL queries and using collections are effective ways to avoid governor limit violations in Salesforce.

- Separating business logic from triggers using a trigger handler pattern ensures better code modularity and testability.

- Employing design patterns like singleton and service layer enhances scalability, maintainability, and code reuse.

- Implementing comprehensive error handling mechanisms improves user experience and application reliability.

- Modularizing code and following the SRP simplifies maintenance and future enhancements.

- Best practices such as writing unit tests, conducting code reviews, and adhering to coding standards are essential for maintaining code quality.

- Proper monitoring and optimization techniques, like caching and asynchronous processing, are critical for improving system performance.

- Avoid hardcoding by using custom settings or metadata to make your code adaptable and flexible.

- Continuous learning and keeping up with Salesforce updates ensure adherence to best practices and evolving trends.

Questions

1. What are anti-patterns in Apex development, and how do they affect code quality and performance?

2. Why is it important to avoid SOQL queries inside loops, and what techniques can be used to address this anti-pattern?

3. How does the trigger handler pattern improve modularity and maintainability in Salesforce triggers?

4. What are some common pitfalls associated with hardcoding values in Apex code, and how can they be avoided?

5. Explain the role of refactoring in removing anti-patterns from Apex code.

6. How can implementing design patterns like singleton and service layer improve code scalability and reusability?

7. What strategies can be used to optimize query performance and stay within Salesforce governor limits?

8. How can error handling mechanisms enhance the reliability of Apex applications?

9. Why is it important to write unit tests, and how do they contribute to maintaining code quality?

10. Describe the principle of separation of concerns and its impact on Apex code maintainability.

11. What tools and techniques can be used to monitor and optimize the performance of Salesforce applications?

12. How does adhering to coding standards and conducting regular code reviews benefit long-term code quality?

Join our book's Discord space

Join the book's Discord Workspace for Latest updates, Offers, Tech happenings around the world, New Release and Sessions with the Authors:

https://discord.bpbonline.com

CHAPTER 12

Future Trends in Apex Design Patterns

Introduction

Future trends in Apex design patterns directs attention toward the passive exploration of emerging patterns and practices in Apex development. This chapter serves as a forward-looking compass, guiding readers through the ever-evolving landscape of Salesforce development. Readers will delve into the proactive examination of emerging patterns, unveiling innovative solutions to contemporary challenges.

This exploration extends to the strategic integration of design patterns with new Salesforce features, enabling developers to harness the full potential of evolving platform capabilities. Furthermore, the chapter delves into the evolving challenges and opportunities in designing Apex applications. It offers insights into adapting to the dynamic nature of technology, ensuring that Apex solutions remain resilient and future-ready.

Structure

The chapter covers the following topics:

- Importance of focusing on future trends
- Exploring emerging patterns and practices
- Integration of design patterns with new Salesforce features
- Evolving challenges and opportunities in designing Apex applications

Objectives

By the end of this chapter, readers will understand the importance of focusing on future trends in Apex design patterns, exploring emerging patterns and practices in Apex development, Integration of design patterns with new Salesforce features, and evolving challenges and opportunities in designing Apex applications. By the chapter's conclusion, readers will be equipped with a forward-thinking perspective, ready to navigate the evolving frontiers of Apex design patterns with confidence.

Importance of focusing on future trends

In the rapidly evolving landscape of Salesforce development, staying abreast of future trends in Apex design patterns is paramount for several reasons, as follows:

- **Innovation and competitiveness**: Embracing future trends allows organizations to innovate and differentiate themselves in the marketplace. By adopting cutting-edge design patterns, companies can develop solutions that are more efficient, scalable, and user-friendly, giving them a competitive edge over their peers.

- **Future-proofing solutions**: By anticipating future trends, developers can future-proof their solutions, ensuring they remain relevant and effective in the long term. This proactive approach helps mitigate the risk of obsolescence and ensures that applications can adapt to changing business requirements and technological advancements.

- **Enhanced performance and scalability**: Future-oriented design patterns often prioritize performance optimization and scalability, enabling applications to handle increasing volumes of data and users without sacrificing speed or reliability. This focus on efficiency and scalability is crucial for organizations seeking to scale their operations and accommodate growing user bases.

- **Security and compliance**: Many future trends in Apex design patterns emphasize security and compliance, helping organizations build applications that meet stringent regulatory requirements and protect sensitive data. By incorporating robust security measures into their solutions, developers can safeguard against security breaches and mitigate the risk of data loss or unauthorized access.

- **User experience and satisfaction**: Future-oriented design patterns often prioritize user experience, focusing on delivering intuitive, seamless, and engaging interfaces that delight users. By adopting these patterns, developers can create applications that are more user-friendly and enjoyable to use, enhancing customer satisfaction and driving user adoption and retention.

- **Adaptability and flexibility**: Future trends in Apex design patterns often emphasize adaptability and flexibility, enabling applications to evolve and respond to changing business needs and market dynamics. By building solutions that are agile and easily adaptable, organizations can pivot quickly in response to new opportunities or challenges, ensuring their continued success in a rapidly changing environment.

In summary, focusing on future trends in Apex design patterns is essential for organizations looking to innovate, future-proof their solutions, enhance performance and scalability, prioritize security and compliance, improve the user experience, and maintain adaptability and flexibility in an ever-changing landscape. By embracing these trends, developers can build applications that are not only effective and efficient but also well-positioned to thrive in the digital age.

Exploring emerging patterns and practices

As Salesforce continues to evolve and expand its capabilities, Apex developers are increasingly exploring new patterns and practices to enhance their development processes and deliver more robust solutions. Exploring emerging patterns and practices is crucial for staying ahead in an ever-changing ecosystem.

Following are the key areas and trends currently shaping Apex development:

- **Modularization and microservices:** With the growing complexity of Salesforce applications, there is a trend towards modularizing Apex code using microservices architecture. This approach allows developers to break down monolithic applications into smaller, independent services that can be developed, deployed, and scaled independently. It promotes reusability, agility, and easier maintenance of codebases.

- **Event-Driven Architecture: Event-Driven Architecture (EDA)** is gaining traction in Apex development for its ability to decouple components and enable real-time communication between systems and services. By leveraging platform events, developers can design loosely coupled, responsive systems that react to events and messages, enhancing scalability and performance.

- **Domain-Driven Design (DDD):** DDD principles are being increasingly applied in Apex development to better align software design with business domains. By focusing on modeling business domains and domain logic, DDD helps developers create more cohesive, maintainable, and understandable codebases. This approach improves collaboration between technical and domain experts, leading to more effective solutions.

- **GraphQL integration:** As organizations seek more flexible and efficient ways to query data from Salesforce, integrating GraphQL with Apex has become a notable trend. GraphQL allows clients to request exactly the data they need, reducing over-fetching and under-fetching of data. It offers a more tailored and efficient approach to data fetching and manipulation in Salesforce applications.

- **Serverless computing:** The adoption of serverless computing models, such as Salesforce Functions, is simplifying the development and deployment of event-driven microservices on the Salesforce platform. Developers can focus on writing functions that respond to events without managing infrastructure, promoting faster development cycles and scalability.

- **Artificial intelligence and machine learning:** Integrating AI and machine learning capabilities into Apex applications is becoming more prevalent, thanks to Salesforce's Einstein platform. Developers can leverage pre-built AI models and predictive analytics to automate processes, personalize user experiences, and derive actionable insights from data within Salesforce.

- **DevOps and CI/CD practices:** Embracing DevOps practices and **continuous integration/continuous deployment** (**CI/CD**) pipelines is essential for streamlining and automating the delivery of Apex applications. By automating testing, deployment, and monitoring processes, teams can accelerate time-to-market, improve code quality, and ensure more reliable releases. The following are some commonly used DevOps tools that can be effectively leveraged for Salesforce Apex development in the context of DevOps and CI/CD practices:

  - **Salesforce CLI (SFDX):** A command-line interface that allows developers to build and manage Salesforce applications efficiently. It supports automation, version control, and CI/CD workflows.

  - **Git**: A distributed version control system that helps teams collaborate, track changes, and maintain version history. Platforms like GitHub, GitLab, or Bitbucket are widely used for repository hosting.

  - **Jenkins**: A popular automation server for building CI/CD pipelines. It integrates well with Salesforce CLI and other tools to automate testing, deployment, and build processes.

  - **Gearset**: A specialized deployment tool for Salesforce. It simplifies CI/CD, offers robust comparison and deployment capabilities, and integrates with Git and other platforms.

  - **Copado**: A native Salesforce DevOps platform that enables automated deployments, version control, and release management with a focus on Salesforce metadata.

  - **Azure DevOps**: A comprehensive suite for CI/CD pipelines, project management, and integration with Salesforce CLI to deploy and monitor Salesforce applications.

  - **CircleCI**: A CI/CD platform that supports automated builds and testing, with capabilities to integrate Salesforce CLI for Apex code deployment.

- **Travis CI**: A continuous integration service that supports testing and deployment automation, commonly integrated with GitHub for Salesforce development.

- **Bitbucket pipelines**: A CI/CD tool integrated within Bitbucket for seamless automation of Salesforce builds and deployments.

- **CodeScan**: A static code analysis tool for Salesforce that checks code quality and security, making it easier to identify issues before deployment.

- **Heroku pipelines**: Part of Salesforce's ecosystem, Heroku pipelines allows teams to deploy apps in stages, from development to production, using a continuous delivery model.

- **Ant migration tool**: A Java/Ant-based tool from Salesforce that facilitates metadata deployment in CI/CD workflows.

- **SonarQube**: A code quality and security analyzer that integrates with Salesforce projects to identify issues in Apex and Visualforce code.

By incorporating these tools into a CI/CD pipeline, teams can achieve automated testing, robust deployments, and better overall project management for Apex-based Salesforce applications.

- **Low-code development:** Salesforce's low-code capabilities are transforming how developers build applications by enabling citizen developers to create solutions with minimal coding. Apex developers are leveraging low-code tools and frameworks to rapidly prototype, iterate, and deploy applications while maintaining governance and security.

Integration of design patterns with new Salesforce features

As Salesforce continues to innovate and introduce new features, integrating established design patterns with these advancements becomes crucial for maximizing their potential and enhancing development practices.

Following is how design patterns can be integrated with new Salesforce features to drive innovation and efficiency in Apex development:

- **Integration with component-based patterns: Lightning Web Components (LWC)** promote a component-based architecture, allowing developers to encapsulate UI elements and logic. Patterns like composite and decorator can be leveraged to compose complex UI components from simpler ones, promoting reusability and maintainability.

- **Integration with microservices architecture:** Salesforce Functions enable serverless computing, allowing developers to write event-driven functions that respond to events within Salesforce. Patterns like microservices and EDA can be integrated to build scalable, decoupled services that react to events in real-time, enhancing agility and scalability.

- **Integration with strategy and adapter patterns:** Einstein analytics and AI capabilities provide predictive analytics and AI-driven insights within Salesforce. Patterns such as strategy can be applied to encapsulate different algorithms for analytics, while adapter patterns can help integrate external AI services seamlessly into Salesforce applications.

- **Integration with chain of responsibility:** Salesforce Blockchain (Hyperledger) facilitates decentralized applications and smart contracts. The chain of responsibility pattern can be applied to handle complex workflows and transactions across multiple parties, ensuring transparency and security in blockchain-enabled solutions.

- **Integration with observer and command patterns:** Apex triggers and asynchronous processing enhancements allow developers to respond to data changes and execute background jobs efficiently. Observer patterns can be used to notify dependent components of data changes, while command patterns can encapsulate and parameterize operations for asynchronous execution.

- **Integration with facade and factory patterns:** Salesforce's low-code tools empower citizen developers to build applications with minimal coding. Facade patterns can simplify complex APIs and integrations for low-code developers, while Factory patterns can standardize the creation of complex objects or processes within low-code environments.

- **Integration with metadata and decorator patterns:** Enhanced metadata capabilities in Salesforce allow for dynamic customization and configuration of applications. Metadata patterns can be integrated to manage and apply metadata-driven configurations effectively, while decorator patterns can enhance metadata objects with additional functionalities or behaviors.

Integrating these design patterns with new Salesforce features not only enhances the development process but also ensures that applications are scalable, maintainable, and aligned with best practices. By leveraging the synergy between established design patterns and innovative Salesforce capabilities, developers can build robust, flexible, and future-proof solutions that meet evolving business needs and technological advancements.

Evolving challenges and opportunities in designing Apex applications

Designing Apex applications presents a dynamic landscape with challenges and opportunities shaping how developers approach Salesforce development.

Following is an exploration of the current and emerging trends influencing Apex application design:

- **Scalability demands**: With growing data volumes and user bases, Apex applications must handle increasing loads efficiently. Design patterns like bulkification and microservices are crucial for scaling applications without compromising performance.

- **Complex business logic**: Salesforce applications often involve intricate business processes that require careful orchestration and management. Applying patterns like service layer and command helps in organizing and maintaining complex logic effectively.

- **Integration complexity**: Integrating Salesforce with external systems and services introduces integration challenges. Patterns such as adapter and facade simplify integration tasks by providing standardized interfaces and encapsulating complex logic.

- **User experience expectations**: Modern Salesforce applications require intuitive user interfaces and responsive experiences. Leveraging **Lightning Web Components** (**LWC**) and UI design patterns ensures usability while adhering to Salesforce UX guidelines.

- **Governance and compliance**: Compliance with regulatory requirements and Salesforce governance limits poses challenges in application design. Patterns that enforce separation of concerns and data security, such as DAO and Proxy, help in maintaining compliance.

Following are the emerging opportunities:

- **AI and analytics integration**: Integrating Einstein analytics and AI capabilities into Apex applications offers opportunities for advanced insights and decision-making. Patterns like strategy and observer facilitate the integration and utilization of AI-driven features seamlessly.

- **Serverless computing**: Salesforce functions enable serverless computing, allowing developers to build scalable, event-driven functions within Salesforce. Patterns such as EDA and command enable efficient handling of serverless functions and event-driven workflows.

- **Blockchain and distributed ledger**: Salesforce Blockchain introduces opportunities for decentralized applications and secure data transactions. Patterns like chain of responsibility and state facilitate the design of blockchain-enabled applications while maintaining integrity and security.

- **Low-code development**: Salesforce's low-code tools empower citizen developers to contribute to application development. Design patterns like facade and factory support the abstraction of complexity, allowing citizen developers to build applications without deep technical knowledge.

- **Enhanced metadata capabilities**: Advanced metadata-driven development in Salesforce enables dynamic customization and configuration. Patterns such as metadata and decorator facilitate flexible application configurations and customization options.

Navigating the evolving challenges and opportunities in designing Apex applications requires a strategic approach that incorporates established design patterns and embraces new Salesforce features. By leveraging these patterns and opportunities, developers can build robust, scalable, and innovative applications that meet the dynamic needs of businesses while staying aligned with best practices and industry standards in Salesforce development.

Conclusion

In this chapter, we learned the importance of focusing on future trends in Apex design patterns, exploring emerging patterns and practices in Apex development, Integration of design patterns with new Salesforce features, and evolving challenges and opportunities in designing Apex applications.

In this book, we explored the transformative role of Apex design patterns in Salesforce development, emphasizing their importance in creating efficient, scalable, and maintainable applications. Starting with foundational principles, we delved into Apex fundamentals, highlighting key concepts such as data types, control structures, and exception handling. By understanding these basics and adhering to SOLID principles, developers can lay the groundwork for modular and robust solutions.

We covered creational, structural, and behavioral patterns, showcasing their applications in solving common Salesforce challenges. Apex specific patterns, such as trigger and handler, bulkification, and exception management, addressed Salesforce's unique needs, while architectural patterns like MVC, DDD, and EDA offered frameworks for scalable and modular design.

The integration of patterns was explored through strategies, case studies, and best practices, demonstrating how combining patterns enhances flexibility and maintainability. We also addressed common pitfalls and anti-patterns, equipping developers with refactoring techniques and strategies to maintain code quality over time.

Looking forward, we explored emerging trends and future opportunities in Salesforce development, underscoring the importance of continuous learning and adaptability. As we conclude, this book serves as a guide to navigating the complexities of Salesforce development with confidence and precision, empowering developers to create solutions that inspire innovation and drive success.

Points to remember

- Staying updated with future trends in Apex design patterns ensures that Salesforce applications remain innovative, scalable, and adaptable to evolving technologies and business requirements.

- Event-Driven Architecture, Domain-Driven Design, and modularization through microservices are key trends shaping the future of Apex development.

- Integrating Apex with new Salesforce features, such as Lightning Web Components, Salesforce Functions, and Einstein, enhances development processes and enables innovative solutions.

- Addressing challenges like scalability, integration complexity, and governance requires strategic use of design patterns such as bulkification, adapter, and service layer.

- Emerging opportunities, including blockchain, AI integration, serverless computing, and advanced metadata capabilities, allow developers to create cutting-edge, future-ready Salesforce applications.

- Leveraging DevOps practices and low-code development tools ensures efficient workflows, high-quality applications, and collaboration between technical and non-technical teams.

Questions

1. Why is it essential for developers to stay informed about future trends in Apex design patterns?

2. How does Event-Driven Architecture contribute to scalability and responsiveness in Salesforce applications?

3. What role does Domain-Driven Design play in improving code maintainability and aligning software with business requirements?

4. How can Salesforce features like Lightning Web Components and Einstein be integrated with established design patterns to enhance development practices?

5. What are the key challenges developers face in designing scalable and compliant Apex applications, and how can design patterns help overcome them?

6. What opportunities do blockchain, serverless computing, and advanced metadata capabilities offer for future Salesforce applications?

Join our book's Discord space

Join the book's Discord Workspace for Latest updates, Offers, Tech happenings around the world, New Release and Sessions with the Authors:

https://discord.bpbonline.com

Index

www.ingramcontent.com/pod-product-compliance
Lightning Source LLC
Chambersburg PA
CBHW061742210326
41599CB00034B/6761